HYSTERICAL!

M000273198

HYSTERICAL!

Women in American Comedy

EDITED BY LINDA MIZEJEWSKI
AND VICTORIA STURTEVANT

FOREWORD BY KATHLEEN ROWE KARLYN

UNIVERSITY OF TEXAS PRESS *Austin*

Copyright © 2017 by the University of Texas Press
All rights reserved
Printed in the United States of America
First edition, 2017

Requests for permission to reproduce material from this work should be
sent to:
    Permissions
    University of Texas Press
    P.O. Box 7819
    Austin, TX 78713-7819
    utpress.utexas.edu/rp-form

♾ The paper used in this book meets the minimum requirements of
ANSI/NISO Z39.48-1992 (R1997) (Permanence of Paper).

LIBRARY OF CONGRESS CATALOGING-IN-PUBLICATION DATA

Names: Mizejewski, Linda, editor. | Sturtevant, Victoria, 1973–, editor. |
    Karlyn, Kathleen Rowe, 1947–, writer of supplementary textual content.
Title: Hysterical! : women in American comedy / edited by Linda Mizejewski
    and Victoria Sturtevant ; foreword by Kathleen Rowe Karlyn.
Description: First edition. | Austin : University of Texas Press, 2017. | Includes
    bibliographical references and index.
Identifiers: LCCN 2017015723
    ISBN 978-1-4773-1451-7 (cloth : alk. paper)
    ISBN 978-1-4773-1452-4 (pbk. : alk. paper)
    ISBN 978-1-4773-1453-1 (library e-book)
    ISBN 978-1-4773-1454-8 (nonlibrary e-book)
Subjects: LCSH: Women comedians—United States—20th century. | Women
    comedians—United States—21st century. | American wit and humor—
    History and criticism. | Feminism. | Feminine beauty (Aesthetics)—United
    States. | Body image in women.
Classification: LCC PN1590.W64 H97 2017 | DDC 792.702/8092—dc23
LC record available at https://lccn.loc.gov/2017015723

doi:10.7560/314517

CONTENTS

"LAUGHTER THAT DOES NOT STOP is hysterical." This straight-forward but evocative statement from the introduction to this book brings to mind the rich tangle of judgments and metaphors commonly associated with laughter. We imagine laughter as waves or ripples spreading across the surface of water, expanding in space while diminishing in time. We speak of laughter as an explosive force that bursts forth or erupts from the body. Laughter can peal or ring like bells, or it can echo after encountering a surface that absorbs its energy, only to bounce it back again and again to its source. Laughter is infectious or contagious, with uneasy suggestions of disease, something we can "catch" as easily as the common cold when our defenses are down and the right bug strikes. At the same time, that infectiousness makes laughter inevitably social, a means of connecting those who share it. These connections—ripples, echoes, felicitous contagions—are at the heart of *Hysterical!* and my enthusiasm for it.

Laughter, like hysteria, lends itself to metaphor because it touches on the ineffable, that which escapes our efforts to pin it down or tame it with reason. That ineffability first lured me to the study of women and comedy some years ago. I was riveted by the laughter that would not stop at the end of Marleen Gorris's fiercely feminist film *A Question of Silence* (1982)—laughter that appeared both hysterical and utterly rational. I was seduced by comedian Roseanne's claiming the last word in the opening credits of her sitcom (1988–1997) with laughter that continued after the images faded, refusing to end on cue. I was tickled by Miss Piggy's grotesque play with the conventions of femininity and captivated by the witty, glamorous women of romantic comedy in Hollywood's Golden Age. I wanted the emotions I felt from all of these instances of laughter: power, pleasure, renewal, release, and often simply delight.

Seeking to understand anything, including laughter, brings us into the realm of the rational, to the explorations and conversations that take place in the critical discourse on a subject. And if the notion of laughter's infectiousness speaks to its inherently social nature, the same is true of scholarly discourse. *Hysterical!* marks a milestone in this discourse. As its introduction notes, scholarship on women and comedy has typically lagged behind the reality of women's presence in the genres of laughter. Yet in the past few decades, that scholarship has expanded like waves of laughter, gathering momentum rather than losing it as it has traveled along the axis of time. The editors of this collection have led the way with their own work and with the contributions they have gathered here. Some scholars in this volume have long been interested in outrageous, "hysterical" women, while others are newer to this topic. Together, they move our collective thinking into new territory by looking back to recover lost histories of women in comedy and forward to new generations of female comic auteurs and performers.

Hysterical! is also a timely response to a moment in our cultural history when, as its introduction notes, "women comedians have achieved an unprecedented level of visibility as performers, writers, and producers." Female-authored comedy now abounds in film and television and on the internet, which has opened vast new possibilities for women drawn to comedy as a means of self-expression, artistic creation, and political work. Both in mainstream venues and on the fringes of culture, funny women are making themselves seen and heard more than ever, defying expectations that women cannot or should not be outspoken, angry, vulgar, and funny—hysterically funny.

In response to this surge of female laughter, a panel of feminist scholars at a recent international conference took up the question of whether unruliness, or the transgressiveness associated with women in comedy, has become the "new normal" in our post-Roseanne, post-feminist world. The question is provocative. On July 25, 1990, Roseanne unleashed a firestorm when she combined a screeching performance of the national anthem with a parody of male gestures associated with baseball. Today such a performance—or at least the vulgar aspects of it—might elicit only a shrug. For me, this is not a sign that female comedy has lost its disruptive power, but of the reverse. Women's laughter has altered what we consider normal, and for the better.

This book was being written while Hillary Clinton was the first woman to be a serious contender for the most powerful political office in our country. However, she and other prominent women in the campaign endured repugnant expressions of misogyny, in addition to the other toxic forces that often accompany sexism. They found themselves reduced to their bodies, their voices judged as shrill and their laughter as excessive. Yet those judgments have been increasingly challenged and recognized for what they are: tired efforts to protect male power by demeaning and intimidating women with the familiar suggestion that they are hysterical, crazy.

In my most recent work, I have wanted to better understand the ruptures among women across time, especially in the context of the mother/daughter relation. I've felt that girls and women of all ages can only benefit from resisting cultural forces that would separate us from each other and the commitments we share. In the classroom, teaching comedy has allowed me to bring a light touch to heavy subjects and to open conversations with my students on ideas that matter to me. Spanning generations of performers and scholars, *Hysterical!* testifies to the power of comedy to stimulate incisive conversations and build connections across the boundaries of time.

As time passes, I've also become increasingly interested in the unacknowledged personal forces that nudge us toward one research project rather than another. I've come to understand that I wanted to work on comedy because of my yearnings to laugh at the absurdities of life, to celebrate its simple pleasures, and above all to discover and connect with kindred spirits. Studying comedy has allowed me to spend time in the company of others, both real and imaginary, whose work has enriched my own and whose presence in my life has made it better. May *Hysterical!* bring similar connections and rewards to you.

Kathleen Rowe Karlyn

ACKNOWLEDGMENTS

WE ARE DEEPLY GRATEFUL to the writers of these essays for their hard work, dedication, trust in us, and joyful spirit of collaboration. We are especially pleased that many of them were able to come together for panels and friendly gatherings at the Society for Cinema and Media Studies conference and at Console-ing Passions. The enthusiasm, responsiveness, dedication, good humor, and straight-up brilliance of this team of contributors have astonished and humbled us at every turn.

A special tribute goes to Kathleen Rowe Karlyn, the godmother of this book and the original unruly woman of feminist comedy scholarship. Kathleen's work set the bar high for those of us who followed, and she has been an inspiration ever since. Her friendship and encouragement have energized us throughout this project.

Many thanks to Jim Burr at the University of Texas Press, who was excited about this anthology from the very start and who was consistently helpful and supportive as we made our way through the many stages of writing, revision, and manuscript preparation. Thanks, too, to Lynne Chapman at the press for her editorial expertise and enthusiasm, and to Leslie Tingle for the extraordinary copyediting that much improved the final manuscript; both Lynne and Leslie worked hard to finesse all the final details. For any errors that slipped through, the responsibility is entirely ours. Also, we much appreciate the suggestions of the press's readers; the specificity and thoughtfulness of their recommendations were crucial in steering the final revisions.

At the Ohio State University, we were fortunate to have Taneem Hussein and Kristen Kolenz as diligent research assistants through the generosity of Jill Bystydzienski and Guisela Latorre, consecutive chairs of the Department of Women's, Gender, and Sexuality Studies. Support from a Coca-Cola Critical Difference for Women grant made it possible for us to collaborate in the early stages of this project.

At the University of Oklahoma, we thank Greg Boyd for his research assistance, and the Honors College Research Assistant Program for sponsoring that work. The OU College of Arts and Sciences and Film and Media Studies programs provided essential travel funding and material support for this project. Many thanks also to Karl Schmidt and Gary Bates for their technical support.

Linda thanks colleagues and staff at the Department of Women's, Gender, and Sexuality Studies who provide an upbeat and invigorating place to work and think. She is especially grateful to Debra Moddelmog, Janice Pogoda, Judith Mayne, and Elizabeth Davis for their generous friendship, support, and laughter through this project and many others, and to George for being, as always, a loving ally and mainstay.

Victoria thanks all her colleagues in the College of Arts and Sciences, particularly Dean Kelly Damphousse, for their unflagging support and encouragement. Special thanks to Joanna Rapf, who has generously provided her mentorship, kindness, insight, and the occasional highly necessary kick in the pants to keep this project moving along. And of course Jim, for everything, always.

Finally, we thank all the hysterically funny women comedians who continue to act up and speak out. We are fortunate that the longer we worked on this anthology, the more relevant it became.

HYSTERICAL!

INTRODUCTION

LINDA MIZEJEWSKI AND VICTORIA STURTEVANT

HYSTERICAL WOMEN

The title of this anthology, *Hysterical!*, has a double meaning. Though the term is used to describe brilliant comedy and the laughter it produces, the idea began as a medical diagnosis used to control women. Born in 1760, but not coming into common usage until about 1818, "hysteria" was based on the Greek word *hystera*, meaning "womb," and described a number of different physical and psychological symptoms that doctors attributed to a blocked or malfunctioning uterus. Paradoxically linked both with sexual frigidity and with frustrated or excessive desire, hysteria explained away a range of female experiences and behaviors, from listlessness to seizures to "excessive" expressions of creativity, intellectualism, sexuality, or anger—all blamed on the uterus. Hysteria gave medical sanction to the idea that women's bodies predisposed them to emotional or irrational behavior. No need to ask a woman why she might be angry, frustrated, listless, tearful, interested in sex, or not interested in sex. The womb provided a ready answer.[1]

The diagnosis has long been discounted, and the term "hysteria" was removed from the American Psychiatric Association's famous DSM (*Diagnostic and Statistical Manual of Mental Disorders*) in 1980. But hysteria still packs a punch as a way to silence and discredit women. The idea that women are prone to irrational emotion puts them in a double bind: speaking up to protest an unfair accusation of hysteria can easily be dismissed as itself hysterical behavior. Not speaking up means acquiescence.[2] The "hysterical woman" persists in late-night comedy or sitcom clichés about irrational wives, pushy mothers-in-law, and crazy or "high maintenance" girlfriends.

The culturally circulated notions that women lose their minds over premenstrual syndrome or are prone to uncontrollable crying at the slightest offense are modern diagnoses of hysteria, and if you turn from the DSM to the urban dictionary, you find "bitches be crazy," a slang catchphrase that crosses racial, class, and cultural boundaries in its usages and citations. Like hysteria, it is a write-off of women's subjective experiences. No need to ask or try to understand why a woman might be upset. Bitches be crazy.

Yet despite its history as repression and misreading, the doubled meaning of hysteria is a provocative model for women's comedy because it's also a history of performance and female spectacle—women acting out and acting up. The diagnosis of hysteria could sanction unruly female behavior, and records show that because their symptoms could be disruptive and violent, hysterics were often accused of willfully outrageous performance. A nineteenth-century French doctor denounced these women as "veritable actresses" who use the diagnosis to undertake "most shameful actions" and "employ the coarsest and often most obscene language and give themselves up to the most disorderly actions."[3] Similar accusations have long been leveled at women comedians, who—while not all coarse—embrace disorder as a strategy of comedy. Moms Mabley, Mo'Nique, Amy Schumer, Sarah Silverman, and Lena Dunham have built their careers on the necessity of breaking down the barriers that say women must not speak about scatological, gynecological, or sexual matters in public. Even less profane comedians such as Fanny Brice, Lucille Ball, or Carol Burnett defy gender norms with their over-the-top clowning and parodies of feminine ideals. Lori Landay, in her study of boisterous women comedians, pinpoints exactly what these ideals entail: "Ultimately, a woman's place is in a feminine body: immobile, fragile, objectified, commodified," she points out, in a consumerist culture that bombards women with images of how they should act and look in order to conform to a narrow ideal.[4]

Our hope for the present volume is to repurpose the term "hysterical," to turn away from the pathologization of female bodily and emotional excess and towards a frank reading of those very same things. We argue that the social meanings of the comic unruly woman are very different from those of her male counterparts, because the history of pathologizing female unruliness has long worked against women's participation in comedy. The edginess of comedy is understood to be something unnatural to women. Consider the rowdy female performances described in this anthology: Fay Tincher's dare-devil stunts, Mae West's linebacker walk, Carol Burnett's athletic pratfalls, Lucille Ball's manic slapstick, Ellen DeGeneres's tomboy pranks, Tina Fey's smirk and acerbic wit. The woman comic's aggression, madcap antics, and loudness are disturbing because, as Kathleen Rowe has argued, she "unsettles one of the most fundamental of social distinctions—that between male and female."[5]

And when that distinction breaks down, women comics are often subject to a backlash where the logic of hysteria reasserts itself. See for instance a recent rash of pseudoscientific claims linking women's supposed humorlessness to everything from lower intelligence to evolutionary advantages. Comedian Jerry Lewis shocked the audience at the 1998 Aspen Comedy Arts Festival when he proclaimed at a question-and-answer session, "A woman doing comedy doesn't offend me but sets me back a bit. I, as a viewer, have trouble with it. I think of her as a producing machine that brings babies in the world." Pundit Christopher Hitchens famously expanded on this idea in a *Vanity Fair* essay proposing evolution as the reason women are innately less funny than men: men needed humor to attract the interest of women, while women, in order to attract the interest of men, simply needed to inhabit exciting bodies. For Hitchens, sexual desire is a male trait because female desire is all about the womb: "For women, reproduction is, if not the only thing, certainly the main thing. Apart from giving them a very different attitude to filth and embarrassment, it also imbues them with the kind of seriousness and solemnity at which men can only goggle."[6] Comedian Adam Carolla put it more succinctly in an interview with the *New York Post*: "Dudes are funnier than chicks."[7]

Like hysteria, the idea that women aren't funny persists because it symptomizes a much larger gender problem. Few would argue against the idea that humor is an essential and healthy human feature. In studies of American college students, both male and female participants have long indicated they value "a sense of humor" in their mates. But when asked to rate the desirability of potential partners based on a photo and a caption supposedly written by that person, the heterosexual female participants rated men with funny captions higher, while the funniness of the caption made no statistical difference in the heterosexual males' ratings of potential partners. Olga Khazan says, "For decades, this response stumped psychologists," until they figured out that men and women generally mean different things by "sense of humor."[8] Liana Hone, William Hurwitz, and Debra Lieberman refined the experiment and were able to demonstrate that "men viewed humor receptivity as a necessity and humor production as a luxury when they were asked to create an ideal long-term partner. For women, it was just the opposite."[9] In other words, young women tend to value a partner who makes them laugh, while young men tend to value a partner who laughs at their jokes. This asymmetry in the social logic of humor as it is currently practiced in certain heterosexual relationships should not be mistaken for an essential difference between the sexes. Media both reflects and shapes our individual psychologies. We would argue that humor is such an essential mechanism for expressing powerful thoughts and feelings, for social bonding and emotional health, and for making it possible to explore otherwise transgressive or taboo topics that it is a signal mark of inequality that the role of the jokester is understood to be a male prerogative. More and better opportunities for women comics to reach audiences, through stand-up, television, and feature films are necessary and important because they also help reverse social myths that a woman's proper or natural role is to appreciate male humor rather than speak her own truth through comedy. To accuse women of being unfunny is to accuse them of being something less than fully intelligent, spontaneous, and human, incapable of using all the tools of communication available to human beings, including the tool of humor.

Humor is also a key political weapon, so there are political implications to the myth that women are less funny: it discourages women from making use of wit and satire to point out injustices and often marginalizes them when they do. In her classic 1994 book *Women and Laughter*, Frances Gray traces the argument that women have no sense of humor back to the seventeenth century and analyzes in detail this myth's role in disciplining and dismissing women's voices. Looking broadly at the ways women's wit has been condemned, ignored, and misread in western cultural discourse, Gray argues that there are roughly five "basic and easily learned" techniques to shut women out of comedy, deny their sense of humor, and therefore silence women's voices. These are all essentially tricks of *misreading*, of undercutting the intentionality and intelligence that are at the core of good comedy and replacing them with negative stereotypes of hysterical feminine behavior. Updating her examples, we find these techniques alarmingly still effective:

1. *Women are criticized for talking too much,* with the implication that the feminine ideal is silence and acquiescence. When women take the stage and use their voices, especially in verbal forms of comedy like stand-up, they inherently risk being labeled loud, coarse, unfeminine, and pushy—in effect, being larger and taking up more cultural space than women should. Backlash against boundary-pushing humor has impacted the careers of Roseanne Barr, Rosie O'Donnell, and Whoopi Goldberg, showing how easily women can be punished for the appearance of excessive or improper speech. These examples also show the weight of race, class, and ethnicity in deeming a woman "too loud" or taking up too much space.

2. *Women are mocked as overserious* and as killjoys to male bonding. Critics have long pointed out that sitcom mothers, for instance, often have the job of disapproving of their husbands' irresponsible behavior. Along the same line, women's objections to sexist or otherwise objectionable jokes can be dismissed as simple humorlessness; the charge is persuasive because it draws on the existing stereotypes.

3. *Women's comedy is dismissed as unintentional or artless.* Funny women have often presented themselves as "dumb" or "naïve" rather than as the conscious creators of comedy, in order to avoid the above power struggles. Gray uses the examples of Gracie Allen and Marilyn Monroe, and it is easy to trace the line forward to Goldie Hawn and Dolly Parton, and to some elements of Sarah Silverman's or Mindy Kaling's comic personas. The stereotype of the untutored female comedian dismisses women's conscious use of wit and satire and reframes the funny woman's talent as a natural accident—as if she could just as easily be a particularly funny child or animal.

4. *Women's comedy is dismissed as trivial* and not included in the canon of great comic actors that privileges aggressive and risk-taking comedy over relational humor and satire. Charlie Chaplin, the Marx Brothers, John Belushi, Richard Pryor, and Louis C.K. are often labeled "geniuses," while their female contemporaries in this volume have been treated as merely talented, when their contributions are remembered at all. As we have worked with the contributors and compiled these chapters, we have frequently marveled at how much of this history of women's comedy does not circulate in popular culture, in YouTube clips shared on social media, or in lifetime achievement awards and references from other comedians.

5. *Women's humor can be reframed as anger and (paradoxically) humorlessness.* The women's movement activists of the 1960s burned

their bras at public demonstrations because it was less violent and aggressive than the older political practice of burning a figure in effigy. It was, in fact, a rather clever joke. Political commentators of the time regarded it instead as evidence of alarming female rage, and the idea of a "bra burner" has entered the public discourse as a slogan for unreasonable feminist humorlessness. Really, what could be funnier?[10]

Arguing for the political power of laughter and the subversive power of comedy, Gray turns to the galvanizing image of the laughing Medusa invented by Hélène Cixous in her famous manifesto for a female writing practice grounded in the body. Women's self-representation has been stymied, says Cixous, by male portrayals of women as either monsters or as the mysterious "dark continent," to borrow Freud's image—a form of nothingness: "They riveted us between two horrifying myths: between the Medusa and the abyss." Rather than be silenced by these stories and images, she says, women need to claim their own vision: "You have only to look at the Medusa straight on to see her. And she's not deadly. She's beautiful and she's laughing." Advocating women to "write the body," Cixous hailed the "admirable hysterics" of previous generations whose bodies spoke back to patriarchy.[11] Cixous never defined feminine writing, écriture féminine, and its implicit essentialism has drawn extensive critique. However, feminists such as Gray have chosen to interpret it as a poetic trope or rhetorical strategy, and the image of the laughing Medusa endures as a feminist icon of bravado and resistance. Gray uses it to imagine the woman comedian inciting "a laughter that does not stop, that works ceaselessly to steal the language, rebuild it, and fly with it."[12]

A "laughter that does not stop" is hysterical, and here we see a connection to hysteria's history as a way to sanction outrageous female behavior and speech. Comedy is a place where inappropriate behavior is allowable and where taboo topics come to light. Unless individuals can own and speak openly about their experiences, craft their stories, and invest them with the rebellious energy of comedy, then those topics remain shrouded in shame and fear—part of the "dark continent." The idea that women's bodies make them crazy (or angry or frigid or humorless) can flourish only in an environment scared and ignorant of women's bodies. And unless and until women's full range of experiences, including medical, scatological, and gynecological ones, are represented in popular entertainment—as male equivalents have been—then their bodies will remain fertile terrain for projected anxieties.

0.1. Tig Notaro,
*Boyish Girl
Interrupted*,
HBO/2015.
© HBO.

These myths are silencing, and comedy is a form of speech that breaks them open. One example that makes a powerful physical impact is Tig Notaro's 2015 stand-up special *Boyish Girl Interrupted*, which opens up a topic often avoided as monstrosity and mystery, to use Cixous's terms. Forty minutes into the sixty-minute set, Notaro tells a story about undergoing a double mastectomy with no reconstructive surgery in order to treat her cancer. Now recovered, she says she enjoyed stumping an airport screener who expected to find breasts when she patted her down. Shortly after this joke, Notaro removes her jacket, and then her shirt, to enthusiastic applause. Barechested, scarred but healthy, she goes on to perform fifteen more minutes of bravura comedy while shirtless, never again mentioning her appearance, just letting the intensity of her naked chest punctuate what are otherwise very ordinary jokes about air travel and high school embarrassments. Her gestures suggest that she is utterly at ease shirtless, as if she hardly notices it, though the audience can hardly notice anything else. The power of this performance is in the way it disables either fetishizing perspectives of the female body that fixate on the breasts (she has none) or medicalized perspectives that would see her as a tragic victim. (She is strong and active, even beautiful.) Comedy is a space where these ideas can crystallize and where audiences can grasp in a moment what it has taken this whole introduction so far to say: female bodies have been shrouded in mystery and ignorance and melodrama for so long that there is a giddiness and a power to throwing off those taboos and making visible what has been suppressed.

That giddiness has helped produce a remarkable moment in the history of American women's participation in stand-up, television, and film comedy. Since 2000 comics such as Tina Fey, Amy Poehler, Ellen DeGeneres, Lena Dunham, Margaret Cho, Wanda Sykes, Amy Schumer, and Melissa McCarthy have achieved mainstream success, as have female-authored comedy projects such as the films *Mean Girls* (2004), *Bridesmaids* (2011), and *Trainwreck* (2015); television series *30 Rock* (NBC 2006–2013), *The Mindy Project* (Fox and Hulu 2012–), *Girls* (HBO 2012–2017), *Orange Is the New Black* (Netflix 2013–), *Jane the Virgin* (CW 2014–), and *Fresh off the Boat* (ABC 2015–); and the internet series *The Mis-Adventures of Awkward Black Girl* (2011–) and *Broad City* (2010–2014), both of which were picked up for television. And for the first time since Lily Tomlin in the 1980s, women have successfully headlined comedy films because of the star power of McCarthy, Fey, and Schumer. Yet scholarship on women in comedy remains too scarce, despite the rich history of these stars' twentieth-century precedents. Little has been written about early twentieth-century comedians Fanny Brice, Mabel Normand, and Fay Tincher; nor has sufficient critical attention gone to later stars like Moms Mabley and Carol Burnett. It seems that every generation is surprised anew at the emergence of funny women, and then a kind of amnesia sets in about women's long and unruly history of participation in comedy and comic performances.

One feature that unites the women in this volume is their "outsider" relationship to political power. Through much of Western history, the joker, clown, or trickster has been a role for misfits, occupying a liminal site just outside the social order. Studies of comedy often cite anthropologist Victor Turner's writings about liminality, which describe the ambiguous state of being in suspension or in a holding pattern in which identities, social roles, and even gender roles can become unfixed. Turner is describing festivals, rites of passage, and seasonal rituals in certain cultures, but he acknowledges that liminality can be used to describe borderline or counterculture experiences in many societies, including the activities of artists and philosophers. The clown or comic, as an insider/outsider, has similar license to challenge and ridicule cultural assumptions and values, and this gleeful antagonism toward the status quo is intrinsic to comedy's power and appeal.[13] The diversity represented in this anthology is critically linked to the disorderly, subversive, and unruly qualities that make these comedians hysterically funny. For half of them, an outsider racial or ethnic status is an important marker of identity: Fanny Brice, Moms Mabley, Wanda Sykes, Roseanne Barr, Whoopi Goldberg, Sarah Silverman, and Margaret Cho. And nearly a third of the stars covered here (Lily Tomlin and Ellen Degeneres, in addition to Sykes, Mabley, and Cho) identify as gay, lesbian, bisexual, or queer.

The disobedient laughter of the oppressed is a powerful tactic of social bonding, but it works for the other team, too. Throughout history, the edginess of comedy has enabled sexist, racist, homophobic, and xenophobic expressions that would otherwise be forbidden. Joining in the laughter at a sexist or racist joke is a way to feel like an insider, smugly aligned against the outliers. Still, the antiauthoritarian nature of comedy guarantees the persistence of defiant laughter against the powers that be, as seen in the prevalence of Jews and African Americans in the history of American stand-up comedy. As Joanne Gilbert points out, minorities can choose to perform their marginality as a rhetorical strategy in comedy, which can "serve as a powerful means of resistance to social, political, and economic inequities."[14] Rebecca Krefting, in her materialist analysis of oppositional comedy, argues that these comedians pay the price for "charged" humor that focuses on social inequality because they are usually less commercially successful than comedians who tap into dominant identifications that audiences have been taught to value.[15] Nevertheless, as Krefting and others demonstrate, traditions of black, Jewish, ethnic, camp, and queer humor illustrate the power of humor from the margins, both as critique of the mainstream and as a source of identity and solidarity. This is exemplified by the performers included in this anthology who tap specific minority traditions—Moms Mabley's and Wanda Sykes's use of tropes from African American humor, for example, and Fanny Brice's and Sarah Silverman's use of their Jewish identities in their work. The rich diversity of women covered in this volume offers ample but not exhaustive evidence of how deeply marginality and difference inform the tradition of women's comedy.

The number of successful women comedians both past and contemporary far exceeds what we cover in this book; we look to future scholars to fill in the gaps, pick up our momentum, and further develop these critical conversations in feminist, media, and cultural studies. Not all of the comedians discussed in this anthology are feminists, nor do we claim women's comedy as an innately feminist enterprise. But the scholars represented here draw on the methods, perspectives, and questions of feminist theory, which involves the foregrounding of gender, race, class, and sexualities in their analyses. The following section summarizes the theoretical trends and milestones that have shaped their work.

CRITICAL MODELS OF COMEDY AND WOMEN'S COMEDY

Jokes and laughter are so central to the human condition that modernity's most influential thinking about them comes from philosophy, psychology, and cultural studies. Not surprisingly, the authors of these studies—Sigmund Freud (1856–1939), Mikhail Bakhtin (1895–1975), and Henri Bergson (1859–1941)—were post-Victorian white men who would have been stumped by Whoopi Goldberg, shocked by Lena Dunham, and bewildered by Tina Fey—not just because they were offended by these womens' language or topics, but because they didn't imagine women and minorities as powerful subjects of their own comedy. Nevertheless, their ideas continue to be influential, and a brief overview of their theories illustrates comedy's complexity and multiple dimensions. To ask why women's humor is excluded from these theories is to point to decades of exclusions from playbills, films, comedy clubs, and anthologies. When feminists set out to claim and think about women and comedy, in scholarship that began in the late 1980s, they had to barge into the critical conversation, ask new questions, and point out how sex and gender make a difference.

Of the three thinkers listed above, feminist theorists have found Bakhtin the most useful because he acknowledges how comedy can work as a subversive force, and he discusses the "messiness" of the lower female body as part of his theory of the carnivalesque. Bakhtin writes of the medieval carnival—a version of which continues in the New Orleans Mardi Gras—as a time when hierarchy was disrupted, social status turned upside down, and the body itself remapped, with the "lowly" butt and stomach celebrated instead of the head and heart. In those celebrations of the grotesque, he says, the "lower stratum" of the female body was important for its ambivalence, the site of both the scatological and the sacred, decay and birth, and thus "the incarnation of this stratum that degrades and regenerates simultaneously."[16] Thus one of the recurring carnival figures was the "pregnant hag," the wrinkled old crone padded up to look like she was in her ninth month. Feminists have pointed out that this type of characterization unfortunately dovetails with biases about the female body as a gross, degraded version of the male body.[17] However, Bakhtin's theories of transgression and reversal, and especially his focus on the body and its social meanings in comedy, have been useful to feminists thinking about the rowdiness, disruptiveness, and lewdness of certain strands of female comedy, such as the bawd and the "rank ladies" of vaudeville and burlesque.

While Bakhtin was interested in laughter as a social force, Freud focused on the meanings of laughter between individuals and the function of jokes in the expression of otherwise repressed impulses. Nevertheless, social and historical contexts shape Freud's ideas; he wrote about his own middle-class Victorian and Edwardian culture, where lewdness and rowdiness were strictly male privileges, so his abilities to think about women and humor were limited by what he thought respectable women could say or hear. Overall, though, he made important insights about the motivations of humor in *The Joke and Its Relation to the Unconscious* (1905), when he describes jokes as mechanisms allowing the expression of repressed and forbidden feelings, in particular hostility and lust. Certainly the repression theory explains the less-than-funny intentions of sexist, racist, and homophobic jokes that are considered acceptable because they're "just jokes." But his theory about sexual humor is more problematic and reveals the deep interplay of class and gender not only in his observations about the bourgeois Edwardians but in the history of women's comedy. Freud defines "smut" as language "directed toward women" with the intention of seduction, but smut is expressed in the company of women only among the lower classes. For "society of a more refined education" the woman who is the object of the obscene remark is of course absent, and the smut among men is expressed as jokes. In fact, the obscene joke is precipitated precisely because the presence of a woman is an obstacle to what can be said, though Freud makes it clear that only women of a certain "educational and social level" pose this obstacle: upper-class men can in fact make obscene jokes "in the company of girls of an inferior class."[18] In this model, women are either absent or silent, the butts of but never the tellers of a dirty joke. Ramona Curry has pointed out that Mae West's dialogue in 1930s comedy films reveals the limitations of this theory,[19] but Freud's insights into smut as a class issue pinpoint a lingering double standard about gender and dirty jokes. In the first part of the twentieth century, women in burlesque and risqué stage productions—the "low" forms of theater—could perform lewd comedy, but with the exception of West, female comedians in mainstream popular culture steered away from smut. Not even second-wave feminism of the 1970s lured women into ribald stand-up comedy where the sex and language taboos were being exuberantly smashed by the likes of Lenny Bruce, George Carlin, and Richard Pryor. More than a century after Freud published his work on smut as male discourse, women stand-up artists—like Sarah Silverman, Sandra Bernhard, Mo'Nique, and Margaret Cho—who use sexually explicit material still have the reputation for being "shocking," whereas the shockwaves for male comedians lost their voltage decades ago.

The philosopher Henri Bergson wrote about laughter in relation to human nature and our deepest tendencies to align the world into patterns that make sense to us or seem "right." So his theories are aligned with Freud's in that he emphasizes how humor is tied to social norms. Bergson published an essay on this in 1900 (cited by Freud in his book on jokes), later expanded into his book *Laughter: An Essay on the Meaning of the Comic* (1911). Bergson was interested in laughter as social complicity: a group recognition and criticism of something perceived as wrong, out of place, or unexpected. He's often cited for his analysis of comedy as the perception of incongruity and absurdity. "Laughter is, above all, a corrective," Bergson argues. Freud thought that not all humor was "tendentious" (hostile and/or smutty), but Bergson finds hostility at the root of laughter: "Its function is to intimidate by humiliating," he writes, anticipating the social satire of *30 Rock*, on the one hand, but also the casual sexism and racism of Andrew Dice Clay, on the other. So while Bakhtin emphasizes comedy's subversive potential, Bergson reminds us of comedy's meaner flip side: "By laughter, society avenges itself for the liberties taken with it. It would fail in its object if it bore the stamp of sympathy or kindness."[20] In short, Bergson focuses on the joker's antipathy towards what's being mocked. And though he doesn't mention power relations, he's pointing to a reason why comedy has been and remains dominated by men: if comedy has the power to humiliate or even to "correct" a wrong, certainly it's no job for a woman, who couldn't possibly have the status or aggressiveness to call out social flubs—as seen in the history of stand-up comedy, an innately aggressive and frequently political format that remains dominated by men.[21]

Comedy as a topic of feminist criticism lagged behind other kinds of feminist academic work in the 1970s and 1980s, perhaps because women were avoiding topics that seemed frivolous. But more than that, feminist criticism hadn't yet become generous enough to include "low" cultural sites like the ethnic humor of Fanny Brice, or the women comedians appearing on *Laugh-In* (NBC 1969–1973), or the burlesque tradition that had produced Mae West—about whom there was deep suspicion that she was a "phallic woman" and an object of the male gaze (though there wasn't *enough* suspicion about the racial/racist dynamics in her movies). But over the next few decades, feminist scholars of popular culture tapped, revised, and reinvented theories of comedy in order to open up discussions of women's comedy, past and present, and to acknowledge its diversity. The following is a brief overview of these feminist critical models, often cited in the essays in this anthology. For easy reference, these theories are identified through specific authors and books, but we emphasize that these scholars and theoretical models are always in conversation with each other. Theories of "the unruly woman" and "the female trickster," for example, position the female comic figure into different frameworks, yielding in turn different questions and insights. But both models begin with the figure of the comic "woman on top" who disrupts gender hierarchies and threatens the status quo. Of the theorists discussed here, three are scholars who were once stand-up comedians—Regina Barreca, Joanne Gilbert, and Rebecca Krefting—so they bring to this conversation exciting insiders' perspectives on women's comedy.

FEMININE HUMOR

The earliest feminist scholars on comedy were eager to seize on comedy's antiauthoritarianism, pointing out that women writers from Aphra Behn to Lily Tomlin have used the power of wit and waggery to critique patriarchal culture. Judy Little's 1983 book, *Comedy and the Woman Writer: Woolf, Spark, and Feminism*, was the first to argue for a literary tradition of women's feminist comedy. Little draws on Turner's concept of liminality and festival role reversal to describe feminist humor that plays with identities and mocks social norms but then refuses to return from "festival" mode, instead pushing for "a radical reordering of social structures, a real rather than temporary and merely playful redefinition of sex identity." The result, she says, is comedy that "can well be called subversive, revolutionary, or renegade."[22] This conclusion is shared by Nancy Walker in her 1988 book, *A Very Serious Thing: Women's Humor and American Culture*. While Little focused on British writers, Walker argues for a tradition of female humorists in the United States, arguing that not all women's humor is feminist, but a "significant part" of that tradition is politically charged, either through a "subtle challenge" to gender roles or through open confrontation of those roles.[23] In the introduction to the 1988 anthology she coedited with Zita Dresner, *Redressing the Balance: American Women's Literary Humor from Colonial Times to the 1980s*, Walker and Dresner go further towards a theory of feminine humor, arguing that because of their unequal status, women have developed a distinctive comic style that is more indirect and oblique than men's. Drawing on Bergson's concept of laughter as a "corrective" device, they argue that women see and laugh about a "lack of balance" in patriarchal everyday life, and their anthology likewise seeks to correct the gender balance of American literary humor's canon.[24] In a later essay, Walker goes further with the political argument, emphasizing the importance of feminine humor as a site of feminist bonding and resistance. American women's humor, she says, has "functioned as a means of establishing and representing a community of shared concerns about oppression."[25] By 1994, four anthologies of feminist criticism about women and comedy had appeared, and the topic had expanded to include stand-up comedy, television, film, and theater.[26] Two of them were edited by Regina Barreca, a feminist critic who drew on her experience on comedy club stages in her 1991 book, *They Used to Call Me Snow White . . . But I Drifted: Women's Strategic Use of Humor*. Barreca wittily argues that the funny woman is implicitly a gender outlaw because she refuses her place as the silent, docile feminine ideal. Twenty-two years later, she reiterates this argument on behalf of a "feminine comedy" that is innately subversive and aligned with the oppressed: "Feminine comedy doesn't attack the powerless; it makes fun of the powerful."[27]

This body of scholarship was enormously important in drawing attention to the gendered nature of comedy and recognizing its feminist threads and potential. These scholars were also responsible for establishing women's humor as a legitimate history and topic for scholarship. The Walker/Dresner anthology, aiming to "re-dress the balance" of American comedy, illuminates and reclaims a long, rich continuum of women humorists from frontier days through Nora Ephron. Thinking about women and comedy this way, Barreca, Little, and Walker draw from second-wave feminism, which understands women as a unified category through which political bonding and activism can occur. But this perspective also shares second-wave feminism's danger of essentialism—casting all women into a monolithic group that doesn't account for the variables of race, sexuality, class, and access to power. The limitations of the Little/Walker/Barreca framework become apparent as more women comedians join the mainstream and enter the public realm from a wide variety of power positions; it would be difficult to categorize mainstream star Chelsea Handler, for instance, within the same oppressed group as lesbian African American comic Gloria Bigelow. Making the point that not all women's humor is progressive, Sean Zwagerman uses right-wing pundit Ann Coulter as an example of a woman using biting political wit that is profoundly antifeminist and often misogynist.[28] In a poststructuralist version of a "feminine humor" approach, Frances Gray draws on Jacques Lacan and Julia Kristeva to describe women as outsiders to masculine culture and thus likely to take special pleasure in playful subversion of hierarchy and order. While Little and others take Cixous's incitement to the feminine sentence more literally, Gray takes "writing the body" as poetic inspiration (as described in the first section of this essay), thus avoiding the problem of essentialism. Gray infuses the concept with specific historical meaning by imagining the woman comedian claiming presence and voice in traditionally masculine spaces: "A woman who both writes and performs, as so many woman comedians do, is making this image [of writing the body] concrete, flesh and blood as well as ink, a lived parable of the possibilities Cixous envisages."[29]

PERFORMED MARGINALITY

Avoiding the problem of essentialism—the idea that women as a group produce subversive female humor—Joanne Gilbert proposes that women's comedy is one strand of a larger category of humor that

comes from the social margins: "Like other marginalized performers, the female comic simultaneously affirms and subverts the status
quo," with the advantage that she is "part of the marginalized majority."[30] In *Performing Marginality: Humor, Gender, and Cultural Critique* (2004), Gilbert focuses on the practice and history of female
stand-up comedy, where the "performance of marginality" is a deliberate rhetorical strategy. Unlike the disadvantages of social marginality, she says, "rhetorical marginality may actually empower" because
it's a chosen stance, "performed or not performed at will."[31] Gilbert
provides a detailed taxonomy of women stand-up comedians from
Moms Mabley through Roseanne Barr, describing their tactics and
personas and noting that all of their self-presentations have equivalents in male comedians. If this is the case, she asks, is there actually
such a thing as female humor? Gilbert is especially skeptical of feminist humor, which, she says, is a term that "seems to be: (1) humor
simply performed by a female; (2) sexist humor directed at males; or
(3) 'marginal' humor."[32] However, this concept of feminist humor is
tethered to some problematic assumptions—namely, that feminism
resides in female bodies and that feminist comedy targets men rather
than patriarchal or sexist ideology. Overall, Gilbert believes comedy
cannot be political because humor itself is an

> "anti-rhetoric," always disavowing its own subversive potential by be-
> ing "just a joke." More important, humor renders its audience passive.
> It disarms through amusing. Laughter is not generally a galvanizing
> force toward political action. What critics who discuss the subversive
> nature of "feminist" humor miss is the fact that humor disarms all
> audiences—it does not discriminate between hegemonic and margin-
> alized individuals.

However, she insists that "performing marginality" is powerful, with
tangible "social and psychological effects."[33]

THE UNRULY WOMAN

Rather than claiming that women's comedy is innately subversive,
Kathleen Rowe focuses on a type of outrageous comic female character that she traces from the Middle Ages to contemporary popular culture. *The Unruly Woman: Gender and the Genres of Laughter* (1995) is about narrative comedy as opposed to stand-up, but her

extensive theorization of the "unruly woman" character has proven useful in describing many kinds of female comic performances. Rowe delivers a feminist critique of Bakhtin's theory of the female grotesque, emphasizing the subversive promise as well as the sexist dangers of this carnivalesque figure. She also draws on historian Natalie Zemon Davis's concept of "the woman on top," to describe female figures who "disrupt the norms of femininity and the social hierarchy of male over female through excess and outrageousness."[34] Rowe identifies the woman on top, or unruly woman, in a tradition ranging from medieval and Renaissance plays through Mae West, Roseanne, Miss Piggy, and romantic comedy films, where the excessive woman is given wide berth because she ultimately takes a traditional place as bride. Citing cultural theories of liminality and dirt as well as theories of narrative, Rowe demonstrates how women are traditionally "emplotted" in stories and how the unruly woman disrupts those plots. For Rowe, the unruly woman is no less than the "prototype of woman as subject—transgressive above all when she lays claim to her own desire."[35] This agency and desire drives the heroine of romantic comedy, Rowe says, but we can also imagine the stand-up comedian channeling "the woman on top" in using aggressive and suggestive language to assert herself.

THE FEMALE TRICKSTER

Like Rowe, Lori Landay identifies a recurring female character type whose cultural meanings across the centuries are deeply tied to ideologies of gender. In *Madcaps, Screwballs, and Con Women: The Female Trickster in American Culture* (1998), Landay taps North American folklore and literary traditions as sources of the female trickster character in popular culture: the sly, resourceful woman who subverts the status quo and outwits her adversaries through deception and fast thinking. Although this character is usually represented as male—the con artist, confidence man, or bad man–outlaw—Landay finds the trickster's doubleness and use of deception especially suited to women in that "the social practice of femininity is a form of trickery"; women are encouraged to "sublimate assertive impulses" and use cosmetics and fashion to look better for men.[36] In *I Love Lucy*, Lucy Ricardo's doubleness as 1950s housewife and wily schemer exemplifies the trickster's duality. The female trickster often shows up in comedy because of her wit and playfulness, and Landay's examples include, in addition to Lucy Ricardo, the heroines of screwball comedies and madcap sitcoms. However, this figure is a larger cultural archetype hovering at the boundaries of gender systems and "imagining what tactics are necessary to escape the system as well as what factors prevent that escape. In short, female tricksters are fantasy figures . . . of resistance, self-preservation, and self-definition."[37] In this rubric, Landay claims Catwoman in *Batman Returns* as a female trickster, as well as figures in folklore, literature, and advertising. Landay emphasizes the cultural specificity of these manifestations, which she finds imbricated in particular historical discourses and controversies about femininity.

FEMINIST CAMP

Camp humor, often traced to the ironic theatricality of Oscar Wilde (1854–1900), has long been considered the domain of gay men, but Pamela Robertson challenges that assumption by tracing a history of feminist camp as a performance style and an aesthetic. In *Guilty Pleasures: Feminist Camp from Mae West to Madonna* (1996), Robertson points out that whereas female stars such as Marlene Dietrich and Judy Garland have always been *interpreted* as camp, attention needs to be directed towards women as active *producers* of camp style and comedy. Robertson finds the feminist component of camp in its gender parody and the conscious performance of sexuality and gender *as* performance, exemplified in the comedic style she delineates from Mae West to *Absolutely Fabulous* (BBC 1992–2012). Drawing on Judith Butler's work on performativity as well as on Joan Riviere's theory of female masquerade, Robertson argues that "what gender parody takes as its object is not the image of the woman, but the idea—which, in camp, becomes a joke—that an essential feminine identity exists prior to the image."[38] Making this move, Robertson addresses the problem that female camp figures can be read as misogynist stereotypes, claiming that a feminist perspective can reread and reinterpret camp history, drawing on camp's inclination toward the recycling of the past. "By recycling feminist camp," she says, "camp spectators, producers, and critics can potentially insure that we never see these stereotypes the same way again."[39] Spectators who "get it" have always been intrinsic to camp history, so Robertson's call for feminist spectatorship develops this dynamic by emphasizing the female audience as well as the ironic performance of femininity.

"PRETTY/FUNNY"

Linda Mizejewski's *Pretty Funny: Women Comedians and Body Politics* (2014) argues that in the twenty-first century, women's comedy has become a key site for feminist discourse and representations of feminism. The concept of "pretty versus funny" springs from the biases of popular culture, which tends to divide women in comedy into the "pretty" ones—actresses with good comic timing who get cast in romantic comedies—and the "funny" ones—comedians who write and perform their own work but aren't considered attractive enough to be leading ladies. Since 2000 that stereotype has been powerfully challenged by the likes of Tina Fey, Sarah Silverman, Amy Schumer, and Amy Poehler; these comedians follow the long tradition of Mae West and burlesque stars who have lampooned and satirized femininity and "prettiness." Given the binary of pretty-versus-funny, "women comics, no matter what they look like, have been located in opposition to 'pretty,' enabling them to engage in a transgressive comedy grounded in the female body—its looks, its race and sexuality, and its relationship to ideal versions of femininity."[40] Mizejewski emphasizes that in American culture, "pretty" overwhelmingly means not just heterosexual but also white, so she is particularly interested in how these diversity issues play across the work of contemporary women comedy stars.

CHARGED HUMOR

In *All Joking Aside: American Humor and Its Discontents* (2014), Rebecca Krefting develops the concept of "charged humor" to describe stand-up comedy that challenges the status quo and aims for social change. Like Gilbert, Krefting includes women comedians as part of a larger category of minorities who bring a marginal perspective to the stage, but she differs from Gilbert in her insistence on the political intent and effects of this comedy. Honoring the pioneering work of Walker and Dresner, Krefting argues that in performances that offer "examples of feeling like a second-class citizen," this type of comedian "charges audience members with complicity toward social inequities, and . . . offers solutions for redressing the balance." This is humor that "springs from a social and political consciousness" with the aim of "creating cultural citizenship."[41] Krefting is especially interested in how audience identification with the performer works as a dynamic in stand-up comedy. She claims identification is a key to the failure of women to be as commercially successful as male come-dians; because women are assumed to be socially inferior, "there is simply no economic incentive for anyone, men and women alike, to learn to identify and 'buy in' to a woman's point of view."[42] Krefting's attention to queer, racial, and ethnic humor is important in "redress-ing the balance" of earlier feminist models of comedy that tended to focus on white women, a tendency of the second-wave feminism in which those theories were based. Krefting's inclusion of people of color, LGBTQ comedians, comedians with disabilities, and Arab and Muslim comedians after 9/11 reveals comedy as a diverse space full of competing and very different voices.

HISTORICAL/CULTURAL STUDIES

In addition to these critical theories of gender and comedy, a num-ber of theater and film histories have provided insights into the social meanings of women's comedy in the nineteenth and early twentieth centuries, producing a valuable genealogy of funny women in Amer-ican culture. The historical and recovery work of these scholars has revealed how early cinema and theatrical venues offered women op-portunities for outrageous performance styles and for the flaunting of large, even grotesque bodies in the face of new trends for dieting and slimness.

Robert Allen's *Horrible Prettiness: Burlesque and American Cul-ture* (1991) characterizes burlesque from the 1860s into the 1920s as the staging of the transgressive female body. He describes the con-troversies about this theatrical venue as "a struggle between spec-tacle and mimesis, display and drama, desire and repression. Ulti-mately, it was a struggle *over* women's sexuality."[43] Along the same lines, Susan Glenn emphasizes the importance of comic women in popular theater during this era; in *Female Spectacle: The Theatrical Roots of Modern Feminism* (2000), she argues that aggressive, outsize comic headliners such as May Irwin and Trixie Friganza signaled the contentions of the emerging women's movement. Stage comedy al-lowed women to act out taboo disruptive behaviors and "helped move women and comedy into the twentieth century."[44] One of the stage comedians cited by Glenn is Marie Dressler, who went from theater to cinema and became MGM's top box-office draw. In *A Great Big Girl Like Me: The Films of Marie Dressler* (2009), Victoria Sturtevant analyzes Dressler's unlikely popularity as a tall, two-hundred-pound woman whose stardom peaked when she was sixty-two. Examining

Dressler's career during the Great Depression, Sturtevant's work captures the specific historical resonance of this comedian and contributes to the larger cultural project of recovering stars and performers who have been forgotten or relegated to footnotes in entertainment histories. Alison Kibler likewise draws attention to forgotten comic stars in *Rank Ladies: Gender and Cultural Hierarchy in American Vaudeville* (1999), which demonstrates how large, ethnic, and disorderly female bodies were both celebrated and reviled in vaudeville comedy. The "wild woman" behavior of the vaudeville female comedians mocked Victorian conventions but also "underscored the degree to which resistance to upward mobility and Americanization was infused with resentment over shifting gender relations."[45]

This comic "wild woman" is included in Henry Jenkins's book *What Made Pistachio Nuts? Early Sound Comedy and the Vaudeville Aesthetic* (1992) as a figure who embodied both fear and excitement about suffragism and the nascent women's movement in the first decades of the twentieth century. In his chapter on representations of the unruly wife in early film comedies, Jenkins's argument aligns with Kibler's observations about vaudeville, in that the wild woman was "both a target of chastising male laughter and a vehicle for liberating female laughter."[46] Rob King likewise devotes a chapter to the role of women and comedy in *The Fun Factory: The Keystone Film Company and the Emergence of Mass Culture* (2008). Focusing on the 1910 film company famous for its comic shorts, King demonstrates how comedy enabled women to embody changing gender roles—and not in a merely symbolic way. Women's engagement in physical comedy was like their newly allowed engagement in sports, he claims, in that "the New Woman had defined herself, in large part, by reclaiming the right to her own embodiment," so that "female comic performance contributed to the somatic iconography through which gendered change was understood."[47] All of these studies emphasize class and ethnicity as key factors in the emergence of early women comedians, greatly enhancing our understanding of women in American comedy.

UPDATING THE THEORIES, REFOCUSING THE SPOTLIGHT

Hysterical! updates and expands critical work on comics such as Mae West, Roseanne Barr, Tina Fey, and Ellen DeGeneres, but this collection also includes scholarly studies of Fay Tincher, Mabel Normand,

Fanny Brice, and Carol Burnett, pioneering comedians who have not been extensively analyzed in feminist and media scholarship. Our anthology begins with chapters on Normand and Tincher, who were renowned comic stars of silent cinema, exemplifying the arguments made by Henry Jenkins and Rob King. Kristine Brunovska Karnick, in "Mabel Normand: New Woman in the Flapper Age," notes that two major movie magazines honored Normand as a fan favorite and "living legend" in 1914 and 1915, even though Normand was all but forgotten by the 1920s. A similar story is told by Joanna Rapf in "Fay Tincher: Female Rowdiness and Social Change." Tincher's wildly athletic comic stunts awed audiences and shot her to stardom between 1914 and 1920. Her Rowdy Ann character remains a classic unruly woman of silent cinema. But Tincher left the movie business entirely in 1928. Both she and Normand defy Hollywood histories that define "comedian comedy" (a style centered on the lone clown figure) as a male tradition ranging from Charlie Chaplin, Buster Keaton, and other key figures from the silent era through the contemporary cinema.[48] The similarities of Normand and Tincher say a lot about what gets excluded from those histories as well as what got excluded from women's comedy in Hollywood after the silent era. Normand and Tincher performed bold physical comedy that was aligned with the athleticism and independence of the New Woman. Fortunately, some of Tincher's and Normand's films are easily accessible, as Rapf and Karnick point out, so that it's possible to see the slapstick female comedian in action in the early days of cinema.

The next two chapters focus on stars who made their mark in vaudeville and on Broadway in the 1920s and 1930s before moving on to other media; both of them engaged in comedy that lampooned traditional womanly behavior. In "Fanny Brice's New Nose: Beauty, Ethnicity, and Liminality," Kristen Anderson Wagner analyzes Brice's ambivalent relationships to femininity, theater, and race. Playing on her position as the Jewish outsider and as the nonglamorous female performer, Brice used her talent for slapstick and mimicry to undermine the racial and gender ideals of the showgirl and glamour girl. Wagner argues, however, that even as her comedy parodied white femininity, Brice retained in her overall career an inclination toward melodrama that acknowledged the costs of marginalization and "made her performances both sympathetic and subversive" (84). Appearing in New York theaters during the same era, Mae West had no such affinity for sentimentality or melodrama except as targets of her campy humor. Kristen Hatch's chapter, "Mae West: The Constant Sinner," explores West's frank representations of female sexual desire in an era when femininity was identified with decorum, restraint, and maternity. Best known for her over-the-top send-ups of glamour, West was also a playwright, script writer, and novelist, as Hatch points out, whose sexually active *"femmes amoureuses"* or "daughters of joy" characters exposed social hypocrisy about female desire. Like Brice, West was aware of the centrality of whiteness in feminine ideals, and though her uses of black performance styles and black actresses are often problematic, West's connections with black women as well as gay men produced a transgressive "equivalency between black women, gay men, and white women . . . that was conveyed through their expressions of sexual desire," Hatch writes. West's popular films of the 1930s and early 1940s marked the end of female comedian comedies for decades. With the predominance of romantic comedy, it was not until Lily Tomlin's films of the 1980s that a woman headlined a comedy film on her own, and Tomlin was an outlier until the films of Melissa McCarthy and Amy Schumer more than a generation later.

Instead, television was the medium where women comedians could flourish, even if they were a minority there, because television relied less on the glamorizing close-up and provided venues and narratives not dependent on heterosexual romance. In short, women could look funny, do raucous slapstick, and engage in stories about work, friendship, and motherhood, as seen in the landmark series *I Love Lucy* (CBS 1951–1957), *The Carol Burnett Show* (CBS 1967–1978), and *Roseanne* (ABC 1988–1997). In "Lucille Ball and the Lucy Character: Familiarity, Female Friendship, and the Anxiety of Competence," Lori Landay emphasizes the significance of *I Love Lucy* in shaping the character-based comedy series that would become the enduring model for sitcoms. Tracing the development of Ball's Lucy Ricardo character, Landay expands her previous work on Lucy as a trickster (described in the previous section) by analyzing the gags, slapstick performances, facial expressions, and voice intonations that made Lucy a comedy icon. Although Lucille Ball did not write her own work, Landay argues that Ball "invented the basic emotional and psychological elements of the Lucy character" by drawing on her previous work in radio and film. While Ball was famous for a singular, long-running character, Carol Burnett was famous for her numerous comic-skit characters and her parodies of glamorous film heroines. In "Carol Burnett: Home, Horror, and Hilarity on *The Carol Burnett Show*," Linda Mizejewski focuses on Burnett's comic, often grotesque, portrayals of Hollywood sirens and on her role as the harried daughter Eunice in "The Family" skits. Lampooning both melodrama and glamour, Burnett "was the star who was *not* beautiful and *not* classy, but her comedy made those ideals ludicrous rather than intimidating," Mizejewski writes. Ten years after Burnett's variety show ended, those ideals were similarly dismissed in the groundbreaking series *Roseanne* in its "depiction of an embattled working-class family, revolving around an overweight, sexy, cynical woman," as Rosie White describes it. In "Roseanne Barr: Remembering *Roseanne*," White revisits the series in light of Barr's celebrity in the following decades, including Barr's decisions about undergoing cosmetic surgery that seem to contradict the meanings of her "unruly" body celebrated by feminist critics of the television show. White points out that the series itself was never free of such contradictions about commodification and class, despite the wit of its social satire and feminist comedy. Analyzing the final season, White reveals the show's self-consciousness about Barr's celebrity status and about the drive of media culture to fetishize both blue-collar identity and feminism, "deploying discourses of class, race, and gender while tacitly denying that such differences *really* matter."

Brenda Weber and Joselyn Leimbach likewise draw on celebrity studies to analyze the star persona of Ellen DeGeneres, whose popular image as "authentic" drives her reputation as a beloved comic, feel-good feminist, and the entertainment world's most visible lesbian. In "Ellen DeGeneres's Incorporate Body: The Politics of Authenticity," Weber and Leimbach explore DeGeneres's popularity across multiple media platforms, made possible because of what they call her "incorporate body . . . a specific fashioning of self that combines and fuses together hybridities of desire and identity under a sign of authenticity." Similar to White's critique of the commodification of marginal identities in *Roseanne*, Weber and Leimbach argue that DeGeneres's embrace of marginality operates within the neoliberal logics of individualism and conspicuous consumption and that she manages the transgressive elements of her persona—her masculinity and her lesbian identity—through comic strategies that evade a political stand. Demonstrating the latter tactic, Weber and Leimbach analyze celebrity encounters on *The Ellen DeGeneres Show* (NBC 2003–), where potentially subversive sexual comedy is defused by ambiguity that undermines sex and gender conventions but reinforces them as well.

As opposed to DeGeneres's skirting of queer and feminist politics, Lily Tomlin and Margaret Cho have publicly claimed those politics as intrinsic to their comedy. In "Lily Tomlin: Queer Sensibilities, Funny Feminism, and Multimedia Stardom," Suzanne Leonard
maps Tomlin's long career onto the development of American feminism and the emergence of queer politics since the 1960s. Leonard
points out the strong thread of social critique in Tomlin's work, beginning with her famous Ernestine character of the 1960s and per-
sisting through her Netflix sitcom *Grace and Frankie* (2015–) four
decades later. Tomlin's 1980 film *9 to 5* remains an icon of "popular feminism"—that is, predominantly white, second-wave feminism
that was focused on equality and civil rights. But Tomlin has also always played diverse characters—gay, male, impoverished, disabled—
that "evince queer sensibilities in that they decenter normative categorization," Leonard argues. While Tomlin and DeGeneres play to
mainstream audiences, Margaret Cho plays to the margins and offers comedy as revolution, as evident in the title of Rebecca Krefting's
chapter, "Margaret Cho's Army: 'We Are the Baddest Motherfuckers
on the Block.'" Krefting claims that Cho's affinities with racial and
sexual minorities, as well as other marginalized groups, have created
a highly diverse audience for her "charged humor . . . that intentionally educates and mobilizes audiences, creates community, and offers strategies for social change." Krefting focuses on the rhetoric of
Cho's comedy as well as the social contexts that motivate her politics, but she is also attentive to Cho's audiences and to the technologies of production that circulate the comedian's work. The latter
are especially important, Krefting points out, because social media
has allowed Cho to take control of her career after her earlier history of racist and sexist treatment at the hands of mainstream media
production.

Bambi Haggins's chapter, "Moms Mabley and Wanda Sykes: 'I'ma
Be Me,'" demonstrates how closely the comedy of Mabley and Sykes
is aligned with that of Cho in seeking to mobilize, instruct, and
speak truth to power. Haggins pairs these comedians not only because of their shared identities as black gay women but because their
careers, generations apart, illustrate the uses of black comedy as a
tool of protest and resistance in two different eras. Mabley began in
the early twentieth-century Chitlin Circuit, the second-tier clubs and
venues available to black audiences and entertainers, and developed
into a powerful voice in the civil rights era. Her folksy "Moms" per-

sona was disarming and authoritative at once, slyly providing imaginary access to national and world forums in comedy albums such as *Moms Mabley at the "UN"* (1961) and *Moms Mabley at the Geneva Conference* (1962). Haggins sees Mabley as the predecessor of Wanda Sykes, noting their shared candor, directness, and defiance in the face of social injustice. Especially striking is the sexual agency evident in their comedy, even though Mabley was not able to make her lesbian identity public as Sykes did in 2008 as part of her protest of Proposition 8, which barred gay marriage in California. For Haggins, only an intersectional approach connecting race, gender, and sexuality can account for the "transgressive and transformative" power of their comedy.

Whoopi Goldberg began her career with socially biting stand-up comedy routines similar to those of Mabley and Sykes, and we continue to see her comic wit in her current role as television talk-show maven. But cinema was where Goldberg went mainstream as a comedian, and her comedy films are the focus of Rebecca Wanzo's chapter, "Whoopi Goldberg in Hollywood: Queering Comic Genre Genealogies." Wanzo's interest is how Goldberg, by way of race and gender, is a bad or awkward "fit" in Hollywood genres, creating a queer and comic dissonance between body and narrative formula. Wanzo argues that "not fitting" is important "not only [for] comic genealogies, but some discourses of Americannesss itself," a dynamic informed and complicated by race: Goldberg "both disrupts idealized constructions and naturalizes a black female presence in genres that are consistently situated in Hollywood as inappropriate for black women stars." One of Goldberg's comedy films is a farce requiring her to perform in drag, but Wanzo uses the trope and figure of drag to read Goldberg's disruptions of other Hollywood genres as well.

As the previous paragraphs indicate, the contributions in this collection focus on comic style, celebrity and stardom, genre, and the politics and technologies of production. So Anthony McIntyre's study of Sarah Silverman is unique in its focus on an aesthetic: cuteness, an affect and style that describes a type of humor but also encompasses a broad range of commodities, star personalities, media images, character types, online videos, and other pop-culture sites. Cuteness is associated with precarity and vulnerability, but Silverman's grotesque and unsettling uses of cuteness expose the power dynamics of this aesthetic, which McIntyre describes as a "neutralizing" of social and economic uneasiness by "providing pleasure in aesthetically consuming vulnerability in others." His chapter also considers the aging female body, pointing out how Silverman, policed and criticized as a middle-aged single woman without children, pushes the cuteness aesthetic concerning children and motherhood to interrogate its ambivalence.

Because this anthology foregrounds the creativity of women comedians and the feminist implications of their work, it fittingly concludes with two chapters on female auteurship and body/feminist politics. These chapters also remind us of how the female comedy auteur is increasingly visible but still a minority in a male-dominated field. The stardom and celebrity of Tina Fey and Lena Dunham are deeply invested in their success as television showrunners, the creators/producers identified with a specific series, making them exceptions in a prestigious cohort that is overwhelmingly male. In addition, Fey's series *30 Rock* is associated with "quality" television, a canon that is likewise dominated by male-driven series and masculinized assumptions about content. In "Tina Fey: 'Quality' Comedy and the Body of the Female Comedy Author," Julia Havas explores how Fey's reputation as a feminist and as a writer of "quality" programming conflicted with her increasingly grotesque physical comedy on *30 Rock*. Many feminists in the media disapproved of the "*embodied* (physical, grotesque) satire, located in the female comedian's bodily performance," Havas points out. Controversies about the show's gender politics were further complicated by Fey's tendency to satirize all gender discourses, including feminism, and by the tendency of quality programming to favor postfeminist rather than feminist agendas. Contested representations of the comic auteur's body are likewise addressed in Maria Sulimma's chapter, "Lena Dunham: Cringe Comedy and Body Politics." Sulimma pinpoints the central dynamic of Dunham's comedy as its disregard for boundaries, evident in the awkward social transgressions of her characters and in Dunham's personal tendency to overshare and to disregard public versus private niceties, as seen in her casual use of her own nudity on her series *Girls*. *Girls* has been criticized for its narrow focus but lauded for its feminist insistence on depicting Dunham's supposedly "nonnormative" nude body—that is, an average-looking body not often seen in mainstream media and thus a target of misogynist criticism. As Sulimma emphasizes, "Her comedy never makes the 'non-normative' body a target, but rather the norm by which audiences and other characters respond to it."

CODA

When we began writing and planning this anthology in 2013, we could not have foreseen the coming boom years for women in comedy. As it turns out, Lena Dunham remains a fitting topic to conclude this book not only because of her taboo-breaking body politics and powerful auteurism, but also because she is emblematic of the unruly women who began to capture mainstream audiences in the following years. Given that a form of popular feminism—contested as it may be—has slowly pervaded the media since 2013, it is perhaps less surprising that in-your-face feminism has made a place for itself on television. Amy Schumer's bawdy comedy on *Inside Amy Schumer* (Comedy Central 2013–) immediately attracted attention with gender-skewing skits such as "Lunch at O'Nutters," a parody of the restaurant chain Hooters. Schumer cranked up her feminist critique in the second season of her show, taking on topics like rape culture and rape in the military. Her 2015 skits "Last Fuckable Day" and "Twelve Angry Men" quickly became feminist classics, savaging sexist representations of women in media. In the latter, a parody of a famous jury drama, twelve relatively unattractive male stars grapple with the question of whether or not Schumer is "hot enough to have her own television show." Meanwhile, for shrewd political comedy, Samantha Bee emerged as the pundit whose brilliance and acidic commentary is acknowledged as the equal of her late-night colleagues Jon Stewart, Stephen Colbert, Trevor Noah, and John Oliver. Formerly a writer and performer for *The Daily Show with Jon Stewart* (Comedy Central 1999–2015), Bee launched *Full Frontal with Samantha Bee* (TBS 2016–) as an unabashedly feminist weekly news show that opens each episode with a hard-hitting satirical monologue, wittily arguing a case about issues ranging from immigration and women's health to the follies of elections and political leaders.

This most recent wave of women comedians exemplifies our claim that diversity and difference are likely to be central in women's comedy, given its investments in issues of marginalization and exclusion. In 2012 Kate McKinnon became the first openly gay cast member of *Saturday Night Live* (NBC 1975–). Her impersonations of Hillary Clinton were a staple of the 2016 presidential election season, matched only by her uncanny performances as Justin Bieber, a coup de grâce of cocky queerness. Meanwhile, Maria Bamford, whose comedy embraces difference and imperfection, regularly deals with mental illness as a topic of her sets and in her Netflix series *Lady Dynamite* (2016–). In television sitcoms, Mindy Kaling broke barriers as the first east Indian American woman to create and star in her own show, *The Mindy Project*, about the romantic adventures of a young obstetrician/gynecologist, a character based on her own mother. And as this anthology goes to press, Aparna Nancherla has accumulated a massive online following and was named by *Rolling Stone* as one of the twenty-five funniest people on Twitter.

However, the comedy scene across all media remains both segregated and stacked, especially against women of color. This is evident in the career of Leslie Jones, who played black venues all over the country for twenty-five years before joining *Saturday Night Live* in 2014, first as a writer and then as a cast member at the age of forty-five. "Every black comedian in the country knew what I could do," she said in a *New Yorker* interview, "But that doesn't mean everyone else was paying attention."[49] Jones was hired because of a media storm protesting the absence of women of color on *SNL*, a telling sign of a shift in cultural awareness of this problem, given the lack of diversity spanning *SNL*'s forty-plus-year history. By the summer of 2016, Jones's star power was considerable enough that she was tapped for network television commercials and for NBC's coverage of the Summer Olympics in Rio de Janeiro. But she was also the target of a vicious, racist internet attack at this time, indicating how mainstream stardom for a large, black, funny actress also entails backlash and fierce resistance. Jones was also part of the all-female lead cast of the *Ghostbusters* remake (2016), which was a high-mark moment for women's comedy, but it drew a line in the sand, too, provoking a sexist smear campaign on social media before the film was even released. No matter the quality of the film itself, the ferocity of the backlash against the very idea of a female remake suggests the intrinsically transgressive nature of women taking on the culturally masculine role of being funny.

As you consider the chapters in this volume describing the extraordinary work of this long line of women comics, we hope you'll keep in mind the ways that these accomplishments were always achieved

0.2. *Vanity Fair* tweets its cover image, September 14, 2015

0.3. Samantha Bee's response to *Vanity Fair*, September 14, 2015

against a cultural backdrop of exclusion and misreading. The recent explosion of funny women on stage, television, film, and electronic media has been a powerful intervention against these exclusions, but there are many ways in which women's comedy is still being ignored, misread, and underestimated. Consider a *Vanity Fair* cover story from late 2015, "Why Late Night Comedy Is Better Than Ever."[50]

Although the article does acknowledge the scarcity of women in late-night television comedy as a problem, the startlingly tone-deaf photo that accompanied it and the Twitter caption frankly revel in the idea of comedy hosting as a man's club, claiming, "We talked to all the titans of late-night television," while pointedly excluding the two women late-night hosts, Chelsea Handler and Samantha Bee. The caption goes on to claim that "late-night is better than ever," implicitly equating quality with masculine exclusivity. Samantha Bee, preparing to premiere her own late-night show, assembled a visual retort: a version of the same photo with herself photoshopped in as a centaur, laser beams coming out of her eyes. The self-representation of a woman comedian as an angry, powerful, mythical creature crashing a boys' club is an apt metaphor for the ways women comics are still required to prove themselves—or even just remind people they exist—over and over again, despite the overwhelming cultural impact and financial success of their work across many media. Bee's unruly response to her own exclusion is consistent with a recent move toward funny women engaging in outspoken self-advocacy. At

a 2016 press conference, Tina Fey blasted back against the suggestion that the work of acknowledging women's participation in comedy is now done: "Every single interviewer asked, 'Isn't this an amazing time for women in comedy?' Fey says. 'People really wanted us to
be openly grateful—'Thank you so much!'—and we were like, 'No,
it's a terrible time. If you were to really look at it, the boys are still
getting more money for a lot of garbage, while the ladies are hustling
and doing amazing work for less.'"[51] The fact that neither Bee nor Fey
takes the trouble to hide her anger is a retort to the logic of hysteria—
the idea that women's emotions disqualify them from public input
on weighty matters. Indeed, their anger sharpens and gives shape to
their input, as they do not flatter and cajole but demand equity in the
public discourse around American popular entertainment.

In the comedy of the women included in this anthology, you can
often glimpse this edgy demand for attention and recognition. It's
the through-line of many of their comic characters and personas: Fay
Tincher's Rowdy Ann, Lucille Ball's Lucy Ricardo, Moms Mabley's
"Moms," Carol Burnett's Eunice Higgins, Whoopi Goldberg's Fontaine, Roseanne Barr's Roseanne Conner, Tina Fey's Liz Lemon, Lena
Dunham's Hannah Horvath. You can hear it, too, in the jokes, rants,
quips, and satire described in these pages, from Margaret Cho's political barbs to Mae West's claims for female sexual pleasure. Women
act out, speak up, and misbehave in these performances, and these
comedians are hysterical.

NOTES

1. The diagnosis was most commonly, though not exclusively, applied to
white, middle-class women who would have been the objects of scrutiny for a
newly developing professional class of physicians heavily influenced by the growing literature on psychoanalysis, which readily pathologized the female body as
inherently unbalanced, a notion sanctified in Josef Breuer and Sigmund Freud's
Studies on Hysteria (1895), trans. James Strachey (New York: Basic Books, 1957).

2. Victoria Sturtevant makes this observation about hysteria in "Getting Hys-
terical: *Thelma & Louise* and Laughter," in *Thelma & Louise Live! The Cultural
Aftermath of an American Film*, ed. Bernie Cook (Austin: University of Texas
Press, 2007), 45.

3. Quoted in Elaine Showalter, "Hysteria, Feminism, and Gender," in *Hysteria beyond Freud*, eds. Sander L. Gilman et al. (Berkeley: University of California
Press, 1993), 302. As Carroll Smith-Rosenberg points out, the suspicion that hysterics were frauds led physicians to a "compensatory sense of superiority and hostility" towards these patients, condemning their "emotional indulgence, moral

weakness, and lack of willpower." *Disorderly Conduct: Visions of Gender in Victorian America* (New York: Oxford University Press, 1986), 204–205.

4. Lori Landay, *Madcaps, Screwballs, and Con Women: The Female Trickster in American Culture* (Philadelphia: University of Pennsylvania Press, 1998), 7.

5. Kathleen Rowe (Karlyn), *The Unruly Woman: Gender and the Genres of Laughter* (Austin: University of Texas Press, 1995), 43.

6. Christopher Hitchens, "Why Women Aren't Funny," *Vanity Fair*, Jan. 2007.

7. Larry Getlen, "The Man's Man," *New York Post*, June 17, 2012.

8. Olga Khazan, "Plight of the Funny Female," *Atlantic*, Nov. 19, 2015.

9. Liana S. E. Hone, William Hurwitz, and Debra Lieberman, "Sex Differences in Preferences for Humor," *Evolutionary Psychology*, Feb. 10, 2015.

10. Frances Gray, *Women and Laughter* (Charlottesville: University of Virginia Press, 1994), 8–12.

11. Hélène Cixous, "The Laugh of the Medusa," trans. Keith Cohen and Paula Cohen, *Signs* 1, no. 4 (Summer 1976): 885–886.

12. Gray, *Women and Laughter*, 185.

13. See Victor Turner, *The Ritual Process: Structure and Anti-Structure* (Ithaca, NY: Cornell University Press, 1969), 110, 112–113, 128. Henry Jenkins uses Turner and liminality in his discussion of the clown figure in *What Made Pistachio Nuts? Early Sound Comedy and the Vaudeville Aesthetic* (New York: Columbia University Press, 1992), 224–225. Judy Little uses this concept as a framework for her argument about feminist comedy in *Comedy and the Woman Writer: Woolf, Spark, and Feminism* (Lincoln: University of Nebraska Press, 1983), 3–6. Also see Rowe, *The Unruly Woman*, 48–49.

14. Joanne R. Gilbert, *Performing Marginality: Humor, Gender, and Cultural Critique* (Detroit: Wayne State University Press, 2004), 5.

15. Rebecca Krefting, *All Joking Aside: American Humor and Its Discontents* (Baltimore: Johns Hopkins University Press, 2014), 6–7.

16. Mikhail Bakhtin, *Rabelais and His World* (1965), trans. Hélène Iswolsky (Bloomington: Indiana University Press, 1984), 240.

17. See Rowe (Karlyn)'s extended engagement with Bakhtin in chapter 1 of *The Unruly Woman*, 25–49, as well as Mary Russo's feminist elaboration of the grotesque, *The Female Grotesque: Risk, Excess, and Modernity* (New York: Routledge, 1994).

18. Sigmund Freud, *Jokes and Their Relation to the Unconscious* (1905), trans. James Strachey (New York: Norton, 1963) 97, 100–101.

19. Ramona Curry, "Mae West and Film Censorship," in *Classical Hollywood Comedy*, eds. Kristine Brunovska Karnick and Henry Jenkins (New York: Routledge, 1995), 227–230.

20. Henri Bergson, *Laughter: An Essay on the Meaning of the Comic* (1911), trans. Cloudesley Brereton and Fred Rothwell (Boston: IndyPublish, 2008), 197, 198.

21. Rebecca Krefting points out the larger social and economic picture regarding this situation, arguing that stand-up comedy is dominated by white, heterosexual men because audiences prefer to identify with comedians who are "comfortably situated within the dominant culture and bearing the privileges of not only legal but social inclusion." *All Joking Aside*, 133.

22. Little, *Comedy and the Woman Writer*, 2.

23. Nancy A. Walker, *A Very Serious Thing: Women's Humor and American Culture* (Minneapolis: University of Minnesota Press, 1988), 13.

24. Nancy A. Walker and Zita Dresner, introduction to *Redressing the Balance: American Women's Literary Humor from Colonial Times to the 1980s*, eds. Walker and Dresner (Jackson: University Press of Mississippi, 1988), xxii–xxvi.

25. Nancy A. Walker, "Toward Solidarity: Women's Humor and Group Identity," in *Women's Comic Visions*, ed. June Sochen (Detroit: Wayne State University Press, 1991), 60.

26. Regina Barreca, ed., *Last Laughs: Perspectives on Women and Comedy* (New York: Gordon and Breach, 1988); Sochen, *Women's Comic Visions*; Regina Barreca, ed., *New Perspectives on Women and Comedy* (New York: Gordon and Breach, 1992); Gail Finney, ed., *Look Who's Laughing: Gender and Comedy* (New York: Gordon and Breach, 1994).

27. See Barreca's descriptions of a feminine humor that is antagonistic or resistant to patriarchy in *They Used to Call Me Snow White . . . But I Drifted: Women's Strategic Use of Humor* (New York: Viking, 1991), 13–21. She makes the remark about power and humor in the preface to *Women and Comedy*, eds. Peter Dickinson et al. (Lanham, MD: Fairleigh Dickinson University Press, 2013), xi.

28. Sean Zwagerman, "A Cautionary Tale: Ann Coulter and the Failure of Humor," in Dickinson, *Women and Comedy*, 171–183.

29. Gray, *Women and Laughter*, 37.

30. Gilbert, *Performing Marginality*, 33.

31. Ibid., 6–7.

32. Ibid., 135.

33. Ibid., 177.

34. Rowe (Karlyn), *The Unruly Woman*, 30.

35. Ibid., 31.

36. Ibid., 11–12.

37. Landay, *Madcaps, Screwballs*, 26.

38. Pamela Robertson, *Guilty Pleasures: Feminist Camp from Mae West to Madonna* (Durham, NC: Duke University Press, 1996), 12.

39. Ibid., 143.

40. Linda Mizejewski, *Pretty/Funny: Women Comedians and Body Politics* (Austin: University of Texas Press, 2014), 5.

41. Krefting, *All Joking Aside*, 25.

42. Ibid., 119.

43. Robert C. Allen, *Horrible Prettiness: Burlesque and American Culture* (Chapel Hill: University of North Carolina Press, 1991), 81.

44. Susan A. Glenn, *Female Spectacle: The Theatrical Roots of Modern Feminism* (Cambridge, MA: Harvard University Press, 2000), 73.

45. M. Alison Kibler, *Rank Ladies: Gender and Cultural Hierarchy in American Vaudeville* (Chapel Hill: University of North Carolina Press, 1999), 77.

46. Jenkins, *What Made Pistachio Nuts?*, 247.

47. Robert King, *The Fun Factory: The Keystone Film Company and the Emergence of Mass Culture* (Berkeley: University of California Press, 2008), 220–221.

48. Steve Seidman defines this type of comedy, based around a central clown figure, in *Comedian Comedy: A Tradition in Hollywood Film* (Ann Arbor: University of Michigan Research Press, 1981). Also see Kathleen Rowe's comments on the gendered implications of this comedy tradition in "Comedy, Melodrama, and Gender: Theorizing the Genres of Laughter," in Karnick and Jenkins, *Classical Hollywood Comedy*, 45–46.

49. Andrew Marantz, "Ready for Prime Time: After Twenty-Five Years as a Road Comic, Leslie Jones Becomes a Star," *New Yorker*, Jan. 4, 2016.

50. David Camp, "Why Late Night Comedy Is Better Than Ever," *Vanity Fair*, Oct. 2015.

51. Ned Ehrbar, "Stop Asking Tina Fey if Women Are Funny" *Metro*, Mar. 2, 2016.

CHAPTER I

MABEL NORMAND:
NEW WOMAN IN THE FLAPPER AGE

KRISTINE BRUNOVSKA KARNICK

AT THE HEIGHT of her career, Mabel Normand (1895–1930) was judged by audiences as the most popular female comedian in Hollywood, and a quarter million *Photoplay* readers voted her their favorite film personality of 1914.[1] In 1915 *Moving Picture World* ran a movie popularity contest, which Normand won as "Female Comedian."[2] As Scott Berg has noted, "In this early world of ephemeral stardom, Mabel Normand was one of the few genuine living legends to walk the earth. Every critic praised her as the greatest comedienne of the silent screen."[3] However, by 1917, a mere seven years into her career, her stock had dropped to the point that *Motion Picture Magazine* ranked Normand 86th out of 104 performers in its "Popular Player Contest." Several other polls conducted in the 1917–1919 period publicized similar results.[4]

The drop in Mabel Normand's popularity, which continued throughout the 1920s, has routinely been attributed to events in her personal life—she was implicated and/or indirectly involved in several Hollywood scandals. Accounts of Normand's life and career have continued to cite her association with embattled comic costar Fatty Arbuckle; her implication in director William Desmond Taylor's murder; a shooting involving her chauffeur and her gun; her association with Wallace Reid at the time of his death from a drug overdose; and charges of her own drug use, all of which have been posited as driving factors in the eclipse of her career. However, the decline in her popularity began in the late 1910s and thus preceded the majority of these events, some by more than five years.

More closely aligned with the slide in Normand's popularity were social and industry trends that increasingly favored a new style of comedienne and a new kind of star. Normand represented a vivacious, active, athletically gifted turn-of-the-century conception of the "New Woman," a figure linked to ideals of autonomy and expanded notions of femininity. Normand portrayed a wide variety of characters in more than two hundred film roles. An especially popular character type was the poor, rural working girl with long ringlet curls and little or no makeup. Early films such as *Mabel's Dramatic Career* (1913), *Won in a Cupboard* (1914), and *Mabel's Busy Day* (1914) portrayed her as physically active and engaged in meaningful labor. *Mabel's Dramatic Career* casts her as a maid. In *Mabel's Busy Day* she is a hotdog vendor. By the late 1910s, however, public desire for that image was giving way to a more pleasure-seeking, consumerist ideal that was ushering in the Jazz Age. Emerging comic roles for women emphasized wealth, fun, and adventure. Young comediennes of the late 1910s and 1920s, including Marion Davies, Constance Talmadge, Olive Thomas, and Colleen Moore, represented the modern, urban woman who wore fashionable gowns, cut her hair shorter (sometimes into a bob), and used cosmetics. Davies portrayed an heiress in the 1919 feature *Getting Mary Married*. In *A Virtuous Vamp* (1919), Talmadge played the descendant of an English aristocrat. Thomas's 1920 film *The Flapper* cast her as a boarding-school student looking for fun, mischief, and adventure. A pivotal moment in this shift from New Woman to modern woman can be seen in the Talmadge comedy *Experimental Marriage* (1919), which tells the story of a New Woman, just married, who lives with her husband only on weekends because her suffrage work demands her full attention during the week. A review of the film described Talmadge as a "thoroughly modern young woman of lovable disposition."[5] The social and political goals of Talmadge's character, Suzanne, express ideals of the New Woman of the earliest years of the twentieth century. At the same time, the film's plot renders those ideals unworkable in contemporary urban America. The end of the film portrays a distraught Suzanne asking to lead a more conventional life.

Similarly, Cecil B. DeMille produced popular sex comedies that featured "the transformation of the sentimental heroine, piously devoted to family and community, as she became a clotheshorse and sexual playmate. An inveterate consumer, she became the symbol of the modern Jazz Age."[6]

Perhaps sensing the shifting social climate, Normand tried to adapt to this emerging trend. Wanting to move away from slapstick shorts, she signed on with the newly formed Goldwyn Studios in 1916 to make feature-length films.[7] Her first films at Goldwyn provide evidence of her desire to refashion her image into a more modern version of the American woman. Normand's early films at Goldwyn rejected the raucous physicality of her earlier Keystone performances. Films such as *Dodging a Million* (1918), *The Floor Below* (1918), and *The Venus Model* (1918) featured young, modern characters and cultures of consumption.

Then, only two years into Normand's career at Goldwyn, Mack Sennett released *Mickey* (1918), a film shot before Normand entered into her contract at Goldwyn. (As this book goes to press, *Mickey* is available online at YouTube.) *Mickey* was an enormous hit. The problem, however, was that *Mickey*'s Mabel Normand was a tomboy-hoyden, a character that had been common for her at Keystone but was exactly what she had wanted to move away from at Goldwyn. Box-office reaction to the film suggested to Goldwyn that audiences preferred this earlier persona of "Mabel." Therefore, while other studios were developing Jazz Age comediennes, Goldwyn began to develop for Normand roles similar to that in *Mickey*. In other words, the very things that made for Normand's great early success contributed to her fading popularity in the wake of newer, more modern styles of comedy.

The height of Normand's popularity had come before the "flapper comediennes" had made their first films. Within this emerging comic environment, Normand seemed an atavistic reversion to earlier feminist ideals and to standards of beauty that were based on healthy bodies and useful lives. Normand's early Keystone shorts had positioned her as a woman of action and athleticism, whose appearance was closer to the Gibson Girl than to the flapper. Normand herself was of the working class and called herself a suffragette. Her audiences knew her as that. She had begun her career as conceptions of the New Woman were adjusting to meet the Jazz Age. As the 1920s approached, her long dark curls, evident in later Goldwyn films as well as in *Mickey, Molly O'* (1921), *The Extra Girl* (1923), and *Suzanna* (1923), were at odds with the short bob that was coming into style. Her typical tomboy attire was at odds with the growing commercial beauty culture. Her character in *Molly O'* was described as "a daughter of poverty struggling against overwhelming odds of environment."[8] By the 1920s movie stars were becoming great influences on American women. In that context the continuing portrayal of Normand in impoverished roles necessarily diminished her cultural capital.

FROM KEYSTONE SHORTS TO GOLDWYN FEATURES

The arc of Mabel Normand's career coincides with dramatic shifts in the social and cultural framework of early twentieth-century urban America. These changes undoubtedly helped to shape Normand's career and star image. The nickelodeons' core working-class and immigrant audiences, which favored physical humor and its relentless attacks on law and propriety, provided a fitting backdrop for the physicality of Normand's early comedy. The rise of the New Woman—in all her permutations and imaginations—included, at the very least, expanded notions of acceptable female and feminine behavior through the growth of social spaces for comic presentation, representation, and transgressiveness. Normand's Keystone films were set squarely within this milieu.

The 1910s films of both comediennes and serial queens featured strong, athletic, ambitious female protagonists who often saved the day. The cycle of suffragette films, some of them comedies, also pointed to women's expanding roles in economic and political life. Film portrayals of active, boisterous female comics provided audiences with models of feminine behavior that echoed arguments about the political and economic empowerment of females and the working class. Women comics challenged traditional gender roles. As Karen Ward Mahar has noted, "Slapstick purposefully violated the bounds of refined middle-class behavior, finding humor in the daily chaos of an urbanizing, heterosocial society, where both men and women inhabited the public realm of work and leisure.[9] A heightened attention to athleticism provided further indication of the ideals that accompanied many early conceptions of the New Woman.

Post-Victorian social changes were clearly shown in advertising, where after 1910 women were depicted as more dynamic figures with more of their activities taking place outside their homes.[10] Sports and physical culture provided a sign of transition away from earlier, Victorian constructions of femininity. "Women's new interests in sports," argues Rob King, "threatened the model of separate spheres by transplanting the arena of female accomplishment from the spiritual realm to the physical."[11] Physical activity became more important not merely as a way to keep healthy but as a way to be modern.

"Women's sporting activities came to imply solidarity with cultural narratives of female modernity," King writes.[12] The variety of performance styles available to and enacted by female comics suggests an openness to experimentation that would, by the mid-1920s, become far more limited. "Female comicality—especially in its slapstick dimensions—offered potent symbols of gender disorder," King argues.[13] The rules for what would be acceptable female behavior in Hollywood films were still in flux in the early to mid-1910s.

Normand's performances in her short films and in *Tillie's Punctured Romance* (1914) display a subtle, understated use of gesture, expression, and movement. At the same time this early work displays a virtuosic athleticism that demonstrates supreme control over body and motion. Normand attributed aspects of her style to early lessons learned at Vitagraph:

> Mabel received from [John Bunny and Flora Finch] instruction on how to act and appear in front of a film camera. Most notably they imparted to her the invaluable understanding that in films natural and understated expression were often more effective than the more loud and formalistic gesturing not infrequently encountered in stage acting of the day.[14]

Understated, well-timed, expressive gestures often found themselves juxtaposed with physically demanding, spectacular stunts. Mabel's stint in an airplane in *Dash through the Clouds* (June 1912), and her climb down a two-hundred-foot rope tethered to a hot-air balloon in *Mabel's New Hero* (August 1913) are indicative of such physical virtuosity.

Comic portrayals of young, active, often working women offered the studios a powerful tool in attracting an important and growing segment of the movie audience. Throughout the 1910s, Miriam Hansen has argued, "industrial attempts to address a female audience are marked by an experimental opportunism which taps a variety of discourses already effective in other media such as women's magazines and pulp fiction."[15] As early as 1910, Kathy Peiss has noted, "Movie producers and exhibitors were tuned in to the 40 percent of the working-class movie audience that was female. They were well aware of the impact of women's attendance on the industry."[16] Serials like *The Adventures of Kathlyn* (1913–1914), *The Perils of Pauline* (1914), and *The Hazards of Helen* (1914–1915), featuring adventurous, physically active heroines, assumed a more modern, egalitarian discourse addressed primarily to young working women. Serials and female-centered comedy shorts promoted female characters who were, much like young women in the audience, "comfortable in the heterosocial spheres of work and commercial amusements."[17]

Normand's move from shorts to feature-length films occurred during a transitional period in the films of comediennes. By the late 1910s, this "New Woman–Style" (as termed by Mahar) comedienne faded from the short-film genre, in great part because of the departure of Mabel Normand and the gentrification of the short comedy.[18] Consequently, as the 1920s approached, film images of women as active and athletic, particularly in slapstick comedies, became relegated to small films in second- and third-run movie houses.

MODERN MABEL'S MOVE TO GOLDWYN

The comedy of the motion picture is in process of evolution. The slapstick and the roughhouse have had their day and played their brief part in the history of the films. The coming comedy will be of better variety and higher standards.
FILM FUN, 1915[19]

The film industry's concerted push towards middle-class respectability coincided with Normand's search for film projects with more developed narrative structure and more refined, genteel, "situation" comedy. In 1916 *Motion Picture Magazine*, in a splashy publicity stunt that was characteristic of the time, reported on Normand's desire to expand her career into new dramatic territory by "burying" her old life:

Mabel Normand recently gave a very original sort of party on her yacht. The invitations to the "burial party" [featured] a casket. . . . The casket was committed to the deep, to appropriate funeral music thus signifying Miss Normand's final good-by to slapstick comedy.[20]

The period 1918–1922 provided Normand with tremendous opportunities to be seen by audiences. Moving forward from her Keystone career and the one- and two-reel shorts that had characterized her work at that studio, Normand hoped to be able to expand on the variety as well as depth of her acting at Goldwyn Studios:

She wants to be a trifle more serious and dignified than they have allowed her to be in the Keystone comedies. She says comedy does not altogether consist of falling downstairs and throwing custard pies, and she believes that she can be just as funny in more dignified situations. The point is that Mabel Normand is tired of slapstick. She feels that she is capable of *better* things.[21]

"Better things" became sixteen feature films produced by Goldwyn during a four-year period. Unfortunately, all but four of the Goldwyn films are lost.[22] Although it would be folly to make a determination about the relative quality of Normand's Goldwyn product using only the few available films, we can learn much from the limited available footage, plot synopses, scripts, reviews, and other surviving documents regarding her career at Goldwyn. Through such material, an image begins to emerge of a comedian whose emphasis on virtuosic physical performance and unparalleled comic timing were placed in the service of two kinds of films. First were early dramatic comedies that were written by "Eminent Authors" untrained in film work; although (reportedly) visually superior to her Keystone product, they often failed at the level of basic storytelling. Second, Normand's later Goldwyn features were both praised and faulted by critics for a reliance on either shopworn or pleasantly familiar (depending on one's perspective) characterizations. These later films featured elements of the physical, slapstick comedy that had brought Normand great fame—just as that comic style was waning.

Although the New Woman of the late nineteenth century was characterized by a push for higher education and an emphasis on social and political activism, the modern woman of the late 1910s and 1920s tended to realign feminist goals around a core of consumerist behaviors.[23] For women, attainment of universal suffrage in 1920 (though California had seen this happen regionally in 1910 and New York in 1917) came at a time when the film industry was selling a lifestyle built around the purchase and enjoyment of goods and services. In other words, turn-of-the-century social ideals, changes, and transformations were becoming commodified within the burgeoning medium of film. Within the environment of expanded possibilities for women, argues James McGovern, "the ensuing decade was marked by a revolution in manners and morals; its chief embodiment was the flapper who was urban based and came primarily from the middle and upper classes.[24]

1.1. *Film Fun* cover
(January 1916).

The covers that graced the fan magazine *Film Fun* in the 1910s present a visual indicator of the shift in what Hollywood considered appealing images of and for women. The majority of *Film Fun* covers featured Charlie Chaplin, but those covers that showed women in the mid-1910s emphasized an active lifestyle, picturing women engaged in physical activities such as fishing, fixing cars, and playing ball. Such images reflected ideals espoused by those writing about the New Woman. By the late 1910s, however, such images had been replaced by far more passive images of female beauty and femininity. *Film Fun* covers after 1918 displayed glamour poses by actresses such as Olga Petrova, Geraldine Farrar, and Norma Talmadge. Moving even further away from the active, athletic female, early 1920s *Film Fun* covers exclusively began to feature pin-up type images by illustrator Enoch Bolles.

The film industry was similarly finding ways to transform images of female empowerment through labor into models for empowerment through consumption. As Rob King has noted, "Popular, working-class comic traditions were decisively transformed by their encounter with, and participation in, the reifying pressures of an emergent mass culture."[25] Perhaps Normand sensed the direction in which female comedy was headed when she signed a five-year contract at Goldwyn Studios in 1916.[26] Goldwyn publicized its ability to show Normand in richer, more dramatic roles, with greater attention paid to story, direction, costume, and setting: "She is the pioneer in her field and her work has been distinctive and distinguished. Goldwyn's plans for Miss Normand contemplate giving her even more distinctive comedies than she has done in the past and the technical and artistic facilities which Goldwyn contributes to all of the productions mean much more for this exceptional artist."[27] Samuel Goldwyn publicized

1.2. *Film Fun* cover (May 1918).

Normand as a serious actress.[28] Her biographer, Betty Harper Fussell, attributed to Goldwyn "supersalesman" status, his genius for packaging being responsible for putting together "Eminent Actresses and Eminent Authors" in order to attract to movies "the carriage trade."[29] Goldwyn explained in a magazine interview the kinds of films Normand would make at Goldwyn:

> Miss Normand can do comedy plays that convey an interesting story in contra-distinction to the comedies that are built upon an unusual situation alone. She is a typical American girl and as such she has built up not only a huge American but an international following as well. We want to star her in typical American comedies. And these comedies must tell a story.[30]

Yet Normand's first film at Goldwyn was the drama *Joan of Plattsburg*, shot in the spring of 1917 as America was headed into World War I. Poor feedback from Goldwyn's salesmen caused a delay in the release of the film.[31] In the meantime, the company shifted its approach, placing Normand in the comedy *Dodging a Million* (January 1918). Normand's own desire to refashion her screen image coincided with Goldwyn's courting of what he referred to as "the carriage trade" by way of Normand's first Goldwyn films. Publicity surrounding the film's release emphasized its style and fashion. Although print journalists had previously described Normand as a woman of style, that emphasis had not often been evident in her Keystone films. At Goldwyn, conversely, Normand's first release was set in a dress shop, where her character was able to wear "some of the fetchingest apparel she ever has been arrayed in for a motion picture."[32] The film featured models wearing designer Richard Hickson's gowns. A movie magazine said of Normand at the time, "She is very fond of beautiful clothes and means always to wear pretty things on the screen in future as in 'Dodging a Million.'"[33] The film seems to have been a significant departure from the roles that had made Normand a star. In *Dodging a Million* she plays an heiress rather than the tomboy-hoyden-slavey type roles that had been so common for her at Keystone. Initially Arabella Flynn (Normand) works as a shop girl while pretending to be an heiress. Stills from the film feature Normand in fashionable attire, as her character dresses in the store's finery and eventually discovers that she is indeed an heiress.

In support of Normand's evolving image of glamour and sophistica-

Goldwyn Pictures

The Box-office Event
of 1918: The Return
of Mabel Normand

FEW stars have ever approached
her in popularity or in drawing
power at the box-office.

Consider, therefore, the tremend-
ously increased value given you by
Goldwyn in a George Loane Tucker
picturization and the return, after
a year's absence from the screen,
of world-beloved

MABEL
NORMAND
in Dodging
A Million
by Edgar Selwyn & A.M.Kennedy

Goldwyn is proud to come to the
rescue of the box-offices of North
America with this wonderful combination of star, story and director
working together for your profit.

Goldwyn
Distributing Corporation
J. F. FLYNN
Detroit Manager
Film Building   Cherry 4655

"DODGING A MILLION"
Is playing this week at the Madison Theatre, Detroit

1.3. Mabel Normand's glamorous new image for her first Goldwyn feature, *Dodging a Million*. In *Michigan Film Review* (February 2, 1918).

tion, fan magazines and newspapers began carrying stories and interviews about Normand's artistic sensibilities and cultural ambitions. Whereas earlier stories had dealt with her personal style and love of decorating, such pieces now emphasized more cerebral interests, and Normand took every opportunity to emphasize the differences between her earlier work at Keystone and her current films for Goldwyn. Whereas she had earlier played very young girl characters, she now ridiculed Hollywood's emphasis on "eternal youth," questioning the desire of actresses to play younger than their years.[34] Whereas her "Keystone Mabel" character could often be characterized as a mischievous hoyden, her new roles promised to be more fashionable. Her earlier work in slapstick would be replaced by more dramatic roles. In trying to convince her audience to see her in a new light, magazine articles written during Normand's first year at Goldwyn often mentioned her serious taste in books and plays and referred to her as a "great reader of the world's best literature."[35] She was quoted in an interview as saying, "You didn't know I went in for deep thinking, did you?"[36]

Normand's third Goldwyn film moved further in the direction of the dramatic. *The Floor Below* (March 1918) cast Normand as Betsy Donnelly, a copygirl turned investigative reporter. In the course of the film, Betsy unravels a series of robberies, meets young missionary Hunter Mason (Tom Moore), and saves him from an unscrupulous fiancée. Normand's Betsy is a modern woman. She works in "the office of a big American newspaper." She dresses in business suits and stylish gowns, and for most of the film her hair is put up in a rather professional-looking bun. While her penchant for playing games and pranks at the office causes her trouble, she is the reporter who gets the story—and the guy—at the end of the film. However, although the film includes many comic moments, it would be difficult to call Normand a comedienne based on her work in it. Her physical performance is far more subdued—even stiff at times—than had been the norm in her short films. There is little of what could be referred to as slapstick in *The Floor Below*. A chase sequence across rooftops and down a fire escape early in the film provides some of the only moments of the kind of physical virtuosity audiences had come to expect in Normand films. In one scene, a playful Betsy hides under a table and teases Hunter by tickling his ankles and dropping small items into his pants cuffs. Despite its subdued physicality, however, Normand's performance is replete with beautiful moments of subtle facial expressiveness, signaling sadness at times and an exuberant happiness at other times. Medium shots of Betsy's face reveal far more about the film's story than do the 125 intertitles that mostly recount lines of dialogue.

Reviews of both *Dodging a Million* and *The Floor Below* were mixed at best. Of *The Floor Below*, *Variety* wrote, "Goldwyn made an error in judgment in selecting a melodramatic scenario for the use of Mabel Normand."[37] Perhaps most pointed were the comments of Linda A. Griffith, writing of Normand's return to the screen in *Dodging a Million*:

> To bring back a star who had been lost to movie fans for a year or more in such a hodge-podge . . . is surely a pity. . . . It would seem that

the least that might be done for an attractive, paying star, such as Miss Normand has always been, would be to reintroduce her in a vehicle worthy of her talents. Whatever *Dodging a Million* is about is more than I know. . . . It seems a pity to kill off favorites in this fashion, but Mabel Normand's popularity will soon be a thing of the past if this is the best that Goldwyn can do for her.[38]

Griffith's critique ends with a warning: "There is nothing distinctive about Miss Normand in *Dodging a Million*, and unless some interest by her managers is taken in her scenarios and the direction of her pictures, her screen life may be short."[39]

The eventual release of *Joan of Plattsburg* proved a success for Goldwyn. Despite, again, mixed reviews, it became the company's first hit film—after eighteen misses.[40] Normand's film output for the remainder of 1918 consisted of five more comedies: *The Venus Model* (June), *Back to the Woods* (July), *Peck's Bad Girl* (September), *A Perfect 36* (October), and the promotional film *Stake Uncle Sam to Play Your Hand* in support of the war effort. *The Venus Model* and *Back to the Woods* moved Normand's image even further away from the Keystone roles that had made her a star. Her characters in both films are of a higher social class and are surrounded by trappings of wealth. *Moving Picture World* referred to *The Venus Model* as "a production replete with movement, interest and unusual beauty."[41] As in Normand's earlier Goldwyn efforts, her character (Kitty O'Brien) in *The Venus Model* begins as a modern working girl, this time in a garment factory, where she makes bathing suits. When she designs a revolutionary bathing suit, "the Venus Model," she is rewarded by being promoted to general manager of the factory, where she turns around the failing business.[42] In *Back to the Woods*, Normand plays teacher Stephanie Trent. As with her earlier Goldwyn films, the critical reception for these comedies was mixed. In reviews of *The Venus Model*, the press referred to the film's subject as threadbare and its themes as hackneyed, though again praising Normand's "lively" performance. The *New York Times* called *Back to the Woods* "average," adding, "[It is] tediously long."[43] Along similar lines, *Motion Picture Magazine* wrote, "They say a rolling stone gathers no moss, but the story of this latest picture of the Normand has rolled through so many movies it must be hoary with age."[44] On the other hand, *Variety*'s review captures precisely the tone that Normand and Goldwyn had planned for her features. The review begins by distinguishing the film from her work at Keystone, dismissing as juvenile the slapstick work that had made her a star:

> The picture also marks a very distinct advance in the work of Mabel Normand, who is the star. Since the earlier days Miss Normand has been regarded as one of the best exponents of screen comedy and nothing more; the farcical, custard-pie-throwing, knockout comedy which will always appeal to something childish that remains in us. In "Back to the Woods," however, Miss Normand's work is marked by an archness and finesse, a lightness of touch, which stamp her as a comedienne of a much higher rank.[45]

When *Peck's Bad Girl* was released two months later, *Variety's* praise of the film again centers on Normand's performance: "Miss Normand is one of the best comediennes on the screen, and there are few artists who can get a laugh with quicker readiness. In 'Peck's Bad Girl' she has a vehicle uncommonly well-suited to her peculiar talents."[46]

In critiquing Normand's last Goldwyn release of the year, *A Perfect 36*, *Moving Picture World* reviewer Robert McElravy summed up neatly what seemed to be the critical consensus regarding Normand's features: that her talent outshined her material. Griffith's review of *Dodging a Million* had earlier expressed the same opinion. McElravy's review praised Normand's "manifest physical charms and general daring," calling her a first-class comedienne: "Her humor springs from a vivid and buoyant personality." He went on, however, to criticize director Charles Giblyn's handling of the humor in the film, as well as the film's screenplay.[47]

During 1918 Normand appeared in no fewer than eight feature films. It would be her busiest year at Goldwyn Pictures. Yet when *Motion Picture Magazine* released its "Motion Picture Hall of Fame" at the end of the year, Normand appeared in 109th place.[48] *A Perfect 36* became Normand's first Goldwyn film not to be reviewed in *Variety*. In the next two years, four more of her films would fall into that category.[49]

MICKEY AND A SHIFT IN STRATEGY

As 1918 came to a close, perhaps the brightest spot of the year for Mabel Normand came with the release—finally—of *Mickey*. Mabel

1.4. Return to an earlier Mabel in *Mickey*. In *Moving Picture World* (February 16, 1918).

Normand's feature film career had actually begun in earnest with the production of *Mickey*. Shot in 1916 at the new Mabel Normand Feature Film Studios with an estimated budget of $125,000, the film eventually grossed $18 million.[50] One newspaper called it "the greatest motion picture ever screened."[51] In discussing her career, Normand once said of *Mickey*, "I dwell on Mickey because it was my best work."[52]

Directed by F. Richard Jones, *Mickey* was the first feature-length comedy to give top billing to a single star comedienne. It retells a well-worn Cinderella story in which Normand (in long, dark curls) plays Mickey, an orphaned tomboy living in the country. Already well established in the public consciousness by the 1910s, the Cinderella myth provided Normand with an abundance of comic possibilities. Whereas the trope of the self-made man expressed the common belief that for men hard work would bring success, its counterpart for women was the belief that beauty would attract wealthy and powerful men into marriage. As Lois Banner expresses it, "Young men in business dreamed of rising to the top through entrepreneurial skill. Young working women dreamed of marrying the boss's son."[53] Normand's earlier Goldwyn films had complicated this idealized scenario by highlighting her own entrepreneurial skill (*The Venus Model*, *Back to the Woods*) and/or her wealth (*Dodging a Million*, *The Floor Below*). *Mickey*, by contrast, hewed more closely to well-worn depictions of the road to female happiness. Normand portrays Mickey as a mischievous child of nature (considerably younger than her own age), unconstrained by the demands of society while growing up the child of a miner in the country. After the death of her father, Mickey is sent to live with her father's business partner, Joe Meadows (George Nichols). Her unrestrained behavior gives him pause, and she is sent to live with unscrupulous relatives in the city to become cultured. This film in many respects presents the Normand character as she had appeared at Keystone—an active, athletic, energetic, mischievous tomboy. Even the name of her mine—Tomboy—hints at the outlines of her character.

In a scene that recalls some of Normand's earliest film moments, suitor Herbert Thornhill (Wheeler Oakman) spies a nude Mickey diving from very tall cliffs nearby and then swimming to shore. In case the extreme long shot of the dives does not provide sufficient indication of her lack of attire, a medium close-up at the end of the scene displays her bare shoulders and arms. Normand's performance in the scene is physically virtuosic. She doesn't simply appear for the benefit of a male voyeur. Although her behavior is risqué and open to the gazes of both Herbert and the audience, the act itself is uninhibited, unapologetic, and unembarrassed. Mickey owns the last shot of the scene as she looks out at the camera, thereby exerting a measure of knowing self-confidence and control over her image. Such control can be seen as evidence of early cinema's refusal to specify male control of the gaze. "Early cinema routinely portrayed women either in possession of a visual gaze or overturning the male mastery of the gaze . . . [and] thus offered up the possibility of an alternative formulation of cinematic desire through the inscription of the woman who looks," writes Lauren Rabinovitz.[54] In such performances, early film comediennes might be seen as subjects rather than the objects of the look. Normand's Mickey takes pleasure in her abilities and in her performance and thus controls her own image. This fascinating moment comes in a film that in many respects presents the Normand character as she had appeared at Keystone—an active, athletic, energetic, mischievous tomboy.

Mickey arrives at the palatial home of her relatives to a show of warmth and support due someone who has something to offer. Her aunt, Mrs. Drake (Laura La Varnie) believes Mickey to possess great wealth from her mine, which can help the family out of financial difficulties. When she learns that Mickey has no fortune, Mrs. Drake instead puts her to work as a servant. Mickey's youthful and unrestrained exuberance and her lack of cosmetics and stylish gowns all provide a fitting contrast to the more stylish look and restrained demeanor of her romantic rival, Elsie Drake (Minta Durfee). Elsie represents the emerging ideal of modernity to Mickey's more active but perhaps outdated image. In fact, Herbert's "love at first sight" glimpse was of a naked Mickey—completely unadorned and supremely active. Such contrasts between Normand's "natural" appearance and more constructed styles of beauty would appear repeatedly in later films. In a scene from *Molly O'*, for example, two stylish women passing Molly on the street scoff at her plain, unadorned appearance.

The critical as well as box office success of *Mickey* had a profound effect on the type of film Mabel Normand would subsequently make at Goldwyn. The emphasis on style, refinement, subtle humor, and the blending of comedy and drama lasted only until *Mickey*'s successful run suggested to the studio that audiences wanted a different type of performance from Normand. Her first film to go into production after the release of *Mickey* was *Sis Hopkins* (February 1919). Based on a Rose Melville play, the film features Normand as a "grotesquely gotten up rube girl," who comes to live with relatives in the city—and who does not become educated and wealthy in the last reel.[55]

The similarities in plot to *Mickey* are striking, as are the differences between this and Normand's earlier Goldwyn features. The elaborate sets that Goldwyn had boasted about were absent in her later Goldwyn films. The *Variety* review of *Sis Hopkins* commented, "The picture for the greater part was inexpensive to produce as the scenes are mostly exteriors with the exception of about four interiors that were not costly."[56] In the same review, mention of a "juvenile rube lover" suggests that Normand was portraying (as in *Mickey*) a character younger than her age. Finally, the fashion-forward costuming that had been most evident in *Dodging a Million* was replaced by grotesque hair and makeup and baggy, ill-fitting work clothes. While waiting for the film's release, one reporter quipped, "Let us hope the

1.5. A shift in strategy at Goldwyn with *Sis Hopkins* (1919).

revised version brings back to us the long-gone inimitable Normand of old."[57] In fact, Normand's next films at Goldwyn would provide precisely that.

Over the next three years, Normand would complete eight more films at Goldwyn. None would approach the success of *Mickey*, though exhibitors made sure to tie Normand's new films to the success of *Mickey*: "In playing 'Sis Hopkins' particular stress must be laid on the comedy angles of the picture and the fact that Miss Normand who starred in 'Mickey' is seen in it."[58]

In most of Normand's post-*Mickey* Goldwyn features, the studio seems to have been reaching back much more aggressively towards the types of characters, situations, and settings that had characterized Normand's earlier career. She often played a character that was perhaps summed up best by a *Motion Picture World* reviewer as "a rural mischief maker."[59] Her performances in *Sis Hopkins, The Pest, When Doctors Disagree, Jinx* (all 1919), and *Pinto* (1920) were all versions of this character. One description of *When Doctors Disagree* referred to her Millie Martin as "the *village gawky hoyden* of Ferryville."[60] In trying to recreate Normand's past screen success, the film also featured a love interest, Walter Hiers (as John Turner), who bore more than a passing resemblance to Roscoe "Fatty" Arbuckle. In *Upstairs* (1919) and *What Happened to Rosa* (1920), she plays urban, working-class mischief makers, and although the success of *Mickey* may have solidified her place as the cinema's chief female mischief maker, none of these films achieved similar success. Critical opinion on most of the films was mixed, though there was little negative criticism aimed at Normand herself. In describing her performance in *When Doctors Disagree*, Rob King writes,

> The merit of this film lies firmly with Normand's performance. . . . It's a film that gives lots of scope for Normand to develop her facial pantomime. A very liberal use of close-ups allows Normand to elaborate a very nuanced kind of facial performance, much more so than in her previous films. . . . In *When Doctors Disagree*, this becomes the basis for something much more Chaplinesque in its delicacy—and perhaps the influence of Pickford can be detected here, too.[61]

However, reviewers would also continue to notice the studio's frugality in the production of Normand's films.[62] Goldwyn vice president and production supervisor Abraham Lehr summed up the studio's position on Normand, when comparing her to the studio's other stars: "Not one of them was as valuable to us as Mabel, whose pictures cost less and brought in more money than anybody's at that time. Why, we didn't even have to buy great pictures for her; her personality made any picture a success with the booking agents even before it was started!"[63] Over time, Goldwyn's initial marketing of Normand's image to "the carriage trade" was shifting to an appeal to a much different audience. A review of *Pinto* called the film "not much of a story to offer to a sophisticated audience."[64] *Jinx*, a *Dramatic Mirror* review observed, was a "pretty good picture for patrons under twelve years of age—in fact, it is a young folk's play from the start and should amuse children."[65]

The difficulties of blending Normand's appeal, Goldwyn's artistic sensibilities, and genre expectations can be seen most clearly in one of her late Goldwyn films, *The Slim Princess* (July 1920). In descriptions that recall some of the characteristics of the earliest Normand/Goldwyn films, reviewers commented glowingly on the film's magnificent sets, costumes, and backgrounds, and they praised its beautiful photography. *Variety* called it "by long odds the handsomest Goldwyn product in some time." However, criticism of the film was particularly pointed, centering on the tension between its comic and dramatic elements and denouncing its forced attempts at slapstick. Set in a fictional kingdom, the film lacks the contemporary iconography that was becoming a hallmark of the emerging style of comedy. Normand's character, Kalora, spends parts of the film in a rubber fat suit. The film's director, Victor Schertzinger, who had previously helmed four of Normand's Goldwyn films, came under particular attack as "showing little imagination," and critics noted that the comedy "didn't get any particular laughs out of the crowd."[66]

Normand would make two more films for Goldwyn after the completion of *The Slim Princess*. *What Happened to Rosa* (April 1921) casts her as Mayme Ladd, a downtrodden, working-class shop girl, "a dreamer whose dull, drudging life has never been brightened by a single gleam of romance." She is enticed or conned into visiting a clairvoyant, who tells her that she possesses the spirit of Rosa Alvaro, a Spanish maiden. Mayme then fully embodies the spirit of Rosa, converting a large shawl into a Spanish costume and attending a masquerade ball, where she meets and is pursued by handsome Dr. Maynard Drew (Hugh Thompson). In an interesting twist on Normand's typical Cinderella roles, this one ends with Mayme having to disguise herself as a dirty young boy and get struck by a car in order to gain access to Dr. Drew. Consistent with descriptions of most of her later Goldwyn films, *Rosa* includes none of the stylish settings, costumes, and makeup that were publicized in earlier Normand/Goldwyn films.

With a year remaining in her contract with Goldwyn, Normand was released to allow her to rejoin Mack Sennett in making *Molly O'*, a film that attempted to replicate the story, character, and success of *Mickey*.[67] Even though its release was delayed due to the Arbuckle scandal, the film was by most accounts a success. Critics noted how far from her early film style her Goldwyn pictures had been. Louella Parsons, awaiting the release of *Molly O'*, wrote, "It is revealing no secret to say that Mabel's last big hit 'Mickey,' was not a Goldwyn picture, that Goldwyn was deplorably wanting in the ability to furnish her with a suitable story, or direction—I shan't presume to say which."[68] A similar sentiment was expressed in a newspaper review from Tarentum, Pennsylvania:

> Frankly, Miss Normand was a disappointment to us in all her vehicles since *Mickey* until we saw her in *Molly-O*. She is the same fascinating, mischievous sprite that first won our admiration, and in our estimation she should stay in productions which have the supervision of Mr. Sennett and the direction of F. Richard Jones, for no other producer seems to be able to give her the opportunity of exercising her unique and wholly splendid talent.[69]

BEAUTY AND THE COMEDIENNE IN THE POSTWAR ERA

Thus Normand's career initially benefited from changes in social attitudes and was ultimately done in by them. As World War I ended, comedies became more sophisticated, and although slapstick films were still being made, the role of women in them changed as well. With Mabel Normand's departure from Sennett Studios, her athleticism in the water was replaced by Sennett bathing beauties—women to be looked at.

By the end of Normand's career at Goldwyn, these divergent conceptions of the New Woman had reached a pivotal moment. A major shift in beauty standards was taking place as was evidenced by the launch, in 1921, of the Miss America pageant. That event, Lois Banner has argued, put forth the powerful notion "that the pursuit of beauty ought to be a woman's primary goal. It also marked a substantial triumph of the fashion culture over feminism."[70] That culture had turned feminist arguments about beauty's potential to free women from cultural constraints into the argument that beauty is a tool available to all who use the right cosmetics or wear the right hairstyles.[71]

In post–World War I America, the growing consumer culture and the changes in women's roles caused audiences to seek out newer, more modern depictions of the American woman. Sporting shorter, sometimes bobbed, hair, the new-style comedienne dressed in more modern garb, sought modern pleasures, and engaged in modern behaviors. Audiences flocked to films such as Constance Talmadge's *A Virtuous Vamp* and *A Pair of Silk Stockings* (1918). Olive Thomas appeared as *The Flapper* in 1920. By late 1918 player polls were already citing new comediennes Constance Talmadge and Dorothy Gish as more popular than Normand. Women's slapstick was softened into a more genteel comedy style appropriate for the new era. This shift, however, was also responsible for the removal of the subversive elements that had been a hallmark of slapstick comedy and had allowed comediennes such as Normand to assault the gender status quo. As Mahar has argued, "The gentrification of highbrow comedies and the relegation of serials and slapstick to the cheaper theaters was a blow to the New Woman onscreen."[72]

Normand's comments about her upcoming films as she arrived at Goldwyn imply a keen understanding of this emerging social climate and an astute desire to foster her own image within the constraints of the new beauty culture. The pre-*Mickey* features she completed at Goldwyn seem to hold to the ideals of that culture. However, their lack of success relative to the eventual triumph of *Mickey* seem to have led the studio towards safer projects employing more established characterizations that some critics would see as stale. The labor, physicality, and impressive achievement inherent in Normand's early Keystone work had given her characters a life and vitality that seems to have been absent from her early work at Goldwyn. When *Mickey* was released, it might have been a throwback to an earlier era, but audiences responded enthusiastically, leading Goldwyn to attempt to replicate that success in Normand's subsequent films. Audiences may not have been able to buy Normand as a Jazz Age heroine, but they were eager to see fresh, Jazz Age faces on the screen. Constance Talmadge had already made her first film by the time Normand went to work at Goldwyn, and it was during her time there that Marion Davies and Colleen Moore made their first films. The age of the flapper was just beginning.

It is difficult to say whether Normand's career would have rebounded after the difficulties and frustrations she encountered at Goldwyn, even if the scandals in which she was implicated had not taken place and had illness not taken her life.[73] It might be tempting to think that as a "female Chaplin" she could have enjoyed the same measure of success by perfecting the style that she had developed at Keystone and expressed later in *Mickey*—as Chaplin continued to do with his "tramp" character into the 1930s. Some critics, recognizing Normand's artistry, continued to write glowingly of later films such as *The Extra Girl* and *Suzanna*, even imploring audiences to "give her a chance."[74] However, the problem may have involved more than scandals and ill health. Changing cultural tastes and newer conceptions of modern womanhood were making Normand's image seem repetitive, staid, and downright old-fashioned. After all, *Molly O'* and the *Extra Girl*, like *Mickey* before them, were all stories of "a poor girl who rises to good luck." *Suzanna* features Normand as a roustabout in an old Spanish colony in California. Such images were inconsistent with the demands of the burgeoning beauty culture of the period. Instead, images of the glamorous, pleasure-seeking modern woman were becoming far more common and attractive to audiences. Distinctions were drawn between the flapper as a determined pleasure seeker and her "older married sister," whose preoccupations had been with political and social activism. The most fundamental condition of change was not sophistication but urban living and the freedom it conferred.[75]

Eventually the type of energetic heroine with whom Normand had found early success was replaced by a new kind of leading lady. Even Mary Pickford's onscreen career was called into question during this period: one critic stated in 1925 that "her supremacy has been in doubt for the past twelve months" and asking whether her place at the top rung of the ladder of fame and popularity was at an end.[76]

It would take a younger generation of film comediennes—such as Corinne Griffith, Colleen Moore, Marion Davies, Carole Lombard, and Constance Talmadge (often recreating not only Normand's comic bits but entire films)—and lessons learned from this earlier period in Hollywood to more successfully negotiate the balance of comedy and drama within the framework of increasingly codified industry expectations and shifting gender roles in the new consumer culture.

The figure of the active and productive New Woman was surely more threatening to the status quo than the figure that would come to replace it, the modern consuming woman. Movies lured postwar audiences into theaters with films that, Marsha Orgeron argues, "embodied and begat excitement, fun, and the spirit of rampant consumerism."[77] It may have been difficult to bring to heel the transgressive behavior of early screen comediennes, but with the new pleasures available to the consuming modern woman, that job undoubtedly became easier.

NOTES

1. "Victory on the Last Lap!," *Photoplay* 6, no. 1 (June 1914): 140–141.

2. This poll is cited in Betty Harper Fussell, *Mabel: The Life of Mabel Normand* (New York: Limelight Editions, 1992), 89. However, Fussell incorrectly cites the source as *Motion Picture World*.

3. A. Scott Berg, *Goldwyn: A Biography* (New York: Ballantine Books, 1989), 71.

4. "Popular Player Contest," *Motion Picture Magazine*, Feb. 1917, 129. Normand's rank in a popularity poll from late 1918 was even lower: 109 out of 422 performers. "The Motion Picture Hall of Fame: The Whirlwind Finish of the Greatest Motion Picture Contest Ever Conducted," *Motion Picture*, Dec. 1918, 12–13.

5. Hanford Judson, "'Experimental Marriage': Ripples of Laughter Break Out All through Delightful Constance Talmadge Comedy," *Moving Picture World*, Apr. 5, 1919, https://archive.org/stream/movwor40chal/movwor40chal_djvu.txt.

6. Sumiko Higashi, "The New Woman and Consumer Culture," in *The Silent Cinema Reader*, ed. Lee Grieveson and Peter Kramer (London: Routledge, 2004), 305.

7. Constance Talmadge's first feature film was produced in 1916; Colleen Moore's starring roles began in 1917; Marion Davies's first film was made in 1917.

8. Clipping, *Willows (CA) Journal*, June 24, 1922, Special Collections, *Molly O'* Scrapbook, Margaret Herrick Library, Academy of Motion Picture Arts and Sciences, Los Angeles.

9. Karen Ward Mahar, *Women Filmmakers in Early Hollywood* (Baltimore: Johns Hopkins University Press, 2006), 110.

10. James McGovern, "The American Woman's Pre–World War I Freedom in Manners and Morals," *Journal of American History* 55, no. 2 (Sept. 1968): 315–333.

11. Robert King, *The Fun Factory: The Keystone Film Company and the Emergence of Mass Culture* (Berkeley: University of California Press, 2009), 215.

12. Ibid.

13. Ibid., 221.

14. William Thomas Sherman, "Mabel Normand: An Introductory Biography," www.mn-hp.com/mn.html.

15. Miriam Hansen, "Adventures of Goldilocks: Spectatorship, Consumerism, and Public Life," *Camera Obscura* 8, no. 1 (1990): 54–55.

16. Kathy Peiss, *Cheap Amusements: Working Women and Leisure in Turn-of-the-Century New York* (Philadelphia: Temple University Press, 1986).

17. Mahar, *Women Filmmakers*, 101.

18. Ibid., 123.

19. *Film Fun* 319, Oct. 1915.

20. Clipping, *Motion Picture Magazine*, Oct. 1916, in William Thomas Sherman, *Mabel Normand: A Source Book to Her Life and Films* (2015), https://archive.org/details/MabelNormandASourceBookToHerLifeAndFilms.

21. *Film Fun* 326, May 1916.

22. The four surviving Goldwyn films are *The Floor Below* (Mar. 1918), *When Doctors Disagree* (May 1919), *What Happened to Rosa* (Apr. 1921), and her last Goldwyn film, *Head over Heels* (Apr. 1922). Only *What Happened to Rosa* is commercially available. In addition to the surviving Goldwyn films, the Mack Sennett productions *Molly O'* (Dec. 1921) and *The Extra Girl* (Oct. 1923) have survived, as has footage from *Suzanna* (Dec. 1922).

23. Stuart Ewen's assessment of workers at the Ford factory is not entirely out of place in this regard. Ewen has argued that Ford's institution of higher pay and shorter hours for workers in 1906 helped create a class of consumers who had

more money to spend and more time during which to enjoy that spending—and thus divert their attention away from the repetitiveness and tediousness of their assembly-line work. Stuart Ewen, *Captains of Consciousness: Advertising and the Social Roots of the Consumer Culture* (New York: McGraw Hill, 1976) 23–30.

24. McGovern, "American Woman's Freedom," 322.

25. King, *Fun Factory*, 211.

26. Normand had recently traveled from California to New York after a break in her personal relationship with Sennett. Undoubtedly more than the pain of a romantic breakup caused Normand to end her business relationship with Sennett. That same year, Chaplin's salary had risen from $125 to $10,000 a week when he signed on with Mutual Film Corporation. Mary Pickford had signed the first "million-dollar contract" in Hollywood at Paramount Pictures. Roscoe "Fatty" Arbuckle, searching for more money and more artistic control, left Keystone the same year as Normand. Normand explained her reasons for leaving Keystone as follows: "I wanted better pictures[.] I was getting tired of grinding out short comedies to bolster up programs in which other stars in other companies, as well as our own, were featured in pretentious films and were paid far more than I was." Sidney Sutherland, "Madcap Mabel Normand, Part 3," *Liberty* magazine, Sept. 20, 1930, 44.

27. "Goldwyn Gets Normand, *New York Morning Telegraph*, July 29, 1917, quoted in Sherman, *Mabel Normand: A Source Book*.

28. Samuel Goldfish renamed himself Goldwyn when he joined brothers Edgar and Archibald Selwyn in the formation of the Goldwyn Company in 1916.

29. Fussell, *Mabel*, 105.

30. "Mabel Normand to Do American Comedy Plays," *Motography* 18, no. 7 (Aug. 18, 1917): 348.

31. Berg, *Goldwyn*, 70.

32. "Fake Couturier Got Camouflage from Real One," *Elyria Evening Telegram*, July 11, 1918, www.freewebs.com/looking-for-mabel/hicksonco.htm.

33. "Storms, Chocolate Cakes, and Vampires Her Delight!," *Pictures and Picturegoer*, Aug. 1918.

34. Agnes Smith, "'Glad to Come Back,' Says Mabel Normand," *New York Morning Telegraph*, Sept. 9, 1917.

35. It was not uncommon practice for studios to publicize the style, intelligence, and scholarly interests of their screen comediennes by writing about their intellectual pursuits.

36. Smith, "'Glad to Come Back,'"; Norbert Lusk, "The Girl on the Cover: Mabel Normand Discloses a New Plan for Making Magnates Laugh," *Picture-Play*, Feb. 1918; Grace Kingsley, "Mabel's Pink Thoughts," *Los Angeles Times*, Mar. 11, 1917, quoted in Sherman, *Mabel Normand: A Source Book*; Randolph Bartlett, "Would You Have Ever Suspected It?," *Photoplay* 14, no. 3 (Aug. 1918): 43–44.

37. "The Floor Below," *Variety*, Mar. 8, 1918, 41.

38. Linda A. Griffith, "The Comments and Criticisms of a Free-Lance, Reenter Miss Normand," *Film Fun* 349, May 1918, 11.

39. Ibid.

40. Berg, *Goldwyn*, 79. In addition, the reviewer for *Variety* made note of Normand's weight gain and explained that she lacked the "spiritual" quality needed

to play a "Joan of Arc type" role: "When it becomes necessary for her to transform herself from materialism to spirituality, she 'isn't there.'" The reviewer also called the overall production "pretentious." "Joan of Plattsburg," *Variety*, May 3, 1918, 41.

41. "The Venus Model," *Moving Picture World*, June 8, 1918, quoted in Sherman, *Mabel Normand: A Source Book*.

42. "The Venus Model," *Variety*, June 14, 1918, 29.

43. Clipping, *New York Times*, July 22, 1918, quoted in Sherman, *Mabel Normand: A Source Book*.

44. "Back to the Woods," *Motion Picture Magazine*, Oct. 1918, 110.

45. "Back to the Woods," *Variety*, Aug. 2, 1918, 37.

46. "Peck's Bad Girl," *Variety*, Sept. 27, 1918, 46.

47. Robert C. McElravy, "A Perfect 36," *Moving Picture World*, Dec. 28, 1918, 1551.

48. "The Motion Picture Hall of Fame," *Motion Picture Magazine*, Dec. 1918.

49. *Variety* did not provide reviews for *A Perfect 36, When Doctor's Disagree, Upstairs, Pinto,* or *What Happened to Rosa*.

50. Mack Sennett, *King of Comedy*, as told to Cameron Shipp (San Francisco: Mercury House, 1954), 208–211.

51. *Lowville (NY) Journal and Republican*, July 24, 1919, quoted in Sherman, *Mabel Normand: A Source Book*.

52. Sutherland, "Madcap Mabel Normand," 44ff.

53. Lois Banner, *American Beauty* (Chicago: University of Chicago Press, 1984), 14–15.

54. Lauren Rabinovitz, *For the Love of Pleasure: Women, Movies, and Culture in Turn-of-the-Century Chicago* (New Brunswick, NJ: Rutgers University Press, 1998), 81–82.

55. "Sis Hopkins," *New York Times*, March 3, 1919, quoted in Sherman, *Mabel Normand: A Source Book*.

56. "Sis Hopkins," *Variety*, Mar. 7, 1919, 67.

57. Clipping, *Photoplay*, Feb. 1919, 146.

58. "Sis Hopkins," *Variety*, Mar. 7, 1919, 67.

59. Clipping, *Motion Picture World*, Apr. 5, 1919, 149.

60. "Looking for Mabel Normand," http://looking-for-mabel.webs.com/rob whendocsdisagree.htm.

61. Rob King, quoted in "Looking for Mabel Normand."

62. The *Variety* review of *Jinx* mentions that it was "not an expensive production." "Jinx," *Variety*, Dec. 19, 1919, 45.

63. Sutherland, "Madcap Mabel Normand."

64. "Pinto," *Dramatic Mirror*, Feb. 5, 1920, quoted in Sherman, *Mabel Normand: A Source Book*.

65. "Jinx," *Dramatic Mirror*, Dec. 25, 1919, 157.

66. "The Slim Princess," *Variety*, July 2, 1920, 27; "Star's Work Stands Out in Weak Comedy Story," *Wid's Daily*, July 4, 1920, 166.

67. Sidney Sutherland, "Madcap Mabel Normand, Part 4," *Liberty* magazine, Sept. 27, 1930.

68. Willis Gold Beck, "Worldly but Not Weary," *Motion Picture Magazine*, Sept. 1921, quoted in Sherman, *Mabel Normand: A Source Book*.

69. Press clipping, *Tarentum (PA) Telegram*, Apr. 18, 1922, quoted in Sherman, *Mabel Normand: A Source Book*.

70. Banner, *American Beauty*, 16.

71. Ibid.

72. Mahar, *Women Filmmakers*, 118.

73. A most compelling argument about the media's fashioning of Normand as a source of cultural authority during her years at Goldwyn and the eventual positing of that status as illegitimate (after the Taylor scandal) can be found in Mark Lynn Anderson, "Reading Mabel Normand's Library," *Film History* 18, no. 2 (2006): 209–221.

74. Fulton Oursler, "Give Mabel Normand a Chance!" *Movie Weekly*, Feb. 2, 1924.

75. McGovern, "American Woman's Freedom," 333.

76. Eugene V. Brewster, "The Coming Screen Year," *Motion Picture Classic*, Oct. 1925, 27.

77. Marsha Orgeron, "Making *It* in Hollywood: Clara Bow, Fandom, and Consumer Culture," *Cinema Journal* 42, no. 4 (Summer 2003): 81.

CHAPTER 2

FAY TINCHER: FEMALE ROWDINESS AND SOCIAL CHANGE

JOANNA E. RAPF

ALMOST FORGOTTEN TODAY, Fay Tincher (1884–1983) was a star in the early years of motion pictures in the United States. An April 27, 1918, headline in *Moving Picture World* proclaimed, "Fay Tincher Becomes 'World' Star," but today she is not even a footnote in standard film history texts. Kalton C. Lahue and Samuel Gill are among the few to acknowledge her significance, writing in their book on the lesser-known comics of the silent era that her work with Al Christie between 1919–1920 "ranked among the best on the screen at the time." They suggest, as have others, that she had "some of the elusive qualities of Mabel Normand" and rightly conclude that her disappearance from the screen in 1928 remains a mystery.[1] Fortunately, one of her Christie films, *Rowdy Ann* (May 25, 1919) is widely available today, allowing contemporary audiences to see the spunk and talent of this unique comedienne.[2]

The comparison with Normand is more precise and interesting than simply the presence of "elusive qualities." Both women in their early careers embodied the idea of the "New Woman," who, as Kristine Karnick describes in the previous chapter, challenged traditional gender roles through athleticism, dress, and portrayal of working-class struggles. As the 1910s came to a close, both women also articulated a clear desire to move from slapstick to more refined comedy, but neither achieved the same success in more sophisticated comedies. Tincher, following the fashion of the time, even unwillingly bobbed her hair in her role as Min, but the subversive element of challenging the status quo was gone, replaced by a new emphasis on tepid domesticity and consumerism.

Unlike Normand, on screen Tincher had three quite distinct personae: first, Ethel, a gum-chewing, no-nonsense stenographer with large spit curls who appeared in a series of shorts based on the popular "Bill the Office Boy" stories by Paul West (1914–1915); second, an athletic, independent young woman in a variety of shorts between 1916–1920; and third, finally, Min, the long-suffering and rather bland wife in Universal's series about the Gump family, based on a popular comic strip by Sidney Smith (1923–1928). In this chapter I will look at each of these three phases of her career, emphasizing the middle period when *Rowdy Ann* was produced—during which, for one-and-a-half years (1918–1919), she even had her own company, Fay Tincher Productions. In this, she invites comparison with other popular comediennes who gave their names to short-lived companies—Marie Dressler, Flora Finch, and, again, Mabel Normand. The World Film Corporation that released the films made by Tincher's production company publicized her unit with this statement: "Miss Tincher writes her own stories (in self defense, as she puts it), chooses her own casts, and directs her own pictures."[3] A photo caption (dated July 20, 1918) under a scene from one of her films, *Some Job* (June 24, 1918), reads: "Fay Tincher is a merciless autocrat when she directs men's activities."[4]

The caption's stress on Tincher's independence and control suggests the fashionable interest in the idea of the New Woman. Although this term initially referred to affluent, college-educated women at the turn of the twentieth century who rejected social conventions and often pursued a life outside of home, by the 1910s, it applied to a new generation of young women who repudiated bourgeois sexual norms and emphasized personal fulfillment.[5] The suffrage movement at this time is entwined with these ideas; when the United States entered World War I in 1917, women were needed more than ever in jobs outside the home and in support of the war effort. The political and social climate was conducive to admiring strong, independent women. The culmination of the struggle for recognition came in 1920 when the Nineteenth Amendment was finally passed, prohibiting any citizen of the United States being denied the right to vote on the basis of sex. Tincher's life, both on-screen and off, embodies and reflects many of these evolving perspectives on women.

In his book on the history of Keystone Studios, Rob King discusses how changes in turn-of-the-century womanhood emerged from a multifaceted set of interactions. One centered on athleticism. He writes, "Women's new interests in sports threatened the model of separate spheres for men and women. For young women across the

social spectrum, the growth of female physical culture not only provided a means to keep healthy, it became a way of affirming their
refusal of traditional gender norms and participating in a modern-
izing process."[6] Film reviews and fan magazine stories stress Tincher's interest in sports, especially boxing, an interest she would ex-
ploit in *Rowdy Ann*. A notice in the *Buffalo Times* (October 25, 1914)
begins, "Film Actress Enjoys Major Ring Battles." In the *Milwaukee Journal* (October 31, 1914), we learn not only that she was "an
ardent 'fight fan,'" but that "she also enjoys baseball and aeroplan-
ing. But her greatest joy is swimming and diving, and she is one of
the champions of the Pacific coast."[7] In June 1915 news stories announced that she won first prize in a bathing suit parade in Venice,
California. The bathing suit, we are told, was "fashioned after the famous 'Ethel' dress she wears while playing the part of the stenographer."[8] It is worth noting that Mabel Normand, too, was promoted as
a swimming star, the "beautiful Diving Venus," and that Normand's
first role in a Keystone film was in *The Water Nymph* (September 23,
1912), where her acrobatic dives outmatch those of the father of her fiancé (played by Ford Sterling), humiliating the male. King observes
that "the bathing girl becomes the emblem of a new world of popular
amusements in which the genteel paterfamilias can participate only
at the cost of humiliation."[9] *Photoplay* editor Julian Johnson mentions both Normand and Tincher, along with Victoria Forde (a star of
western films), as tomboy role models: "Every boy imitates Charles
Chaplin. Your tom-boy girl—anywhere—is sure that she's a Mabel
Normand, or a Victoria Forde, or a Fay Tincher."[10]

Between 1914 and 1920 Tincher consistently played strong, independent women, anticipating something of the uniqueness, strength,
confidence, and even dominance of men later embodied by the revolutionary Mae West in the early years of the talkies. Unlike West,
however, Tincher never pretended to be a sex symbol to men; she was
never the *femme amoureuse*, as Kristen Hatch describes Mae West
in the following chapter of this volume. From what we know of Tincher's work, she rarely put herself in a "romantic" situation, prefer-
ring roles that allowed her self-sufficiency unusual in female characters of the time. For example, a review of *The Love Pirate* (January 30,
1915), a two-reel Komic Reliance-Majestic release, describes what we
might now call "a feminist perspective" in its critique of women who
act childishly and illogically in order to please men: "Without dep-
recating noble women, and without belittling our ideals of woman-

hood, the story points out a very common weakness that is liable to remain a serious weakness in the gentle sex until they are given equal opportunity with men from babyhood."[11]

Unlike Mabel Normand, Tincher was never really a "slapstick" comedienne. She is quite explicit about this in an interview with Margaret Denny: "There's nothing funny about getting hit in the face with a pie, if there's no reason for it."[12] Most of what we know about Tincher's film roles comes from reviews in the trade magazines, but it's clear she didn't play the victim, the foil, or a flailing ingénue. Defining herself as a "comedy actress who takes her work seriously," Tincher told Denny that she was offered roles involving "cheap, vulgar, dime-novel comedy—slapstick, the managers call it," but she refused them. The "Office Boy" series allowed her a dignity, what she called "real humor . . . clean, and sweet, and *funny*."[13]

TINCHER'S UNCONVENTIONAL BEGINNINGS

Tincher began her career in amateur theater. Born in 1884 to an affluent family in Topeka, Kansas, she went to Chicago after high school to study at the Ziegfeld Musical College. There she did some work in light opera with the Henry W. Savage Company. A June 1905 picture in *Munsey's* magazine shows Tincher and Bertha Engel as the "Sing Song Girls" in a production of *The Sho-Gun*, described by the *New York Times* on April 1, 1904, as "the nearest approach to the Gilbertian style of opera the American stage has had in many years."[14] She continued her career in vaudeville and musical comedies in New York; by 1906 she had joined Joe Weber's company, where she initially appeared as Annette, a performer, in *Twiddle-Twaddle*, which ran for the first five months of the year. Between October 10 and December 7, 1907, she played Chip Chase, a student, in Weber's *Hip! Hip! Hooray!* There is a picture of her along with Suzie Pitt in the *New York Standard* with the caption, "Studying Hard at Doolittle College." The brief story continues, "The curriculum of Doolittle College is explained more fully in 'Hip! Hip! Hooray!' at Weber's Theater, where several other equally studious and equally shapely students may easily be seen."[15]

The rather raucous personal lives of these young showgirls emerges in a well-publicized story that reflects Tincher's savvy ability to promote herself, an ability that allowed her to move from the anonymity of the chorus to a featured player.[16] After an evening that involved a good deal of drinking, she is unsure as to whether or not, on a dare, she had actually married a wealthy Connecticut bachelor named Ned Buckley. The *New York Sun* ran a headline, "She's Afraid She's Married. Fay Tincher, Chorus Girl, Gets Lawyer to Find Out," and the story of the escapade is long and detailed:

> "The Merry-Go-Round" company was in Atlantic City week before last, and Buckley was down there too. Miss Tincher goes further than that and says that Buckley was very nice to her in the three years she was with Joe Weber's company. So when on the return of the company to New York, or to be exact, when on Sunday night last young Buckley came around with his touring car and suggested taking Miss Tincher and a few of her friends and a few of his down to the Chateau des Beaux-Arts at Huntington for supper, the little chorus girl consented.

The supper was fine, and the group of friends seemed to have the idea that Buckley wanted to marry Tincher. "Everybody began to tell the little chorus girl to forget her coyness and say yes." Taking a chance, and assuming the minister was not real, and no doubt having drunk a good deal, she agreed to the ceremony on the spot. But then the question was, "Had she really wed?"[17] In a 1908 story in the *Philadelphia Times*, under the headline "Wed or Not? That Is The Query Confronting Chorus Girl Hamlet," Tincher is described as having been "conspicuous" in the chorus of "The Merry-Go-Round." The story continues that she

> rested her little head first in one hand and then in the other yesterday as she soliloquized, like Hamlet, upon a momentous question. "Am I married," she asked herself, dolefully, as she gazed down Broadway, "or am I single?"[18]

The *New York World* begins a story, "Doesn't Know Whether She's Married or Not. Am I Mrs.? Or Miss?" In this piece Tincher is quoted as saying, "Not that Ned would not make a desirable husband for any girl who wished to marry. . . . But I do not want to marry him nor any man."[19] And as far as we know, this marriage was a sly hoax that gained her a lot of publicity and Tincher never married.

She claims her film career began by accident. She was sitting in a booking office one day with a friend when a man came in and after staring at her for a while, asked if she had ever worked in pictures. When she said no, that she had not even seen a moving picture, he suggested she meet D. W. Griffith. The meeting did not go well, according to Tincher's publicity account in a contemporary *Photoplay* article. Griffith asked her to show different emotions, but his only reaction was to look at her with "a sort of smile." When he made some kind of sarcastic remark, Tincher got mad: "I told him I didn't care for moving picture work; that I hadn't asked for a job; that he had invited me to call, and that I didn't purpose to be treated that way." Griffith, delighted with her feistiness, jumped up and announced, "You're the one I've been looking for. . . . You're just the type." According to Tincher, he recognized that her coloring was ideal for black-and-white cinematography:

> Now take that type—Miss Tincher there—she is a distinct type, all black and white, black hair, black eyes, all the rest is white. You can't go wrong on such a face, for it's only black and white. It won't show shadows as the blonde type will.[20]

In later years Tincher liked to credit Griffith with inspiring her with the idea of her trademark black-and-white costumes that eventually earned her the nickname, "The Girl o' the Stripes." A 1918 story in *Motion Picture Classic* reads as follows:

> When Miss Tincher first met David Wark Griffith at a dinner-party they were discussing Motion Pictures.
>
> "Now, there," suggested Mr. Griffith, indicating Miss Tincher, "is an ideal combination for the screen—black hair, white skin, black eyes, white teeth—black and white, effectively combined, is the best possible combination for screen purposes.
>
> Having just signed a contract to work under Mr. Griffith's direction, Miss Tincher lent his words the honor of close attention. And thus was born the inspiration for "The Girl o-the Stripes," as Miss Tincher has since become known.[21]

Griffith cast her as Cleo the Vamp in *The Battle of the Sexes* (April 12, 1914), with Lillian Gish, Owen Moore, Donald Crisp, and Bobby Harron, although sadly only a fragment of this film survives. It was the first film that Griffith made for Harry Aitken's Reliance-Majestic, an organization he joined after leaving Biograph in 1914.

FAY TINCHER

2.1. Fay Tincher as "Girl o' the Stripes." Postcard courtesy of the author.

Tincher also became a part of Reliance, relocated with the company to California in 1914, and may have appeared in some of their releases before becoming popular as a comic star on her own.

Like so many press releases, these stories of Tincher's beginnings in film are probably, at least in part, apocryphal and may be further examples of her ability to manipulate publicity. Steve Massa, who has written the only critical essay on Tincher to date, has found evidence of two films in which she appeared in 1913, shot in New Jersey and released through Universal Éclair American.[22] And she seems already to have been working as part of the Griffith-supervised unit, Komic Comedies, making one-reel shorts under the direction of Edward "Eddie" Dillon by March 1914 when Battle of the Sexes was released. Many of these short films were written by Anita Loos, Griffith's favorite scenario writer, a smart, talented, and forceful personality who would go on to fame as the author of the best-selling Jazz Age novel, *Gentlemen Prefer Blondes* (1925), subtitled *The Intimate Diary of A Professional Lady*. In these Komic shorts (whose credits also included future horror director Tod Browning) Tincher plays a variety of roles that Loos may well have shaped, including a lady drummer, a country maid yearning to be an urban vamp, a brash shop girl, and a headstrong socialite. Massa sees the unifying aspect of these roles as her "no nonsense demeanor and feistiness which were in comic contrast to her tiny stature."[23]

She, like Loos and Mae West, was only a little over five feet tall, but she knew how to dominate the frame. Her positioning in *Rowdy Ann* illustrates this beautifully. An iris-out into a medium shot introduces Ann on horseback, immediately putting her in charge.

Shortly after, when we see her with her mother, the mother is sitting in a chair while Ann is standing, reinforcing her power. In an ensuing boxing match with her villainous suitor, discussed below, the camera tilts down with her to a low-angle shot as she discovers his weakness—a bad foot—a weakness that enables her to get

2.2. Fay Tincher with Edward Dillon and Chester Withey in *Faithful to the Finish* (1915). Photograph courtesy of the author.

2.3. Fay Tincher in the title role of *Rowdy Ann* (1919).

2.4. Fay Tincher puts herself in the dominant position with a classmate in *Rowdy Ann* (1919).

the upper hand as she steps on it. Tincher quite consistently includes scenes where others are sitting and she is standing. Towards the end of *Rowdy Ann* there is a subtle variation of this tactic as Ann and a classmate are discussing their friend's disastrous engagement to a flimflam man. The classmate is in an armchair, but Tincher places herself in the dominant position by sitting on the arm of the chair. Mae West used similar devices to place herself in the dominant position in a scene.

TINCHER AS ETHEL IN THE "BILL THE OFFICE BOY" SHORTS

Shortly after Komic Comedies was formed, the unit acquired the rights to the "Bill the Office Boy" stories. The first film in this series, *Bill's Job*, was released on July 5, 1914, and twenty-two more were released in the following year. They starred Tammany Young as Bill, the office boy with a penchant for chaos and destruction, and Tincher as Ethel. A story in *Photoplayers Weekly* gives the history of the series and tries to account for its success:

> Eleven months ago, Edward "Komic" Dillon was assigned to the producing of a series of Paul West fiction stories, and without the usual aid of a brass band, he made them a success from the very start. Since then, one has been released on the Mutual program every other week, and at the present writing Director Dillon is busily engaged staging episode Number Twenty-three. One reason for the immediate success of this Komic serial is due to the fact that each episode contains a complete story itself, yet each bears a resemblance to the following one—but in characters only—not in continuity of the general theme.[24]

Working much like a TV series today, the "Bill the Office Boy" shorts appealed especially to young women who admired Ethel's sense of adventure and her ability to stand on her own. A review of one of Tincher's films in the *Chicago Herald* looked back at her success as Ethel by stressing her warmth and humanity:

> The office force in the audience had been led on beautiful, idealistic, heroines so long that when a natural true-to-life portrayal came along they recognized it at once. Girls must be either idealistic or fraternize, and here was a "stenog" who was human to the core. So the vast army of typists took her to their bosoms and named her a star.[25]

A 1914 clipping from the *Chicago Tribune* notes, "Fay Tincher in her general exaggeration of everything from pose to spit curls, as Ethel, the stenographer in the Komic release of the Paul West 'Bill' stories, has achieved one of the funniest, jolliest character bits in present film experience. . . . There is a zest and brightness about her work that makes it genuinely a pleasure to watch."[26] Always aware of the need to make herself noticed, she did it through her distinctive dress, hair, and what is called, in theatrical terms, "bits of business." Tincher said, "My part wasn't very big and I wanted to make it stand out so I thought, 'How can I dress most effectively,' and then I thought of what Mr. Griffith had said about all black and white, and I had it."[27]

A 1917 story in *Motion Picture Magazine* about Tincher describes her surprising stardom this way:

> When the first "Bill" comedy was flashed on the screen, the audience saw a "stenog" who wore a series of "spit" curls and chewed gum "all over the office." The stenographer wasn't meant to be the star of the cast, but the distinctive way in which she carried her role made her one overnight.[28]

Other reviews in the clippings file at the New York Public Library emphasize just how unusual she was:

> She is a striking brunet [sic] with remarkable powers of facial expression. The role of the adventuress seems to be her forte. (*New Orleans States*, August 11, 1914)

> Fay Tincher is a funny woman, not only fun loving, but funny in the sense of out of the ordinary. (*Buffalo Times*, October 25, 1914)

> Large dark brown eyes, black hair, a beautiful complexion and lovely features, possessed of these adjuncts Fay Tincher nevertheless persists and revels in making herself look awkward, no makeup, no matter how grotesque, is too difficult for her, nor does she care how it makes her look provided it accomplishes her purpose—to make people laugh and be happy. (*Milwaukee Journal*, October 31, 1914)

She was obviously a smart and skilled performer. One contemporary journalist describes her as "one of the cleverest comediennes filmdom proudly possesses," and adds:

Clever would be putting it mildly in describing the talents of Fay
Tincher. Her tendency to grasp almost immediately just what
the director calls for in difficult scenes is admired by many. . . .
Miss Tincher is without a doubt the most popular girl within studio
bounds, and her popularity is deserved.[29]

In one of the last of the "Bill" releases, *Ethel's Disguise* (May 2,
1915), Tincher had the opportunity to cross-dress in a role, something
she had done occasionally during her theatrical career. *Photoplayers
Weekly* announced that "the Griffith-Komic comedienne in 'Ethel's
Disguise,' dons the clothes of a dashing young hero." While in costume, the studio's publicity story goes on, she was mistaken as a pro-
spective chauffeur for an elderly lady who was seated in a limousine
across the street from the studio. "Fay thought she would continue
the joke, and asked for a fabulous sum for her weekly services. The
reply she received was a very discouraging one."[30] The *Fargo Daily*
for June 20, 1915, has a picture of her dressed as a boy, with a hat and
cane, presumably from *Ethel's Disguise*. The caption reads, "'Playing Boy' For Films Heaps of Fun," and quotes Tincher as saying, "It's
more fun being a boy in a movie comedy than chewing a whole pack-
age of gum."[31]

During this era when women were challenging their traditional
positions within society and expanding the kind of roles they played
in the new and not fully respectable medium of film, female to male
cross-dressing, although not common, did occur, especially in comedy. The beautiful Dorothy Devore, for example, played a young man
in *Know Thy Wife* (December 30, 1918), while Polly Moran played
Sheriff Nell in a series of shorts between 1917–1920. In his book on
Keystone, Brent Walker singles out Moran as embodying the "new
take-the-bull-by-the-horns attitude" among women, growing out
of their "new spirit of political and social awareness."[32] This would
characterize Tincher also.

TINCHER'S INDEPENDENCE, COMIC REORIENTATION, AND "ROWDY" ROLES

Around 1915 screen comedy was changing as studios worked to appeal to more middle-class, sophisticated audiences and gain greater
respectability. King traces this move towards more narrative-based,
situational, and sentimental comedies, such as the successful "Fatty
and Mabel" series starring Roscoe Arbuckle and Mabel Normand.[33]

The development of the Chaplin persona from a knockabout comic to his "Little Tramp" character reveals a similar comic trajectory, and as she became more established as a star, Tincher's ideas about comedy similarly reflect this reorientation.

> I see that comedy on the screen will have to be taken seriously and raised to a much higher level than it has been so far, if it is to be permanent, and I'm glad of this chance to put myself on record as having said so. . . . Comedy-drama is growing in importance every day, and that is the thing I want so much to work into.[34]

Her initial foray into what she calls "comedy-drama" was as Dulcinea in *Don Quixote* (February 27, 1916), the first film she did for the Triangle Film Corporation, which had been formed in 1915 when Harry and Roy Aitken merged Griffith's Fine Arts Studio with Mack Sennett's Keystone Studios and the companies of Thomas Ince. Interestingly, another powerful comedienne of this era, Marie Dressler, was considered for the role, but Griffith felt she was too stout and too old. The diminutive Tincher was perfect. Her costar was De Wolf Hopper, probably best known today for his recitation of the popular baseball poem "Casey at the Bat" and for being the husband (1915–1922) of the woman who became the notorious Hollywood gossip columnist Hedda Hopper. *Don Quixote* was heralded as his movie debut after a lengthy stage career, but the film was poorly received and unfortunately it is now lost. In his 1927 memoir, in which he talks about the making of the film (it took twelve weeks), he comments that "present-day audiences" would only recognize three members of the company: "Monte Blue, George Walsh and Fay Tincher," who had risen "to a considerable fame as a comedienne and character woman."[35]

The story of *Don Quixote* is summarized in *Motion Picture Magazine*, and Tincher graces the cover riding a mule.[36] It is clear from reviews that Tincher transformed Cervantes's simple farm girl into a headstrong, adventurous, and commanding presence. Julian Johnson in *Photoplay* described the film itself as "misbegotten" and "unworthy," but he added that "from this welter of keystonery by an undertakers' convention, Fay Tincher's Dulcinea shines like a starbeam from another century. . . . [She] visualized Cervantes."[37] In an earlier review, Johnson also observed that she made the role of Dulcinea "into a female Charley [sic] Chaplin" rather than playing it as a more traditional Lady Godiva type. The review continues:

The comedy as a whole is not so much reminiscent of Cervantes as of Mutt and Jeff. For Dulcinea herself, I have nothing but praise; Fay Tincher's performance is little short of wonderful. All things considered, she surpasses Hopper. A young woman who can do this sort of thing deserves stardom.[38]

The *New York Review* echoes Johnson's enthusiasm: "Fay Tincher was 'made' as a moving picture comedienne by her performance as Dulcinea." The writer goes on to say that "one reason why the young woman succeeds in the delineation of eccentric roles is, undoubtedly, that she is a bit bizarre—in personal tastes as well as in methods of acting."[39]

"A bit bizarre" hits exactly the right chord. Tincher was unconventional both onscreen and off. After the success of her role in *Don Quixote*, a "film that established Fay Tincher as one of the great film actresses," she announced that she would work only five more years (which would take her up to 1921) and that "after that I'm going to travel."[40] And indeed there is a gap in her filmography right around 1921, but I would argue that it might have something to do with the temper of the times and Will Hays' public crusade to clean up Hollywood following the Arbuckle scandal, as I will suggest at the end of this essay.[41]

She did three more pictures with Hopper, *Sunshine Dad* (April 16, 1916), on which Tod Browning receives screenplay credit and in which she plays the Widow Marrimore; *Mr. Goode, the Samaritan* (May 29, 1916), where she is Shortie Sal, a crook's girlfriend; and *Rough Knight* (June 1916). Tincher was well received, but Peter Wade in *Motion Picture Magazine* comments, "*She pulled the stroke-oar for Hopper,* who has since acknowledged that he was not cut out for silent comedy."[42] Hopper returned to the stage, while Tincher went on to star in a series of shorts directed by Edward Dillon for Triangle–Fine Arts.

The Dillon-directed series ended in December 1916, and there is a gap in Tincher's career. Peter Wade's 1917 story in *Motion Picture Magazine* says, "At the present moment this little bundle of nerves, vivacity and 'human' comedy has retired on her honors."[43] The emphasis on "human" highlights Tincher's forte as something other than a slapstick comedienne; however, "retired" may not be quite accurate. She seems to have been developing ideas for her own production company, Fay Tincher Productions, which would release its films through the World Film Corporation. The first two were *Main 1-2-3* (May 27, 1918) and *Some Job* (June 24, 1918).[44] These were shot

2.5. Fay Tincher with Chester Withey in *Sunshine Dad* (1916). Photograph courtesy of the author.

on the east coast and directed by Al Santell, although Tincher seems to have a hand in here too.

At least one more short is known to have been made by Fay Tincher Productions, *O, Susie Behave* (July 22, 1918), but comedy shorts were no longer the mainstay of the film industry and performers who wanted to be taken seriously—and Tincher did —looked to features. Her company was short-lived, and her next appearance is in a dramatic feature (now lost), *The Fire Flingers* (April 21, 1919). Although not funny, she still plays a "tough" character as the review in *Variety* indicates: "Hard and tough with a 'you better give me' look, she presented a very real type. . . . Miss Tincher wore a good looking shirt waist and suit and later had on a long fur cape. She also wore too much lip rouge."[45] There is a picture of her in this outfit in *Theatre Magazine* giving her costar, Rupert Julian, that "hard and tough" look. In the story she is enthusiastic about playing a "heavy," but not the Theda Bara kind of vamp. Her vamp she describes as "ingenuish," a vamp with a sense of humor. This vamp is in control and can hold a man. "She laughs at him, even as she is seeking to allure him—and he adores it."[46] A woman laughing at a man is rare on-screen, even today. Laughter is connected with power; hence, it is far more common to find men laughing at women rather than the other way around. Tincher recognizes the power of laughter and uses it in creating "a new style of vamp" (*Variety*, May 28, 1919). But she also says she hopes to play more dramatic leads because "screen farce has never appealed to me." Yet being a comedienne kept catching up with her. Comedy is transitory, but "drama is life," Tincher noted, and added, "I want to portray life" (*Theatre Magazine*, June 1919). However, I would argue that one of the unique aspects of her comic roles was that they did portray "life," that they were, as the *Variety* review of *The Fire Flingers* says, "real."

But comedy caught up with her once again, and in May 1919 she signed with Al Christie Productions. Christie was one of the founding fathers of screen comedy. Like Mack Sennett, he was from Canada, and he had his first success with a one-reel "Mutt and Jeff" series beginning in 1910. *Photoplay* announced her signing:

> Fay Tincher, she of the black and white stripes and spit curls of the once famous Griffith studio comedies, is with us again but minus stripes and curls. She is Al Christie's new star and the veteran comedy producer is directing her personally. Miss Tincher's vehicle will be two reelers similar to those that made her famous in the old days.[47]

Tincher made about nine two-reelers with Christie, and significantly they include *Rowdy Ann* (May 25, 1919). Christie utilized the unconventional and active Tincher as a wild western cowgirl, not only in *Rowdy Ann* but also in *Dangerous Nan McGrew* (September 1919), *Wild and Western* (October 1919), and *Go West Young Woman* (December 1919). From reviews, she seems to have played a similar character in all these pictures. For example, in *Dangerous Nan McGrew* we are told, "She packed a pistol. But it was her eyes that were dangerous, not her pistol."[48]

In *Rowdy Ann* the running gags in the film involve roping, shooting, and fighting. Ann packs a pistol everywhere but never hurts anyone. She is adept at shooting holes in cowboy's hats, lassoing her father and the villain, and punching men and women alike. The film does not have much of a structure or even a coherent story. It is tied together by the flimflamming villain Ann runs into on the train as she is being shipped off to boarding school to become a lady, and perhaps by the obviously gay dance instructor (played by Eddie Barry, a character actor and Christie regular) who is also on the train and is a horrified observer of Ann's tactics. As mentioned above, Ann is introduced on horseback as a cowhand on her father's ranch. But when some of the cows break free, she has to fetch her father from the saloon, which she does by roping him and shooting holes in the hat of an elderly cowboy at the bar. That done, we are introduced to the "villain," Handsome Hank, who, we are told, "coveted the ranchman's *manly* daughter" (italics mine). Just as she did in her real life in 1908, she nixes the "Romeo stuff," knocks her rough suitor down, shoots at him, and watches as he falls into a stream. The wimpy ranch foreman also desires Ann. She seems to like him in a platonic sort of way (she even gives him a peck on the cheek as she gets on the train to go east to boarding school), and he wants revenge on Hank. This sets up an uneven boxing match between the two men. In real life, as already mentioned, Tincher had always enjoyed boxing. In *Rowdy Ann* she breaks up their fight as a title card says, "Stand back, boys, I want to lick this guy myself." And she does. Hank has removed one wet boot before the fight starts, and there is then a continuity error in the film as he fights the foreman, Jimmy, because we briefly see Hank with both boots on. This is significant only because when Ann takes over the fight, she shrewdly observes that Hank has a badly bruised and bunion-covered foot. There is an expressive close-up of Tincher's quizzical face, and we realize what she is thinking when she stamps on Hank's foot, causing him to pull back and wince in pain. This enables her to give him a good wallop, and using this tactic, she succeeds in knocking him out just before her father enters to take her away. But in a parting gesture, she perfectly shoots more holes in the hats of the on-looking cowhands.

Upset about the unladylike life Ann is living, her parents send her east to school. At this point in the film, the western adventure of the first half disappears completely, and we hear no more of her parents, Handsome Hank, or the wimpy foreman. There is the sequence on the train, mentioned above, where she "outs" the flimflam man, and her gun-toting ways alarm Professor Leavitoff, the dance instructor en route to Ann's school. There is also, by today's standards, a racist routine, where she thinks the black porter is trying to seduce her with loving words and she chases him over the tops of the train cars and off into a field. But this part of the film also simply stops—we never find out what happened to the porter—and we cut to the dance instructor arriving at Ann's school to tell the headmaster about his hair-raising train trip.

2.6. Fay Tincher reacts to the sight of Handsome Hank's foot as she fights him in *Rowdy Ann* (1919).

The rest of the film takes place at the school, where the most prolonged sequence establishes Ann's "manly" ways in contrast to the clumsy dance instructor and his bevy of young ladies in diaphanous dresses absurdly leaping around a rather barren landscape. Ann herself has put on one of these short, flimsy garments, but she has kept her boots, pistol, holster, and cowboy hat. She approaches the group with a swagger. Shot from the rear, we see her, hands on hips, stop the dancers in their tracks. The girls laugh at her and Ann resorts to the only defense she knows: she punches them. Professor Leavit-off runs from the fight to get the headmaster, who succeeds in subduing the ruckus. Ann gives up her gun and takes off her boots, and this seems to be her transition to becoming a lady and wearing dresses. In the concluding sequence, she saves an heiress classmate from an unfortunate marriage with the flimflam man Ann exposed on the train. Again using her roping skills, she lassoes him from her dormitory window. The police, who have been on his trail, then nab him in front of the surprised young women and the always-mortified dance instructor.

Structurally, the situation in the film is slightly reminiscent of what we see later in Buster Keaton's *Steamboat Bill, Jr.* (Charles Reisner, May 20, 1928), only in that film we have the reverse. Willy (Keaton) comes back from the east all dandified and has to learn to shed those ways and become a man so that he can win the girl at the end. In *Rowdy Ann*, Ann's makeover into one of the girls does not enable her to find a guy. We never see her return to her family, and significantly, it is a film without romance. It ends (somewhat like the Marie Dressler feature *Tillie's Punctured Romance* [December 21, 1914]) with a scene of female bonding. The rich girl, who had previously scorned Ann, is now grateful to her for saving her from an unfortunate marriage, and the last scene has Ann, the rich girl, and another friend playfully throwing pillows at each other. There is really no resolution other than an affirmation of female friendship that seems to have no connection to the male world of the first half of the film.

Commenting on this unusual ending, Andrew Grossman observes that Tincher "subversively resists her feminization (and thus socialization) through to the film's very end, at which point the kindly but ineffectual cowboy with whom we assumed she'll be romantically paired has been forgotten altogether." He concludes: "In *Rowdy Ann*, using the masculinized trappings of the Western, Tincher not only transcends standard norms of femininity but, more exceptionally, enters the realm of asexual, asocial play that was generally the exclusive terrain of the socially subversive male silent clown."[49]

Her "play," her comedy in this film, is not in response to an attraction to a man, as Mae West's comedy was, or even as Marie Dressler's was in a film such as *Tillie's Punctured Romance*, which ends with two women (Dressler and Mabel Normand) embracing as their former love interest (Charlie Chaplin) is carted off. In *Rowdy Ann*—and we may assume in the other "cowboy" films she made for Christie, who was fond of utilizing cross-dressing—the wellspring of the comedy is simply the leading lady's rejection of the expectations of female behavior. In fact, the introductory title card to the DVD of *Rowdy Ann* mentions that Tincher challenged "conventional notions of femininity that earned her the reputation as one of the best comediennes of the silent screen."[50]

LONG-SUFFERING MIN

In 1920 Tincher stopped making western comedies. She appeared in a few more two-reelers for Christie, including *A Seaside Siren* (July 25,

1920), in which she is again dressed as a man. The plot summary (the film is lost) in *Motion Picture News* (June 22, 1920) describes Tincher's role as a maid who is asked to impersonate the young woman for whom she works so that the woman can elope with her lover. Tincher manages to horrify the guests at the seaside resort by her "rough attentions to a husky coast guard," then she escapes wearing a suit of men's clothes "about ten sizes too large." In 1921 she did promotional tours for Christie, but her active, independent, on-screen career seems to have gone by the boards.

From 1923 until 1928, Fay Tincher became known almost exclusively as Min Gump. Universal made close to fifty of these two-reel comedies over the five-year stretch. A review in *Motion Picture News* aptly points to the routine nature of these shorts: "The comedy for the most part is of a rather inferior calibre [*sic*] and offers nothing in the way of original gags or action."[51] Trade magazines in 1924 and 1925 report that she was not happy about having "to bob" her hair to match the cartoon image.[52] According to Steve Massa, "Min's character was supportive, long-suffering, and unfortunately very bland." Although Sidney Smith thought of her as "the brains of the family," brains do not necessarily make for comedy, and existing footage shows that Tincher was overshadowed by her costar Joe Murphy as Andy Gump.[53] In a thought-provoking article in *Picture-Play* magazine entitled "Where Are the Funny Girls?," Gordon Gassaway aptly remarks, "It's the rooster in man that is funny. The hen[s] of the species do not cop the laughs."[54] In the Gump series, Tincher played the hen.

Why was she stuck in this mediocre role, and why did she virtually disappear after the series ended in 1928? One reason put forth is that because of her sexual preferences she may have been on censorship czar Will Hays' blacklist that rumor says was created in the wake of the Arbuckle and William Desmond Taylor scandals in 1921 and 1922. The dates fit that theory and would also, at least in part, account for Marie Dressler's effacement. The acerbic Anita Loos commented in later years:

> The heroines of many of my half-reel farces were played by Fay Tincher, who has been long forgotten. Ideal for those rowdy scripts, Fay required no acting ability. Let's say that she had the pert allure of a "Patsy" and could be a provocative target for slapstick. Fay was anything but a sex symbol, and—in those days before lesbians came out

of the closet—her fans never dreamed that their rambunctious little idol harbored a preference for g-i-r-ls![55]

Although little is known about Tincher's private life, Loos's remarks must be taken with a grain of salt (Massa suggests even a "salt block"), for she could be quite vicious towards people she did not like, especially after they had died, and she admits she was never very close to Tincher.[56] But she does reiterate Tincher's forte for "rowdy scripts." Asked once who was her favorite author, Tincher replied, "James Barrie," an indication, the interviewer suggested, "of her real personality."[57] Whatever her "real personality" was—and we know little of her personal life—there was no doubt an element of whimsy to it and perhaps also an affinity for Barrie's most famous creation, the androgynous Peter Pan.

A second reason is simply that comedy changed in the 1920s. Female slapstick clowns of the 1910s, such as Alice Howell, Louise Fazenda, and Polly Moran took on supporting roles as comedy blended with drama in an effort to appeal to more sophisticated audiences, as previously discussed. Although Tincher's career involved the three distinct and very different screen characters—the stenographer Ethel, the cowgirl Rowdy Ann, and Min Gump—they were all "brainy," uninvolved in romance, and not stereotypically "feminine."

What happened to this unique performer? The last report I could find before her death was from 1932. Ramon Romero, in an article about forgotten faces of Hollywood, describes her as a "prominent comedienne of the Sennett-Keystone and Christie comedy days. But what is she doing now? Working as a cashier at a drugstore." A history of silent film stars reports that in the same year she returned to Los Angeles (possibly from Chicago?) when her sister died of acute alcoholism.[58] Tincher herself died at the age of ninety-nine in 1983 in Brooklyn, New York, and is buried in an unmarked grave in Silver Mount Cemetery on Staten Island. What she did and where she lived for the fifty-one years between 1932 and her death is unknown.

Although most of her films are lost, what we know of them and of her from the trade papers allow us to see her uniqueness, her savvy, her skill at self-promotion, and her awareness of how comedy was evolving during the teens. Her story is of a remarkably independent woman who made a substantial career for herself independent of a husband or male mentor or lover and who reflected the emerging social, political, and economic power of women in the early twentieth century. She was truly a subversive comedienne, believing that a woman not only could, but *should* laugh at a man from a position of strength and control, a laugh that even today is rare on-screen. Like Fanny Brice, both on-screen and off she freely defied ladylike expectations—most explicitly, as discussed above, as Rowdy Ann and Dulcinea—and offered her audiences a challenge to traditional gender norms. Unrecognized, she is still a harbinger for the female comics who followed her—such as Fanny Brice, Mae West, Moms Mabley, Lily Tomlin, Roseanne Barr, Whoopi Goldberg, Margaret Cho, and others—and she is a poignant reminder that subversive comedy does not only belong to the male clowns who populate the comic canon.

NOTES

1. Kalton C. Lahue and Samuel Gill, "Fay Tincher," in *Clown Princes and Court Jesters* (London: Thomas Yoseloff, 1970), 368, 372.

2. Because so many shorts came out during a single year, it is common to include both the year and month of release when they are known.

3. Steve Massa, "Some Job: The Film Career of Fay Tincher," in *Lame Brains & Lunatics* (Albany, GA: Bear Manor Media, 2013), 165.

4. The photo is in the Fay Tincher file, Billy Rose Theatre Collection, New York Public Library for the Performing Arts (hereafter cited as FT BRTC).

5. For a full discussion of the emergence of the New Woman, see Margaret Gibbons Wilson, *The American Woman in Transition: The Urban Influence, 1870–1920* (Westport, CT: Greenwood Press, 1979).

6. Rob King, *The Fun Factory: The Keystone Film Company and the Emergence of Mass Culture* (Berkeley: University of California Press, 2009), 215.

7. *Buffalo Times*, Oct. 25, 1914; and *Milwaukee Journal*, Oct. 31, 1914, both in FT BRTC.

8. FT BRTC.

9. King, *Fun Factory*, 217–220.

10. Julian Johnson, "Close-Ups," *Photoplay* 8, no. 5 (Oct. 1915): 105. Forde was a comic actress who started in shorts in 1910, specializing in westerns. Beginning in 1914 she worked with Al Christie but left the movie business in 1919 after marrying Tom Mix.

11. Louis Reeves Harrison, "The Love Pirate, A Two-Reel Reliance Presenting Woman's Character from a Utilitarian Standpoint," *Moving Picture World*, Feb. 13, 1915, n.p.

12. Margaret Denny, "How Fay Tincher Regards Her Profession," *Motion Picture Magazine*, Aug. 1916, 78.

13. Ibid., 77, 78.

14. FT BRTC.

15. *New York Standard*, Nov. 15, 1907, FT BRTC.

16. It's worth noting that Fanny Brice was also shrewd about her publicity, as discussed by Kristen Hatch in chapter 3 of this volume.

17. *New York Sun*, Aug. 7, 1908, FT BRTC.

18. *Philadelphia Times*, Aug. 7, 1908, FT BRTC.

19. *New York World*, Aug. 7, 1908, FT BRTC.

20. John Lloyd, "Let Fay Try It!," *Photoplay* 10, no. 1 (June 1916), 54–55.

21. *Motion Picture Classic*, Feb. 1918, FT BRTC.

22. Massa, "Some Job," 150.

23. Ibid., 156.

24. Bennie Lubinbille Zeidman, "The Unexploited Series That Exploited Itself," *Photoplayers Weekly* 2, no. 7 (Apr. 23, 1915): 7–8.

25. Review of "The Calico Vampire," *Chicago Herald*, Oct. 25, 1916, FT BRTC.

26. FT BRTC, n.d.

27. Lloyd, "Let Fay Try It!," 55–56.

28. Peter Wade, "The Girl on the Cover," *Motion Picture Magazine*, Apr. 1917, 167.

29. Zeidman, "Unexploited Series," 8.

30. *Photoplayers Weekly* 2, no. 6 (Apr. 16, 1915): 11.

31. FT BRTC.

32. Brent E. Walker, *Mack Sennett's Fun Factory* (Jefferson, NC: McFarland, 2013), 90.

33. King, *Fun Factory*; see chapter 4, "Made for the Masses with an Appeal to the Classes," 143–179.

34. Denny, "How Fay Tincher Regards Her Profession," 78.

35. De Wolf Hopper, *Reminiscences of De Wolf Hopper: Once a Clown, Always a Clown* (Boston: Little Brown, 1927), 151.

36. Robert J. Shores, "The History of Don Quixote," *Motion Picture Magazine* 11, no. 1 (Feb. 1916): n.p. A story on the making of the film in *Moving Picture World*, Nov. 17, 1915, n.p., indicated that "Miss Tincher has taken great delight in her rides on the animal." FT BRTC.

37. Julian Johnson, "The Shadow Stage," *Photoplay* 10, no. 4 (Sept. 1916): 122.

38. Julian Johnson, "The Shadow Stage," *Photoplay* 9, no. 4 (Mar. 1916): 110.

39. *New York Review*, 1916, FT BRTC.

40. Lloyd, "Let Fay Try It!," 56.

41. Roscoe Arbuckle was accused of the rape and death of Virginia Rappe following a riotous party in San Francisco in September 1921. Although he was eventually acquitted, the scandal ruined his career and was a harbinger of a stricter environment of censorship in the Hollywood community.

42. Wade, "Girl on the Cover," 167.

43. Ibid.

44. FT BRTC.

45. *Variety*, May 28, 1919, n.p., FT BRTC.

46. *Theatre Magazine*, 1919, n.p., FT BRTC.

47. *Photoplay*, May 1919, FT BRTC.

48. Clippings file, FT BRTC.

49. Andrew Grossman, "Fay Tincher," *Senses of Cinema* 23 (Dec. 2002), http://sensesofcinema.com/2002/the-female-actor/symposium3/#tincher.

50. *Slapstick Encyclopedia, Vol. 4*, IMAGE Entertainment. DVD.

51. Anonymous, "Uncle Bin's Gift," *Motion Picture News* 28 (Sept. 8, 1923): 1245.

52. See "Immortalizing Andy," in *Picture-Play* magazine 12, no. 6 (Aug. 1925): 99.

53. Massa, "Some Job," 171.

54. Gordon Gassaway, "Where Are the Funny Girls?" *Picture-Play* magazine 18, no. 4 (June 1923): 86.

55. Anita Loos, *Cast of Thousands* (New York: Grosset and Dunlap, 1977), 30–31.

56. Massa, "Some Job," 157.

57. Anonymous, "Fay Tincher—An Ingenuish Vampire," *Theatre Magazine*, June 1919, 389.

58. Ramon Romero, "The Town of Forgotten Faces," *New Movie Magazine*, Aug. 1932, 39; Billy H. Doyle, *The Ultimate Directory of the Silent Screen Performers: A Necrology of Births and Deaths and Essays on Fifty Lost Players* (Metuchen, NJ: Scarecrow Press, 1995), 79.

CHAPTER 3

MAE WEST: THE CONSTANT SINNER

KRISTEN HATCH

If you want to tell people the truth, you'd better make them laugh. Otherwise, they'll kill you.
OSCAR WILDE

To play a bad woman successfully, which means to use the West technique, means playing it with comedy. Audiences must be compensated for accepting certain things from the Diamond Lils. Their indignation must be turned to laughter.
NEW YORK EVENING POST

IN 1936 THE *NEW YORK DAILY NEWS* informed readers that Mae West was the "highest paid gal in the US," earning well over $300,000 a year, leaving Constance Bennett and Marlene Dietrich trailing far behind in second and third place at half her salary.[1] West had signed a contract with Paramount in 1932, and despite Hollywood's misgivings about the suitability of her humor for movie audiences, she enjoyed an unusual degree of control over her films, selecting the cast and director and approving costumes as well as writing the scripts. One newspaper quipped that her full title should be "writer-director-actress-costume designer-comedy constructionist-film editor-property director-unit business manager-make-up artist-singer-producer-talent scout."[2] Indeed, when Henry Herzbrun took over production at Paramount in 1935, he complained that the company had given too much control to its star directors, Cecil B. DeMille and Josef von Sternberg, and to its most notorious star, Mae West.[3] In short, West enjoyed a privileged position in Hollywood, despite the fact that she represented a considerable risk to the studio—having already been arrested for bringing "indecent" material to the stage—and despite her unconventional ap-

3.1. Mae West was one of the most widely recognized women of the early twentieth century. *Movie Mirror* (April 1935). Author's collection.

pearance (for a movie star at least); in the words of Louella Parsons, she was "fat, fair, and I don't know how near forty."[4]

West had earned this privileged status through her considerable success as a playwright, novelist, and performer in the 1920s and early 1930s. Three early plays—*Sex* (1926), *The Drag* (1927), and *The Pleasure Man* (1928)—gained her an arrest record and considerable notoriety. However, it was her production of *Diamond Lil* (1928), in which she starred as the unofficial queen of the Bowery, that transformed her into one of the most celebrated performers and writers on Broadway. In 1930 West published her first novel, *Babe Gordon*, which was later retitled *The Constant Sinner*, and in 1932 she published a novelization of *Diamond Lil*. All this was before she began her celebrated film career, writing and starring in *She Done Him Wrong* (1933), *I'm No Angel* (1933), *Belle of the Nineties* (1934), *Goin' to Town* (1935), *Klondike Annie* (1936), *Go West Young Man* (1936),

Every Day's a Holiday (1937), and *My Little Chickadee* (1940). After 1934 her films may have been subject to the dictates of the Motion Picture Production Code, but her persona lived on outside her film work. Through this body of work and the considerable publicity surrounding it, Mae West established herself as one of the most widely recognized women of the early twentieth century.

West's popularity was due in large part to her campy humor. Her one-liners and double entendres continue to amuse by challenging our assumptions about female desire. She upended popular mores by celebrating female sexual pleasure in respectable, middle-class venues. Ultimately, her performances as what she termed the *femme amoureuse*, a figure commonly condemned as a "fallen woman," represented a condensation of all the forbidden sexualities that both fascinated and horrified white, middle-class Americans in the early twentieth century. With her undulating walk, rolling eyes, and purring speech punctuated by groans of pleasure, she was an amalgam of the outsiders—black, gay, and working-class—whom religious, political, medical, and juridical leaders sought to eliminate from the American body politic. Through her writing and performances she captured the contradictions of a society that enjoyed the spectacle of transgression while seeking to suppress its transgressors. And her plays and films offered an impassioned argument against sexual shame.

FEMME AMOUREUSE

Mae West's humor and, indeed, her very persona were defined by her outspoken endorsement of sexual promiscuity for women. In her stage and film performances, West brought an utterly new image of female sexual pleasure to middle-class audiences who were accustomed to encountering "fallen" women in melodramas like *Camille* (1936) or *Blonde Venus* (1932), in which female sexuality inevitably leads to suffering. Writing in the 1930s, Gilbert Seldes celebrates West's challenging the view that female sexuality is inherently dangerous:

> Her invitation, "Come up and see me sometime," as delivered in a gurgling voice, suggests for the first time on any screen that mutual satisfaction will result from the encounter. She destroys the idea that women have no satisfaction in love, and at the same time the idea that men's lives are ruined by love.[5]

West's celebration of female sexuality was especially remarkable given the fact that promiscuity, particularly among the white, working-class women, was taken by the medical and legal professions as a sign of racial degeneracy and was cause for sterilization during the early twentieth century. West's novels and plays engaged indirectly with this eugenic discourse, offering an alternative view of the sexually voracious woman and a critique of the society that condemns her. For West, female sexual pleasure was more than a punch line. It was also a means of empowerment.

Much of Mae West's humor arose out of the comic reversals produced by her characters' sexual voracity. In *I'm No Angel*, a fortune-teller gazes into her crystal ball and tells Tira (West), "I see a man in your life." Tira complains, "What? Only one?" Similarly, in *She Done Him Wrong*, Captain Cummings (Cary Grant) asks Lady Lou (West), "Haven't you met a man who could make you happy?" Lou replies, "Sure. Lots of times." These jokes rely on the expectation that women long for marriage and (presumably) monogamy and that an unmarried woman is an unhappy woman who longs for her one true love. By asserting that lots of men have made her happy, West endorses the immediate pleasures of sex over the abstract ideal of marriage. The joke remains funny because we continue to hold to the belief that sex offers only transient pleasure while marriage brings true happiness, regardless of evidence to the contrary.

West's frank pleasure in sex combined with her refusal to countenance marriage or motherhood was particularly transgressive during the 1920s and 1930s, when eugenic beliefs shaped medical practice and American jurisprudence. One of the better-known illustrations of the devastating effect of eugenic beliefs on white, working-class women in the United States came to light with the Supreme Court decision in *Buck v. Bell* (1927), which upheld a medical doctor's right to forcibly sterilize an eighteen-year-old girl who had become pregnant out of wedlock.[6] In her history of gender and eugenics in twentieth-century America, Wendy Kline argues that it was often a woman's sexual conduct rather than any mental deficiency that led to her being sterilized "for the good of the race." Within eugenic logic, a woman who was sexually active outside marriage was "a biological threat to the health and advancement of the race. . . . Her sexual behavior indicated her primitive savagery—trapped in the mind of an adolescent, she was both mentally and morally deficient and a threat to the race."[7] Kline's analysis of the records of the Sonoma State Home in California, which sterilized twenty thousand people between 1909 and 1963, demonstrates that the women sent there for "sexual delinquency" were generally guilty of no more than sexual desire. "The most common indicator of female sexual deviance found on patient records was the term 'passionate,'"[8] a word that West would happily apply to herself and the characters she played.

In her novels, plays, and films, West offered an alternative framework for understanding women whose pleasure in sex was unmotivated by marriage or motherhood, identifying such women as "femmes amoureuses" or "daughters of joy." West understood sexuality in terms similar to those of the eugenicists, attributing sexual behavior to heredity, but she rejected the idea that such women represented the deterioration of the race. In her 1930 novel *The Constant Sinner* (originally titled *Babe Gordon*), she explains:

> Nature creates different kinds of females and makes them perplexingly contrary to a moral law that assumes all female flesh to be the same. As a matter of fact there are women so constituted that physically and mentally they have no desire for men and therefore become old maids, or enter nunneries. There are women who live a normal, conventional sex life and enter into marriage and motherhood. And then there are women so formed in body and mind that they are predestined to be daughters of joy. These women, whom the French call *"femmes amoureuses,"* are found not alone among women of the streets, but in every stratum of society.[9]

With this description of the spectrum of female (hetero)sexuality, West attributes sexual behavior to "nature," much as eugenicists understood behavior in terms of evolutionary development. However, she implicitly refuses the notion that the femme amoureuse was a "degenerate" who threatened the progress of civilization. Instead, she asserts that such women could be found across all social strata.

Similarly, West described the speakeasies of Harlem during Prohibition not to demonstrate that the neighborhood's black inhabitants were innately primitive, as eugenicists would have it, but as a "sensual oasis in the sterile desert of white civilization where people can indulge in unconventional excesses."

> The old, old story of civilization's lusts was being retold in Harlem. The lusts that ancient Rome and Athens could not purge from

their proud and disciplined cultures—the flesh cry that has persisted through all time—found expression and release in the region of New York's black belt. Harlem is the Paris of the Western Hemisphere.[10]

Thus, whereas eugenicists would assert that restraint and progress go hand in hand, West suggests that the "flesh cry" has persisted unabated across millennia. Further, West explains that Harlem's "hellholes flourish side by side with high-colored respectability."[11] That is, they are not representative of all the inhabitants of the black neighborhood of Harlem. Rather, in the confines of the black ghetto, respectable families live side-by-side with disreputable neighbors.

Moreover, far from bringing about the downfall of women and society, as countless novels, plays, and films about "fallen women" would have it, sexuality was a source of power for the women within West's oeuvre: "History's pages reveal the power of these women who thrive on love, whose lives are centered on men."[12] Indeed, West had a long-held fascination with powerful and promiscuous women. According to newspaper publicity, her library consisted "almost entirely of biographies of famous women of history."[13] In 1937 she pitched the idea of starring in a film about Catherine the Great to Paramount. She had a very different image of the empress from the one portrayed by Marlene Dietrich in *The Scarlett Empress* (1934). Instead of a "hollow-cheeked doll," West planned to portray Catherine "as a warm, gay, very sensual woman, and yet a monarch who was a skillful politician and master statesman."[14] The studio passed on the idea, but West developed her script into a play, *Catherine Was Great*, which premiered on Broadway in August 1944. In her autobiography, West explains, "I frankly characterized [Catherine] as a *pre-incarnation* of myself. A Slavic-Germanic Diamond Lil, just as low in vivid sexuality, but on a higher plane of authority."[15]

"I USED TO BE SNOW WHITE, BUT I DRIFTED"

While eugenicists sought to segregate or sterilize promiscuous working-class women, gay men, and African Americans for the betterment of the American gene pool, urban members of the white middle class, pursuing illicit thrills, actively sought contact with the "degenerate" and "primitive" denizens of the nation's growing cities. West's stardom was a direct outcome of the early twentieth-century practice of "slumming," whereby members of the white middle class visited nightclubs and cabarets where "Negroes" and "pansies" performed. Slumming became particularly popular in the 1920s as a result of Prohibition. In 1919 Congress enacted the Volstead Act, outlawing the sale of alcohol in the United States and inaugurating the period of Prohibition, which lasted until 1933. However, the law was widely unpopular, and many otherwise law-abiding Americans continued to purchase alcohol at illicit speakeasies, often in poor neighborhoods. During Prohibition, middle-class white patrons flocked to black neighborhoods in search of gin and thrills, helping to inspire what Langston Hughes decried as a "Negro vogue."[16] Mafia-owned speakeasies in poor neighborhoods also provided a venue in which gay men and women could gather, and these, too, became a source of entertainment, prompting a "pansy craze."[17] West and others helped to bring black and gay male performers to Broadway and Times Square, where they reached an even larger middle-class audience. Attending her plays and films, audiences could go "slumming" in the comfort of the theater. The *New Republic* noted that West's controversial play *Sex* appealed to the "special tastes" of "people who looked on at the performance with raw thrills, or with the amused scandalization [*sic*] of slumming parties."[18] And *Life* magazine noted that the play attracted "soft-purring limousines [that] roll up with theatre parties of gentry, out 'just for a lark.'"[19]

West began her career at a time when stage entertainments catered to white audiences divided by class, and to a large degree her success arose from her ability to transgress boundaries and bring forbidden performances to legitimate venues.[20] In the early twentieth century, burlesque offered somewhat disreputable entertainment that catered to men. Vaudeville provided relatively cheap entertainment to white men and women. The Keith Circuit, where West was one of the few women to perform a solo act, took pains to achieve respectability. And Broadway attracted well-off, white audiences who could afford the higher ticket prices. However, West's performances challenged these distinctions, bringing burlesque-style performances to vaudeville, Broadway, and eventually Hollywood. She made a name for herself in vaudeville in 1912 by performing a "cooch" dance—a dance style associated with burlesque—while seated in a chair. Scandalized reviewers of her 1926 production of *Sex* pointed to the play's burlesque elements as a sign of its vulgarity. It was a "nasty red-light district show—which would be tolerated in but a few of the stock burlesque houses in America. . . . [It is] the nastiest thing ever dis-

3.2. Audiences identified Mae West's distinctive silhouette with burlesque. *Go West Young Man* (1936). Author's collection.

closed on a New York stage (and that takes into consideration the re-cent burlesque stock company down at the Chelsea Theatre)."[21] One anonymous reviewer wrote, "It has the earmarks of the sordid bur-lesque skits of years gone by . . . and even [there] few plays of such crude and immoral scenes and dialogue were tolerated."[22] *The Plea-sure Man* was "a sickening excess of filth," in part because of its "ham-greased imitation of Burlesque."[23] Even her films made un-der the auspices of the Motion Picture Production Code evoked bur-lesque. *Goin' to Town* had the "innuendoes of a burlesque show. . . . Miss West fairly outdoes herself as a rather vulgar retailer of indeli-cate wisecracks."[24] And when her curvaceous figure began to influ-ence Paris fashion, several newspapers identified West's distinctive silhouette with burlesque.[25]

Much as she brought burlesque performance styles to more legiti-mate venues, West brought elements of the "Negro vogue" to vaude-ville, Broadway, and Hollywood. She was often credited with intro-ducing the "shimmy," a dance attributed to black women, to the stage. *Theatre Magazine* quipped, "Those who do not know African tribal customs credit—or damn—[Mae West] with the invention of the shimmy."[26] The dance was considered so outrageous that the lights were turned out during her performances in Boston and Atlanta so that audiences would not be subjected to the "vulgar" dance.[27] West likewise brought the performance styles associated with African Americans to the Broadway stage. For example, the second act in *Sex*, which takes place in Trinidad, was described as looking "ever so much like that Harlem cabaret we had seen further downtown and in more celebrated art centers."[28] Her performance of "Sweet Man" in the play was "very Harlem and with a jazz dance right out of the eff-sharp department."[29] And in her films she sang "dirty" blues songs associated with singers like Ma Rainey and Bessie Smith, whose lyrics suggested that men were good for sex and little else.

West's appropriation of the performance styles of unacknowledged black women is but one example of a long history of what James Snead has described as a process of "exclusionary emulation," whereby a white performer's emulation of a black performer contributes to the latter's exclusion from the scene of performance.[30] Mae West became a star, in part, by adapting the performances of African American dancers and blues singers who remained relatively unknown. From nineteenth-century blackface minstrelsy through recent examples of twerking and beyond, white performers have gained more profit and notoriety from practices associated with the supposed authenticity of black performers than have black performers themselves. And West's performances certainly fit this pattern.

Nonetheless, West's adaptation of jazz song and dance to vaudeville, Broadway, and Hollywood served an important function beyond erasing black performers from popular culture. On the one hand, West's invocation of African American performance styles suggests that she helped to make songs and movements associated with the "Negro vogue" appear less dangerous to middle-class audiences. On the other hand, though, she also helped to obscure the differences between white and black women, particularly in relation to sexuality. As Pamela Robertson points out, "West's affiliation with African American culture serves in part to underscore her identification with the marginal and her status as a transgressive woman within the mainstream representation of sexuality."[31] Recalling the play *Sex* in 1934, Zora Neale Hurston noted that "Mae West in *Sex* had much more flavor of the turpentine quarters than she did of the white bawd. I know that the piece she played on the piano is a very old jook composition."[32] Hurston's description of West as having "more flavor of the turpentine quarters than she did of the white bawd" and *Variety*'s description of her performance as "very Harlem" suggest that she was capable of evoking African American sexuality through the movement of a distinctively white body.

African American women played a key role in West's humor as well. West's papers contain several boxes of handwritten gags, which she scrawled across reams of paper as she lay in bed. Reading these gags in succession, it becomes clear that her jokes developed around a handful of stock figures: the suitor, who was often too young, too eager, or too drunk; the blue blood who sought to censor her, though if he were a man he might be seduced by her; and black maids who share her polygamous desires but need advice to express them fully.[33] It is not surprising to find that the suitor plays a large role in her humor. Her persona was built around the idea that she was desirable to all men and unwilling to settle for any one of them. Nor does the presence of the blue blood come as a surprise, given West's frequent run-ins with censors. However, the consistency with which her jokes invoked a black maid is rather curious.

Further, publicity for West often made mention of West's "off-and-on the screen maid," Libby Taylor, whose picture was included in newspaper articles about the star.[34] Indeed, West was so strongly associated with her maid that when a bus line hired an actress to impersonate West as a promotional stunt, the impersonator was accompanied by a "colored maid."[35] Hedda Hopper emphasized the unusual camaraderie between West and Taylor when she reported that West was accompanied to the premiere of *I'm No Angel* by "her colored maid who has been faithful to her for years. The maid was gotten up in white velvet and orchids. Nor was it a hand-me-down from Mae's own wardrobe. It was a special dress for a special occasion."[36]

Several scholars have noted that the presence of black maids in West's films produces a visual contrast that draws attention to West's shimmering whiteness. At the same time, they note, West and her maids enjoy an interracial camaraderie that is rarely found in Hollywood film of the studio era.[37] Perhaps the only equivalent, as James Snead points out, would be Shirley Temple's performances alongside Bill Robinson.[38] As Pamela Robertson writes, West "simultaneously

3.3. African American women played a significant role in West's star persona.
Mae West and Libby Taylor in *Belle of the Nineties* (1934). Author's collection.

foregrounds her racial difference from the maids and her gendered
identification with them in what Stuart Hall describes as a double
move of 'othering' and identification typical of racist discourse."[39]

Within the context of West's humor, though, the black maid plays
a somewhat different role from that of comrade or foil. West's jokes
involving black maids function to produce a comic inversion in
which West assumes the role associated with the types of moral reformers who fought to censor her. Within the racial logic of eugenics,
white women were meant to bring moral uplift to immigrants, the
poor, and the "racially inferior." West reversed this, offering instead
a sensual pedagogy to her maids. In her films, it is the black maids
who advocate propriety and the white woman who counsels pleasure.
In *She Done Him Wrong*, her maid, Pearl (Louise Beavers) expresses
the familiar argument for wearing fresh underclothes: "I wouldn't
want no policeman to catch me without my petticoats." West, however, advocates for pleasure rather than propriety when she suggests
that it might be fun to be caught without undergarments: "A police-

man? How 'bout a nice fireman?" Similarly, in *Belle of the Nineties* when her maid, Jasmine (Taylor), wonders "What kind of husband do you think I should get?" West's character replies with the usual reversal: "Why don't you take a single man and leave the husbands alone?" Again, the black woman's propriety is overturned by the white woman's promiscuity.

THE GREATEST FEMALE IMPERSONATOR OF ALL TIME

While West shocked critics by bringing the dance styles of Harlem cabarets to vaudeville, she scandalized Broadway by reproducing elaborate drag balls in *The Drag* and *The Pleasure Man*, which she wrote but did not perform in. While the frank depiction of prostitution in *Sex* repelled many reviewers, who described it as "nauseating," "vulgar," and "smut,"[40] it was the plays featuring female impersonators that invited police raids and a brief jail sentence. And while black women were a significant and very visible part of Mae West's star persona, prior to the revitalization of her career in the 1970s West seldom appeared alongside drag queens, though camp humor was central to her performances. Much as her performances helped to establish an affiliation between black and white working-class sexuality, West's alignment of the femme amoureuse with gay men points to their shared status as outsiders and "degenerates."

Just as West's adaptation of black performance styles is part of a larger history of "exclusionary emulation," so her popularity as a camp performer accompanied the disappearance of gay and effeminate men from public performance venues. Inspired by *Sex* as well as other controversial plays that frankly depicted illicit sexual behaviors, the Wales Padlock Law of 1927 authorized the New York police to close down a theater for a year if it were found to depict or deal "with the subject of sex degeneracy or sex perversion." Similarly, in the 1930s the Motion Picture Production Code dictated that Hollywood films could not even hint at the existence of homosexuality.[41] Even the word "pansy" was eradicated from Hollywood scripts. However, Mae West persisted in bringing the camp humor associated with gay men's performances to Broadway and Hollywood audiences.

West's indebtedness to gay men's performance is easily recognized by contemporary audiences by virtue of her long afterlife as a camp icon. Her double entendres and pithy witticisms are the soul of camp.[42] As early as 1934, *Vanity Fair* writer and editor George Davis, cautioning West against imagining that she had the ability to enact anything other than her familiar persona, celebrated West's resemblance to the female impersonator and comic Bert Savoy:

> I can pay you no greater tribute, dear lady, than to say [you have] healed the wound in my heart caused by the death of the one and only Bert Savoy. I love you, Miss West, because YOU are the greatest female impersonator of all time.[43]

Indeed, as Robertson notes in her exploration of West's camp aesthetic, West's trademark phrase, uttered at the end of *Diamond Lil* and repeated in several of her films—"Come up and see me"—echoed Savoy's line, "You must come over."[44]

West's alignment with gay men points to their shared status as sexual outsiders. Her description of the femme amoureuse is echoed in the words of a sympathetic doctor who treats gay men in her 1927 play *The Drag*. Indicating his patient, the doctor explains, "The man has done no wrong. He's only what he was born to be—a sexual invert." Arguing with a judge who believes that "degenerates" should be segregated from American society by being quarantined on a deserted island, the doctor replies that it would take a very large island. "Nature seems to have made no distinction in bestowing this misfortune [same-sex desire] upon the human race. We find this abnormality among persons of every state of society. It has held sway on the thrones of kings, princes, statesmen, scholars, fools! Wealth, culture, refinement makes [*sic*] no difference. . . . It is as strong today as it was centuries ago."[45] Again, as with the femme amoureuse and the pleasure grounds of Harlem, the "invert" has existed throughout history and within all strata of society, contradicting the eugenicists' view that such behavior signals evolutionary regression.

Just as West embodied the movements and voiced the desires of black women in her performances of the shimmy and dirty blues, so she aligned herself with gay men in her expressions of sexual desire. West's plays *Sex* and *The Pleasure Man* were controversial, in part, because they were about gay men who, much like West herself, were unashamed of their unorthodox desires. In these plays, gay men often tell jokes at the expense of straight men who are oblivious to their double entendres. In *Sex*, for example, one of the drag queens suggests to a taxi driver, "Ride me around a while, dearie, and then come back for her [indicating his gay male companion], if you're so inclined."[46]

Like the gay men who appeared in her stage plays, West often played a sexual aggressor to "innocent" straight men. In *Go West Young Man*, for example, she plays Mavis Arden, a Hollywood star who is diverted from her planned tryst with a politician because her car has broken down in a small town. Looking out the window of the boarding house where she has taken refuge, she catches sight of the handsome mechanic, Bud (Randolph Scott), who is fixing her car, and she decides that, perhaps, the weekend won't be a complete waste. "What large and sinewy muscles," she purrs to herself as she and the audience look at the handsome man's muscled arms. Mavis sets out to seduce the oblivious yokel. Dancing with him to the accompaniment of the radio, her hand travels down his back, reaching for his buttocks. Here, as in *The Drag*, the straight man is the butt of a shared joke because he is unable to recognize that he is the object of unconventional desire.

West functioned as a stand-in for the myriad performers whose more threatening bodies—black, effeminate—were all but eliminated from public view in the 1920s and 1930s. However, in so doing she did not erase these outsiders; rather, she suggested solidarity between herself and them. West's performances implied a dissolution of boundaries between black and white bodies and homosexual and heterosexual behaviors. Her persona helped to establish an equivalency between black women, gay men, and white women, an equivalency that was conveyed through their expressions of sexual desire.

"THE FINEST WOMAN THAT EVER WALKED THE STREETS"

With her corseted figure evoking the Gay Nineties and her indebtedness to the outmoded style of burlesque, West's performances could be dismissed as mocking the past rather than critiquing modern society. However, the censoring of her plays and films suggests that West's persona was quite threatening indeed. Rather than offering a safe substitution for the forbidden figures of black women and white, gay men, Mae West's singing, dancing, and camp humor undermined notions of white femininity that were foundational to racial ideology in the early twentieth century. More than that, she used her position of relative privilege to skewer the hypocrisy of a society that condemned her behavior while flocking to her performances.

More often than not, the femme amoureuse was the moral center of West's plays and films, many of which take aim at the hypocrisy of a sexual double standard that condemns women for behavior that would be accepted in a man. As Lady Lou (West) quips in *She Done Him Wrong*, "When women go bad, men go right after them." Like Babe in *The Constant Sinner*, many of West's characters hold to the belief that "if a man can have as many women as he wants, there is no reason why a woman should not do the same thing."[47] The double standard is quite literally put on trial in *I'm No Angel* when Tira (West) sues her former fiancé, Jack Clayton (Cary Grant), for breach of promise. Clayton's defense rests on the fact that Tira has seduced many men, but she turns the tables when she cross-examines the men in her past and reveals that they were no less guilty of promiscuity than she and that no harm has come of their love affairs.

Indeed, West's characters often attribute their cynicism about love to their treatment by men. In *Sex*, Margie tells Agnes,

> Ever since I've been old enough to know Sex I've looked at men as hunters. They're filled with Sex. In the past few years I've been chattel to that Sex. All the bad that's in me has been put there by men. I began to hate every one of them, hated them, used them for what I could get out of them, and then laughed at them.[48]

And in *She Done Him Wrong*, Lady Lou explains her philosophy: "Men's all alike, married or single. It's their game. I happen to be smart enough to play it their way." Perhaps this is why she does not represent marriage as a reward to be earned but something to be avoided, a false prize in a rigged game.

High society slummers, too, come in for invective in West's work. They make their appearance in several of her novels, plays, and films. In *I'm No Angel*, Tira is visited in her dressing room by a bevy of obnoxious slummers. And in *Goin' to Town*, too, West's antagonist is a society woman who cheats at horse racing and is engaged in an affair with a gigolo, but who condemns West's character as a whore. In *Sex*, a wealthy society matron, Clara, is picked up by a pimp, Rocky, during a night of adventure in the red-light district. Clara coos in delight, "This is so thrilling. I love it because it's so . . . unconventional. . . . It's such a departure from the usual course of life! So daring!" (48). However, West's character, Margy, objects to her using the underclass as a source of entertainment and derides the hypocrisy of the middle-class woman who would shun her on Park Avenue: "She's one of those respectable society dames who poses as decent, and is looking for the first chance to cheat without being found out" (54). Rocky spikes Clara's drink in order to rob her, leaving her for dead in Margy's apartment. Margy revives her, and hypocritical to the end, Clara betrays the prostitute, accusing her of drugging and robbing her rather than admit to the police she entered the apartment with a pimp. "I don't count, I suppose," complains Margy, "because I'm what I am" (56).

Mae West's plays and films are particularly critical of the ideology promoted in the "fallen woman" film, which portrayed female sexuality as a source of suffering. West's novels, plays, and films suggest instead that it is not female promiscuity that is a social problem but sexual shame. In *Goin' to Town*, for example, her character tells a young man, "For a long time I was ashamed of the way I lived." "You mean to say you reformed?" he asks. "No, I got over being ashamed."

West's humor may have been her primary attraction to audiences, but she also used melodrama effectively to critique the society that would condemn her as a "fallen woman." The fallen women was a stock character on stage and in films of the 1920s and 1930s. Peter Brooks demonstrates that melodrama developed in the eighteenth and nineteenth centuries in response to the secularization of European society; as the church withdrew from political life, melodrama emerged as means of exploring moral problems. Linda Williams builds on this work, arguing that Hollywood melodrama orchestrates its characters and narrative situations—its villains and victimized heroes, its nostalgic longing for a "place of innocence," and its "dialectic of pathos and action"—in order to produce "moral legibility," a clear framework for asserting the moral legitimacy of specific values and ideologies.[49]

In melodramas about fallen women, the idealized family home is often the "place of innocence" to which the characters long to return. The fallen woman—the woman who turns to prostitution for noble reasons—is often the victimized hero, her suffering the focus of the film's drama. In *Blonde Venus*, for example, Marlene Dietrich stars as Helen Faraday, who engages in an affair with a wealthy man (Cary Grant) in order to raise money to save her husband from radium poisoning. At the film's end, after a period of abjection in which Helen is separated from her child and forced to walk the streets, the family is restored. Inversely, men may suffer for their infatuation with seductive and greedy women, as in *Baby Face* (1933), in which Barbara Stanwyck sleeps her way to the top of the bank where she works, eventually bringing down the entire organization.[50] In either case, the "place of innocence"—the idealized location to which characters long to return or the place that is lost over the course of the film— is the single-family home, presided over by a benevolent father. Although such films were quite controversial in the 1930s—Lea Jacobs has demonstrated that the popular cycle of fallen women films played a central role in the development of the Production Code—they did, for the most part, uphold the ideal of the patriarchal family and assert the moral legitimacy of such values as monogamy, female chastity outside marriage, and women's devotion to caregiving and self-sacrifice rather than the pursuit of sensual pleasure.

While West helped to transform the gold digger from a dangerous figure into a figure of fun, she also relied on the fallen woman as a source of pathos. Her play *Sex*, for example, is about a prostitute, Margy (West), whose idea of "rising to the top of her profession" is to become the kept woman of a wealthy man. Margy takes on the role of mentor to a younger prostitute, Agnes, who is ill-suited to the profession and longs to return home to "the old folks and the little white cottage." The sound of church bells drives Agnes to tears: "Those bells, every time they ring it seems as if—Oh I—can't stand it Margy, I can't stand it. Back home the little old church—"[51] However, while the play invokes the image of the idealized home that is so central to melodrama, West punctures the fantasy by warning Agnes of the narrow-mindedness that characterizes that home: "When you get back home, old girl, you'll be buying a through ticket back here, mark my words. They won't let you go straight. They'll hold you up as an example. I tried it. I know." Margy's advice proves true. Agnes returns home only to discover that "they forgive you but they won't let you forget" (65). In the end Agnes kills herself, her death dismissed as that of "just one of those poor wretches that follow the fleet" (70). Here, what is being made "morally legible" is middle-class bigotry and the damaging effects of sexual shame.

A similar character appears in *Diamond Lil* and its film adaptation, *She Done Him Wrong*. The story is set in the 1890s in Suicide Hall, a Bowery saloon so named because of the number of women who have ended their lives there. Diamond Lil (West) is the mistress of the saloon's owner, Gus Jordan, who unbeknownst to her is engaged in the trafficking of women.[52] A despondent woman, Sally, arrives in the saloon with the intention of killing herself, and Lil coaxes her story out of her. She is pregnant and unmarried, too ashamed to return to her parents and convinced that her father wouldn't allow her back in any case. As in *Sex*, the fallen woman pays dearly for the moral hypocrisy of a society that punishes women for engaging in premarital sex. Sally is sold into sexual slavery. As Lea Jacobs points out, the film takes a deliberate jab at the fallen woman genre when Lil dismisses Sally's plight: "Some guy done her wrong. The story's so old it should've been set to music long ago." Indeed, the old story has been set to music in countless blues numbers. The refrain of West's signature song, "Frankie and Johnnie," for instance, is "He was her man, but he done her wrong." And, of course, the film's title—*She Done Him Wrong*—reverses genders, celebrating Diamond Lil as the woman who triumphed when "she done him wrong."

The Drag offers a variation on the themes of sexual shame and moral bigotry, suggesting an equivalence between the suffering of the fallen woman and that of the gay man. The play, subtitled *A Homosexual Comedy in Three Acts*, is about a physician, Dr. Richmond, who treats gay men for psychiatric illness. A despondent young man, David, comes to him for help and explains to Richmond:

> I was attracted by my own sex. How was I to know it was wrong, when it seemed perfectly natural to me. . . . I soon realized that I was not like other men. I sought those of my own kind as companions. I realized that we were outcasts. I suffered. I rebelled. I fought with myself—but it was stronger than I. Then I gave in. . . . There were others like me. Oh, we all fight in the beginning, but it was no use. (102)

David explains that he was happy, briefly, after he fell in love: "We lived together. We were happy. The curse didn't seem to matter so much. . . . No normally married couple were happier than we were" (102). Their happiness was short lived, however, because his partner's family insisted that their son marry a woman: "He owed it to them. To his name." And to compound the pain, his former partner has taken up with another man. David explains that in his anguish, he attempted suicide, which is what brought him to the doctor. Later, the doctor advocates for the legalization of homosexuality, arguing that current laws "force [men] into secrecy and shame for being what they cannot help being . . . branding them as criminals and so lead them into the depths of misery and suicide" (108).

The Drag considers the question of how society should treat its sexual misfits. The doctor and his friend, Judge Kingsbury, engage in a debate about the nature of "sexual inversion." Whereas the doctor advocates treating gay men with empathy—"The charity of our hearts is the only love which they can ever know"—the judge responds in horror and asserts that such "things" "should be herded together on some desert isle—" (107). When the doctor objects to treating gay men as criminals, the judge responds that homosexuals must be contained for the good of society: "The law has forced this vice into a corner, just as it has forced prostitution into shady byways" (108). A third position is offered by one of the play's drag queens, Clem, who compares David's shame with her own refusal to be cowed by society:

> Yesterday, you know LM, that sentimental moll. . . . Well, she calls me up and asked me to come right over, she's hysterical. Well, I goes over and there was the poor queen ready to jump out of the window. Of course, I knew what was the matter. She needed a jab. She's been taking heroin and morphine by the barrels. The trouble with her is she's sensitive of what she is. Now, I don't give a goddamn who knows it. Of course, I don't go flouncing my hips up and down Broadway picking up trade. . . . But of course, I don't pass anything up either, dearie. I'm out to have a good time as well as the next.[53]

The lively vernacular of this speech is far more vivid than the conversations in which the doctor and the judge debate the place of gay men in American society. In these words we hear echoes of Margy and Lil, the cynical, insouciant prostitutes who have dismissed the moral laws of a society that oppresses them and instead derive their power from pursuing sexual and other pleasures.

In the end, it turns out that David's ex-lover is none other than the judge's son and the doctor's son-in-law, who has ruined the happiness of both David and the doctor's daughter by succumbing to social pressure and entering into a sham marriage. In this sense, he shares a key characteristic of the villains in Mae West's melodramas: he is dishonest about his sexual desires, such hypocrisy being the height of villainy in Mae West's moral universe.

CONCLUSION

During a period when racial and sexual outsiders were all but eliminated from public view, Mae West stood out not merely as a substitute for those bodies—black and effeminate—that had been made to disappear, but also as the voice for those whom reformers hoped to eliminate altogether during the Progressive era and into the 1930s. It should come as no surprise, then, that her name should become shorthand for the immorality of Hollywood that these reformers sought to repress. Under the restrictions of the Production Code, and with the centralization of authority at Paramount due to the imperative that the company turn a profit during the Depression, West lost much of the power that had made her among the most successful women in the world in the early 1930s. Nonetheless, she continued writing and performing until her death in 1980.

NOTES

The chapter epigraph is from Charles Parker Hammond, "She's No Angel," *New York Evening Post*, Feb. 18, 1933. Mae West Scrapbook, 1913–1937, Billy Rose Theatre Collection, New York Public Library for the Performing Arts (hereafter MWS BRTC).

1. "She's the Top," *New York Daily News*, Jan. 8, 1936, MWS BRTC. The previous year, 1935, she had earned over $480,000, second only to William Randolph Hearst and well ahead of Bing Crosby, Hollywood's highest paid male star. Simon Louvish, *Mae West: It Ain't No Sin* (New York: St. Martin's Griffin, 2007), 301.

2. Unidentified clipping, *Brooklyn Daily Eagle*, May 30, 1936, MWS BRTC.

3. Henry Herzbrun, Letter to Adolph Zukor, Mar. 5, 1935. Adolph Zukor Collection: Folder 15, 1935 correspondence, Margaret Herrick Library, Academy of Motion Picture Arts and Sciences (AMPAS), Los Angeles.

4. *Los Angeles Examiner*, June 13, 1932.

5. Gilbert Seldes, *The Movies Come from America* (New York: Charles Scribner's Sons, 1937), 35.

6. Carrie Buck became pregnant at the age of seventeen after being raped by her foster brother. For a compelling history of the decision and the legal and medical thinking that lay behind it, see Adam Cohen, *Imbeciles: The Supreme Court, American Eugenics, and the Sterilization of Carrie Ann Buck* (New York: Penguin Press, 2016).

7. Wendy Kline, *Building a Better Race: Gender, Sexuality, and Eugenics from the Turn of the Century to the Baby Boom* (Berkeley: University of California Press, 2005), 29.

8. Ibid.

9. Mae West, *The Constant Sinner* (London: Virago Press, 1995), 5. Interestingly, despite her long association with gay men, West overlooked the possibility that some women desire women.

10. Ibid., 103. West's philosophy of a sexual spectrum should not be taken to indicate that she did not share the dominant racial ideology of the time, which associated African Americans with backward "primitivism" and understood Europeans and European Americans to be more evolutionarily advanced.

11. Ibid., 103.

12. Ibid., 5.

13. "Mae West Adapts Library to Film Use," *New York American*, Feb. 3, 1936, Mae West Clippings, BRTC.

14. Mae West, *Goodness Had Nothing to Do With It* (Englewood Cliffs, NJ: Prentice-Hall, 1969), 196.

15. Ibid., 197.

16. Langston Hughes, "When the Negro Was in Vogue," in *The Collected Works of Langston Hughes*, vol. 13, ed. Joseph McLaren (Columbia: University of Missouri Press, 2002), 175.

17. In *Slumming*, Chad Heap examines the discourse surrounding such slumming expeditions to demonstrate that white outsiders often built a sense of affiliation with the white middle class through their visits to these enclaves. There, patrons were able to flirt with forbidden behaviors while at the same time projecting their illicit desires onto the black inhabitants of neighborhoods like Harlem and Chicago's South Side, thereby disavowing the transgressiveness of their own behaviors even as they indulged them. Heap also argues that the practice helped to produce gay communities that crossed boundaries of race and class. *Slumming: Sexual and Racial Encounters in American Nightlife, 1885–1940* (Chicago: University of Chicago Press, 2010).

18. Stark Young, "Diamond Lil," *New Republic*, June 27, 1928, 146.

19. "All About *Sex*," *Life*, May 20, 1926, Mae West Clippings, BRTC.

20. Marybeth Hamilton provides a thorough and fascinating account of Mae West's career in the context of these various performance venues. See *"When I'm Bad, I'm Better": Mae West, Sex, and American Entertainment* (Berkeley: University of California Press, 1997).

21. "*Sex*," *Variety*, Apr. 28, 1926, 79.

22. Unidentified clipping, Mae West, Robinson Locke Collection, BRTC.

23. Gilbert W. Gabriel, "Pleasure Man: Something of a Description of the Somewhat Indescribable," unidentified clipping, Oct. 2, 1928, Mae West Clippings, BRTC.

24. Howard Barnes, "Goin' to Town," *New York Herald Tribune*, May 11, 1935, Mae West Clippings, BRTC.

25. See Alice Hughes, "Hour-Glass Rules Style for the Fall," *New York World Telegram*, July 31, 1933; "Mae West Sharp Trader," *New York World Telegram*, Sept. 13, 1933. Both are found in Mae West, Robinson Locke Collection, BRTC.

26. "Mae West," *Theatre Magazine*, Nov. 1921, Mae West, Robinson Locke Collection, BRTC.

27. *Variety*, Sept. 1919; Apr. 1921; May 1921.

28. Review of *Sex*, unidentified clipping, Mae West Clippings, BRTC.

29. "Mae West, 3-Star Special in *Sex* Play," *Variety*, May 5, 1926, 26.

30. James Snead, *White Screens, Black Images: Hollywood from the Dark Side* (New York: Routledge, 1994), 60. West did make an effort to include black performers in her films. For example, she insisted that Paramount hire Duke Ellington and his band to perform in *Belle of the Nineties* at considerable expense to the studio.

31. Pamela Robertson, "Mae West's Maids: Race, 'Authenticity,' and the Discourse of Camp," in *Camp: Queer Aesthetics and the Performing Subject, A*

Reader, ed. Fabio Cleto (Ann Arbor: University of Michigan Press, 1999), 402. Robertson argues that blackness functions within white camp as a means of signifying authenticity.

32. Zora Neale Hurston, "The Characteristics of Negro Expression" (1934), in *"Sweat,"* ed. Cheryl Wall (New Brunswick, NJ: Rutgers University Press, 1997), 69.

33. Mae West's papers are held at the Margaret Herrick Library, AMPAS (hereafter West Papers).

34. *Belle of the Nineties,* Paramount press release, West Papers.

35. "Mae West Impersonator as Bus Line Shilless, *Variety,* Jan. 16, 1934, BRTC.

36. Unidentified clipping, 1933, Hedda Hopper Papers/Metro-Goldwyn-Meyer, f. 280, Margaret Herrick Library, AMPAS. Hopper does not acknowledge that Libby Taylor played a role in the film.

37. Donald Bogle, *Toms, Coons, Mulattoes, Mammies, and Bucks: An Interpretive History of Blacks in American Film* (New York: Viking Press, 1973), 45–47; Snead, *White Screens,* 67–68; Ramona Curry, *Too Much of a Good Thing: Mae West as Cultural Icon* (Minneapolis: University of Minnesota Press, 1996), 12–17, 87.

38. Snead, *White Screens,* 67.

39. Robertson, "Mae West's Maids," 398.

40. Robert Coleman, *"Sex* an Offensive Play," *New York Mirror,* Apr. 30, 1926; Walter Winchell, *New York City Graphic,* Apr. 28, 1926; unidentified clipping. All are from Mae West Clippings, BRTC.

41. The Motion Picture Production Code began to be enforced in 1934 when, in a successful attempt to stave off government censorship and quell calls to boycott movies, the Hollywood studios agreed that they would not exhibit films that had not earned a seal of approval from the Production Code Administration. The code remained in effect through the 1950s and was replaced by the ratings system in 1968.

42. West's indebtedness to camp humor is discussed in Curry, *Too Much of a Good Thing;* Hamilton, *"When I'm Bad I'm Better";* and Pamela Robertson, *Guilty Pleasures: Feminist Camp from Mae West to Madonna* (Durham, NC: Duke University Press, 1996), 23–54.

43. George Davis, "The Decline of the West," *Vanity Fair,* May 1934, 82.

44. Robertson, *Guilty Pleasures,* 31.

45. Mae West, *The Drag,* in *Three Plays by Mae West: Sex, The Drag, The Pleasure Man,* ed. Lillian Schlissel (New York: Routledge, 1997), 107.

46. Ibid., 101.

47. West, *Constant Sinner,* 5.

48. Mae West, *Sex,* in *Three Plays,* 68.

49. Linda Williams, "Melodrama Revised," in *Refiguring American Film Genres: Theory and History,* ed. Nick Browne (Berkeley: University of California Press, 1998), 42–88. See also Linda Williams, *Playing the Race Card: Melodramas of Black and White from Uncle Tom to O. J. Simpson* (Princeton, NJ: Princeton University Press, 2001); and Christine Gledhill, "Rethinking Genre," in *Reinventing Film Studies,* eds. Linda Williams and Christine Gledhill (London: Edward Arnold, 2000), 221–243.

50. The film's ending was changed at the insistence of the Hays office, which demanded that Stanwyck's character suffer some form of punishment for her sins. In the release print, Lily (Stanwyck) realizes that she loves her husband (George Brent) just in time to save him from suicide. She returns her riches to the bank, and she and her husband move from their fashionable Manhattan apartment into a modest home.

51. West, *Sex*, in *Three Plays*, 40.

52. Diamond Lil's name was changed to Lady Lou in the film in order to appease audiences who objected to the idea of West's scandalous play being adapted for the screen.

53. In the play, drag characters use the feminine pronoun to refer to one another, thus Dave and Clem are "she." West, *The Drag*, in *Three Plays*, 120–121.

CHAPTER 4

FANNY BRICE'S NEW NOSE:

BEAUTY, ETHNICITY, AND LIMINALITY

KRISTEN ANDERSON WAGNER

IN A 1923 NEWSPAPER ARTICLE, Fanny Brice explained that she was having plastic surgery to reshape her nose because "in noses as in life, one wearies of the too familiar. Charm lies in the unexpected. Besides, I am tired of having to fit my hats to the curve of my nose rather than the needs of my temperament."[1] In this and other articles she joked that "everything about me has stopped growing except my nose," and claimed that "I couldn't take a drink of water with any comfort. I couldn't keep my nose out of the glass."[2] She insisted she was having the surgery purely for aesthetic reasons, because she was "consumed with a passion for a straight nose," and not to advance her career: "I'll tell you—it's not for my work—my nose suits my work all right. They get along fine together. It's for my soul that I'm having this thing done."[3]

Newspaper writers reported on her stated reasons and then speculated about her "real" motivations for undergoing the procedure. Several articles noted that the surgery would bring her nose "back to normalcy," which would help in her quest to be taken seriously as a dramatic actress:

> It appears that the real reason for the reconstruction of the nose was not the desire to buy hats for the temperament, but to act in plays of a different type.
>
> Miss Brice, already successful in homely comedy for which the old nose was an asset, now wants to branch out. In the drama of the drawing room the nose might distract attention from the play. . . . Other artists would accept the limitation and go on doing comedy; Miss Brice boldly decides to abolish the inhibitory nose.[4]

Neither were the racial implications of Brice's surgery lost on the press. While several articles obliquely referred to her desire to change her nose "from Roman to Grecian," Brice claimed that Eddie Cantor, who was also Jewish, told her, "'Some people cut off their nose to spite their face; but you cut off your nose to spite your race.' As if he had any room to talk!"[5] One Jewish weekly paper commented approvingly on Brice's surgery, arguing that "many Jews have names and noses that they might like to have beautified. To which we have no particular objection. One can be a good Jew and a good American citizen by any name and by any nose."[6] Despite Brice's protestations to the contrary, the press understood that there was more to her plastic surgery than a simple desire to keep her nose dry when she took a drink. By joking about her reasons for the procedure, she shows a reluctance to share her true motives with the public, but the fact that she allowed the event to receive so much press in the first place points to her willingness to publicly reveal her insecurities about her appearance.[7]

On Fanny Brice's nose we can find the convergence of three interconnected strands that came to define her public and private lives, and about which she clearly felt a great deal of ambivalence: her position as a comedienne, her physical appearance, and her ethnicity. Although famous for comedy, she longed to be taken seriously as a dramatic actress and made repeated attempts to be recognized as more than just a comedian. While her decision to have plastic surgery points to an insecurity about her looks, she played up her supposed homeliness in her routines, putting herself on display as a sort of antispectacle, and frequently burlesqued the trappings of traditional femininity. And as the daughter of Jewish immigrants, her ethnicity would become a central part of her act as she assumed a Yiddish accent to deliver comic monologues and songs; yet throughout her career she sought to distance herself from her Jewishness in order to broaden her appeal. In each of these categories Brice occupies a liminal position, a marginal space from which she can use her status as insider/outsider to critique and disrupt social structures. Henry Jenkins describes the comic performer's "freedom that comes from straddling cultural categories,"[8] and Brice's liminality, her positioning within and between the categories of comic/dramatic, pretty/ homely, white/nonwhite, gave her the opportunity to both question and deflate their importance. In Brice's multilayered performances she could use her liminal position to make fun of what she was while simultaneously burlesquing what she wasn't, a strategy that made her performances both sympathetic and subversive.

The tension between "pretty" and "funny" informed much of Brice's comedy and career. Although these would seem to be unrelated traits, for women "pretty" and "funny" have long been considered mutually exclusive categories; as Linda Mizejewski argues, "In the historic binary of 'pretty' versus 'funny,' women comics, no matter what they look like, have been located in opposition to 'pretty.'"[9] While this binary can be limiting to comediennes, there is room for transgression in performances that ridicule traditional femininity, and Brice—like a great many other comediennes who occupy a liminal space outside of idealized conceptions of femininity—made idealized femininity itself the source of much of the humor in her act, playing characters who couldn't, or wouldn't, live up to societal expectations for how women should look, sound, and behave. In this way, Brice was using her insider/outsider status to challenge restrictive gender expectations for women. A similar dynamic was at work when Brice made her ethnicity a centerpiece of her comedy. In giving her comic characters a Yiddish accent, Brice was complicating her audiences' expectations about minorities and immigrants. While much of the comedy in Brice's performances was based on the seeming incongruity of a Jewish immigrant aspiring to the rarefied world of ballet dancers and opera singers, her characters were generally sympathetic figures rather than disparaging stereotypes. With ethnicity, as with comedy and femininity, Brice's comedy was rooted in liminality, as Brice could use her position as an American-born daughter of Jewish immigrants to critique and disrupt anti-Semitic cultural currents.

These contradictions in Brice's life and career are particularly evident in her performances with the Ziegfeld Follies, where her otherness—her ethnicity, her unconventional looks, and her humor—was emphasized by her positioning alongside the idealized, homogenized beauty of the Ziegfeld Girls. As Linda Mizejewski has noted, "Brice's comic genius was her embodiment of everything the Ziegfeld Girl was forbidden to be: spontaneous, loud, clumsy, ethnic, Jewish."[10] In burlesque, vaudeville, the Follies, and her films, Brice played characters who tried, but failed, to achieve the type of idealized femininity represented by Ziegfeld chorines such as Marilyn Miller, Ann Pennington, and Lillian Lorraine, a femininity characterized by beauty, self-control, and whiteness; by appearing alongside the Glorified American Girls of the *Follies*, the aberrant femininity of Brice's characters was highlighted. But although these performances brought her fame and universal acclaim, Brice herself was clearly uneasy with her status as the anti–Ziegfeld Girl.

"I WAS GOING TO BE A GREAT DRAMATIC ACTRESS"

Fanny Brice began her professional career in burlesque, and it was there that she developed what would become her signature performance style of comic songs sung in a Yiddish accent and accompanied by broad movements. *Variety* called her "an all over the stage comedienne" who added "to the humor of the lyrics with her arm and body movements," and the *New York Times* praised her "accent and stupendously shrill voice and . . . her broad grimaces and stiff-jointed bucking and plunging."[11] Brice excelled in manic physical comedy, using her long, thin limbs and her expressive face to illustrate the actions in songs such as "Sadie Salome, Go Home!" and "Becky Is Back in the Ballet." This emphasis on physical comedy further set her apart from the languid beauty of the Follies showgirls, who, clad in elegant gowns, slowly paraded down steep flights of stairs in a deliberate and somewhat unnatural gait known as the Ziegfeld Walk.[12] In fact, revues such as the Follies were structured so that comedy routines alternated with extravagant production numbers, heightening the disparity between the fast-paced comedy and the more static chorus and showgirl sequences.[13] While slapstick comediennes were not uncommon on stage and in motion pictures in the 1910s and 1920s, comedy, especially physical comedy, was still considered by many to be a specifically masculine mode of performance, unsuitable for women's delicate sensibilities. In 1927 *Moving Picture World* summed up widely held beliefs about women's supposed distaste for physical comedy, claiming that "slapstick comedy with man-made laughs, and broad masculine humor seldom please the woman patron. . . . The reason that Our Gang comedies are such a great success is because here is humor that is gentle and that the feminine heart can interpret and enjoy."[14] Yet women have long used humor to address what Nancy Walker and Zita Dresner describe as "a concern with the incongruities between the realities of women's lives and the sentimental or idealized images fostered by the culture."[15] Juxtaposed

4.1. Fanny Brice (ca. 1916).

with the sentimental and idealized Ziegfeld Girls, Brice's portrayal of "the slightly crossed eyes, the broad grin and the comic awkwardness of a gawky east side young lady"[16] can be seen simultaneously as a failure to live up to societal expectations of traditional femininity and a rejection of those expectations. Fanny Brice, Eva Tanguay, Fay Tincher, Mabel Normand, Marie Dressler, and numerous other early twentieth-century comediennes were rejecting the notion that women couldn't or shouldn't perform physical comedy, and through their work they became "highly visible examples of women defying expectations regarding ladylike behavior and proper femininity, contradicting notions of how women should behave, and proving that they were capable of succeeding in a 'masculine' genre."[17]

Yet, despite the subversive potential of her work, Brice wanted to be more than "just" a comedienne. Like many female comics in the early twentieth century, Brice was reluctant to be known solely for comedy and longed to be taken seriously as a dramatic actress:

> I want to do more pretentious things than I have done. I'm ambitious, like every actress. I know I can act, and I want to show the public what I can do. It's a more difficult matter, for the public doesn't want to accept me in any other role than a comic one. If I can give a matinee performance of A Doll's House, I'll convince the most skeptical.[18]

By the late 1910s Brice was intent on showcasing her dramatic abilities but had some difficulty finding the right vehicle. She starred in a play titled Why Worry? in 1918 that was conceived as a drama but had evolved into a comedy by opening night, giving her very little opportunity to act outside her comic wheelhouse. In 1926 she had another chance to emote, this time in a play for the legendary Broadway producer and director David Belasco. Like Why Worry?, the Belasco play, titled Fanny, ultimately was more comedy than drama, with serious scenes coexisting uneasily alongside broad comedy. J. Brooks Atkinson of the New York Times noted that "Fanny contrives now and then to manage an emotional scene or two to humor Fannie's whim," and added that "perhaps Miss Brice believes that in such moments her art rises to nobler, exalted inner shrines of the theatrical heaven. In fact, perhaps it does." But, Atkinson declared, the best moments occurred when Brice "puts the play out of her mind completely" and embraces the comic persona that audiences had come to love.[19] As another critic put it, "Only her 'broad grins, Jewish mannerisms, and slangy speech' kept the audience from 'running out into the street.'"[20]

Her most successful attempt to prove her dramatic abilities came when Florenz Ziegfeld asked her to sing an adaptation of a melodramatic French torch song in the Follies of 1921. "My Man," which would become her signature song, was unlike anything in her repertoire. Ostensibly a piece about a Parisian street girl lamenting her lover's mistreatment, it was understood by audiences as a reflection of Brice's own troubled relationship with her husband, Jules "Nicky" Arnstein. Brice performed the number wearing a dirty, torn dress, and while her other songs called for broad gestures and mugging, she stood perfectly still when she sang "My Man," leaning against a flickering lamppost with her eyes closed. The performance was irresistible to critics and audiences alike, with the opening night applause so wild that Brice claimed, "It wasn't a theater I was standing in, it

4.2. Fanny Brice performing "My Man" in *The Great Ziegfeld* (1936).

was pandemonium. I can feel my body shake now with the thunder of it."[21] Interestingly, some audiences apparently were unsure of how to read Brice's performance, as a reviewer in Boston noted:

> When she swung into "My Man," the impression she had left with her previous burlesques remained to such an extent that there were several snickers. It didn't seem possible she was going to be serious. But she was, and for a passing heart throb there are few things better than that "My Man" number.[22]

Despite this temporary confusion, Brice had clearly found an effective dramatic vehicle. At least one writer felt that "a Belasco could visualize Miss Brice elaborating the character portrayed in 'My Man' into a serious play that might give the American stage a female Warfield," and Brice herself told a reporter about a "gorgeous idea" she had for a play based on a similar type of tragic woman,

> which will render row upon row of handkerchiefs in the audience absolutely unfit for further use. . . . I shall have the curtain rise on a courtroom. A voice off stage will be heard saying, "I pronounce this

woman guilty. Woman, have you anything to say?" And there I'll be, the condemned woman in the prisoner's box. The scene itself will be the story of why the woman killed the man she loved.[23]

Brice's attempts to parlay her "My Man" success into dramatic stardom were largely unsuccessful, but she continued to mix pathos and comedy in her subsequent stage and film work. This was especially true in her first two films, the part-talking Vitagraph feature *My Man* (1928) and *Be Yourself* (1930). In both of these films she plays a long-suffering woman in love with a man who treats her poorly. Both films are liberally sprinkled with comedy songs ("I'm an Indian" and "I Was a Floradora Baby" in *My Man* and "It's Gorgeous to Be Graceful" and "Is There Something the Matter With Otto Kahn?" in *Be Yourself*) and dramatic numbers ("My Man" and "If You Want the Rainbow, You Must Have the Rain" in *My Man* and "When a Woman Loves a Man" in *Be Yourself*), giving her ample opportunities to perform a wide range of emotions. Interestingly, the advertisements for *My Man* play up the pathos, claiming that the movie is "a tense drama full of tragedy and comedy," and that audiences will be "Lifted to soul-stirring emotional climaxes" as they witness "the marvelous art of Fannie Brice—her subtle humor—her sympathy— her deep understanding of Life, its loves, hopes, tragedies, triumphs." Audiences, however, may have seen something completely different, as Delight Evans, reviewing the film for *Screenland*, described *My Man* as "gay, infectious, lowbrow entertainment—a grand, rowdy, combination movie-musical comedy-vaudeville show."[24] The studio must have thought the pathos angle would be more marketable to audiences across the country, and yet the inclusion of broad comedy numbers such as "I'm an Indian" and "Mrs. Cohen at the Beach" indicate that Evans's review is an accurate description of at least parts of the film.[25] Brice appeared in only a handful of films, none of which attempted to blend comedy and pathos to the same degree as these first two starring vehicles. And while audiences insisted that she include "My Man" and other melodramatic songs in her stage routines for the rest of her career, they were most eager to see her play comedy. As Florenz Ziegfeld bluntly told her, "They'll never take you home because of your tears, but because of your laughter."[26]

Brice was like a great many other comediennes in her ambivalence toward comedy. Fan magazines commonly played up the idea of the "'tragic comedienne'—the performer who longs to trade the indigni-

ties of comedy for the refinement of drama."[27] Louise Fazenda, Polly
Moran, and Charlotte Greenwood were among the actresses who, like
Brice, were said to have landed in comedy only after failing to find
success in dramatic roles. Fazenda, for example, described the "terrible irony of fate if you began with the aspirations of a Bernhardt
and ended as a clown,"[28] and Greenwood told how she "wanted to be
a great dramatic star or prima donna, but all that time I was fighting against nature. It took me all that time to realize that I wasn't
built to shine as Ophelia or the Merry Widow."[29] Similarly, Brice referred to "the field of comedy that was forced on me by 'Sadie Salome's' success" and claimed that her career "started like a catastro-
phe. I was going to be a great dramatic actress."[30] Certainly, drama
was considered by many to be more respectable than comedy, especially physical comedy, and it's easy to see why this would be appealing to Brice. Her status as both insider and outsider—as a Follies star
but not a Ziegfeld Girl, as a daughter of Jewish immigrants who is almost, but not quite, white—left her in an uncertain, liminal position,
and mainstream success in a respectable genre would have "meant
acceptance by the dominant culture she so much wanted to be a part
of."[31] But while she never completely abandoned her dramatic ambition, Brice did acknowledge the importance of comedy to her career,
saying in 1925, "I'm always going to act and what's more, I'm always
going to be a comedienne. I know my business too well to give up the
one thing in the world that brought me success—comedy."[32]

Although Brice insisted that her nose job was unrelated to her dramatic aspirations, newspapers speculated—no doubt rightly so—that
a major motivation for the surgery was her desire to be taken seriously as an actress. Her looks were intrinsically linked to her comedy; her biographer, Barbara Grossman, notes that "audiences found
her funny as soon as she appeared on stage. Before she even opened
her mouth, she convulsed them because she looked so comical. She
was a sight gag and she knew it,"[33] and while Brice was certainly not
an unattractive woman, she used her body to full comic effect, performing physical routines that drew attention to her thin, awkward,
angular frame and employing facial expressions that made use of her
large mouth and nose. In fact, female comics have long built their
acts around the ways that they deviate from conventional standards
of beauty by creating comedy out of the supposed flaws in their appearance. Sophie Tucker, for example, poked fun at her weight in a
song titled "Nobody Loves a Fat Girl"; Charlotte Greenwood would

nonchalantly kick her long and exceptionally limber legs up to her own, or her partners', shoulders; and Marie Dressler, who was described in the press as "homely," "elephantine," and "as plain as an old size-eight shoe," would throw her large frame around the stage in violent pratfalls and stunts that made a joke out of her excessive size.[34] Similarly, in the *Follies of 1910*, Brice performed in "a white satin gown that fitted like a silk stocking," making her already thin frame appear even skinnier. Brice then used a comic bit to draw even more attention to her appearance:

> I was painfully thin and my dress fitted like a vise. The last roar that met my ears came when I pulled my skirt up over my knees and then, peering down on legs that looked like two slats, put my hand over my eyes in one despairing gesture and stalked off.[35]

By creating comedy out of her appearance, Fanny Brice was drawing on a well-established tradition of female comics who "derived their comedy from their failure to meet traditional standards of feminine beauty," a strategy that many comediennes continue to use today.[36]

"I WAS FUNNY, BUT NOT GOOD LOOKING"

While burlesque was known for its broad definition of beauty, "its 'beef trust' chorines with legs like 'stuffed black clubs,'"[37] the Follies and other Broadway revues featured a more homogenized version of beauty, and Flo Ziegfeld was known for promoting a very narrow definition of acceptable femininity that few women could attain: "Five per cent of all American women are beautiful. Five of every hundred conform to the established canons of perfection in loveliness. Fifty per cent are pretty, pleasing or personable. . . . Over the remaining forty-five per cent we will draw the veil of kindly silence. I want to live long."[38] Brice, as one of the 95 percent of women who, presumably, weren't beautiful, would have fit in with the wide range of body types and femininities on display in burlesque, but she certainly would have suffered by comparison to the women with whom she shared the stage in the Follies, women who were hired because they fit Ziegfeld's very narrow beauty standards.

This same dynamic would follow Brice to Hollywood, where she made several unsuccessful efforts to launch a film career. Poor screen tests prevented her from signing with the William Fox Picture Company in 1915, a fact that is unsurprising given that she wasn't pretty enough for leading-lady parts in motion pictures, and her considerable vocal talents would have been lost in the silent cinema. Had she been willing to appear in the kind of knockabout comedies made by Keystone or Hal Roach, she might have followed in the footsteps of Polly Moran, Alice Howell, Gale Henry, and other stage comics who transitioned to film. It's unknown why she chose not to, but the kind of rough, lowbrow physical comedy expected of slapstick film comics was certainly less glamorous, more physically demanding, and likely lower paying than her stage work. With the advent of talking pictures in the late 1920s, however, Warner Bros. was interested in repeating the success of Al Jolson's *The Jazz Singer* (1927), and Brice was placed under contract. By this time Brice had already had plastic surgery to reshape her nose, and she also had her teeth capped after being dissatisfied with how they looked in a screen test, but despite these efforts to make herself more conventionally attractive, she faced the same problem as in the Follies—she was simply not as beautiful as the other leading ladies in Hollywood. Her looks, as well as her undeniable ethnicity, undoubtedly contributed to the fact that her films were not terribly successful and her screen career never really took off.

It's not surprising that Brice may have felt that she needed to be more conventionally attractive in order to be taken seriously as a dramatic actress. Then, as now, beauty and humor were thought to be mutually exclusive qualities. Closely related to the notion that comedy was incompatible with femininity was the idea that women could be either pretty or funny, but seldom both. As a result, women performers who were considered unattractive were frequently pigeonholed in comedy and had fewer options than pretty actresses to work in other genres. The Follies were structured around this pretty-versus-funny binary. Ziegfeld built his shows around "girls and laughter," and it was clear where Brice fell in that equation; as she once told a reporter, "Ziegfeld thought I was funny, but positively not good-looking."[39] Although *Funny Girl*, the 1964 musical loosely based on Brice's life, implies that Brice was hired to appear in the chorus as a Ziegfeld Girl and only turned to comedy when she realized she wasn't as pretty as the other girls, she was in fact hired specifically as a comedienne, something that the Follies' publicity and structure made very clear.[40] This pretty/funny dichotomy was likely behind Ziegfeld's reported displeasure with Brice's plastic surgery. Newspapers reported that the operation could cause her to lose her job with the Follies, and Brice recounted Ziegfeld's vexed reaction to her new look:

> "What did you do that for?" he demanded.
> "Well, I thought it might make me a little better looking," I explained.
> "'Better looking,'" he thundered; "I can get all the good-looking girls for $60 a week. I'm paying you $2,000 and part of it was for that nose. And now you've lopped off a yard or two of it!"[41]

Because so much of Brice's comedy was derived from her appearance, Ziegfeld was clearly worried that any changes to her appearance could hurt the effectiveness of her act, especially when those changes were tipping the scales toward pretty—and therefore away from funny. And, in fact, there was some agreement that Brice was somewhat less funny after her nose job, although it was probably only partly due to the fact that she no longer looked as funny as she once had. It's likely that her longing to play dramatic roles was much more of a factor, possibly causing her to be more restrained and less manic onstage. As Ziegfeld put it, "I want Fanny to make 'em laugh—that's what I pay her for. But you can see for yourself that she doesn't do it. She's become serious and that's fatal for a funny woman."[42]

Brice must have hoped, on some level, that her surgery would help her to shift her identity from homely comedienne to beautiful tragedienne. At the same time, she regularly parodied beauty, art, and other trappings of idealized femininity in her performances. According to Mizejewski, the pretty/funny dichotomy allowed comediennes "to engage in a transgressive comedy grounded in the female body—its looks, its race and sexuality, and its relationships to ideal versions of femininity. In this strand of comedy, 'pretty' is the topic and target, the ideal that is exposed as funny."[43] This was certainly true for Brice, whose characters aspired to be refined, beautiful, and serious, but failed absolutely. And yet, in her characters' failure was her own performative success.[44] Although she was closely identified with her characters, she managed to maintain a distance from them, through "sly winks," "knowing glances," and "conspiratorial grimaces."[45] This performance strategy allowed her to align herself with the audience, so that she could comment on her characters at the same time she was playing them. As Barbara Grossman argues, this technique "signaled that she shared the audience's awareness of the character's silliness because she was separate from that character. . . . She parodied her subject by calling attention to the disparity between the character's perception of herself and the way others viewed her."[46]

Brice's characters often aspired to be or perceived themselves as graceful, refined, and attractive. In the song "Sadie Salome, Go Home!," which she first performed in 1909, her character was a Jewish girl who wanted to be "an actress lady on the stage" but ended up as a Salome dancer, in a parody of a risqué dancing craze that had swept the nation since the New York premiere (and closure after one performance) of Richard Strauss's controversial opera *Salome* in 1907. The most scandalous part of the play, the sensual and exotic Dance of the Seven Veils, was imitated and parodied endlessly, and although the fad was starting to fade by the time Brice performed "Sadie Salome," she could still use the dance to parody both the Salome craze and silly girls who saw themselves as the glamorous and daring dancer. "Sadie Salome" was the first song Brice sang using a Yiddish accent, adding an ethnic dimension to the disjuncture between lowbrow Sadie and her highbrow aspirations. In her performance of the song, she wriggled and jumped around—she would later claim that she did this the first time because her costume was riding up "you know where" and she was "trying to squirm it away"[47]—and her awkward movements further served to lampoon the graceful and sensual dance. Besides "Sadie Salome," she parodied numerous other dances and dancers throughout her career. In "Becky Is Back in the Ballet," which she first performed in 1915, she wore "a short ballerini [*sic*] skirt and pink fleshings and essay[ed] some toe pirouettes with disastrous results."[48] Included in the performance was a burlesque of prima ballerina Anna Pavlova in "The Dying Swan"; as in her Salome number, Brice's Dying Swan was clumsy and awkward, a far cry from the lithe and ethereal Pavlova. The contrast between Becky and Pavlova was certainly highlighted when Brice performed the number in the Follies, with the Ziegfeld Girls standing in for Pavlova's idealized grace. A similar dynamic had the potential to occur when she performed the song in vaudeville, as one reviewer noted that Brice "is following Ruth St. Denis at the Palace, making this number more pronounced as a burlesque."[49] Brice used "Becky," as well as later ballet numbers, to "[poke] fun at Pavlova, graceless girls like Becky, and the pretentiousness of classical dance,"[50] and, additionally, to poke fun at the idea of women as refined and graceful. She played other characters who similarly tried, but failed, to emulate idealized femininity, including classical singers ("Is There Something the Matter With Otto Kahn?" and "When Priscilla Hits High C"), chorus girls ("I Was a Floradora Baby"), Theda Bara–style vamps ("I'm Bad" and "I'm a Vamp from East Broadway"), modern dancers ("Modernistic Moe"), brides ("I Don't Know Whether to Do It or Not"), and even burlesque strippers ("Countess Dubinsky"). In "Sascha, the Passion of the Pasha," she plays a nice Jewish girl who is kidnapped and forced to join a harem, but soon becomes the sultan's favorite wife. The sexual references in the song are far from subtle:

Oh, how he appreciates
A little kosher meat
And speakin' about the art of sheikin'
The sultan's wife is a wonderful life
Provided you don't weaken

Sascha's apparent delight in sharing her "kosher meat" with her sultan puts her at odds with societal expectations for feminine modesty, especially concerning sex, and Brice played up the innuendo with knowing looks to the audience, playful eye rolls and a sly grin.[51] "I Don't Know Whether to Do It or Not" (also known as "The Yiddish Bride") finds Brice as a bride on the morning of her wedding, wracked with indecision about whether or not to go through with the ceremony:

And I don't know whether to do it or not
I'm thinkin' it out with all the brains I got
Should I be a wife or lead the single life
One's a curse, the other's worse
How can a woman make a choice?
I promised him I'd marry him today
But why? Why should I throw myself away?
I'll be sorry if I do it, but what'll I do?
If I don't do it, then I'll be sorry, too.
Should I go, go. Yes, no, I don't know.
Don't know whether to do it or not.

Just as Sascha fails to be demure and innocent in her frank enjoyment of sex, the bride fails to be the submissive blushing bride. Instead, she questions why she should "throw myself away" on marriage, which is

4.3. Fanny Brice
as "The Yiddish
Bride" (ca. 1916).
Photograph courtesy
of the New York
Public Library.

a "curse." Unlike "Oh! How I Hate That Fellow Nathan!"—in which
Brice played a woman with a long list of reasons to hate her erstwhile
fiancé ("He used to say that he would lay down and die for me, but
he wouldn't stand up and work for me")—"I Don't Know Whether
to Do It or Not" gives no reason for the bride's reluctance other than
her own trepidations about married life and her desire to stay single.
Even "Second-Hand Rose" ("I'm wearing second-hand shoes/Second-
hand hose/All the girls hand me their second-hand beaus") is about a
woman who fails at the feminine tasks of shopping and consumption
and instead gets all of her possessions (and men) second hand. The
subversive nature of these performances lies in the fact that Brice
emphasized her characters' awkwardness, their obvious inability to
live up to impossible standards of idealized femininity that require
women to be refined, beautiful, elegant, sexy (but not too sexy), and
graceful. By emphasizing this, she called attention to the fact that the
slinky sex symbol, the graceful dancer, and the rest were constructed
categories of femininity that didn't include all women.

In her performance style Brice created distance between herself and the characters she played, but her personal and professional lives sometimes became entangled, positioning Brice as a woman who, like the characters she played, fell short of idealized feminine standards. For example, she talked about pawning her jewelry early in her career in order to buy costumes for her stage show and about giving her street clothes to other girls in the chorus in exchange for dancing lessons, giving up items that women were supposed to covet in order to pursue a career, something that women weren't supposed to desire.[52] Roberta Mock has argued that "audiences demanded this intertextual slippage between the personal and the public, and Brice's broad comedy and social commentary was not sufficient to provide it."[53] What gave audiences the intertextual slippage they desired was hearing about Brice's rocky marriage to her second husband, Jules "Nicky" Arnstein.[54] The press reported constantly on details of their marriage, from the alienation of affection suit brought against Brice by Arnstein's previous wife to the numerous times she was forced to pawn her jewelry to pay for his legal expenses.[55] Brice was clearly figured as the long-suffering victim in these stories, the faithful wife who stood by her husband, visiting him in prison and sending him "daily endearing telegrams and letters" while raising their two young children and finding the courage to perform night after night.[56] While she sometimes played the victim for comedy (as in the song "Oh! How I Hate That Fellow Nathan!"), she shrewdly used the publicity surrounding her marriage to Arnstein as the basis for her performance of the song "My Man." Brice claimed that Ziegfeld had no particular motive for giving her the song: "To be honest, no one thought of connecting this song of the forlorn apache girl with my personal life. It was a fine number, sung all over Paris. Ziegfeld and I never dreamed what it would do to an audience at just this time."[57]

And yet it was immediately clear that the song was meant to capitalize on her troubled marriage. As Norman Katkov says, Channing Pollock, who wrote the English translation of the song "might have taken [the lyrics] from the newspaper accounts of Fanny's courtship of Nick. Which he could have written only for Fanny. Which detailed, with keyhole clarity, what went on behind the closed doors of her life.[58] Arnstein's frequent troubles were heavily reported in the press and were therefore very familiar to audiences, who would undoubtedly link Brice's problems to the song's lyrics:

Oh, my man, I love him so, he'll never know
All my life is just despair, but I don't care
When he takes me in his arms
The world is right, all right!
What's the difference if I say I'll go away,
When I know I'll come back on my knees someday?
For whatever my man is, I am his forever more!

Brice sang a number of other songs that exploited her personal life in a similar way, including "I'd Rather Be Blue over You (Than Be Happy with Somebody Else)," "When a Woman Loves a Man," and "Weren't We Fools?" The Fanny of the failed marriages and troubled life became just as much a character as Sadie, Becky, and Sascha, and, like those other characters, Brice played up her failure to perform idealized femininity—in this case, her inability to maintain a healthy relationship with a man. Also, Brice came to see Tragic Fanny, like her other characters, as ripe for parody. In the *Follies of 1936* she sang "He Hasn't a Thing Except Me"; the scene resembles "My Man" at the beginning, right down to the lamppost against which Brice is leaning. However, the lamppost walks offstage before she begins to sing, and the lyrics are a comic laundry list of the lover's shortcomings: "The one thing he's mastered/is just getting plastered"; "His talk isn't flow'ry/it's straight from the Bowery." At one point Brice speaks directly to the audience:

> Well, you get the idea. You know I've been singing about this bum for twenty-five years. Sometimes he's called "Oh, my Gawd, I love him so" or "He's just my Bill" or "You made me what I am today," but he's always the same low-life and he's always doing me dirt and I just keep on loving him. Can you imagine if I really ever met a guy like that what I would do to him? Why I'd—it's no use talkin'—that's my type.[59]

Despite her longing to play drama, and despite the successes she had with "My Man" and other poignant songs that clearly took advantage of audiences' interest in and knowledge of her personal struggles, Brice still understood that she was, first and foremost, a comedienne, and as such, she had to be willing to poke fun at what was pretentious and overblown, even if that meant poking fun at herself and her own act.

"DISTINCT HEBREW CLOWNING"

A significant way that Brice burlesqued pretension and idealized femininity was through the use of dialect comedy. Although Brice was the daughter of Jewish immigrants, she didn't speak Yiddish, and in fact her first use of ethnic humor was in the form of "coon" singing. Coon songs, which were generally comic songs or sentimental ballads about life in the Old South, were a holdover from nineteenth-century minstrel shows. Although their popularity was in decline in the early 1900s, "by the 1890s . . . coon shouting was chiefly considered a Jewish composer's and Jewish women's performance venue—with [Sophie] Tucker and Fanny Brice being the last and most famous."[60] While blackface was not a requirement for coon shouting (in fact, Brice likely only appeared in blackface once in her career), an exaggerated and stereotyped African American dialect was an essential part of the performance, and Brice made use of this accent when she sang these songs.[61] She began using a Yiddish accent in her act with "Sadie Salome, Go Home!" in 1909; when she went to Irving Berlin for some new material for an upcoming benefit performance, he played his "Sadie Salome" for her, singing it with a Yiddish accent. She emulated Berlin with resounding success, and, like her broad physical comedy and her unconventional looks, the Yiddish accent quickly became a characteristic of Brice's performances. And like her comedy and looks, her ethnicity set her apart from the glorified femininity of the Ziegfeld Girls, who were very specifically white; as Mizejewski notes, "Femininity itself is racialized, and its idealized versions are white, a crucial element in the pretty/funny dynamic of women's comedy."[62] Not only was there a division between beautiful and funny in the Follies, there was also a division between white and nonwhite, with the white-appearing Ziegfeld Girls (regardless of their actual race or ethnicity) serving as a contrast to Jewish performers such as Brice, Nora Bayes, Eddie Cantor, and Sophie Tucker, and African American comedian Bert Williams, who was "compelled to perform in the 'straitjacket' of blackface and racial dialect."[63] This racial division contributed to the insider/outsider dynamic for Jewish and African American performers in the Follies, who were simultaneously a part of the show and set apart from the show's main attraction. Brice's Yiddish dialect, then, was another example of her creating comedy out of her characters' inability to live up to idealized feminine standards; just as her characters were too funny and too funny-looking to compete with the Follies chorines, they were also too Jewish. So while Brice's reliance on ethnic comedy may have been limiting in some ways, it also gave her the freedom to address issues such as femininity, beauty, and class from the liminal position of outsider, allowing her to both participate in and parody traditional femininity.

The rise in racist and prejudicial attitudes in the United States in the 1920s, evident in a resurgence of the Ku Klux Klan, the passage of restrictive federal immigration laws, and "a cultural climate permeated by 'scientific' racism and eugenic thought"[64] would have given minority performers such as Brice some impetus to appear less ethnic offstage and to create a clear distinction between actor and character. It's highly likely that this was a motive for her plastic surgery, as she reshaped the end of her nose to make it less obviously Semitic, or, as the press put it, she had her "hooked" nose "made over into what the plastic surgeons term a 'normal' nose."[65] Fifteen years before her surgery she had changed her last name from Borach to the less-ethnic-sounding Brice, and although she claimed that it was because she was tired of people calling her "Borax" or "Borache," as with her nose job she was almost certainly trying to appear less Jewish in order to appeal to a wider audience. As it turned out, a year after her first appearance as Fanny Brice in 1908, she began incorporating Yiddish dialect and humor into her act and so would come to be known for her ethnicity despite the new name, although, as Grossman points out, she continued to hope for acceptance from non-Jewish audiences.[66] She may have also hoped that erasing her ethnicity from her name and face would be beneficial in her attempts to be taken seriously as a dramatic actress. Indeed, in her act she used her Yiddish accent strictly for comedy numbers, dropping it for dramatic pieces such as "My Man" or sometimes singing one verse straight and then following up with a comic second verse with the accent. Brice was creating humor out of the contrast inherent in a vamp or ballerina speaking in a thick Yiddish accent, which "raised expectations about the type of behavior to be presented and then made the character's actual behavior seem wonderfully incongruous."[67] When she dropped the accent, it seemed more like authenticity and less like she was playing a character, and so audiences likely felt that they were getting a glimpse of the real Fanny Brice when she sang the pathos-filled numbers that were supposedly based on her personal life. The same motivation to appear less Jewish was certainly behind her attempts to distance herself from Jewishness offstage, as when she insisted that she used a Yiddish accent in her act but "didn't even understand Jewish, couldn't talk a word of it."[68] In statements like this she was emphasizing the difference between Fanny Brice, the performer, and the characters she played. And while Brice never denied being Jewish, she wanted to make sure that her audiences understood that she was, first and foremost, American.

The issue of ethnicity became even more vital when she embarked on her film career, since comedy that went over in multicultural cities such as New York and Chicago was a tougher sell in less diverse rural areas. Henry Jenkins talks about the "de-semitization" of Jewish comedian Eddie Cantor when he went to Hollywood as "one aspect of a complex process by which stage stars were repackaged in order to appeal to a broader national audience."[69] For Brice, this process meant limiting her Yiddish accent to her comic songs and only using it in dialogue sequences for the sake of a joke. In the film *My Man*, Brice played Fannie Brand, who works in a costume shop while raising her two siblings, including the very blonde, very gentile Edna (played by Edna Murphy). Fannie is not specifically Jewish in the film, although her employment in the garment industry, as well as her use of the Yiddish accent in some of her songs and in her "Mrs. Cohen at the Beach" monologue, creates the opportunity for her character to be read as Jewish, just as Eddie Cantor's "screen persona could be at once Jewish and non-Jewish depending upon the desired audience."[70] A similar multiple reading can be found in *Be Yourself*, in which "Fannie Field" only uses her Yiddish dialect in her comic songs and in her dialogue with her obviously Jewish brother, Harry (Harry Green), who, unlike his sister, speaks with a heavy accent. Like *My Man*, *Be Yourself* offers opportunities for Jewish audiences to interpret her character as Jewish, while non-Jewish audiences can easily find different meanings in her performance. *Everybody Sing* (1938) sidesteps the Jewish issue entirely by making Brice's character, Olga Chekaloff, Russian. While Olga could be read as a Russian Jew, unlike Brice's earlier films there is nothing specifically Jewish about Olga's character. It's not surprising that Brice was refigured as Russian rather than Jewish at this point; by 1938 her film career was foundering badly, and a large part of the blame was placed on the notion that her ethnic comedy was not relatable to audiences across the country. *Variety* wondered in 1928 "if certain localities are apt to chill on the star's distinct Hebrew clowning,"[71] and it appears that, despite efforts to downplay her ethnicity, Brice ultimately proved too Jewish for film audiences.

A scene from *Be Yourself* provides an excellent opportunity to examine the interplay between comedy, femininity, and ethnicity in Brice's work. The film features Brice as Fannie Field, a nightclub singer who manages a boxer named Jerry (Robert Armstrong). As Fannie falls in love with Jerry, she faces competition from Lillian (Gertrude Astor), a beautiful gold digger. Lillian makes her move on Jerry at Fannie's nightclub, joining him at his front-row table, clinging to his arm, and convincing him that he'd look "swell" if he had his battered nose "fixed." Her maneuvers are cut short when Fannie appears onstage dressed as a ballerina in a white tutu with fur-trimmed bodice and a sleek feathered headpiece and sings "It's Gorgeous to Be Graceful." This number, like her earlier song "Becky Is Back in the Ballet," parodies the grace and beauty of classical ballet, with Brice skipping awkwardly around the stage, arms and legs akimbo, her bobbing head and turned-out toes more reminiscent of a pigeon than a swan. The lyrics ("Oh, it's gorgeous to be graceful/To flit and float and fly!") serve to heighten the contrast between Fannie's gawky choreography and her character's perception of herself as lithe and graceful:

> I want to be a dancer, my spirit's fancy free,
> And trip the light fantastic gracefully.
> I long to be so slender and so slim,
> To show my limb to him and him and him.
> My dress is a cocoon
> If I don't breathe I'll swoon
> Oh, I can't get the darn thing off too soon!

As in so many of her other songs, in this number Brice plays a woman who tries, but fails, to live up to impossibly idealized standards of beauty and femininity while also exposing the artifice behind those standards. Although Fannie's ballerina longs to be beautiful and desirable, displaying her long legs for the men in the audience, she concedes that the bodice that makes her "so slender and so slim" is also uncomfortably tight, making it impossible for her to breathe. Here the bodily ideal of the slender ballerina clashes with the bodily reality of a living, breathing woman, and as Fannie pulls at her dress, crying, "I'll take it off! No, I wouldn't! Yes, I will!," she is voicing the thoughts of every woman who's suffered for the sake of beauty in

4.4. Fanny Brice performing "It's Gorgeous to Be Graceful" in *Be Yourself* (1930).

a constricting dress or shoes that pinch and bind. The number concludes with a dance solo to Camille Saint-Saëns's "Le Cygne," in a direct reference to *The Dying Swan* ballet. Brice emulates the fluttering arm movements and mincing steps of Anna Pavlova and other prima ballerinas, and although Brice's expressive hands are quite graceful, her bent knees, slouching posture with hips thrust forward, and over-the-top expressions effectively burlesque the conventions of classical ballet. As Fannie dances a man appears with a bow and arrow and shoots her in the back, and instead of crumbling delicately to the ground like Pavlova, Brice grimaces broadly and clutches her chest, then convulses melodramatically and limps offstage. As Fannie clowns, Lillian looks idly around the room, unable to contain her boredom. Lillian is played by Gertrude Astor, a tall, blonde beauty who could easily have been a Ziegfeld chorine, and her humorlessness, her beauty, and her whiteness, serve to distance her from Fannie and position her closer to the idealized femininity that Brice parodies in this song.

Like her other comic numbers, Brice performs "It's Gorgeous to Be Graceful" with a Yiddish accent, drawing humor from the disjuncture between the audience's assumptions about working-class immigrants and the upper-class refinement of ballet. The song also includes a direct reference to Brice's nose job, as she taps her nose and slyly glances at the audience while singing, "In public I'm Venetian/ But Grecian on the sly," recalling press descriptions of her surgery as changing her nose "from Roman to Grecian." Immediately after Fannie's performance, Jerry visits her in her dressing room and, catching a glimpse of himself in the mirror, wonders how much it would cost to fix his nose. The camera cuts to a close-up of Fannie, as she matter-of-factly tells him, "I imagine it'll cost plenty," in what could be read as a reference to the problems she faced after her own surgery. *Be Yourself* was released seven years after Brice's surgery, but it's likely that many audience members would have understood these references, given the amount of publicity her nose job had received and the fact that it was frequently referred to in articles about her. Just as her humor, her appearance, and her ethnicity had become the defining characteristics of her performance style, her plastic surgery, which so perfectly encapsulated these themes, had become a defining event for her.

CONCLUSION

Fanny Brice's ambivalence about her comedy, her looks, and her ethnicity was resolved to some extent when she moved from stage to radio, where from the mid-1930s until her death in 1951 she played a precocious, troublemaking four-year-old named Baby Snooks in a weekly radio program. Brice had occasionally played a child character, sometimes called Babykins, for her stage act beginning in the 1910s, but "none of these characters was as fully realized as Baby Snooks. The terrible toddler emerged on radio and was the first character Brice developed specifically for that medium."[72] When she played Snooks onstage, as in the *Follies of 1934* and the *Follies of 1936*, she was funny at first sight, sporting an enormous bow on her head; a short, starched baby-doll dress; and ankle socks with patent leather Mary Janes, and she used her expressive face and body to mug at the audience and cavort around the stage. On the radio, however, she had to rely on her voice alone. Brice delivered Snooks's lines with a childish lisp, giggling impishly or asking her increasingly flustered father (played on the radio show by Hanley Stafford) "Whyyy, Daddy?" and crying hysterically when she didn't get her way.

4.5. Fanny Brice
as Baby Snooks,
with Judy Garland,
in *Everybody Sing*
(1938).

The specific demands of radio meant that she would no longer be called on to perform physical comedy and that her looks wouldn't be an issue. And because Snooks didn't have an accent, Brice was able to leave Jewish comedy behind her. At the same time, she was never able to capture the transgressiveness of her stage act on the radio, as she had to soften her act for mass consumption; in playing a child she could no longer parody femininity, class, and beauty in the same biting way. Especially in her appearances with the Ziegfeld Follies—where her manic, gawky, ethnic presence was a stark counterpoint to the Glorified American Girls—she was able to expose and burlesque impossible cultural expectations for women. Although Brice continually tried to distance herself from the attributes that came to define her comic persona, throughout her long career she was able to confront the many cultural limitations facing female comics, and her subtly subversive performances helped to challenge popular conceptions of idealized femininity.

NOTES

1. "Plastic Surgery for the Stage," *New York Times*, Aug. 16, 1923, 14.

2. "Fannie Brice's Nose to Be Scaled Down," *New York Times*, Aug. 15, 1923, 10; "Serio-Comic Adventures of Fannie's Nice New Nose," *Springfield (MO) Republican*, Nov. 25, 1923, 26.

3. "Designs for Fannie Brice's New Nose Not Completed," *(Harrisburg, PA) Evening News*, Aug. 15, 1923, 13.

4. "Fanny Brice under Knife," *New York Times*, Aug. 16, 1923, 2; "Plastic Surgery for the Stage," 14.

5. "Fannie Brice Wants New Nose," *Mount Carmel (PA) Item*, Aug. 18, 1923, 2; "Serio-Comic Adventures." The line about cutting off her nose to spite her race is typically attributed to Dorothy Parker; it's possible that Cantor was repeating a line that was already well known, or that Brice was giving credit for the clever quip to her friend.

6. "Aristocratic Names and Beautiful Noses," *Wisconsin Jewish Chronicle*, Aug. 17, 1923, 4.

7. Barbara Grossman points out that Brice originally planned to have her surgery in early August 1923 but postponed the procedure because the intense press coverage of the sudden death of President Harding on August 2 would have left little room for coverage of Brice's new nose. This change in dates indicates a desire to maximize publicity and, according to Grossman, "suggests a certain desperation on Brice's part, a desire to take control of her life and work with one decisive act." See Barbara Grossman, *Funny Woman: The Life and Times of Fanny Brice* (Bloomington: Indiana University Press, 1991), 133.

8. Henry Jenkins, *What Made Pistachio Nuts? Early Sound Comedy and the Vaudeville Aesthetic* (New York: Columbia University Press, 1992), 225.

9. Linda Mizejewski, *Pretty/Funny: Women Comedians and Body Politics* (Austin: University of Texas Press, 2014), 5.

10. Linda Mizejewski, *Ziegfeld Girl: Image and Icon in Culture and Cinema* (Durham, NC: Duke University Press, 1999), 6.

11. Sime, "Winter Garden," *Variety*, Jan. 31, 1913, 22; Sime, "Ziegfeld 'Follies,'" *Variety*, June 15, 1917, 18; J. Brooks Atkinson, "Miss Brice Enlists in the Drama," *New York Times*, Sept. 22, 1926, 30.

12. Mizejewski, *Ziegfeld Girl*, 97.

13. Ibid., 32.

14. Beth Brown, "Making Movies for Women," *Moving Picture World*, Mar. 26, 1927, 342.

15. Nancy Walker and Zita Dresner, introduction to *Redressing the Balance: American Women's Literary Humor from Colonial Times to the 1980s*, eds. Walker and Dresner (Jackson: University Press of Mississippi, 1988), xxvii.

16. Atkinson, "Miss Brice Enlists," 30.

17. Kristen Anderson Wagner, "'Have Women a Sense of Humor?': Comedy and Femininity in Early Twentieth-Century Film," *Velvet Light Trap* 68 (Fall 2011): 35.

18. Quoted in Grossman, *Funny Woman*, 151.

19. Atkinson, "Miss Brice Enlists," 30.

20. Quoted in Grossman, *Funny Woman*, 163.

21. "Fanny of the Follies," part 3, quoted in ibid., 127.

22. Len Libbey, "Boston," *Variety*, Dec. 1, 1922, 24.

23. Con, "Palace," *Variety*, Nov. 3, 1922, 19; Katherine Lipke, "Hail to Fanny Brice," *Los Angeles Times*, Sept. 7, 1924, B13.

24. "Irresistible Fannie Brice in *My Man*," *Photoplay*, Mar. 1929, 7; "Fannie Brice Steps from the Screen to Sing and Talk to You," *Motion Picture Magazine*, Mar. 1929, 15; Delight Evans, "*My Man*," *Screenland*, Mar. 1929, 48.

25. The film *My Man* is lost, but the Vitaphone discs with the soundtrack still exist.

26. Quoted in Anthony Slide, *The Encyclopedia of Vaudeville* (Westport, CT: Greenwood Press, 1994), 63.

27. Kristen Anderson Wagner, "Silent Comediennes and 'The Tragedy of Being Funny,'" in *Researching Women in Silent Cinema: New Findings and Perspectives*, ed. Monica Dall'Asta, Victoria Duckett, and Lucia Tralli (Bologna: Dipartimento delle Arti—DAR, Alma Mater Studiorum Università di Bologna, 2013), 231–245, http://amsacta.unibo.it/3811.

28. Louise Fazenda, "Me by Myself: The Confessions of a Comedienne," *Motion Picture Classic*, May 1919, 69.

29. "Don't Fight against Nature," unidentified clipping, ca. 1917, Charlotte Greenwood clipping file, Billy Rose Theatre Collection, New York Public Library (hereafter BRTC).

30. Fanny Brice, "The Feel of the Audience," *Saturday Evening Post*, Nov. 21, 1925, quoted in Grossman, *Funny Woman*, 34; George Benjamin, "Fanny's Follies," *Modern Screen*, June 1938, 37.

31. Grossman, *Funny Woman*, 241. For insider/outsider status and liminality, see Jenkins, *What Made Pistachio Nuts?*, 223–226; and Mizejewski, *Pretty/Funny*, 38–42.

32. Quoted in Grossman, *Funny Woman*, 158.

33. Grossman, *Funny Woman*, 43.

34. Charles Darnton, "'So Long Letty' Almost as Broad as It Is Long" *(New York) Evening World*, Oct. 30, 1916, 13, BRTC; W. Stephen Bush, "Tillie's Tomato Surprise," *Moving Picture World*, Oct. 16, 1915, 463; Jane Kutten, "The World's Best Friend," *Motion Picture Magazine*, Jan. 1931, 31. For more on Marie Dressler's comedy, see Victoria Sturtevant, *A Great Big Girl Like Me: The Films of Marie Dressler* (Urbana: University of Illinois Press, 2009).

35. Quoted in Grossman, *Funny Woman*, 41.

36. Kathleen Rowe (Karlyn), *The Unruly Woman: Gender and the Genres of Laughter* (Austin: University of Texas Press, 1995), 122; see also Mizejewski, *Pretty/Funny*.

37. Grossman, *Funny Woman*, 21.

38. Florenz Ziegfeld Jr., "How I Pick Beauties," *Theatre Magazine*, Sept. 1919, 158, quoted in Angela J. Latham, *Posing a Threat: Flappers, Chorus Girls, and Other Brazen Performers of the American 1920s* (Hanover, NH: University Press of New England, 2000), 107.

39. Florenz Ziegfeld Jr., *San Francisco Examiner*, Apr. 16, 1911, quoted in Grossman, *Funny Woman*, 42; *New York Herald Tribune*, Aug. 14, 1938, quoted in ibid., 43.

40. Interestingly, a 1948 magazine article refers to "twenty-five years ago, when she was one of Ziegfeld's famed beauties," indicating that there was some rewriting of her history with the Follies even during her lifetime. See Mary Jane Fulton, "Sweet Dignity," *Radio Mirror*, Jan. 1948, 57.

41. "Serio-Comic Adventures," 26; see also "Loses Nose and Salary?," *Lincoln (NE) Evening Journal*, Aug. 16, 1923, 1.

42. Quoted in Grossman, *Funny Woman*, 150.

43. Mizejewski, *Pretty/Funny*, 5.

44. The distinction between narrative failure and performative success is made by Patricia Mellencamp in her discussion of Lucille Ball and Gracie Allen: see "Situation Comedy, Feminism, and Freud: Discourses of Gracie and Lucy," in *Star Texts: Image and Performance in Film and Television*, ed. Jeremy G. Butler (Detroit: Wayne State University Press, 1991), 325–326.

45. Quoted in Grossman, *Funny Woman*, 102.

46. Ibid., 103.

47. Fanny Brice, quoted in Norman Katkov, *The Fabulous Fanny: The Story of Fanny Brice* (New York: Knopf, 1953), 51.

48. Jolo, "Fannie Brice," *Variety*, Sept. 10, 1915, 13.

49. Sime, "Fannie Brice," *Variety*, Feb. 11, 1916, 18; Ruth St. Denis was a well-known modern dancer and founder of the Denishawn School of Dance. Although the varied nature of vaudeville meant that Brice undoubtedly followed a wide variety of acts on her tours, it's intriguing to think of the ways that vaudeville acts would have unintentionally (or perhaps intentionally) commented on and referenced one another, creating meaning from the juxtaposition of the acts.

50. Grossman, *Funny Woman*, 98.

51. "Sascha, the Passion of the Pasha" was included in *Be Yourself* but has been cut from currently circulating copies. However, clips of Brice singing the song can be found in the documentary *Broadway: The American Musical* (PBS 2004).

52. A.E.K., "Fannie Brice and Her Adventures," *New York Dramatic Mirror*, Apr. 22, 1914, 20; Benjamin, "Fanny's Follies," 90.

53. Roberta Mock, *Jewish Women on Stage, Film, and Television* (New York: Palgrave Macmillan, 2007), 104.

54. Her first marriage to a barber named Frank White (1910) was short-lived and according to Grossman was likely a publicity stunt: see Grossman, *Funny Woman*, 36.

55. "Fanny Brice in Alienation Suit," *Variety*, July 12, 1918, 3; "After Fannie Brice's Husband," *Variety*, Feb. 27, 1920, 6.

56. "Arnstein out of Jail, Joins Wife in Chicago," *New York Times*, Dec. 23, 1925, 2; see also "Court Gives Fanny Brice Her Divorce," *Los Angeles Times*, Sept. 15, 1927, 9; "Fannie Brice Sues 'Nicky' for Divorce," *Los Angeles Times*, Sept. 13, 1927, 3.

57. "Fannie of the Follies," part 3, quoted in Grossman, *Funny Woman*, 125. "Apaches" in this context refers to members of violent nineteenth-century Parisian street gangs. The apache was a popular character type in the early twentieth century, appearing in films such as Louis Feuillade's 1915 serial *Les Vampires*, as well as in the popular apache dance, which typically simulates a fight between a prostitute and her pimp. Clara Bow performs an apache dance in the 1925 film *Pa-*

risian Love. Fanny Brice's abused and despairing apache girl would have been a familiar character to audiences at the time.

58. Katkov, *Fabulous Fanny*, 137.

59. Quoted in Grossman, *Funny Woman*, 215–216.

60. Pamela Brown Lavitt, "First of the Red Hot Mamas: 'Coon Shouting' and the Jewish Ziegfeld Girl," *American Jewish History* 87, no. 4 (Dec. 1999): 259.

61. She also had at least one vaudeville routine that included "picks," or "pickaninnies," a group of young African American performers who would serve as backup dancers and singers; see Dash, "Fanny Brice and 'Picks,'" *Variety*, July 3, 1909, 20. For "pickaninny acts" in vaudeville, see M. Alison Kibler, *Rank Ladies: Gender and Cultural Hierarchy in American Vaudeville* (Chapel Hill: University of North Carolina Press, 1999), 119–125.

62. Mizejewski, *Pretty/Funny*, 23.

63. Kibler, *Rank Ladies*, 118.

64. Elizabeth Haiken, "The Making of the Modern Face: Cosmetic Surgery," *Social Research* 67, no. 1 (Spring 2000): 81.

65. "Surgeon Removes Hook from Fannie Brice's Nose," *Brooklyn Daily Eagle*, Aug. 16, 1923, 10; "Fannie Brice's Nose to Be Scaled Down," 10.

66. Grossman, *Funny Woman*, 24.

67. Ibid., 226.

68. Ibid., 27.

69. Jenkins, *What Made Pistachio Nuts?*, 182.

70. Ibid.

71. Quoted in Grossman, *Funny Woman*, 178.

72. Ibid., 197.

CHAPTER 5

LUCILLE BALL AND THE LUCY CHARACTER: FAMILIARITY, FEMALE FRIENDSHIP, AND THE ANXIETY OF COMPETENCE

LORI LANDAY

LUCILLE BALL (1911–1989) WAS one of the most beloved and influential women comedians in American culture. Her television series *I Love Lucy* ran Monday nights on CBS as a half-hour situation comedy from October 1951 to May 1957 and is one of the most well-known and persistently popular television shows in the world. (*The Lucille Ball–Desi Arnaz Show* aired in monthly, hour-long specials from November 1957 until April 1960.) The series Ball made after *I Love Lucy*—*The Lucy Show* (CBS 1962–1968) and *Here's Lucy* (CBS 1968–1974)—were top-rated shows (although Ball's last attempt at a television series, *Life with Lucy* [ABC 1986], did not fare well). The four series with "Lucy" characters hinge, of course, on Ball's character Lucy. (There are five series if you count *The Lucille Ball–Desi Arnaz Show* as a separate series, although in it Ball played the character Lucy Ricardo, and there are even more Lucys when one-off specials like *Lucy Calls the President* [CBS, 1977] are included.) Although the circumstances (and writers) changed over the years, what remained was the character's propensity for getting into wacky situations during which Ball could perform comedy. The Lucy character reinvents and renews the trickster: a recurring, shape-shifting, boundary-crossing, liminal culture hero (or heroine) in folklores and popular cultures around the world who embodies and enacts central social conflicts. In the home-centered sitcom, Lucy uses trickery, disguise, and cunning to make her own money, get onto her husband's show, or escape his restrictions. As a specifically female trickster in a popular story cycle in the new medium of television, and with the Lucy character, Lucille Ball embodied the television character whom everyone "loved," and she shaped the emerging expectations of series television so that character was at its center.[1]

The character Lucy, whom Ball created and revised during her sit-com career, plays such a major part in the development of comedy on television and in American culture writ large that we need to isolate it, examine it, and appreciate its significance. This chapter examines how the Lucy character contributed to establishing familiar charac-ters as central to the sitcom in particular and to the emerging tele-vision culture in general. I chart the development of the character across the series, investigate its sources, and analyze it as a trickster character who functions as a female culture hero of 1950s postwar domesticity even as it acts as a clown figure whose comedy draws on an anxiety of incompetence. Finally, I will discuss what is perhaps the most enduring and resonant aspect of the Lucy phenomenon: the strong female friendship that originates between Lucy and Ethel in *I Love Lucy* and continues in Ball's and Vivian Vance's collaborations until Vance's death.

In the 1950s situation comedies were not necessarily the most popular television genre; *I Love Lucy* had many elements that made it outstanding, many of them behind-the-scenes production factors. But in the series' narrative, in the popular discourses of the time (and since), its success hinges on Lucy. The character is the result of type-casting in films based on Lucille Ball's looks and voice; of radio and vaudeville stage performances in front of live audiences that encour-aged her growth as a performer; and of an extraordinary physical abil-ity for comedy honed by much practice. Ball rejected storylines and dialogue that did not fit her conception of her character Lucy, and the writers who wrote for her over the arc of her career (and the others who followed within the patterns they established) quickly learned the parameters. Lucy might not understand how the world worked, but she never intentionally hurt anyone. She might be terrible at a long list of jobs, but she was never portrayed as a bad mother. Her de-sires might take her outside the home, but the home always looked television-good, even if its everyday, ordinary state was contrasted with times when Lucy tried to make it look different for visitors or in publicity for Ricky's career.

THE LUCY CHARACTER

When we look at television performers today, we can see that their personas are based on familiarity. Lucy was one of the characters that shaped how audiences relate to television characters in general. Because television is experienced in the home, and television characters are seen repeatedly over many weeks and years, television performers are perceived as part of everyday life, in contrast to film actors, whose star images emphasize their difference from ordinary people.[2] Even in the 1940s, before television, when Lucille Ball appeared in movies, publicity about her emphasized that she was a "regular person" more than a glamorous star. It would be overstating it to say that the way Lucille Ball presented herself as being more similar to the character Lucy, with everyday problems of domestic life, than to a glamorous movie star, created the more immediate star image of the television performer, but the fusion of the Lucy character with Lucille Ball in the public's imagination, encouraged by publicity materials like articles in newspapers and magazines, certainly furthered the conflation of character and performer that characterizes television.

Ball maintained that the Lucy character was consistent across her career, and instead of delving into the ways in which the characters from the later series might be less satisfying because they have fewer facets than in *I Love Lucy*, let's look for what does stay the same. First, Lucy gets into wacky situations because she wants something or wants to do something. Unwilling to accept either the status quo or the obvious, "normal" way of behaving in the given situation, Lucy ends up doing something extraordinary, and Lucille Ball performs physical comedy. The character is defined at a crossroads between ordinariness and extraordinariness, competence and incompetence, observer and participant. In addition, Lucy the female trickster calls our attention to the shifting boundaries of gender, public and private, sacred and profane, domestic and worldly. Lucy the character must remain in the middle of the story cycle for the series to continue, the housewife who is not content with her lot, whose bristling against strictures is funny because it is enacted through exaggerated situations and slapstick, in a comic context in which not too much is at stake.

Looking over the trajectory of the Lucy character, we can see that its comedy is often based on ideas about women's incompetence or ditziness, Lucy's inaccurate self-image, and the contradictions that develop from the social norm of women being valued primarily for their appearance. In each instance of the Lucy character, there is a gap between how Lucy sees herself and how we see Lucy. Lucy habitually has a moment of confidence when she thinks she is doing fine, but then the situation veers out of her control. Even then she thinks she can possibly get away with it. We laugh at her, but we also recognize great vulnerability that is very human that the Lucy character exposes for us, and we laugh at ourselves, at our own foibles and misapprehensions. For example, in the well-known and beloved candy-wrapping scene in "Job Switching" (*ILL* May 30, 1952), Lucy is momentarily able to keep up with the accelerating conveyor belt before it goes too fast, which is funny, and the character is in comic dialogue with one of the most famous scenes of film comedy, Charlie Chaplin's conveyor belt scene in *Modern Times* (1936, discussed below). But what's funnier is what she does in order to appear to be in control of the situation: stuffing the chocolates in her shirt, hat, and mouth. The expression on her face of wide-eyed innocence and our knowledge of where the chocolates are create one of the most iconic images of the Lucy character.

The chocolate factory conveyor-belt scene works so well because the audience's familiarity with the Lucy character heightens their expectations. The structure of situation comedy necessitates repetition of established rules that govern the emotional range of what the audience can experience from the plots, themes, and characters. Television studies scholar Roberta Pearson highlights the importance of stability for television characters; although she is discussing characters in contemporary television drama serials, her insights are helpful for understanding the nature of character from the foundational stage of television as well:

> For literary and dramatic critics, development has often meant that the protagonist grows, achieves a higher degree of self-awareness and makes life-transforming decisions. But the repetitive nature of the television series dictates a relative state of stability for its characters, whose failure to perform key narrative functions and to interact with other characters in pre-established fashion could seriously undermine a series' premise.[3]

At a time when variety shows were a popular genre, without stable characters in situations beyond the star's persona, the situation comedy that *I Love Lucy* pioneered hinged on character and, more specifically, on Ball's creation and performance of that character.

As the central comic character, Lucy is distinct from the other characters, and kinds of characters, in the series. A few categories of persons emerge in the series alongside the Lucy character: there

5.1. Lucille Ball and Vivian Vance in "Job Switching," *I Love Lucy* (1952).

are ordinary people, people in show business, and then there is Lucy, who is extraordinary but is not in show business. We can understand Lucy as a trickster who seeks a third way when society offers a binary opposition; we can also understand the Lucy character as a construct formed in response to Ball's movie-star career (as Alex Doty suggests).[4] And we can understand Lucy as a character who expresses the traits of optimism, creativity, and ingenuity.

Lucy embodies these hopeful qualities, although the character is repeatedly denied the achievement of her goals, particularly when she wants a job outside of the home or to be in show business. In *I Love Lucy*, she sometimes is offered a part but doesn't take it because it would upset the domestic arrangement of the Ricardo household. Lucy's singing is routinely mocked, when Ball's comedy relies on off-key performance, but her dancing usually passes muster, especially after she works very hard, as she typically does when she seeks out a teacher in the specific style. She is a dilettante: expert in nothing but ready to jump into anything, certain that she can fake it or learn it in a few hours, and Lucy does remarkably well. She has moments of great competence, even when they are framed in a wider failure, such as in "Job Switching," when we see her wrap the chocolate candies on the conveyor belt quickly, before resorting to snatching them and stuffing them in her blouse, hat, and mouth. In the fourth season of *The Lucy Show*, Lucy had a run of success, in drag, as stuntman "Iron Man Carmichael," a job she didn't want to do because she sustained too many bruises. And in what might be the most bizarre Lucy premise ever, in the final episode of the fourth season of *The Lucy Show*, Lucy suddenly has superhuman strength, enough to lift a one-ton computer off Mr. Mooney's foot. (Believe it or not, that a computer weighed a ton was not the improbable part of the setup in 1966.) She could rip the door off her refrigerator and crush tin cans, all because of an overactive adrenal gland. There was no mention of the experience at the start of the next season.

As *The Lucy Show* and *Here's Lucy* turned to different writers who took the Lucy character for granted, the zany situations from which Lucy must extricate herself become more circumstantial than the result of Lucy's personality, and her optimism and frequently brilliant schemes are replaced by naiveté and clearly doomed plans. When we watch some episodes of *The Lucy Show* after writers Madelyn Pugh Davis, Bob Carroll Jr., and Bob Weiskopf left, it is clear that different writers were dropping Lucy into situations that were not consistent with the development of the character to that point. By the fourth season, Lucy Carmichael's children were no longer even mentioned, and the setup of Lucy as an ordinary housewife was eclipsed. We might think this is catching up with the times, making Lucy more modern, but it was regularly paired with making her stupid. Ball hired Milt Josefsberg, a head writer who excelled at sketch comedy, but Lucy's strengths, the Lucy character, and the sitcom were not suited for sketch comedy. There are good gags for the Lucy character in the late 1960s, but they are not as organically connected to the character's personality. Writer Bob Weiskopf asked, "I don't want to sound mean, but where was Lucy in all this? Why didn't she demand better writing for herself? She certainly was in charge."[5]

SOURCE OF THE LUCY CHARACTER

Nevertheless, even at its most instrumental and least multifaceted, the Lucy character does what the ordinary person would not and, like other trickster figures, embodies possibility. Ball explained, "I never found a place of my own, never became truly confident until, in the

Lucy character, I began to create something that was truly mine. The potential was there. Lucy released it."[6]

To be sure, Ball was not the sole "author" of the character Lucy, which was the result of a collaboration among Ball, the producer and writer Jess Oppenheimer, the writers (especially Madelyn Pugh [later Davis, who wrote for Ball for much of her career] and Bob Carroll Jr.), and Desi Arnaz and other Desilu individuals involved in the production and aesthetic decisions that shaped *I Love Lucy* and television itself. Oppenheimer takes credit for making Ball's radio character Liz Cugat (renamed Liz Cooper) funnier when he made her similar to the impulsive child character Baby Snooks, played by Fanny Brice on the radio show he produced before he took over Ball's radio show *My Favorite Husband* (CBS Radio 1948–1951) after its first few episodes.[7]

The performative and comic roots of the Lucy character originate in a character from the touring nightclub act Ball and Arnaz developed in the summer of 1950 in order to convince sponsor and network decision makers that audiences would accept a television couple played by an American woman and a Cuban man. The act can be attributed to several creators: Pepito the Clown, who coached Ball and invented the xylophone and trick cello that were the models for other trick props that highlighted her comic facility with objects; Pugh and Carroll, who wrote a sketch Ball and Arnaz performed; and Arnaz, who expanded his "Cuban Pete" number to include a part for "Sally Sweet." In the original description of the pilot episode of *I Love Lucy*, Oppenheimer specified that Lucy "does a bang-up job" when she replaces a missing Pepito in an audition, but "she foregoes the chance at a career that is offered her in order to keep Ricky happy and closer to his dream of normalcy."[8] It's not until the thirteenth episode of the first season of *I Love Lucy*, "The Benefit" (broadcast January 7, 1952), that Lucy's lack of talent (with her off-key singing) becomes a central plot point, but other "show-business" skills like dancing, telling jokes, and being a "pretty girl" are not called into question. There are a variety of reasons why Lucy doesn't get the part, or chooses not to take the part, in the show, but lack of talent is not the main one in the first season. In fact, getting into show business is not even the most frequent plot in the series.[9]

Ball created her "spider" voice—the trademark *eewww* sound she made when caught or when a plan didn't work out—in performing a radio commercial for Jell-O, but the "spider" became a characteristic Lucy sound and expression. The physical comedy for which Lucille

Ball is so justly celebrated was all scripted by her writers, and one of the few women writers in television at the time, Madelyn Pugh Davis, tried out all the physical stunts as they were writing them. Although the setups and dialogue often were lifted from the *My Favorite Husband* radio scripts written by Oppenheimer, Pugh, and Carroll, the physicality of the television series was a new element for the radio writers, albeit not to experienced film actors Ball and Arnaz.

The *I Love Lucy* scripts show how the writers employed Ball's trademark facial expressions, using key words in the stage directions like "SPIDER" (originating in the Jell-O radio commercial), the indignant look they called "CREDENTIALS," and several others. Ball's expressive lexicon was part of the paratextual information available to fans; an *L.A. Times This Week Magazine* article, "Lucy's Ready-Made Faces," details the code words with illustrations and a snippet from a script. Part of the extensive Desilu publicity machine that ensured *I Love Lucy* fans would know enough about the production and personal contexts to strengthen their identification with and investment in the characters and performers, the article attributes Lucy's faces to the actress. "'All our key words do,' says Jess Oppenheimer, 'is remind Lucy to duplicate something invented in the past. Then we just sit back and wonder at the great talent making our thought come to blossom.'"[10] Ball certainly did not invent the catchphrase (long a staple of vaudeville, stand up, and radio), but she did make that kind of repeated expression associated with a character into a visual as well as aural code of comic representation.

By examining Ball's pretelevision career, we see that Ball invented the basic emotional and psychological elements of the Lucy character before *I Love Lucy*. The aural aspects may stem primarily from radio, but the visual and kinetic facets of her performance are evident in the film characters she played in *Miss Grant Takes Richmond* (1949) and *The Fuller Brush Girl* (1950), both directed by Lloyd Bacon. The "kinesics"—the expressions, movements, comportment, and gestures that an actor can contribute to the creation of characters[11]—of the Lucy character are frequently based on Lucille Ball's use of her eyes and other facial elements that occur in a sequence. Ball showed us Lucy's hopes and ambitions in her face and invited us to experience empathy with the stages of Lucy's schemes and performances, when Lucy keeps going even though things have taken a bad turn. We see when Lucy's perception of herself is still winning out over the re-

5.2. In *Miss Grant Takes Richmond* (1949), Lucille Ball demonstrates many of the comic eye, facial, and body mannerisms that would become central to the Lucy character.

ality we can observe—when her misplaced perception tells her that she is doing a great job of putting one over on everyone, whether it is Miss Richmond pretending to type (although the typewriter ribbon has comically come loose), or her confident smile as her legs kick out the Charleston instead of the ballet barre exercise in "The Ballet" (ILL February 18, 1952) or her acting as if there is nothing amiss as she careens through the party on roller skates. These moments are followed by a glance up and to the side, those big eyes under the long lashes reminding us of the context she is in, giving us the opportunity to look at her while she looks away. So much of the Lucy character is in Ball's eye mannerisms, which suggest her relationship to her body, her lack of full control over it; even when she does control it, her ability gets her body and herself into situations in which she will fit. The incongruities the Lucy character embodies—beauty and the grotesque, competence and ineptitude, desire and limitation, being special and being ordinary—are juxtaposed in the comic climaxes.

If part of creating the Lucy character lies in Ball's kinesics, and her brilliant application of them for comic purposes, then we should also acknowledge the role that her public persona played in the Lucy character. P. David Marshall writes,

> Type or typage as a form of casting has always been an element of film and theatrical performance; but it is the seriality of performance—the actual construction of a personage that flows between the fictional and real person—that allows an actor to claim a persona that can be exchanged within the industry. . . . Television produced with regularity character-actors where performance and identity became indissoluble partly because of the sheer repetition and the massive visibility of these seriated performances.[12]

Moreover, Ball's public persona highlighted her as a domestic person. Magazine and newspaper articles repeat Ball's wish to be a "housewife" and her claims that she is a homebody, that she wishes she were a hairdresser. The public persona she presented in the early 1950s was very much of an ordinary woman who was interested in her marriage and children—and, oh, also, this little show she did near her house and with her husband. The media representations do not emphasize her glamour as a movie star, as they typically did in the 1930s and 1940s, when she appeared in dramatic as well as comedic roles. To be sure, television stars are more frequently seen as ordinary and accessible personalities, made familiar by the regular and intimate practices of television watching, in contrast to the exceptional, distant, inaccessible film star,[13] but Ball made accessibility part of her persona at a very early stage in television, perhaps already influenced by a similar experience of how people perceived her as a radio star versus a film star.

The Lucy character is also defined in contrast to celebrities and is frequently motivated by wanting to meet a celebrity. Much of the Hollywood arc in the third season of *I Love Lucy* involves Lucy's unusual interactions with stars; in the fourth season of *The Lucy Show*, when Lucy Carmichael moves to California, she repeatedly tries to get close to stars. In addition, there are episodes in all the series in which guest stars play themselves or other characters, and Ball's interactions with them onstage and on film reinforce her place in a social circle of stars as well as her professional ties. Stars are portrayed in the Lucy series as if they belonged to an elite club to which Lucy desperately wants access: in "The Tour" (*ILL* May 30, 1955), Lucy ends up hiding under a bearskin rug in actor Richard Widmark's house while he asks Ricky about the rumors he's heard about Lucy—because she wanted the actor to autograph a grapefruit.

In all the Lucy series there are many brilliant moments when Lucy the fan ignores the invisible wall between ordinary person and star in order to meet (and have a comic conflagration with) a star. Sometimes stars played themselves, or sometimes they played the characters for which they were famous, like George Reeve as Superman in "Lucy and Superman" (January 14, 1957) or Jackie Gleason as Ralph Kramden and Jack Benny as himself on "Lucy Visits Jack Benny" on *Here's Lucy* (September 30, 1968). Carol Burnett shows up as both herself and also as a terrifically wacky roommate for Lucy. But none was as bizarre as when Lucy met Lucille Ball in *Here's Lucy* ("Lucy Meets Lucille Ball," March 4, 1974). Lucy tricks her way into Ball's dressing room, squirts on some perfume, and caresses her elegant gowns before, thanks to split-screen special effects, Lucille Ball (in a brunette wig) enters. In their brief conversation, Ball is able to plug her movie *Mame* and her perfume. A scene more interesting as a curiosity and spectacle than for any insight into television personality and star image, it still does what the Lucy character had always done: insist that Lucy is separate from but also connected to Lucille Ball, as if she were two different people who could find common ground (if Lucy's antics did not get in the way).

BEAUTY INTO BUFFOON

Another strain of popular discourse from the early 1950s marveled at the juxtaposition of Ball's showgirl appearance and the comic getups and actions she performed on *I Love Lucy*.

A *Life* magazine article entitled "Beauty into Buffoon" wondered at Ball's readiness to look ugly, move awkwardly, and take a pie or seltzer in her "fine face" for a laugh, and this sentiment is echoed through many articles in the popular press.[14] Ball used her dancer's body to perform in ways that contrast with expectations based on her appearance, although in concert with her character. Even in the pregnancy shows, when the writers couldn't use the word "pregnant" and the network and advertising executives had wanted to hide her body, there was a great routine of Lucy cleverly figuring out how to use the nearby furniture to heave her pregnant body up from a chair in the episode "Ricky Has Labor Pains" (*ILL* January 5, 1953).[15] The

Life article juxtaposes pretty Ball in a "formal portrait" with funny photographs from the set of "The Ballet": Lucy dressed as the (male) clown in baggy pants and hat and caught in the ballet barre in her tutu. Linda Mizejewski writes, "In the historic binary of 'pretty' versus 'funny,' women comics, no matter what they look like, have been located in opposition to 'pretty,' enabling them to engage in a transgressive comedy grounded in the female body—its looks, its race and sexuality, and its relationships to ideal versions of femininity. In this strand of comedy, 'pretty' is the topic and target, the ideal that is exposed as funny."[16] When Lucy impersonates gender types, such as the ballerina in "The Ballet," the character embodies a female subjectivity that exceeds the parameters of the feminine ideal. In "The Ballet," the pretty ballerina literally becomes the target of Lucy's seltzer spray (and Ricky the object of the pie in the face). In the scene in the ballet studio, Lucy Ricardo, costumed in the kind of tutu a girl might wear to dress up as a ballerina, cannot conform to the 'pretty' ideal in comportment, movement, or temperament. When the strict ballet teacher counts out a battement tendu exercise, Lucy's body catches the rhythm, and then her facial expression changes from uncertainty to confidence, from work to play, and she swings into the Charleston, a buoyant smile spreading across her face as her knees bump and stretched legs kick out front and back. The interruption of ballet—ideal feminine performance—with the popular 1920s dance is an example of what Patricia Mellencamp identifies as one of the times that although Lucy's attempts *"narratively* failed, with the result that she was held, often gratefully, to domesticity, *performatively* they succeeded."[17]

Moreover, Ball challenges 1950s paradigms of domesticity and femininity through her comedic use of popular culture and physicality.[18] Throughout this scene, the Lucy character creates comedy with what the great novelist and thinker Arthur Koestler called bisociation, the clash of two disparate frames of reference that causes us to think in a "double-minded, transitory state of unstable equilibrium."[19] Bisociating ballet and the Charleston brings the classical portrayal of the ballerina as lighter than air into sharp contrast with the popular modern, grounded dance. The classical dance form defies gravity to portray the ballerina as lighter than air; yet when Lucy gets tangled up in the ballet barre later in the scene, gravity again has her; she is angular, not curved like a ballerina. This is only one of the many times Lucy's body refuses to conform to the ideal feminine movements or comportment; Lucy's inflexibility and incompetence in these moments, even when she thinks she is doing so well (as when she breaks into the Charleston), characterize her contravention of the line between pretty and funny as surely as her costumes and makeup do.

LUCY AS TRICKSTER

Lucy's comedy is always transgressive, but perhaps not deliberately. The character thinks she might fit in and always thinks she will get away with it no matter how wacky the scheme. As I've discussed elsewhere, Lucy Ricardo is a trickster, and a specifically female one who plays fast and loose with the shifting boundaries of gender in American culture in the 1950s.[20] In contrast to the conventional hero, who attains his objectives through might and power, or to the conventional heroine, who achieves her goals by being good, beautiful, and chosen or saved by the hero, a trickster gets what he or she wants through deception, tricks, disguise, and cleverly breaking the rules. Almost every culture has trickster figures in their folklore. Some are small animals who can outwit larger and stronger animals, like Coyote in southwestern Native American oral traditions or Brer Rabbit in African and African American folklore, and some are human, such as the peasant trickster Till Eulenspiegel of German folklore. Characteristically, tricksters love discord and disruption, and they disturb the status quo. Tricksters embody the uncertainties, failures, and hopes of a culture. Sometimes the trickster becomes the dupe when the tricks backfire.

My argument is that part of the reason why *I Love Lucy* was so phenomenally popular is that it updated and reinvented the trickster for the new medium of television, situating her in the domestic context in which television and television culture prevailed. Lucy the trickster can see and create new possibilities for herself where those following society's rules would only see the status quo. If women are prevented from overtly achieving their goals, then they have no choice but to opt for covert tactics. In the genre of comedy, and in the form of the television situation comedy that *I Love Lucy* helped establish, the character Lucy uses trickery to preserve autonomy in the home and to try to gain agency in the public sphere. In the post–World War II world reflected in the distorted mirror of television comedy, female trickery works in domestic settings but not as often outside the home.

For example, Lucy successfully deploys trickery to get Ricky to stop regimenting her time in the home in "Lucy's Schedule" (*ILL* May 26, 1952) but she only undermines herself with her scheme in "Mr. and Mrs. TV Show" (*ILL* November 1, 1954). In "Lucy's Schedule," Lucy colludes with Ethel and Ricky's boss's wife to convince the men that putting their wives on a strict schedule is a terrible idea. Lucy and the other women preserve their autonomy in the home, maintaining a sexual division of labor. In "Mr. and Mrs. TV Show," Lucy pulls a trick she thinks will teach Ricky a lesson about falsely claiming it was his idea to include her in the husband-and-wife breakfast television show that will star them. First we see a rehearsal, where the characters perform idealized versions of themselves, personas for public consumption that have little in common with the characters' usual dress, comportment, diction, and behavior. Lucy thinks it's another dress rehearsal when it's really the live broadcast, and her trick of saying terrible, unflattering things about the sponsor and appearing in a burlap bag and fright wig instead of a glamorous outfit backfires and she loses what she has always wanted, to be on television and in show business. Here the laughs are because Lucy is not only refusing to do what she should be doing in the television show, presenting a romanticized performance of everyday domestic life, but she has also deliberately made herself particularly hideous. Beauty into buffoon indeed!

"Mr and Mrs. TV Show" is similar to a first-season episode "Men Are Messy" (*ILL* December 3, 1951) but with television instead of a magazine. Lucy out-tricks herself when she tries to make a point to Ricky about how messy he is by trashing their apartment and dressing like a hillbilly for a photographer because she thinks he is from a musicians' magazine and the story will only be seen by people who know Ricky. However, the photographer is really from the popular *Look* magazine, and Lucy is humiliated when she appears on the cover. As usually happens to the trickster, the trick is on her. These two episodes also reveal the artifice of the media, that television and magazines are tricks, at the same time that they reify them. The representation of television in "Mr. and Mrs. TV Show" and the depiction of how Lucy sets the apartment as if it were a stage (and of course it is a set on a stage) expose what we see on the television screen and the page as constructions. In "Mr. and Mrs. TV Show," in the scenes that are part of the show-within-the-show, Ricky and Lucy look straight into the camera to address the viewer, and we see the

5.3. Lucy the trickster's trick backfires on her in "Mr. and Mrs. TV Show," *I Love Lucy*, 1954.

characters acting in a fake, idealized way, looking at each other adoringly rather than the way we usually see them, informal and in conflict. These episodes call attention to how media is constructed, albeit in a simplified way, and make the rest of the series' audiovisual style seem more "natural."

It makes sense that a trickster figure would thrive in the new medium of television and in the genre of the television sitcom. What the Lucy character brings to the established cultural figure of the trickster, though, is the first fully articulated female trickster who features in a story cycle at the very center of a culture, in this case, American culture in the 1950s. We see Lucille Ball's perpetuation of the Lucy character throughout her career, and we can also see how female trickery becomes a staple of female comic characters beyond the Lucy character. Seeing Lucy as a trickster both universalizes her—putting her alongside the plethora of tricksters throughout time and across cultures—and also particularizes her, when we think about the specific ways in which women's power in the home and in society was depicted in the 1950s in the series, and we consider how Lucy gets around the limitations imposed upon her by her husband and social role. Another important factor to Lucy's portrayal as a trickster is that she is not shown as a talented singer or performer, or depicted as having any other marketable skills: she has to get onto the show or get other kinds of attention or find ways of getting her own money through trickery. Thus Lucy's incompetence when she attempts to cross the boundaries of domesticity is an essential feature of her character.

LUCY AS CLOWN: THE COMEDY OF INCOMPETENCE

A clown is not really a character in any realistic sense; a clown (with his or her wig, makeup, and clothes that are too baggy or shoes that are too big) is marked as outside the norms of society. The Lucy character is half-clown, half-character; she is a clown in the new form of situation comedy. Her trademark red hair, false eyelashes, and red lipstick sit atop fifties dresses—until she puts on a costume or wig.

Ball's homages to the male icons of silent comedy, Charlie Chaplin and Harpo Marx, locate her in the tradition of great film comedy. For example, as noted above, Chaplin's film *Modern Times* inspired the accelerating factory conveyor belt that speeds the chocolates by Lucy and Ethel in the *I Love Lucy* episode "Job Switching." In *Modern Times* the Tramp is a factory worker who has to tighten bolts on an assembly line; to do the job well, he has to be like a machine. Lucy reprises the mirror routine from the Marx Brothers film *Duck Soup* (1933) with Harpo Marx ("Harpo Marx," *ILL* May 9, 1955); in *Duck Soup* Harpo is dressed up like his brother Groucho Marx and pretends to be Groucho's mirror reflection when he is really on the other side of a large door frame. It is a classic comic routine that many *I Love Lucy* viewers would have recognized, and by putting herself in Harpo's place in the mirror routine with Harpo in Groucho's role, the Lucy character again participates in a wonderfully funny performance that is in comic dialogue with other great comic performances. Moreover, the setup to the scene is consistent with the Lucy

5.4. Clockwise, from top left: Chaplin in *Modern Times* (1936), skating and on the assembly line; Ball and Harpo Marx in *I Love Lucy* (1955); Ball dressed as Chaplin in *The Lucy Show* (1962).

character's interest in appearing to have high status, because she is dressed as Harpo to trick her visiting friend into thinking she knows lots of celebrities. Ball also impersonated Chaplin on *The Lucy Show*—baggy pants, mustache, hat, cane, and all—and, like Chaplin in *Modern Times*, she performed on roller skates in a bit that, like Chaplin's, plays with lack of control. With these performances that connect her to the great comedians of film, Ball deliberately placed herself alongside the male stars of comedy; she was not just the Lucy character.

However, even though failure and incompetence are frequently the sources of comedy for the male comic figure, the Lucy character is pigeonholed by it. It is a different thing for a male character to be foolish, inept, clumsy, or naïve, because not all men are stereotyped with those qualities. Yet women's incompetence in the public sphere is the expected outcome of women's ambition to do something outside the home. In all of the series the Lucy character embodies a comedy of incompetence, and as a consequence of the paradoxes of the feminine mystique, of a particularly female kind of anxiety of competence. When we contrast Chaplin's Little Tramp and Ball's Lucy, for example, there are many similarities: for instance, both are tricksters who reject authority to pursue their own version of how life should be and what their role should be in it. However, overall the Tramp stands outside society and Lucy within it. The Tramp chooses not to participate in aspects of society he thinks are pointless; Lucy seems not to understand fully how little she fits in as opposed to not caring whether she does or not. Her self-image, comically inaccurate at times, is of someone who is poised, on top of things, and getting away with it all. That's part of her Americanness, that she always thinks she is pulling it off, that she has so much confidence in her ability even when she doesn't have the ability.

Let's contrast how Chaplin and Ball use the same physical device: roller skates. In *The Rink* (1916) Chaplin uses his skating skill for romantic pursuit and to best the larger man. In *Modern Times* the Tramp's skating ability—even unbeknownst to his blindfolded self— is an example of his dexterity and luck as he avoids skating off the edge (although it was a glass floor and a trick shot instead of a dangerous stunt).

In the department store where he works as a night watchman, the Tramp puts on a blindfold, showing off to impress the woman (Paulette Goddard). What the Tramp doesn't know is that he is skating dangerously close to the edge of a second-floor balcony that doesn't have a railing. He teeters on the edge only to glide back to safety, but then he rolls to the edge again. That the Tramp does not know he is in danger, and the dramatic irony of his carefree skating to the precipice of the railless edge, "lifts the sequence out of the mere physical exhilaration and hypnotic motion of the skating in *The Rink* (1916) and suggests a metaphor that uniquely applies to the tramp character Charlie has created. Even when Charlie seems to be in complete control, he is merely one step from disaster. Ironically, he loses his control only when he discovers his danger."[21] The Tramp is a terrific skater, and although the stakes are different than in *The Rink*, the performance is about competence and control.

In contrast, Ball's performance on roller skates in the "Lucy and the Good Skate" episode of *The Lucy Show* (September 21, 1964), is all about inflexibility. The setup is that Lucy's feet are so swollen that she cannot take off her roller skates to go to the formal country club dance, so in characteristic Lucy fashion, she thinks she can get away with wearing them under her long dress and no one will really notice. The source of the comic situation is the inverse of the Tramp's; Lucy overestimates her ability to fit into a social situation and also is a terrible skater with no control. With eyes wide open instead of blindfolded, and thinking others are somehow incapable of seeing everything, she rolls into the dance, unable to stop or turn. The wheels of the skates propel Lucy in whatever direction someone pushes her, and her facial expressions and upper-body dance moves as she trades partners (or is sent from one to the next) are set to a lilting "Blue Danube Waltz" punctuated with crashing sound effects. This bit of physical comedy exemplifies Henri Bergson's idea of comedy coming from a human acting like a machine, when a person is inflexible, automatic, or rigid; Bergson said laughter is caused by "something mechanical encrusted upon the living."[22] The scene moves from the comic to the absurd when Mr. Mooney, Lucy's authoritarian boss, played by Gale Gordon, takes Lucy for an elegant spin around the dance floor instead of his customary bellowing chastisement.

How do we understand this scene in the wider context of the Lucy character? We have the characteristic physical comedy. We have Lucy's belief that she can do the most bizarre things and somehow get away with it. In this episode, as in others, her perception of herself differs from how others perceive her, and her preconception of the results of what she sets in motion with her actions is wildly, hilariously, off the mark. We can dig into production history to understand how such a scene was created. Writer Garry Marshall (who applied much of what he learned writing for Lucy to *Laverne and Shirley* [ABC 1976–1983]) recalled how the episode originated. "The framework for *The Lucy Show* was to write a broad physical-comic last scene for her (as we did in an episode called "Lucy [and] the Good Skate" in which she attends a formal dance on roller skates) and then write a script that would motivate her to that ending scene. Lucy's physical comedy was at its strongest when she got stuck in some place that she shouldn't be. As writers, our job was to get her into a jam so the audience could watch her wiggle out."[23]

In the later instances of the Lucy character (like the roller-skating Lucy in *The Lucy Show*), the situation primarily focuses on the Lucy character. In *I Love Lucy*, although the writers were certainly writing towards a comic scene for Ball, they also were writing for the four main characters, and how they interacted, and who was teamed up with Lucy and how. They paid more attention to the diegetic world of the characters' relationships. Producer Oppenheimer explained,

"We were looking for a situation where Lucy's and Ricky's problems and differences of opinion were the same ones that most of our audience had encountered. We called it 'holding up the mirror.'"[24] It is certainly the distorted mirror of situation comedy, a funhouse mirror that exaggerates and elides, but especially when you watch the episodes as they originally aired (not the ones that aired in syndication that were edited to make time for commercials, which may have been our first encounter with the series). There is, if not quite a logical setup, at least a setup with a certain comic logic consistent with the diegesis of the series. This is what thins out in the later Lucy series. Still, the Lucy character gets to the physical comedy by crossing the boundaries between observer/participant, ordinary person/celebrity, socially conforming/extraordinary throughout the character's manifestations in different series.

LUCY AND ETHEL/VIV

Lucy's friendship with Ethel is an important representation of female friendship, and the collaboration between Lucille Ball and Vivian Vance outlasted *I Love Lucy* and Ball's marriage and partnership with Desi Arnaz. Like marriage in the series, the friendship is not portrayed as an idealized relationship. The two women trade barbs, mostly based on the others' oft-exhibited character traits, such as Lucy's lies that inveigle the friends into various schemes, or Ethel's eating or eavesdropping. They often experience friction over jealousy and competition; in "Lucy and the Good Skate," Lucy and Viv are both interested in the same attractive man, and although Viv lengthens Lucy's dress so it will cover the roller skates and helps her get to the dance, when they are both vying for the man's attention, Viv gives her a good push that sends Lucy careening out of the way. Just as the comedy of married life established in *I Love Lucy* (and previously in the radio show *My Favorite Husband*) stems from conflict and resolution, sometimes within the couple and sometimes between the couple as a unit and an external force, the comedy of female friendship features both the rifts between the two women (repeatedly enacted in comic performances requiring teamwork from the actresses) and moments when the two women act in concert in a scheme. Lucy's wackiest moments are funniest when they also involve Ethel/Viv; the two women play off of each other and, as one scholar notes, "It is Lucy's relationship with Ethel, and not her occasional successful forays into public life, that were perhaps the most liberating aspects of the series. When Lucy returned home after turning down jobs, she also returned to Ethel."[25]

Ball and Vance had extraordinary timing and chemistry. Vance described their relationship: "She and I were just like sisters. We fought like sisters and made up the same way. We shared a rare sense of balance, Lucille and I, much like the instinct of a diver who judges precisely the right moment to leave the springboard. . . . We could take off together, singing or dancing, matching the notes and the steps, without having to think about it."[26] What had been just one of the pairings in *I Love Lucy* became the central relationship in *The Lucy Show*, with widowed Lucy Carmichael and divorced Vivian Bagley sharing a house with their children. The wacky situations in which Lucy and Viv became entangled were regularly prompted by them having to pinch pennies to make ends meet. As the series changed over the seasons (writers Madelyn Pugh Davis and Bob Carroll left the show in the middle of the second season over a disagreement, and Vance left as a regular at the end of the third season), the dynamic between the two women suffered. Vance left the series for personal reasons, and Ball had other costars, including Carol Burnett as the shy librarian who hilariously comes out of her shell in the fifth season, but none of the new characters had the same depth of relationship with Lucy.

The relationship between Lucy and Ethel/Viv may not have been equal in billing, but for the characters, it was mutual. Vance's character is quickly and willingly sucked into Lucy's optimism, and it prevents her from descending into the cynicism for which her zingers show a propensity. Lucy elevates the daily life of Ethel/Viv above the mundane; Ethel/Viv's life with Lucy keeps her involved in playful, imaginative situations that she is clearly willing to be in but would never initiate.

Lucy, of course, needs Ethel/Viv not only as a co-conspirator, but also for much more, because it is only with her friend that she can be herself. In contrast, Lucy's interactions with Ricky (and although less emotionally important, with Mr. Mooney and the other men in the other series) are performances, rife with schemes and impersonations intended to manipulate them into denying her less or keeping them from being angry with her. It is only Ricky's "love" that keeps the whole situation on the side of comedy. Lucy's relationship with her friend becomes more central in *The Lucy Show*, but it is present

5.5. The twenty-five-year collaboration of Lucille Ball and Vivian Vance. Left:
I Love Lucy (1953); right: *The Lucy Show* (1964).

throughout *I Love Lucy* in Lucy and Ethel's unwillingness to separate
even when Lucy and Ricky move to Connecticut, and it's apparent
whether or not the two characters are teaming up or fighting. It is a
powerful representation of female friendship, in which the friends do
make mistakes and look stupid, but they sustain each other anyway.
Lucy's female friendships suggest that the female trickster doesn't
have to be a loner, to choose between autonomy and social connections like the male trickster does. The success of Ball and Vance reinforces the popularity of comic teams and puts that dynamic in a
central place in the sitcom genre.

Even in their last collaboration, a one-hour special, *Lucy Calls the
President* (CBS November 21, 1977), the combination of friction and
friendship is evident. The premise of the show, written by Bob Carroll and Madelyn Pugh Davis, is that President Jimmy Carter is going
to come to the Lucy character's house (this time Lucy Whittaker, a
housewife in small-town Indiana). This provides the setup for various
comic interactions between Lucy and many of her costars from all
of the series, including Gale Gordon, Mary Jane Croft, Mary Wickes
(who played the ballet mistress in "The Ballet" and various parts on
The Lucy Show and *Here's Lucy*), and Vivian Vance as her next-door
neighbor. When a nervous Lucy and Viv start to bicker over how to
decorate the cake for the president, their conflict swiftly shifts into
comic absurdity: Lucy first gestures tauntingly with the grip of her
tube of cake icing; then Viv says, "You wouldn't dare"; Lucy replies,
"Maybe not, but I'd sure like to." Viv then steps out from behind the
cake, as if a gunslinger, hands on imaginary holsters, and says, "Two
could play that game." The exchange is overheard by the president's

security man in the living room: "You're going to have to shoot first," so he rushes in, gun ready, just as the two women are squirting each other in the face with the icing; in the comic conclusion, they turn to the security man and shoot him with the icing.

Is this cutting-edge comedy? No, of course not. The scene is a not-so-new twist on old shtick. The actresses do not conform to the usual television parameters of age, attractiveness, and body shape; seeing Ball and Vivian Vance, who had suffered some facial paralysis from a stroke, trade barbs and face off in the kitchen falls short of conventional television eye candy. But to Lucy fans, who care more about the relationship between the characters and who possess so much extra-textual knowledge about the decades-long collaboration between the actresses, it's funny and pleasurable because it's familiar, because it's Lucy and Viv, Ball and Vance. If the fans were to imagine Lucy and Ethel/Viv growing older, this is what those characters would have been like at this point in their lives. It's no surprise that they shoot each other with the icing, or even that the authority-figure security man gets it in the face, but the way they comport themselves as cowboys in a saloon fight is not predictable and is wonderfully silly. Vance and Ball may not have been able to do some of the physical stunts they did earlier in their collaboration, but their timing is still good, and there they are again together, doing some crazy thing that is funnier when two people are in it together. It's imaginative and playful for them to have the icing fight. The characters participate in the tradition of the female trickster partnership one last time. It is this combination of deep knowledge of the other and venting conflict through physical comedy without challenging the solid foundation of the relationship or falling into sentimentalism that they reprise here in Vivian Vance's final television performance.

Placing female friendship at the center of the situation comedy and making the best friend an essential element of women's comedy on television is part of Lucille Ball's legacy. When I look at the official CBS *I Love Lucy* page on Facebook, for example, I see the theme of friendship resonate through the thousands of comments on posts, including replies to the question, "What's one lesson you've learned from *I Love Lucy*?" As Ball iterated the Lucy character over the different series, Lucy always had important female friendships with characters played by Carol Burnett, Ann Sothern, and Mary Jane Croft, as well as Vivian Vance, charting the way for women in comedy to collaborate on stories and humor of their own. In the Lucy series and in the myriad examples that follow, female comic characters develop in relationship with each other, from duos such as Mary and Rhoda in *The Mary Tyler Moore Show* (CBS 1970–1977), *Laverne and Shirley* (ABC 1976–1993), *Kate and Allie* (CBS 1984–1989), Tia and Tamera in *Sister, Sister* (ABC 1994–1995, WB 1995–1999), Patsy and Edina in *Absolutely Fabulous* (BBC 1992–2012), and Abbi and Ilana in *Broad City* (Comedy Central 2014–); to foursomes like *Designing Women* (CBS 1986–1993), *The Golden Girls* (NBC 1985–1992), and *Sex and the City* (HBO 1998–2004).

Moreover, the Lucy character is one of the elements in the development of television culture that constructs the audience's relationship with the familiar characters they come to love. Just as Lucy and Ethel/Viv could count on each other, we the viewers can count on the Lucy character not just to get into those crazy situations but to react in a certain, distinctively Lucy way: with optimism and confidence even when there is absolutely nothing in the environment or situation to foster them. In a 1996 episode of Ellen DeGeneres's situation comedy *Ellen* (ABC 1994–1998), Ellen overcomes her fear of a mammogram with a strategy for managing stressful situations shared by her cool friend (played by Janeane Garofalo): remember *I Love Lucy* episodes. This is only one trace of how the Lucy character continues to resonate in women's comedy and in television culture. What is required from a character in situation comedy—that he or she remains in the situation and that we can become attached to the character as we watch him or her week after week, year after year (or these days, over whatever time period we choose)—is part of the character Lucille Ball created at the very beginnings of situation comedy and television culture. Lucy's sense of herself as capable right up until the final moment makes her heroic. That she is there in the next episode, the next series, trying again, well, we may smile at that as savvy television viewers, but there is also something heroic about that, too. Lucy is tenacious, and no, she never did learn that she shouldn't or couldn't, and she never accepted the place she was put. We really wouldn't want her any other way.

NOTES

1. Ball was also one of the most prominent women on the business side of television in its first few decades, first as a co-owner of Desilu Productions (the first independent television production company) from 1950 until 1962, when she bought out Desi Arnaz to become the first woman CEO of what had become a

major movie as well as television production company. By 1967, when Ball sold her shares of Desilu to Paramount Studios for $17 million, she had successfully led the company's gamble on groundbreaking television series *Mission: Impossible* (CBS 1966–1973) and *Star Trek* (NBC 1966–1969). She established her own production company, Lucille Ball Productions, in 1968 to make *Here's Lucy*; she not only produced the show but also directed several episodes (uncredited) and went on to direct pilots for her company. In a time when women were only grudgingly given credit for acting as an art form, Ball pursued an active role in all aspects of television.

2. Characters and character types associated with actors are among the essential elements that the film, radio, and television industries use to create the images of stars. As Richard Dyer explains, a star image is a "complex configuration of visual, verbal and aural signs" from many types of media that form how audiences perceive a star. The characters a star portrays, the performance style, publicity material, advertisements, and the genre and medium in which they appear all contribute to the star image." See Dyer, *Stars* (London: BFI, 1998), 34.

3. Roberta Pearson, "Anatomising Gilbert Grisson: The Structure and Function of the Televisual Character," in *Reading CSI: Crime TV under the Microscope*, ed. Michael Allen (London: Tauris, 2007), 55–56, quoted in Jason Mittell, *Complex TV: The Poetics of Contemporary Television Storytelling*, pre-publication edition (MediaCommons Press, 2012–2013).

4. Alexander Doty, "The Cabinet of Lucy Ricardo: Lucille Ball's Star Image," *Cinema Journal* 29, no. 4 (1990): 3–22. doi:10.2307/1225313.

5. Stefan Kanfer, *Ball of Fire: The Tumultuous Life and Comic Art of Lucille Ball* (New York: Knopf, 2003), 255.

6. Quoted in Kathleen Brady, *Lucille: The Life of Lucille Ball* (New York: Billboard Books, 2001), 197.

7. Scholar Miranda Banks considers Oppenheimer to be an early version of what we now call a showrunner, a term that originated in 1990 in the trade press for a television series writer-producer who gives the series its creative vision, structure, and direction, and Oppenheimer sees himself in this way in his writings. See Miranda J. Banks, "I Love Lucy: The Writer-Producer," in *How to Watch Television*, ed. Ethan Thompson and Jason Mittell (New York: NYU Press, 2013), 245. Television studies scholar Thomas Schatz, however, provides another way to understand how a cultural artifact like a television series or character is made. He focuses on Desilu and specifically on Desi Arnaz in his discussion of how the independent production company shaped *I Love Lucy* and television production and programming in the 1950s; for Schatz, the narrative content stems from the production context:

> Clearly the economy of production design—the limited sets and locales, the four-character constellation, the repetitive plot structure of each episode—did not undermine the show's appeal. On the contrary, the very simplicity and formulaic nature of *I Love Lucy* was essential to its success, particularly in the way it concentrated the entire narrative enterprise on Ball's hare-brained, hustling, mock-heroic housewife, the inimitable (though much imitated) Lucy Ricardo. Ball's character was the source of conflict and comedy in each series

installment, and her chronic domestic anarchy clearly struck a chord for the millions of TV viewers caught up in America's postwar baby/family/housing boom. (Schatz, "Desilu, I Love Lucy, and the Rise of Network TV," in *Making Television: Authorship and the Production Process*, ed. Robert J. Thompson and Gary Burns, 123–124. [New York: Praeger, 1990.])

8. Jess Oppenheimer, with Gregg Oppenheimer, *Laughs, Luck, and Lucy: How I Came to Create the Most Popular Sitcom of All Time* (Syracuse, NY: Syracuse University Press, 1996), 139.

9. In the first season, fourteen episodes revolve around Lucy wanting to get into show business, and in five of those episodes she was motivated by wanting to help Ricky's career. Fifteen of the first season's episodes had to do with marriage or domestic situations, six with the battle of the sexes, and one pits the Ricardos against the Mertzes. In the second season, five episodes involve Lucy wanting to get into show business; in two of those episodes she is motivated by wanting to help Ricky's career. Nineteen are marriage/domestic plots, including six of the seven pregnancy shows. The seventh pregnancy show also features Lucy wanting to get into the act. Four are battle-of-the-sexes plots, and three are Ricardo versus Mertz.

10. Leslie Lieber, "Lucy's Ready-Made Faces," *L.A. Times This Week Magazine*, May 9, 1954, 31.

11. Virginia Wright Wexman, "Kinesics and Film Acting: Humphrey Bogart in *The Maltese Falcon* and *The Big Sleep*," *Journal of Popular Film and Television* 7, no. 1 (1978): 42–55.

12. P. David Marshall, "Seriality and Persona," *M/C Journal* [online] 17, no. 3 (June 11, 2014): n.p., http://journal.media-culture.org.au/index.php/mcjournal /article/viewArticle/802.

13. John Langer, "Television's 'Personality System,'" *Media Culture & Society* 4 (1981): 167.

14. *Life*, "Beauty into Buffoon," Feb. 18, 1952, 93–97.

15. Lori Landay, *I Love Lucy* (Detroit: Wayne State University Press, 2010), 73.

16. Linda Mizejewski, *Pretty/Funny: Women Comedians and Body Politics* (Austin: University of Texas Press, 2014), 5.

17. Patricia Mellencamp, "Situation Comedy, Feminism, and Freud: Discourses of Gracie and Lucy," in *Studies in Entertainment: Critical Approaches to Mass Culture*, ed. Tania Modleski (Bloomington: Indiana University Press, 1986), 88. See also Alexander Doty, "The Cabinet of Lucy Ricardo: Lucille Ball's Star Image," *Cinema Journal* 29 (1990): 3–22.

18. Lori Landay, "*I Love Lucy*, Television, and Gender in Postwar Domestic Ideology," in *The Sitcom Reader: America Viewed and Skewed*, eds. Mary M. Dalton and Laura R. Linder, 87–97 (Albany: SUNY Press, 2005); Landay, *Madcaps, Screwballs, and Con Women: The Female Trickster in American Culture* (Philadelphia: University of Pennsylvania Press, 1998).

19. Arthur Koestler, *The Act of Creation* (New York: Macmillan, 1964), 36. Koestler explains that the single joke has one "explosion"; in contrast, a continuous experience of comedy happens when "a humorous narrative oscillates between two frames of reference" (38). I see the situation of *I Love Lucy* as biso-

ciating the frame of reference embodied by the Lucy character and the frame of reference of normative behavior as the extended oscillation, punctuated by the comic explosions of jokes and physical comedy.

20. See, for instance, Landay, "*I Love Lucy*, Television, and Gender"; Landay, *Madcaps, Screwballs, and Con Women.*

21. Gerald Mast, *The Comic Mind: Comedy and the Movies*, (Indianapolis, IN: Bobbs-Merrill, 1973), 86.

22. Henri Bergson, *Laughter: An Essay on the Meaning of the Comic* (1914), trans. Brereton Cloudesley and Fred Rothwell (Rockville, MD: Arc Manor, 2008), 24.

23. Garry Marshall, with Lori Marshall, *Wake Me When It's Funny: How to Break into Show Business and Stay* (New York: HarperCollins, 1997), 68.

24. Oppenheimer, *Laughs, Luck, and Lucy*, 180.

25. Lynn C. Spangler, *Television Women from Lucy to Friends: Fifty Years of Sitcoms and Feminism* (Westport, CT: Praeger, 2003), 36.

26. Frank Castelluccio and Alvin Walker, *The Other Side of Ethel Mertz: The Life Story of Vivian Vance* (Manchester, CT: Knowledge, Ideas & Trends, 1998), 199.

CHAPTER 6

CAROL BURNETT: HOME, HORROR, AND HILARITY ON *THE CAROL BURNETT SHOW*

LINDA MIZEJEWSKI

CAROL BURNETT (1933–) was featured in one of the most famous sight gags in television history as part of a *Gone With the Wind* parody on her award-winning variety series *The Carol Burnett Show* (CBS 1967–1978). In the 1976 sketch "Went With the Wind!," Burnett as "Starlet O'Hara" bustles offstage to whip up a fancy dress from velvet curtains, an iconic scene from the classic book and 1939 movie. But when "Starlet" reappears, she's wearing the entire window contraption—the curtain rod strapped across her shoulders and the curtains tied at her waist with the cord. An enchanted "Rat Butler" (Harvey Korman) exclaims, "That gown is gorgeous!" "Starlet" beams and bats her eyelashes. "Thank you," she says. "I saw it in the window and just couldn't resist it."

The curtain-rod gimmick is a brilliant image of women weighted down by the expectations of both domesticity and glamour, two central themes in Burnett's comedy and often spoofed on *The Carol Burnett Show (TCBS)*. Widely acknowledged as an influential and powerful pioneer of television comedy, Burnett was one of only two women ever to host a network variety show, a musical/comedy revue genre popular in the 1950s and 1960s. Her show won twenty-two Emmy Awards and became a ratings gold mine for CBS, though Burnett had been warned by television executives that hosting a variety show was "not really for a gal," given its lineage of shows built around the likes of Sid Caesar, Jack Benny, Dean Martin, and Red Skelton.[1] Proving herself as both witty comedian and amiable host, Burnett opened every show with an impromptu five-minute chat with the audience. An audience member once asked for her measurements, and she replied, "37-24-38—but not necessarily in that order."[2] Burnett's long career included film, made-for-TV movies, television specials, and Broad-

6.1. Carol Burnett in the "Went With the Wind!" skit, *The Carol Burnett Show* (1976). CBS/ Photofest. © CBS.

way, but *TCBS* is the focus of this essay. As a prime-time vehicle for a female comedian, its robust eleven-year run is unmatched, and it contains her most celebrated and accessible work in roles ranging from the bored secretary Mrs. Wiggins to the Queen of England and "Starlet O'Hara." *TCBS* is also where, in "The Family" sketch series, Burnett developed her most famous character, Eunice Higgins, the shrill Texas housewife who yearns to go to Hollywood to be a star.

Burnett often referred to herself as a comic actress rather than a comedian, and it's true that a brilliant team of writers headed by Arnie Rosen and later by Ed Simmons produced top-notch material for *TCBS*; "The Family" series was written by Dick Clair and Jenna McMahon. However, according to Burnett's interviews and observations made by her biographer, her creative input on the show stepped up after she was influenced by the women's movement in the 1970s and began campaigning for the Equal Rights Amendment.[3] So while *TCBS* steered clear of the era's political hot buttons—Vietnam, Watergate, civil rights—the feminist slant is occasionally blatant, as in the well-known skit in which Burnett as a frazzled housewife is viciously attacked and eventually killed by the out-of-control advertising icons for laundry detergent and floor cleaner; Burnett said that she herself wrote this skit with her husband Joe Hamilton.[4] Burnett was also responsible for the assembly of a talented, tight-knit comic ensemble and for the nurturing and mentoring of her young costar Vicki Lawrence. Just out of high school and with no professional experience, Lawrence wrote to Burnett in 1967, asking for advice about show business and enclosing a photo to show how much she resembled the comic star. Burnett took her on the show as "Sis," intending to do comic versions of her relationship with her own much-younger half-sister Chrissy, whom she'd helped to raise.[5] Groomed by Burnett, Lawrence grew to be an accomplished, Emmy Award–winning comic actress over the eleven years of *TCBS* and continued her role in "The Family" sketches in her own sitcom, *Mama's Family* (NBC 1983–1990).

Most of all, the creative force Burnett brings to every sketch and character of *TCBS* is her skill as a high-energy performer. For the *Gone With the Wind* parody, the idea for the curtain rod came from the show's celebrated fashion designer, Bob Mackie, but the heart of the sketch is Burnett's demonic mimicry of Southern charm, which mines her talent for grotesque facial expressions and aggressive physical comedy. Burnett was notorious for her fearless stunt work. The sketch scenes compiled in the PBS American Masters biography, *Carol Burnett: A Woman of Character* (2007) show her ability, from the very start of her career, to hurtle herself to the ground, throw herself against a wall or out a window, and skillfully deliver and receive fake punches, slaps, blows, and knock-backs to and from fellow actors. In a 1962 interview, she dismissed the "outmoded . . . necessity to be ladylike" but acknowledged that many people believe "being funny is unfeminine."[6] Her indifference to feminine ideals was perhaps most evident in her willingness to comply with the frequent audience request for her Tarzan yell. Cupping her hands to her mouth, Burnett would boom out the warbling Tarzan yodel made famous by muscular Johnny Weissmuller in 1930s matinee adventure movies. The Tarzan yell was one of her signature bits, revealing her enormous versatility in performing variations of gender. David Marc notes that

Burnett could be a "slapstick mama and a refined lady of the stage," capable of both "opera and soap opera."[7] She could sashay like Vivien Leigh, but she could also yell like Tarzan.

Critics have lauded the subversive 1950s comedy of Lucille Ball as the zany housewife, but Burnett's comic flouting of femininity in sketch comedy has received far less attention, perhaps because variety shows are usually dismissed as gutless, middle-brow entertainment.[8] While the choreographed musical numbers of *TCBS* now look dated, the comedy sketches have a compelling edge not found on other variety shows of the era, especially when Burnett performs violent slapstick versions of the crazed housewife, drama queen, or diva. The effect is often unsettling. Comparing Burnett to Lucille Ball, Susan Horowitz points out that despite Lucy Ricardo's rebellious antics, *I Love Lucy* (CBS 1951–1957) retained the fiction of an ideal home and loving marriage, a sharp contrast to Burnett's "absurd theatre of cruelty."[9] The examples are numerous. Burnett's demented "Nora Desmond" in a *Sunset Boulevard* (1950) parody gets an offer to do bedbug commercials and eventually stabs the befuddled ad salesman, her beloved butler, and herself. In a *Rebecca* (1940) parody, a ghoulish talking head appears on a dinner platter to nag the heroine about her failures. And in "Went With the Wind!," Burnett's "Starlet" gut-punches "Rat," slams the door on Melanie's hand, breaks a chair over the back of a Yankee, and tumbles down the stairs twice within five minutes. "I adore doing violent slapstick," Burnett told a journalist in 1976.[10] And because they involve emotional rather than physical violence, "The Family" sketches are even more disturbing, as every dinner, birthday, and board game ends in vicious arguments. The writer Harold Brodkey wondered in 1972 how a show as upbeat as *TCBS* could convey such "horrors" and how a comedian as sunny as Burnett could exhibit so much "savagery" in her performances.[11]

This essay focuses on the gendered inflections of that question—the relationship between Burnett's beloved star persona and the "horrors" conveyed in her performances in the film parodies and "The Family" series, the best-known sketches on *TCBS*. The horrors inevitably involve violent undertows of domestic life or grotesque versions of femininity. Burnett brings to these performances two personal elements that she widely discussed without sentimentality throughout her career and that became discourses central to her stardom: her looks and her hard-scrabble background. *TCBS* parodies and "The Family" sketches are deeply inflected with the class and gender ideals against which Burnett's unlikely stardom was pitched; she was the star who was *not* beautiful and *not* classy, but her comedy made those ideals ludicrous rather than intimidating, as suggested by her quip about her measurements. The film parodies are especially critical of the narrow stories available to women in melodrama and "the woman's film," where pursuits of glamour, romance, and domestic bliss invariably make women miserable. As opposed to satire or caricature, parody imitates a well-known text, and its success is dependent on its ability to capture the contradictions, conventions, and unspoken assumptions of the original. Because parody subverts dominant and "legitimate" texts, putting them to "illegitimate" use, it's a key dynamic in Burnett's comedy, enabling witty, alternative versions of women's roles and stories. "The Family" is not a parody of a particular text, but it's fueled by the dynamics of maternal melodrama, notably the class conflicts in mother-daughter films such as *Stella Dallas* (1937) and *Mildred Pierce* (1945). Ironically, Burnett's Eunice in "The Family" suffers from a narrow life made more wretched by her conviction that a happier world awaits her in Hollywood.

Freud has told us that horror begins at home, which is also the site of family melodrama. In *TCBS* parodies and "The Family" series, the domestic scenes of family or romance all go terribly wrong, and the comedy plunges into uncomfortable chasms.[12] At some point, the shrieking arguments of Eunice and Mama make us cringe, and the lunacy of "Mildred Fierce" is unnervingly close to everyday maternal devotion. These performances "hit too close to home," to borrow Freud's terms in "The Uncanny": horror resides in the collapse of the familiar and unfamiliar, the *heimlich* (homelike) and *unheimlich*, revealing something we have always known and producing the discomfiting effect of uncanniness.[13] The image of "Starlet" sewn into the curtain fixtures captures, in an uncanny way, the atrocious implications of women being "domesticated." Parody itself involves the uncanny with its doubling effect, returning us to a familiar scene and exposing what it had concealed; Burnett as the double of Scarlett O'Hara, Mildred Pierce, or Norma Desmond confirms our uneasy suspicions about the desperation of these characters and the liminal freakishness of glamour.

All good comedy hovers on horrific truths about the human condition, and Burnett's comedy targeted the truths of women's conflicted stories, expectations, and ideals—beginning with her own. "The first

6.2. Carol Burnett in the "Nora Desmond" skit, *The Carol Burnett Show* (1972).

time I ever forgot I was homely," Burnett said in 1963, "was the first time I heard an audience laugh."[14] My interest here is the cultural rather than the psychoanalytic implications of that statement, but it's worth considering, on many levels, what Burnett did with "homeliness" on *TCBS*. The homely scenes of domestic life in the comedy sketches become uncanny sites of absurdity and violence. But her homeliest character, Eunice, is also the most touching; "The Family" sketches often end with a glimpse of the loneliness and sadness of Eunice's life, inviting us to recognize what's identifiable in her craziness. And when Burnett doubles as funny-looking versions of movie icons like Vivien Leigh or Joan Crawford, she taps what's familiar and unfamiliar about the cruel demands of femininity and the uncanny convergences of grotesquery and glamour.

HOME AND HOMELINESS

As a 1950s comedian, Burnett followed the tradition of Martha Raye (1916–1994), Nancy Walker (1922–1992), and Imogene Coca (1908–2001), comic television actresses known as unruly loudmouths and "character types," a euphemism for actresses not considered attractive enough for romantic roles. Raye and Coca were famous for their expressive, rubbery faces, and Raye in particular was known for the size of her mouth—as Kathleen Rowe has pointed out, an important facial feature of female comedy, signaling bawdiness, voraciousness, and back talk.[15] Like Raye, Burnett could twist her face into hideous shapes and could use her powerful voice to yell, squawk, and wail;

not surprisingly, she got her big television break in 1959 as a fill-in for Raye on *The Garry Moore Show* (CBS 1958–1967). Burnett claims that for the first fifteen years of her career, she depended on her ability to make funny faces as the basis of her comedy. It was well into the 1970s and the success of *TCBS*, she reports, before she reconsidered this tactic: "I started to realize I didn't have to do it, that I was a mature woman who could still be funny without crossing my eyes all the time," adding that "a growing security," as well as the influence of the women's movement, made her stop mugging and "putting down" her looks.[16] I have argued elsewhere that women in American comedy have been categorized in a pretty-versus-funny binary: the "pretty" ones (inevitably white or light-skinned) who do romantic comedy and the "funny" ones who lampoon and satirize notions of "prettiness." Burnett's remark, in the same interview, that she "had a great face for mugging" and assumed "that's what they wanted," shows that she knew her place in mainstream twentieth-century entertainment, where women were strictly classified by their appearance—beautiful or funny-looking.[17]

Because of that expectation, the topic of Burnett's looks shows up often in interviews, press coverage, and biographical material at the beginning of her career. "Miss Burnett is resigned to the fact that the TV cameras do not flatter her," said a 1960 *New York Times* piece. In 1963 a *Life* magazine profile catalogued her "anteater nose," "endlessly receding chin," and a lower lip that sticks out "like a hitchhiker's thumb." Her biographer spends three pages on the topic, quoting colleagues about how Burnett was determined to "uglify" herself for television. An associate producer remembers that her attitude was, "Yeah, I know I'm not pretty. In fact, I can make myself even uglier. Watch this!"[18] Funny-looking male comics of the era, like Bob Hope and Danny Kaye, could be leading men in romantic comedies, but comic women who were not Doris-Day-cute or Marilyn-Monroe-gorgeous had fewer platforms. For Burnett, the parodic mimicry of cuteness and gorgeousness was a powerful option; her "syrupy" imitation of Doris Day was such a "mean parody," according to Joe Hamilton, that Day's son launched a complaint.[19]

The elusiveness of Hollywood glamour haunted Burnett's early life and clearly influenced her later comedy. "I had a very beautiful mother, and I'm sure it came as a shock to her that she didn't give birth to a beauty," she said.[20] Louise Burnett moved herself and her young daughter from Texas to make it big as a writer in Hollywood, where Louise's dreams and beauty were quickly burned out by bad decisions and alcoholism. Living on the edge of poverty, Burnett escaped to the cinema seven or eight times a week, she says, while she grew up to look nothing like the stars she loved onscreen, describing herself as "five foot six, with buckteeth, stringy brown hair, and ninety pounds wringing wet."[21] Burnett's first ambition was to be a Hollywood journalist, and she says her mother encouraged her along those lines as her only possible entry into show business, telling her, "No matter what you look like, you can always write."[22] But her experiences in a musical comedy workshop in college changed her mind; when she announced to her family that she intended to be an actress, "they wanted to hit me with a reality stick," she told a journalist. In the same interview, Burnett speaks of her joy in eventually getting to play parodies of the roles made famous by Lana Turner and other screen idols of her childhood, noting the pleasures of donning wigs, padding, elaborate costumes, and killer eyelashes—in effect, proving the "reality stick" of glamour most likely comes out of a cosmetics box.[23]

Class is the other key element in the film parodies (especially the melodrama spoofs) and in "The Family" sketches, and class is likewise a central theme of Burnett's star persona. Anxieties about respectability and class status have been foundational to melodrama from its eighteenth-century beginnings through Dickens and *Downton Abbey* (PBS 2010–2015). In classics like *Gone With the Wind*, the heroine loses either moral compass or romantic happiness as she struggles out of poverty, and in maternal melodramas like *Mildred Pierce*, the mother-daughter relationship is the loss suffered as the price of success. Burnett's rise-from-poverty history packs in all the standard plot points. While her mother slid into addiction and failure, Burnett was raised in a one-room apartment by her maternal grandmother, "Nanny," an irrepressible presence with whom she shared a deep, lifelong bond. Both her mother and her estranged father, also an alcoholic, died when Burnett was a teenager. Money was always a problem. When Burnett was a child, Nanny sometimes took her along on her cleaning-lady jobs at the Warner Bros. studio, but it was a secret because "if the Relief Lady found out, the checks would stop coming."[24] The seedy apartment and degenerate parents were intrinsic to Burnett's origin narrative from the start; the extensive 1963 *Life* magazine profile that described her "anteater nose" provided the whole story down to the detail of how young Burnett didn't have closet space in Nanny's room and hung her clothes on a rack above the bathtub—in all, material for a star-is-born weepie.[25]

The most direct citation of Burnett's down-at-heels background is the iconic cleaning-lady character she played on *TCBS*, always referred to as Charwoman. Burnett's version of the melancholy clown figure offered a specifically gendered twist, given that femininity is usually configured as not just white but middle or upper class.[26] Charwoman was part of the show's logo, suggesting an unpretentious view of Hollywood from the bottom up. In an animated cartoon playing over the show's opening credits every week, the caricature version of Charwoman cleans and scrubs the television studio and then accidentally stumbles into the spotlight, suggesting a metaphor for Burnett's early career and an acknowledgement that she was an actress who, in most circumstances, would have been playing obscure "character parts" rather than headlining a show. As early as 1972, Burnett claimed that although she had liked the original skits, she "hated" the Charwoman character and continued it only because it had become popular.[27]

Burnett's discomfort with the character signals the difference between the sad-sack Charwoman and Burnett's own representations of her childhood and girlhood, which eschew both melodrama and sentimentality. She wrote her own story first as a memoir, *One More Time* (1986), and then, with her daughter Carrie Hamilton as a cowriter, a fictionalized stage comedy, *Hollywood Arms* (2002), produced by Hal Prince. *Hollywood Arms* is a coming-of-age story that was praised for humor based on "warmly portrayed everyday fallibility" and "funny-sad sparks that keep both the farcical and the maudlin at bay." The same could be said of the memoir, which never slides into self-pity.[28] Likewise, journalists writing up the 1960s and 1970s interviews that established Burnett's star-origin narrative noted that her stories of her bleak childhood are matter-of-fact and sometimes funny but never bitter. In later interviews Burnett included the unsavory details: "If she'd been drinking, my mother would cuff me across the face. And she could be pretty gross."[29] But not until the 1980s did Burnett admit to journalists that years of therapy were helping her deal with her anger toward her parents. Speaking to NPR in 2003, Burnett describes her mother as a "mean" and "vicious" drunk and remembers slinking off into a corner to draw pictures while her mother battled it out with Nanny.[30] It's difficult not to recall, with these descriptions, the emotional tensions of the Eunice-versus-Mama "Family" sketches, as well as Burnett's personal stake in the film parodies of unhappy families, excessive women, and failures of femininity. The tenaciousness of the Charwoman character demonstrates how Burnett could not, in fact, completely escape sentimentality in representations of her background and persona, but she is best remembered for her performances that skewer sentimentality, melodrama, and other traditional modes of telling women's stories.

HORROR AND MELODRAMA

In "Stolen Serenade," *TCBS*'s parody of *Broadway Serenade* (1939) and other doomed-diva movies, Burnett as the fallen former star Lily Du Lane gasps through an over-the-top deathbed scene in a hospital poverty ward. Lily repents her evil ways and asks forgiveness of her friends, who instead throw snow in her face and ignore her pleas: "My pulse just stopped! Call the doctor!" As she dies, the entire bed is lifted up toward heaven and Lily sprouts oversize angel wings, which she flaps as she sings a cloying, sputtering version of Burnett's theme song, "I'm So Glad We Had This Time Together." While Burnett sang the theme song as a heartfelt closure to every show, the parody version tips into sloppy mawkishness. Likewise, the sketch lampoons melodrama's sensationalized deathbed scenes, epitomized in theatrical and film versions of Charles Dickens and Harriet Beecher Stowe in which angels materialize to carry virtuous souls up to heaven. In "the woman's film," where melodramatic tactics prevail, deathbed scenes redeem fallen women like Sheila (Lana Turner) in *Ziegfeld Girl* (1941), or they canonize saintly but doomed mothers as in *Imitation of Life* (1959), or they end the stories of spunky women who refuse to know their place, like Jenny (Ali MacGraw) in *Love Story* (1970). In "Lovely Story," *TCBS*'s version of the latter film, the despondent husband throws himself on the bed with "Jinny," knowing she has "five minutes to live," mimicking the film's famous scene when the Ryan O'Neal character climbs into bed with his dying wife to embrace her one last time. But in "Lovely Story," the over-the-top gesture turns horrendous when he accidentally hurries her death through "excessive trampling," as the doctor explains.

All this suggests how *TCBS* movie parodies were keenly attentive to film history and to the excessiveness of melodramatic conventions, which comedy can flip from the heartrending to the hysterically funny. Parody has long been acknowledged as a strategy with political potential, given that it critiques the original text and can expose its ideological underpinnings. Parody can be subversive, critics point out, when it challenges the original by undermining the power structure on which the original is based.[31] In *Gone With the Wind*, the curtain episode demonstrates Scarlett's determination to deliver the illusion of glamour and prosperity, but in "Went With the Wind!" glamour is foregrounded as an illusion so obviously manufactured that the rods and pulleys poke out. With its recurring joke about how often the slave "Sissy" (Vicki Lawrence) is slapped by "Starlet," the sketch also exposes the racist violence upon which the original book and movie were structured.

Certainly the tropes of melodrama are ripe for parody—intense confrontations, sharp reversals of fortune, extremes of virtue and villainy, and emotional spectacle—a mode of storytelling which, as Linda Williams points out, is evident in multiple Hollywood genres from the war film to the sports movie, but which is often identified with "the woman's film" and with soap opera.[32] Historically, women have been drawn to these forms because they take women's problems seriously without positing romance and marriage as the happy-ending answer. Instead, romance, marriage, and the family are sites of conflict and anxiety in melodrama, and these stories often end sadly—if not at a deathbed, then with loss and stoic recognition that the contradictions of gender and heterosexuality can't be resolved.[33] Scarlett loses Rhett, Mildred Pierce loses her daughter, Norma Desmond loses her mind. *TCBS* parodies were especially attuned to these specifically gendered appeals and perils. The "Mildred Fierce" character is blindly enthralled by her rotten daughter Veda, who scoffs at her mother's successful business, "Mildred's Fatburgers." Not until Veda spells it out for her does Mildred finally realize that Veda is having an affair with Mildred's own husband. "Okay, okay, I don't have to have a brick fall on my head," Burnett's Mildred says. Immediately a half-dozen bricks fall out of the ceiling directly on her head. Similarly, the sketch "When My Baby Laughs at Me," a send-up of *When My Baby Smiles at Me* (1948), satirizes the long-suffering, masochistic heroine who, in this version, sings excruciating torch songs about her love for her no-good husband: "To stuff a man's turkey, to roast a man's meat/To kiss a man's boo boo, to kiss a man's feet/What else is a woman for?" Burnett croons.

Along the same lines, in a parody of the Gothic melodrama *Rebecca* (1940), Burnett plays the hapless heroine tortured by her repeated failure to match the elegance and beauty of her husband's first wife. *Rebecca* has long been a favorite "woman's film" for its exploitation of female insecurities about femininity, epitomized as the class-specific ability to be the mistress of the Manderley estate. Spoofing the torments endured by the heroine, as well as the horror-film genealogy of the Gothic, *TCBS*'s version has her sit down to dinner and lift a domed platter lid to find the talking head of the relentless Mrs. Danvers (Lawrence) on the plate, carping at her for her shortcomings. These sight gags and hyperpathetic song lyrics are played as broad comedy, but they point to the equally heavy-handed devices, emotional violence, and borderline grotesquery of "the woman's film." Burnett's biographer reports that as *TCBS* developed in the 1970s, Burnett "wanted to make a statement with her comedy," telling her staff she wanted sketches that had "something to say"[34]—not surprising, given the popularity of politically oriented sitcoms such as *All in the Family* (CBS 1971–1979) developed in that decade.

Burnett could play melodramatic heroines whose suffering is ludicrous and funny because of the close relationship between melodrama and comedy, as Rowe points out in her analysis of the heroines of melodrama and romantic comedy. Both narratives pivot around transgressive women who "desire too much" and act on these desires, she tells us. Thus the two narratives each contain potential versions of the other, given the threat of loss embedded in comedy and the failed happy endings implicit in melodrama.[35] While Rowe's argument aimed to direct feminist critical attention away from "the woman's film" and toward romantic comedy, her observations are particularly relevant to the film parodies of *TCBS*, which likewise reveal the comic potential in melodramatic scenarios.[36] As "Mildred Fierce," Burnett bluntly expresses the idyllic mother-daughter longing at the heart of maternal melodrama. "I'll pay off the mortgage and then we can spend the rest of our lives together just snuggling," she rhapsodizes to wicked Veda, who nearly vomits at the prospect. The humor of this exchange is also its horror; maternal melodrama rarely acknowledges the "happy ending" of the maternal fantasy— no less than symbiotic union with the daughter—or recognizes the daughter's revulsion about this possibility. Also, in *TCBS* parodies, the punishment of the transgressive woman is satirized or completely diverted. In "Raised to Be Rotten," *TCBS*'s version of *Born to Be Bad* (1950), the devious gold digger Christabel (Burnett) is finally driven out of the sumptuous home she tries to usurp, true to the grim ending of the original movie; but in the happier ending of the parody, she first pickpockets the master of the house, loads up all the fur coats she can carry on her back, and steals a strand of diamonds straight from the neck of her rival.

The "Went With the Wind!" sketch vividly foregrounds melodrama's punishment of women who defy traditional gender roles as well as melodrama's focus on the horrific demands of femininity and respectability. In the original book and film, Scarlett O'Hara's breathless flirtations are necessary to camouflage her gritty determination to get Rhett Butler's money, while she grudgingly allies herself with the saintly Melanie for the sake of respectability—the status given to women who know their place. But as Rowe points out, comedy too is a powerful mode for the excessive woman precisely because it can accommodate outrageous female behavior. In "Went with the Wind!" "Starlet" disguises neither her greed nor her contempt for polite society; as soon as she and "Rat" are pronounced husband and wife, she reaches into his pocket to pull out a wad of money. Confronted with Melanie's saccharine affection, "Starlet" rolls her eyes and says, "Why don't you just stick your head in the punchbowl? I'm sure it could use a little more sugar." "Went With the Wind!" also satirizes melodrama's punishment of the transgressive woman who refuses the feminine world of love and family. In a troubling episode in the original book and movie, Scarlett falls down the stairs and suffers a miscarriage just as she's about to find happiness with Rhett. "Went With the Wind!" ups the ante by having "Starlet" tumble twice, first accidentally punched by "Rat" and then deliberately shoved by Melanie—a "theater of cruelty" that presses the question of how often Scarlett/Starlet needs to be disciplined for her ambitions. Burnett's "Starlet" contorts herself into hilarious parodies of the Southern belle, but she also roils with anger that she's stuck with respectability and childbirth while "Rat" is able to go out and become a millionaire.

"Went With the Wind!" is the only *TCBS* parody that acknowledges the whiteness of classic melodramatic heroines, given the centrality of racism in the Mitchell book and 1939 film. Both original texts strikingly gloss over the violent effects of slavery—with one exception. The only time a slave is struck in *Gone With the Wind* is when Scarlett slaps skittish young Prissy across the face during the siege of Atlanta, an action supposedly acceptable as a standard way to stop hysteria. "Went With the Wind!" cannily hones in on this detail, casting Lawrence in whiteface as "Sissy," who is repeatedly slapped across the face by "Starlet," suggesting that her main job as a slave is to be slapped by a white woman. Eventually, "Sissy" realizes she can slap her own face with the same result. But "Sissy" is the triumphant character at the end. "Starlet" slams the door on "Rat" before he can finish his famous last line, and when she complains to "Sissy" that she doesn't know what his last words meant, "Sissy" delivers the line as her final rebuke to her clueless mistress. "Frankly, Starlet, I don't give a damn," she says, delivering a mighty smack to "Starlet's" face and giving Sissy/Prissy the last word and last slap in this slapstick version of the movie.

"THE FAMILY"

In "The Family" sketches, the horrors of "home" are manifest not through slapstick violence but through the chilling revelations of women's lives distorted by the constraints of gender, family, and imagination. Burnett delivers her most "savage" performances of femininity as the Texas blue-collar Eunice, her most complex character and the one that most closely draws from Burnett's personal life. In a 1976 interview given while she was still playing the part, Burnett describes herself as "very emotionally tied up" with Eunice: "I really, I think, draw her from my mother . . . this pitiful frustration of a woman who is basically smart, who yearns for the finer things of life but has held herself down by blaming circumstances."[37] Embittered and middle-aged, Eunice had imagined a career in Hollywood but instead is stuck in her hometown, married to Ed, a low-life hardware-store salesman (Korman), and—recalling Burnett's cantankerous Nanny—deeply tied to her nagging Mama (Lawrence). Eunice dresses like a drugstore-variety Southern belle, her hair crimped into rigid permanent waves and a floppy cloth flower tucked into her belt, but her flimsy masquerade as good wife and good daughter invariably collapses into bellowing arguments with Ed and especially with Mama, who never thought Eunice would amount to anything anyway. Eunice's resentments are cruelly magnified by her prettier, perkier sister Ellen (Betty White), who had always been Mama's favorite and has married into money. The sketches sometimes play the rivalry as broad comedy; in "Mama's Birthday," Ellen's gift to Mama is a mink shawl while Eunice gives her a fancy flyswatter from Ed's hardware store. But Burnett often performs the aggrieved sister with

6.3. Carol Burnett as Eunice Higgins, *The Carol Burnett Show* (1967–1978). CBS/ Photofest. © CBS.

far more subtlety; when she and Mama visit Ellen's fashionable house just as guests are about to arrive, Eunice settles her rear end into the plush sofa with an evil, self-satisfied grin, fully aware she is fouling the swank furniture just by sitting on it ("Ellen's Anniversary").

The class and gender failures coalesce; the unloved daughter and not-pretty sister, Eunice fumes at the second-rate status of her life. The fake wood of the new salad bowl given to her by Ed is so cheap, she yells, that "the Wishbone dressing eats right through it" ("Sorry"). David Marc describes "The Family" sketches as "surgical penetrations into the soul of supermarket coupon/hair curler/laundromat life in America."[38] The "soul" of that world is female: it will be Eunice, not Ed, who cuts the coupons and totes the clothes baskets to the laundromat, all the while dutifully "keeping herself up" with curled hair and white platform shoes. Eunice's complaint about the salad bowl is part of a longer tirade in that episode about the rotten deal she's gotten because she's a woman. "All you do is get me kitchen appliances because all I do around here is housework," she hollers at Ed. "You sit down and fill your stomach, and then you watch TV and fall asleep. Once in a while you might feel a bit romantic, and that's supposed to be some big *thrill* for me," she hoots, rolling her eyes and drawing out the word "thrill" in a mockery of ardor. Raving that she's criticized and tormented instead of being appreciated, Eunice begins to break down; her face first crumples and then blazes with pure rage as she starts tearing up sofa pillows. The seriousness of Eunice's anger and the tension of the scene is unbroken until Mama, who had been listening to all this in stunned silence, makes a flat diagnosis in her Texarkana twang. "You are really nuts," she says. "Somebody blew your pilot light out. You've got splinters in the windmills of your mind." Her deadpan, cliché-ridden assessment of Eunice's breakdown is both appalling and hilarious—an apt description of the overall kinetics of "The Family."

In a 1983 interview Burnett said there was nothing funny about the stories and dialogue of "The Family" skits and, in fact, a great deal that was "sad." The comedy, she claimed, lies purely in the exaggerated Texas drawls, the facial expressions, and the body language. The cast once did a straight read-through of one of the sketches without all the mugging, and the effect was "devastating."[39] Her anecdote reveals not only the thin line between the humor and the horrors of these sketches but also Burnett's aptitude for performing the "devastating" as comedy. Writers Dick Clair and Jenna McMahon created "The Family," but Burnett and Lawrence often discuss how they transformed the characters on their own, turning them into Texans and swapping roles, so that Lawrence, the younger actress, played the old woman while Burnett got the more complicated role of Eunice, inflecting her with the details of Louise Burnett, down to Eunice's tendency to reach for another beer when she's angry.[40] Eunice's drinking never escapes the critical eye of Mama. When Mama snipes at her about it—"That's your fourth beer today!"—Eunice turns on her with murderous fury. "And I'm gonna tell you something, I needed every one of 'em!" ("Mama's Accident").

Burnett's doubling as her own mother gave "The Family" sketches the emotional depth found in the comedy tradition of pathos that runs from Charlie Chaplin to Louis C.K. "We wrote Eunice as a thoughtless woman, but Carol put vulnerability into her," Clair said.[41] The farcical arguments sometimes slip into genuine anguish, and the skits often end on a jarring note. In "Friend from the Past," Eunice's fun afternoon with her divorced friend Midge (Joanne Woodward) is ruined by Mama and Ed. "I'm so sorry you gotta leave," Eunice says at the end to her departing friend, but Midge replies, "I'm so sorry you gotta stay." When Midge is gone, Eunice slowly and venomously knocks over a tray table, takes Ed's beer from his hands, and sits quietly drinking it, seething, her feet up on the coffee table. We realize that she is seeing herself as Midge has seen her, that she too is sorry she "gotta stay," and that Midge's life alone—which she admits is sometimes lonely—is happier than Eunice's life with her family. Marc succinctly pinpoints this dynamic of "The Family" when he writes about "The Restaurant" episode, in which a dinner at a posh establishment is so disastrous that Eunice, Ed, and Mama are asked to leave; the last shot shows Eunice pausing in the doorway: "Her look of mortification is pathetic and overpowering, an aesthetic counterweight to the slapstick gags of the sketch."[42]

The "counterweight" is the undertow of female anger and disappointment that makes these sketches far riskier, as comedy, than the movie parodies, which portray overblown scenarios—Tara, Manderley, inheritance plots—and grand passions that are easy targets for laughs. "The Family" instead pinpoints the horrors and cruelties of everyday life. In "The Anniversary," Eunice and Ellen argue about who will end up "stuck" with Mama as she ages, and in "The Attic," Ellen spitefully reveals to Eunice that her childhood pet rabbit didn't run away but became the "fried chicken" they'd had for dinner that night. In "The Flashback," we learn that Eunice and Ed "had to get married," in the parlance of the day, and in the same episode, Mama reveals that her own marriage and the birth of Eunice had come about in exactly the same way. The comedy resides in frumpy Mama and uptight Eunice sharing common stories of runaway lust, as well as the irony that Eunice had given herself to Ed ten years before as a way to escape the terrible mother who is still planted in Eunice's living room. But the sketch also delivers a mirthless glimpse of two generations of women wedged into lives they didn't choose. Eunice and Mama never resolve their cagey disputes, and the dysfunctional parenting continues with Eunice's animosity toward her own sons, whom she refers to as "no-neck monsters," recalling Mary Shelley's foundational imagining of horror as reproduction gone dreadfully wrong.

HORROR TO HILARITY: RE-IMAGINING THE FAMILY

The violence and ghastly moments of *TCBS* sketches were palatable for 1960s and 1970s audiences because they drew against the exuberant and upbeat tone of the show. The affectionate camaraderie of the comic ensemble—Burnett, Lawrence, Korman, and Tim Conway—was a huge factor in this dynamic; they clearly enjoyed working together and were having fun. Viewers looked forward to the moments when an especially outrageous line or gag by one of them succeeded in making another one laugh and disrupt the skit (as happens, for instance, in "Sorry" when Mama tells Eunice that someone blew her pilot light out, and Burnett struggles to keep her composure). In her NPR interview, Burnett said she wanted her own variety show so she could have a repertory company that was like a "family."[43] Ironically, then, the portrayals of abject dysfunction in "The Family" sketches were animated by Burnett's assembled kinship of tight-knit comic actors, beginning with Burnett's figurative adoption of Vicki Lawrence to play her little sister on the show. So while Eunice and Mama embodied the uncanny doubles of Burnett's mother and grandmother, squabbling about lost dreams and thwarted ambitions, another kind of doubling allowed Burnett to nurture a "sister" into stardom.

Most of all, as this suggests, Burnett could offer horror and heartbreak on *TCBS* because the show was anchored in the larger narrative of Burnett's stardom, in which the limitations of looks, home, and family were subsumed by the boundary-breaking generosity of comedy. The funny, alternative women's stories on the show were of a piece with the alternative kind of stardom Burnett embodied with her skewed relationship to glamour and class. The Burnett/Lawrence story, after all, is the feminist version of the catty melodrama *All About Eve* (1950), with its scheming ingénue usurping the desperate, aging star. No matter how "savagely" Burnett played out the horrors of home and family in the sketches, she bookended each episode of her variety show with homey personal touches, the opening chat with the audience and the sign-off tug of her left earlobe—the latter a tradition she had begun on *The Garry Moore Show* in the 1960s. It was a signal to her beloved Nanny back in California; Burnett had promised her a secret sign, though she widely shared the secret with audiences and journalists. Decades after Nanny's death, Burnett continued to use it as a farewell gesture on her television specials and other public appearances, acknowledging the importance of her grandmother in her life. The beauty of the gesture is its plainness or homeliness, signaling a family bond and also the singularity of Burnett's comedy and stardom.

NOTES

1. Carol Burnett, *This Time Together: Laughter and Reflection* (New York: Three Rivers, 2010), 81. The other woman who hosted a variety show was Dinah Shore, but *The Dinah Shore Show* (NBC 1951–1956), was discounted as a precedent, Burnett says, because it was "mostly music"—that is, it was built around Shore's stardom as a singer and was focused on its musical lineup, as opposed to the focus on comedy in Burnett's show.

2. Susan Horowitz cites the measurements quip as part of her argument about the importance of failed feminine ideals in Burnett's comedy in her essay on Burnett in *Queens of Comedy: Lucille Ball, Phyllis Diller, Carol Burnett, Joan Rivers, and the New Generation of Funny Women* (London and New York: Routledge, 1997), 68. Horowitz's essay on Burnett is the only extant analysis that takes Burnett's work seriously and notes the barely repressed anger of many of Burnett's sketch characters, especially in *TCBS* film parodies, which, she concludes, are always about "idealized femininity as a source of pain and humor" (77). Overall, she lauds Burnett's "willingness to expose the insecurities that plague most women" (81).

3. Susan Dworkin notes Burnett's "passion" for soap opera in "Carol Burnett: Getting On with It," *Ms.* 12, no. 3 (Sept. 1983): 90; and Burnett speaks in detail about *TCBS* film parodies and her love for classic movies in "Carol Burnett: The Fresh Air Interview," *Fresh Air* (NPR, Nov. 15, 2013): *Newspaper Source*, EBSCO-host. Burnett discusses the influence of her mother in "The Family" sketches and her growing confidence in participating in writing and production meetings, identifying herself as "women's lib" in Richard Meryman, "Carol Burnett's Own Story," *McCalls* 105 (1978): 167. J. Randy Taraborrelli, an unauthorized biographer who was granted extensive access to Burnett's family and colleagues, writes about Burnett's feminism in *Laughing Till It Hurts: The Complete Life and Career of Carol Burnett* (New York: William Morrow, 1988), 302–305, 365–366.

4. Harold Brodkey, "Why Is This Woman Funny?," *Esquire*, June 1972, 198.

5. Taraborrelli, *Laughing*, 241–242.

6. Pete Martin, "Backstage with Carol Burnett," *Saturday Evening Post* 235, no. 10 (Mar. 10, 1962): 36.

7. David Marc, "Carol Burnett: The Last of the Big-Time Comedy-Variety Stars," *Quarterly Review of Film and Video* 14, nos. 1–2 (1992): 151.

8. In their history of television, Barbara Moore, Marvin R. Bensman, and Jim van Dyke proclaim that "the variety show epitomized square, middle-class, Midwestern America, and it didn't survive television's makeover into something sophisticated, urban, and hip during the 1970s," glossing over *TCBS*'s solid ratings' successes for its entire run, ending in 1978. *Prime-Time Television: A Concise History* (Westport, CT: Praeger, 2006), 161. Yet as Terry Teachout has argued, *TCBS* had a "more modern feel" than other variety shows because of Bur-

nett's youthfulness and her roots in Broadway rather than vaudeville. "Saturday Night Strive," *Commentary* 136, no. 1 (2013): 72. Marc argues that Burnett carried the variety show genre many years past its prime, becoming, "an otherwise-withering genre's most popular and enduring star" ("Carol Burnett," 150). Also see Marc's account of the rise of the variety show and Burnett's earlier television experience leading up to *TCBS*, 149–152.

9. Horowitz, *Queens of Comedy*, 76.

10. Meryman, "Burnett's Own Story," 168.

11. Brodkey, "Why Is This Woman Funny?," 124–125.

12. Horror is often hilarious; William Paul describes how audience laughter during horror movies reveals the ambivalence, contradiction, and grotesquery that are the common ground of comedy and horror. See *Laughing Screaming: Modern Hollywood Horror and Comedy* (New York: Columbia University Press, 1994), 67–68. These are also the characteristics that make these genres both rich and risky for women, as decades of feminist scholarship on the horror film and on comedy have emphasized.

13. Freud's account of the uncanny emphasizes the ambivalent relationship between the *"heimlich"*—the familiar, belonging to the home—and *"unheimlich,"* the unfamiliar, demonstrating how the meanings of each are embedded in the other. "The Uncanny," in *The Collected Papers of Sigmund Freud*, ed. Philip Rieff and trans. Alix Strachey, 10:21–30 (New York: Collier, 1963). The uncanny, says Freud, often involves recurrence or involuntary return to a previous scene as well as the effect of the doppelganger or double (10:40–43), suggesting a relationship to parody. For Freud, the ultimate source of the uncanny is the ultimate home: female genitalia. When a man dreams of a familiar place where he has been before, "we may interpret the place as being his mother's genitals or her body" (10:51).

14. Ernest Havemann, "Only Girl Who Acts with Her Back and Front, Too: Carol Burnett," *Life*, Feb. 22, 1963, 87.

15. Kathleen Rowe (Karlyn), *The Unruly Woman: Gender and the Genres of Laughter* (Austin: University of Texas Press, 1995), 37.

16. Dworkin, "Carol Burnett," 43.

17. Linda Mizejewski, *Pretty/Funny: Women Comedians and Body Politics* (Austin: University of Texas Press, 2014), 3–6, 21–24; Dworkin, "Carol Burnett," 43.

18. John P. Shanley, "Carol Burnett Doubles on TV and Broadway," *New York Times*, Mar. 6, 1960; Havemann, "Only Girl Who Acts," 86; Taraborrelli, *Laughing*, 136. A 1976 article in the *Saturday Evening Post* describes an Australian actress who finally meets Burnett in person and gasps, "Why, she's beautiful!," having expected "a leering, glaring, howling, sneering, sniveling, puckering, smirking, wheezing, and whimpering" woman comic who plays extreme caricatures. Frederic Birmingham, "A Carol Is a Song Is a Burnett," *Saturday Evening Post*, Sept. 1976, 54.

19. Brodkey, "Why Is This Woman Funny?," 126.

20. Nora Ephron, "Carol Burnett, Cockeyed Optimist," *Good Housekeeping*, Oct. 1968, 74.

21. Meryman, "Burnett's Own Story," 126.

22. Ibid., 165.

23. "Carol Burnett," *Fresh Air*.

24. Carol Burnett, *One More Time: A Memoir* (New York: Random House, 2003), 116.

25. Havemann, "Only Girl Who Acts," 88–89.

26. Burnett played her as a recurring character on *TCBS*, sometimes sitting on her bucket to sing a sad song; in other numbers, she fantasizes about being a burlesque queen or showgirl and is magically transformed into elegant clothes and a role in a grandly choreographed dance. The latter numbers always end with the fantasy fading away and Charwoman humbly continuing her scrubbing and mopping, a startling reminder that Hollywood-style dreams are doomed to fizzle out.

27. Brodkey, "Why Is This Woman Funny?," 194.

28. John Simon, "Affectionately Yours," *New Yorker*, Nov. 11, 2002, 106. Burnett made the same restrained public response to her daughter Carrie Hamilton's struggles with drug addiction in the 1970s and early 1980s. Carrie went into recovery but then was diagnosed with lung cancer and died in 2002 before the premiere of *Hollywood Arms*, the play she'd written with her mother. In 2011 Burnett published *Carrie and Me: A Mother-Daughter Love Story* (New York: Simon and Schuster), taking control of the story as she had with events earlier in her life.

29. Both Birmingham, "A Carol," 56, and Havemann, "Only Girl Who Acts," 89, note the upbeat tone of her early descriptions of her childhood. The more graphic description appears in Meryman, "Burnett's Own Story," 165.

30. "Carol Burnett," *Fresh Air*. Burnett speaks of going to therapy to handle anger about her parents in Harry F. Waters, "A Comedy Comeback," *Newsweek*, June 18, 1990, 64.

31. See Linda Hutcheon's widely cited argument for the subversive potential of parody, *The Politics of Postmodernism*, 2nd ed. (New York and London: Routledge, 1989), 89–113. Also see Mary Ellen Brown's discussion of the specific appeals of parody for women, which includes Robert Stam's comment on the ability of parody to assume the "force" of the original. *Soap Opera and Women's Talk: The Pleasure of Resistance* (Thousand Oaks, CA: Sage, 1994), 136.

32. Linda Williams, *Playing the Race Card: Melodramas of Black and White from Uncle Tom's Cabin to O. J. Simpson* (Princeton, NJ: Princeton University Press, 2001), 15–17.

33. See Peter Brooks's widely cited analysis of the conventions of melodrama and the "melodramatic imagination," in *The Melodramatic Imagination: Balzac, Henry James, Melodrama, and the Mode of Excess* (New Haven, CT: Yale University Press, 1976), 1–23. Feminist film theory in the 1970s and 1980s was particularly interested in melodrama and the woman's film as key sites in women's culture. See Christine Gledhill's summary of the prime lines of inquiry on this topic, "The Melodramatic Field: An Investigation," in *Home Is Where the Heart Is: Studies in Melodrama and the Woman's Film*, ed. Christine Gledhill (London: British Film Institute, 1987), 5–39. Ien Ang points out melodrama's appeal to the experience of women in patriarchy who are faced with unending contradictions and unsolvable conflicts and suggests that feminism itself carries a melodramatic "edge," featuring women who refuse to give up when faced with "the yawning gap between desire and reality," in "Melodramatic Identifications: Television Fiction

and Women's Fantasy," in *Television and Women's Culture: The Politics of the Popular*, ed. Mary Ellen Brown (London: Sage 1990), 88.

34. Taraborrelli, *Laughing*, 318.

35. Kathleen Rowe (Karlyn), "Comedy, Melodrama and Gender: Theorizing the Genres of Laughter," in *Classical Hollywood Comedy*, eds. Kristine Brunovska Karnick and Henry Jenkins (New York: Routledge, 1995), 49–51.

36. Along the same lines, in her study of soap opera fans, Mary Ellen Brown finds that frequent laughter is the response of even the most ardent devotees, given the genre's bizarre plot twists and outrageous character behavior. Far from watching soaps "in dreary silence," says Brown (133), fans are likely to approach these texts with a sense of play that is ambivalent, acknowledging the absurdities but remaining seriously invested in the characters and stories. See *Soap Opera and Women's Talk*, 133–152. On *TCBS*, soap operas were parodied in the sketch series "As the Stomach Turns," the title of which referenced the long-running soap opera *As the World Turns* (CBS 1956–2010). "Stomach Turns" played on the general sensationalism and outlandish plots of soap operas but was not, overall, as clever as the film parodies, which targeted specific details and characters of movies.

37. Meryman, "Burnett's Own Story," 167.

38. Marc, "Carol Burnett," 155.

39. Dworkin, "Carol Burnett," 91.

40. For details of how Burnett and Lawrence took on these characters and made them their own, see Horowitz, *Queens of Comedy* (77), Taraborrelli, *Laughing* (318–321), and Meryman, "Burnett's Own Story" (167). During her appearance at the ceremony for Burnett's Mark Twain Prize, Lawrence recollects that she and Burnett established the tone and Texas accents of their characters when they stopped in the ladies room together before the first read-through of the script. "Carol Burnett: The Kennedy Center Mark Twain Prize," PBS, Nov. 24, 2013.

41. Taraborrelli, *Laughing*, 318.

42. Marc, "Carol Burnett," 155.

43. "Carol Burnett," *Fresh Air*.

CHAPTER 7

LILY TOMLIN: QUEER SENSIBILITIES, FUNNY FEMINISM, AND MULTIMEDIA STARDOM

SUZANNE LEONARD

I always wanted my comedy to be more embracing of the species rather than debasing of it.
LILY TOMLIN, *METROWEEKLY* INTERVIEW, 2006

BEGINNING WITH THE highly celebrated characters she created for the television variety show *Laugh-In* (NBC 1969–1973), Lily Tomlin has for over forty years held a central position in the history of women in comedy. A popular biography of the comedian is tellingly titled *Lily Tomlin: Woman of a Thousand Faces*, a sentiment that bespeaks her uncanny ability to so thoroughly transform her body through gesture and voice that she appears virtually unrecognizable. Tomlin's extraordinary talents have been on display in a dizzying array of media formats, including stand-up routines, stage and cabaret shows, comedy television specials, recordings, documentaries, caper films, romantic comedies, primetime television dramas, and animated children's series. Despite these extreme variations, Tomlin's overriding modus operandi is both stable and abiding: she embodies quirky outsiders who nevertheless have much to convey about the establishment. As Suzanne Lavin writes, Tomlin's is a comedy of "satiric substance."[1] This sensibility has, no doubt, been fueled by the extratextual significance of Tomlin's personal life: a lesbian comedian whose sexuality was an open secret long before such identities were culturally embraced, Tomlin's career has been underwritten by her longtime professional and personal partnership with Jane Wagner, with whom she has collaborated on much of her comedic material.

Tomlin's long-spanning career has been punctuated by a range of performative clusters that alternately anticipate, echo, and emphasize American feminist thought since the 1960s. Specifically, this chapter analyzes Tomlin's signature personas, one-woman shows, and iconic film appearances, mapping her storied career along a trajectory that includes the onset of second-wave feminism, the development of gay rights activism, and the mainstreaming of both of these movements. Tomlin's early performances presage feminist and queer sensibilities, and her later ones continue to register these commitments. While few of her characterizations could accurately be labeled feminist, Tomlin's performances nevertheless defamiliarize gender norms in such a way as to render these conventions strange, objectionable, and even at times absurd. Specifically, her assemblage of varied identity performances reinforces the notion that genders and social identities take heterogeneous forms, an observation that frequently results in biting social critique. In the process of calling for gender and sexual equality, Tomlin likewise indicts corporate greed, cultures of surveillance, overconsumption, pollution, intolerance, and the abuses of power that tend to stymie social justice and civic progress. Her comedy promotes views that are inclusive and forward-thinking, and she elegantly combines trenchant commentary with humanistic warmth.

ONE RINGY-DINGY: CHARACTER SKETCH AND SOCIAL CRITIQUE

Tomlin's signature personas—eccentric women (and even children) who revel in their idiosyncrasies—both reveal and at times belie her position as an activist. A performer who uses comedy to convey the constrictions of living in a highly gendered world, Tomlin's social commentary repeatedly takes the form of showcasing the inanities of normative ways of thinking. Tomlin's myriad characters—which run the gamut from housewives to the homeless, and now number in the fifties[2]—range from childish to zany to whip smart. All, however, tend to elevate the minutiae of women's lives to material for investigation and insight. Many also maintain highly critical perspectives of institutionalized authority, regardless of whether that authority rests with something as overriding as patriarchy or as quotidian as an overbearing parent.

Well respected for her chameleon-like versatility, Tomlin immerses herself fully in her characters rather than engaging in cheeky impersonation, and often (though not always) transforms herself without the accoutrements of clothing or makeup. Describing her technique and the sort of personas she creates, Tomlin has said that "my comedy is actual life with the slightest twist or exaggeration," adding, "I construct a compressed accuracy, a character essence that is as true and real as I can get it. . . . I know they are out there somewhere. I just imitate them."[3] Tomlin's verisimilitude likewise informs the widely held perception that she is an artist with a deeply humanist bent. When Tomlin was awarded the distinguished Kennedy Center Mark Twain Prize for American Humor in 2003, the prize included the following description: "Her comedy is meaningful because, like Twain's, it expresses truths we already recognize unconsciously, and it allows us to embrace our frailties without shame or embarrassment. . . . Lily Tomlin's communication with her characters creates an undeniable intimacy with her audiences, giving everyone a feeling of connectedness in the process."[4] Such intimacy and connection has been her abiding legacy.

Tomlin likewise specializes in what biographer Jeff Sorenson calls "the forgotten, unglamorous, lost souls,"[5] and her characters routinely exist at the margins of society—one of her most abject, Trudy, is a bag lady. Tomlin has also portrayed an angsty teenage runaway, a disillusioned feminist, a male lounge singer, a quadriplegic, and an opinionated prostitute. Conveying respect for characters who are seldom at the center of cultural discourse, Tomlin expresses a philosophy grounded in a sense of empathy. As she has said, "I don't necessarily admire them, but I do them all with love. After all, in private, we're all misfits."[6] Her partner, Jane Wagner, with whom Tomlin created a number of these personas, characterizes Tomlin's ethos thus: "Lily is after something beyond formulas—not sketches, not naturalism, not black comedy. Call it maybe docu-comedy, something that reveals human nature—absurd, touching, grotesque, and overwhelming."[7] Despite her tendency to afford her characters at least some degree of sympathy, Tomlin nevertheless has an uncanny ability to satirize them in service of making larger political points.

This interest in drawing out the larger sociocultural implications of her character's foibles is perhaps best evidenced by the persona for whom Tomlin is the most famous—Ernestine the telephone operator. Tomlin created this character when she joined the cast of *Laugh-In* in late 1969, and Ernestine has had considerable longevity as a cultural icon since that time. Sporting a tight forties hairdo and a gussied-up wardrobe, Ernestine blissfully lacks awareness of her annoying quirks, particularly her penchant for the sort of doublespeak characteristic of customer service. "Have I reached the party to whom I am speaking?" she asks, without self-consciousness. The nosy spin-

7.1. Ernestine, the inquisitive telephone operator, *Laugh-In* (1969–1973). NBC/ Photofest. © NBC.

ster, who often snorts her way through a conversation, perfectly en-capsulates Tomlin's admission that she likes playing characters who "don't fit in, but think they do."[8] Ernestine registers as both charm-ingly naïve ("you'll pay when what freezes over?") and yet inappro-priately emboldened ("Do the Mr. and Mrs. sleep together? Well, pre-tend you have to check a wire. Go take a look.")[9] As this last quote illustrates, Ernestine's sexual repression informs her characteriza-tion, and Tomlin has been explicit about the relationship between this reality and Ernestine's bullying tactics. Describing how she cre-ated the character, Tomlin notes that Ernestine's threats are "an ex-pression of her own highly repressed sexuality. That made her click, in my mind. . . . Suddenly, without planning it, I physicalized her. My whole body drew in. My mouth pinched in, and the voice came from her nose, and the laugh emerged as a snort, because her face wouldn't allow her to really laugh. Suddenly, there she was, hiding behind her switchboard, the ultimate obscene phone-caller!"[10] Tomlin's insight into the physicality of characterization confirms how completely and thoroughly she embodies the people she portrays and how attuned she is to their (often disordered) psychology.

An unabashed apologist for the phone company, Ernestine's carte blanche access to personal details of her customer's bank accounts, phone records, and financial holdings speaks not merely to her sense of entitlement but also, more suggestively, to her employer's status as a behemoth monopoly. Frequently, her one-sided conversations expose what frustrated customers long suspected—the phone company's power ensures them immunity from criticism or oversight: "We realize that, every so often, you can't get an operator, or for no apparent reason your phone goes out of order, or perhaps you get charged for a call you didn't make. We don't care!"[11] Likewise, while customer intimidation constitutes a job requirement (one with which Ernestine happily complies), the underlying critique of such strong-arming underscores both the hubris of a faceless bureaucracy and the inevitability of its power: "Mr. Veedle, there's no reason on earth for you to feel personally persecuted. We may be the only phone company in town, but we screw everybody!"[12] Ernestine's false enthusiasm only underscores her sadism; gleefully, she uses her professional position to assert authority that is likely lacking in her personal life.

One particularly prescient skit, included on the album "This Is a Recording," from 1971, illustrates *Time* magazine's description of Ernestine as "the Mussolini of the switchboard."[13] Ernestine has sparred with a number of famous men (including Henry Kissinger, Frank Sinatra, President Nixon, and Gore Vidal), and here she chastises J. Edgar Hoover (pronounced by Ernestine as "Jedger") for "some of the abuses of your instrument," namely the fact that he and his agents have engaged in wiretapping. Acknowledging without compunction that she has access to this information because the phone company has been spying on *him*, she (quite unselfconsciously) reminds Hoover that it is a crime to use a phone for annoying or harassing purposes. This litigious tone shifts noticeably, however, once Ernestine admits that "There's no reason for your people to skulk about, electronically speaking. You can get all the information you need from us. Probably a lot more accurately too." Ernestine's transition from moral arbiter to accomplice highlights again the abuses of totalizing power and serves as a now-chilling premonition of the 2013 NSA scandal, where Edward Snowden revealed to the American public a secret government operation that quietly collected troves of phone data. While Ernestine's comedic intervention nodded to the historic abuses of power advanced under a notoriously calculating and vindictive FBI director, the alliance she suggests between government surveillance and corporate malfeasance has proven disturbingly accurate in the ensuing years.

Tomlin's interest in criticizing the misuse of power also frequently reveals the gendered nature of these violations, an observation that circumscribes Tomlin's characterization of Mrs. Judy Beasley, the buttoned-up housewife from Calumet City, Illinois, who serves as a product tester. Always meticulously coiffed, Mrs. Beasley is both defined and constrained by her attempt to approximate an idealized femininity, and Tomlin is vocally critical of how patriarchal norms contribute to producing repressed women who cannot express their true feelings: "I see these very stiff, inhibited women who move and act so much like my character Mrs. Beasley, and I think it's criminal," Tomlin said in 1977. "This is what the culture has done to a lot of women—made them so uptight, so uncertain, so thwarted. It's a matter of power and powerlessness."[14] This blatantly feminist critique is made manifest in skits such as the one where Mrs. Beasley peddles Gr-r-r Detergent, during which she painfully illustrates the strain of trying to maintain a perfect façade, as normative femininity demands.[15] Extoling the virtues of this household product in a clearly scripted introduction to a televised commercial, Mrs. Beasley reveals that the detergent contains an additive called "carnivore," which seeks out and gobbles up stains like a "tiny piranha fish," a comment which provides the first hint of her unrest.

Mrs. Beasley's modulated movements and understated affect quickly give way to a staggering realization. Declaring that she will test the detergent on her own family laundry, she proceeds to wade through dirty diapers and grass-stained chinos, only to discover lipstick stains on her husband's collar. In a phrase that uncomfortably blurs the lines between the psychological rupture created by this sight and the properties of the detergent, she announces, "Gr-r-r! You only need half a cup because, because it's concentrated. See, um, you can actually feel it coming on. For weeks and weeks now, he's been so indifferent, no matter how hard I tried to please him." The slippage between Mrs. Beasley's emotions at discovering her husband's infidelity and her descriptors of the detergent continue, as does her escalating indignation, when she comments: "Because it's concentrated you save money because you use less and less, and less time at home, all those nights he said he was going bowling." In this clever play on words, Mrs. Beasley's attitude toward her husband's selfish and self-serving betrayal conflates with the properties of the detergent—conveniently titled to reflect her rising anger. Frustrated that she has been left alone every night "like some kind of fool," she proclaims, "Well, the hell with you" and rips up a negligee he gave her as an anniversary gift. The skit ends with another stunning revelation: she tells the washing machine, an appliance that has become anthropomorphized into her husband, "Well, you want to know something? Billy isn't yours!" As Patricia Nelson maintains, "What we are watching . . . is the collapse of a regular woman's understanding of her life," a destruction punctuated by the sudden announcement that Mrs. Beasley may have some secrets of her own.[16] Initially appearing on Tomlin's 1973 television special, *The Lily Tomlin Show*, the Gr-r-r Detergent dramatization reinforces the feminist movement's scathing indictment of domesticity, a critique that was by then gaining traction in the mainstream press.[17]

Tomlin's flatness at the beginning of her skit suggests that she employs an acting technique akin to Brechtian distanciation (a strategy meant to alienate audiences and make them think about a performance's content), which also anticipates experimental feminist film texts such as Martha Rosler's *Semiotics of the Kitchen* (1975) and Chantel Ackerman's *Jeanne Dielman* (1975). In both films a woman appears entirely within the space of the domestic, and an understated affect masks a seething rage, a dislocation expressed through sound and gestures rather than through explanation. Rosler's piece registers initially as an ordinary primer on kitchen utensils such as eggbeaters, forks, and graters, until one realizes that each demonstration includes ineluctably jarring sounds and definitively hostile motions that include chopping, pounding, and stabbing. The final subset of the sequence, "xyz," in turn, features a series of slashing motions that betray a frightening suggestion of self-immolation.

In Chantel Ackerman's three hour and fifteen minute opus, protagonist Jeanne Dielman, a middle-class widow who is also a prostitute, engages in a set of pedestrian domestic chores over the course of three days. These include cleaning, tending to her teenage son, and cooking potatoes—all virtually without dialogue—as she works in the interstices of the day to entertain johns who periodically arrive at her door. Slowly documenting her increasingly disordered routine, the film climaxes with her quiet and unexpected murder of one of the johns. All three of these representations point not only to the cathartic power of anger but also to the fact that an awareness of gender inequity fuels these women's brimming rage. Contextualizing this observation in philosophical terms, Elizabeth Spelman explains that subordinate groups have been discouraged from looking positively or clearly at their anger, and hence, "The systematic denial of anger can be seen as a mechanism of subordination, and the existence and expression of anger as an act of insubordination."[18] Together with these other examples of feminist expression, Mrs. Beasley's mounting shock and cruel awareness signify that anger over women's mistreatment in the domestic sphere can be a productive beginning for consciousness raising.

It is perhaps not incidental that Mrs. Beasley rises *to* political activism in the social satire *The Incredible Shrinking Woman* (1981), a film written by Jane Wagner in which Tomlin plays both the central character, cheerful housewife Pat Kramer, as well as Beasley. Both live in the aptly named California suburb Tasty Meadows, a plasticized and pastel-laden land populated by product-dependent inhabitants. After being sprayed with toxic perfume marketed by her husband, an advertising executive, as well as enduring chemical exposure to various other household products framed as being as banal as they are nefarious, Pat inexplicably finds herself shrinking, to the point where she begins living in a doll's house and suffers assaults by household pets and full-sized dolls. (Though the conceit is somewhat preposterous, it should be said that *The Incredible Shrinking Woman*'s environmental critique has proven both prescient and inspirational. Todd Haynes's 1995 film *Safe*, about a privileged California housewife who begins suffering from a full-scale chemical insensitivity, mined similar territory to much greater critical fanfare.)

The notion of the shrinking housewife as a symbol for the shifting status of modern women in the 1980s is, to the film's credit, self-consciously acknowledged as a rather obvious metaphor. In one sequence, a barrage of television commentators speculate on whether Pat has shrunk because "the role of the modern housewife has become increasingly less significant" or because "her role as homemaker was belittling when she looked at herself through society's eyes." Pat's shrinking also quite explicitly comments on the punishing nature of domestic labor, as encapsulated by the fact that Pat's out-of-control children and selfish if generally well-meaning husband typically run roughshod over her. Her newly diminutive stature underscores this general invisibility and inconsequential position except as provider of goods and services (buying food, cooking dinner, servicing her husband sexually), and her shrinking, not incidentally, makes it all but impossible for her to perform these functions. Indeed, the film explicitly foregrounds these deficits with sequences that depict Pat's failed attempts to make breakfast, discipline her children, or connect erotically with her husband. Once sidelined in this way, she has very little value in the family, a plot point that underlines the extent to which women are the casualty of a system that demands their instrumentalization.

This critique of gendered domesticity is further accentuated by the fact that Pat employs a Hispanic domestic worker in her home, Concepcion, who is at first roundly ignored by Pat and her neighbors, but whose role becomes more fraught when Pat becomes increasingly incapable of caring for her house or family. In the wake of Pat's shrinking, Concepcion begins dressing more provocatively, falls prey to the bribes of corporate forces trying to use Pat's illness to their own advantage, and approaches her domestic duties with thoughtless self-involvement to the point where, when Pat falls into the garbage disposal, Concepcion's failure to notice the slip imperils Pat's life. According to Chadwick Roberts, this reversal of fortune between the two women is meant to be read satirically, as a send-up of white privilege and the way it has historically exploited racial divisions of labor. He argues, "It is because domestic womanhood has for so long been defined directly through the labor of women of color that Pat's 'bad-white-body' betrayal is so ironic. She is treated as garbage in her own home and must watch as her white privilege follows her down the drain."[19] The film hence highlights how mythologies of perfect domesticity are troublingly premised on both gendered and racialized inequities.

Though it features a series of outlandish narrative twists—which include a plot by a gaggle of doctors and scientists to use Pat's blood to shrink enemies and ensure world domination and a rescue by an enormous ape who frees Pat from captivity in a hamster cage—*The Incredible Shrinking Woman* nevertheless presents a piercing indictment of what Roberts calls "the oppressive powers of consumer capitalism and patriarchy, and the absurdities of medical and consumer science."[20] By targeting the overbearing nature of male corporate power, the film unveils the entirely amoral nature of competitive consumer capitalism as well as its willingness to sacrifice human health on the altar of profit. For example, despite the fact that

Pat receives decisive, if again absurd, confirmation that her affliction can be traced to a combination that includes "tap water, the flu shot, the perfume, the glue, the solvent, your bubble bath, talcum powder, shampoo, hair conditioner, scenting lotion, hand lotion, mouthwash, hairspray, breath spray, feminine hygiene spray . . ." (and the list goes on), at the urging of her husband and his boss, she decides against revealing this information when she appears on *The Mike Douglas Show*, and does not warn the public that they may be similarly imperiled. Coupling Pat's restrained and demure behavior in this instance with the film's opening scene, where a male announcer with a microphone forces grocery-shopping women to praise the virtues of a clearly processed and chemically laden cheese spread, Sara Hosey contends that the film foregrounds "male control of female speech."[21] Although women frustrate men by saying things that men find inappropriate, she argues that "men retain the symbol and tool of public speech as embodied in the microphone and ultimately decide which speech is valid or acceptable."[22] This observation that women lack vocal or institutional power resonates throughout the film, as Pat's classically feminine virtues of self-abnegation are literalized in her shrinkage. In effect, her diminished body suggests that when women's voices become eviscerated, so do they.

Though Pat never raises her voice in protest, Mrs. Beasley does. Mrs. Beasely initially appears in the film peddling an Avon-like product named Flo-Naturalle (supposedly a natural alternative to more virulent substances) and, in keeping with her general status as a busybody, chastising a neighbor for letting her dog poop outside and not cleaning it up. Pat's unfortunate situation spurs Mrs. Beasley to more worthy causes. As she pushes a cart carrying a minuscule Pat through the supermarket, Mrs. Beasley asserts, "This is chemical warfare and I want to show you what we are up against." Reading off incomprehensible labels that confirm the unnatural composition of all the processed food in the store, all the while fending off gawkers enthralled with the shrinking woman's appearance there, Mrs. Beasley yells, "Don't you have something you want to shop for? A little poison maybe?" Though the over-the-top nature of the film's plotline may undercut its environmental critique, in fact it does dialogue in a rather prophetic way with widening concerns over the relationship between processed and genetically modified food (the province of agribusiness), the pantheon of potentially hazardous chemicals that comprise household and everyday products, and rising health afflic-

7.2. Bag lady Trudy, from the opening scenes of *The Search for Signs of Intelligent Life in the Universe* (1991).

tions. Attesting to the film's broader interest in the extent to which business interests eclipse the well-being of the average person, Tomlin has commented that "the movie is a valid response to a world in which corporate superpowers get bigger and bigger while the consumer feels progressively smaller and more helpless."[23] Tomlin's articulation of this sobering reality again speaks to the larger targets of her comedy, which in this case include institutionalized patriarchy, corporate greed, and blind conformity. In keeping with Tomlin's critical ethos, the next sections examine how such insights fuel critiques of sexual and gender norms and foreground a queer critical perspective.

SHAPE-SHIFTING, MARGINALIZED PERSONAS, AND THE POWER OF VOICE: TOMLIN'S QUEER CULTURAL POLITICS

In a 2003 profile of Tomlin in *Lesbian News*, she recounts being a guest on *The Tonight Show* with Johnny Carson in the 1970s. Faced with his comment, "You're not married. Don't you ever want to have children?" Tomlin politely told him no. When his incredulity prompted continued prodding on the subject, she bit back: "Well, who has custody of yours?" Tomlin knew full well, of course, that Carson had children by his first wife and was by this time on his third or fourth marriage. In the profile she remembers that in "1973, it was not even considered normal to say you didn't want children."[24] Tomlin's willingness to articulate the unpopular, and to both buck and question conventional feminine expectations, has been central to her scripting as a queer comedian. This attribution has been developed in part as a result of her personal life, but also, more importantly perhaps, in conjunction with her offbeat characterizations. For years, in fact, she and Wagner were simply referred to in the press as creative collaborators and roommates. (The couple did marry in 2014, however, after forty-two years together.)

Though she has long been a celebrity, Tomlin's public appearances neither confirmed nor denied her homosexuality; instead, they illustrated precisely the sort of shape-shifting so palpably evident in her professional output. On the one hand, Tomlin has never shied away from gay causes or resisted alignment with gay discourses. She sat for a long interview in 1976 with gay film critic Vito Russo, for example, which was then published in the *Advocate*. She appeared in the HBO movie *And the Band Played On* (1993) as a health official negotiating the AIDS epidemic, a politically conscious film intended to draw attention to the disease's sidelining by government officials and a mostly indifferent public. Tomlin also provided a voiceover narration for *The Celluloid Closet* (1995), a tour de force documentary based on Russo's book of the same name. The ambitious and now landmark film examines gay and lesbian characters and themes in the history of American cinema and identifies how such characters were coded, demonized, marginalized, or made to appear as victims.[25] To give a sense of the liminal space that Tomlin's sexuality has nevertheless occupied for the bulk of her career, consider this: in another interview with the *Advocate* in 2005, the preamble notes that though she has been active in promoting gay causes, "this interview marks one of the few times she's ever spoken with the gay media."[26]

Tomlin also tells a stunning narrative that well encapsulates her attitude towards public displays of sexual identity, a tale that explores how these energies ultimately translate back into her comedic work. As she describes it in the *Advocate*, in 1975 she was making the album *Modern Scream* and received a call from her publicist saying that if she was willing to come out, *Time* magazine would put her on the cover. She refused, citing her discomfort with the idea of being typed as a gay celebrity, and recalls that during that period, such topics were simply not discussed publically.[27] She did, however, incorporate a telling sequence in her album, where Tomlin plays an interviewer from an entertainment magazine who is interviewing the real life Lily Tomlin. As she explains it:

> So in the interview there's a little hunk in that album where the interviewer says, "In your recent movie"—this was not long after *Nash-*

ville; I was just generic, but most people would think of that film—
"how did it feel to play a heterosexual?" "I've seen these women all
my life, I know how they walk, I know how they talk," that kind of
stuff, see? Because that was my answer to the magazine making that
approach to me.[28]

As this story illustrates, Tomlin provocatively turned the tables on
the mainstream press in her comedic work, suggesting that heterosexuality was a performance she had studied and mimicked. (In *Nash-
ville* Tomlin poignantly portrays a lonely, gospel-singing mother of
two deaf children who has a brief, disappointing affair with a wom-
anizer.) As Jennifer Reed writes, the pretend interview sequence
"challenges the inevitability of heteronormativity."[29] Incisively anticipating Judith Butler's work on gender performativity, Tomlin's employment of comedy as rejoinder bespeaks how gender critique can
take more theoretical forms.

Traces of Tomlin's status as a "queer performer" can, in this regard, be best teased out in comedic output that denaturalizes heterosexuality, sensibilities that link as well to Tomlin's feminism. In her
book-length investigation of Tomlin's work with Wagner, Reed explains, "The interrogation of that which appears natural, the shifting
between categories, the opening up to what is beneath the normative,
and doing that with the consciousness of gendered power relations, is
the life force that queer feminism offers to dominant culture."[30] Studies of Tomlin's status as a queer performer have tended to focus, as
Reed does, on her one-woman shows, all of which have been created
in collaboration with Wagner. In each, Tomlin adopts multiple roles,
shifting between ages, genders, sexualities, voices, and mannerisms.
Such techniques not only demonstrate the multiplicity of experience
but also suggest a refusal to be bound by identity categories.

Tomlin's 1977 one-woman Broadway show *Appearing Nitely*, for
instance, features a collection of monologues where Tomlin enacts
fifteen characters without the aid of set, props, or costume changes,
and yet depicts a stunningly disparate array of personas in terms of
their age, gender, abilities, and socioeconomic status. Describing the
effect on the audience of encountering so many personalities in such
short order, Reed explains that "it moves us away from the construction of a unified or even essentialized version of self, and toward a
fragmented and multiple sense of self."[31] As Reed has argued elsewhere, Tomlin's one-woman shows disrupt the idea of "woman" as a
stable signifier, and her technique is aligned in this way with queer

and lesbian feminists, as well as with feminists of color, who sought to destabilize fixed categorizations. Quoting Butler, Reed suggests that Tomlin's performances are part of the larger shifting discourse that worked to "render it [the concept of 'woman'] as 'a site of permanent political contest.'"[32] Tomlin's oeuvre hence denaturalizes identity as a fixed categorization and suggests that generative insights accompany the process of plumbing the vagaries of selfhood.

Such destabilizations can be seen amongst different characters in *Appearing Nitely*, as evidenced in a sequence with Crystal, a wheelchair-bound quadriplegic who nevertheless considers herself superior to those she calls the "walkies." Though she knows that bystanders pity her condition, Crystal's fearless ethos prompts her to reject such lamentations. She cheerfully recounts, "One year seven months now I'm on the road coast to coast, all by wheelchair. When I get to California I will go hang gliding off Big Sur. I will be the first quadriplegic to do so, possibly the last."[33] Crystal does not, however, sugarcoat her situation; instead, she soberly reminds audiences, "Each morning twelve million of us slam our dead old bony asses into a wheelchair and sit. When I say sit, I mean sit. Might as well. Once you get to where you need to go you can't get through the door anyway. Too narrow. I had a friend, got caught."[34] Presenting a clear challenge to ableism, portrayals such as Crystal's evince queer sensibilities in that they decenter normative categorization. As Suzanne Lavin explains, Tomlin and Wagner focus on characters "whose positions as misfits cast a fascinating light on what we consider normal. From outside the mainstream, these figures see into the hypocrisy, greed and intolerance that mark the dominant culture."[35] As Crystal does, a number of Tomlin's characters remind audiences that many bodies reside outside standardized parameters, yet the world provides few accommodations for difference.

Tomlin and Wagner's play *The Search for Signs of Intelligent Life in the Universe* (originally performed in 1986, adapted into a film in 1991, and reprised on Broadway in 2000) likewise typifies their interest in the pedagogical power of the offbeat character who challenges conventional norms, described by Tomlin as "the person who doesn't do what we're all supposed to do, yet is perfectly confident in nonconformity."[36] Narrated by Trudy (a character who has a number of similarities to *Appearing Nitely*'s Tess), a creative consultant–turned-bag lady, *The Search for Signs of Intelligent Life in the Universe* provides both the audience and Trudy's inquisitive alien acolytes with a tour through the cosmic mysteries of humanity. Trudy exhibits multiple eccentricities—for one, she wears an umbrella hat that she claims picks up snatches of people's lives and conversations, which provides a loose organizing structure for the play writ large. Trudy is outside the dominant culture and yet recalls a time when she was squarely within it; she credits her vision with a series of extraordinary inventions, including the color scheme for Howard Johnson's, laugh tracks, and plastic goose eggs that hold panty hose. "Trudy offers the audience a view of life from the margins," affirms Jill Dolan. "Through her encounters with aliens, the audience sees life on earth from an estranged Brechtian perspective that leaves nothing safely ensconced in common sense."[37] Trudy's status as outside normative construction (and particularly normative sexuality) is in turn key to the production's queer sensibility: as Reed argues, Trudy is queer in that she is "characterized without reference to a man or desire for a man," and hence she "breaks the rules of heteronormativity."[38] Much like Tomlin's real-life disinterest in proclaiming herself a spokeswoman for a single cause, Trudy stands slightly outside her community and brings a critical perspective to its happenings and populations.

Tomlin's queer politics also connect more broadly to her interest in social justice. She refuses to privilege one age, race, religion, or creed above another, or as Patricia Nelson persuasively claims: "The use of character-based comedy . . . allowed the familiar face of Lily Tomlin to be poor, rich, heterosexual, homosexual, from Middle America, from Los Angeles, black and white—even as the comforting familiarity of Tomlin's presence told her viewers that this difference, even when it was scary or sad, didn't need to be alienating."[39] Tomlin's relentless commitment to, in Nelson's words, commenting "intersectionally about gender, race, poverty and the environment as well as sexuality," identify her as "America's conscience on matters of difference and compassion."[40] Crucially, Tomlin fights this battle in the realm of her characters, offering a comedic vision less dependent on identity politics than on an expansive view of humanity. The final section of this chapter examines how this ethos informs a sensibility that promotes gender equity in service of all.

FEMALE CHARACTERS AND THE SEARCH FOR A POPULAR FEMINISM

In a clear dressing down of phallic potency, Tomlin's five-year-old character Edith Ann once referenced a boy who takes his "peenie"

7.3. The iconic trio: Jane Fonda, Lily Tomlin, and Dolly Parton in *9 to 5* (1980).

out at school, describing her reaction with a dismissive, "Its not so interesting. . . . I've seen it lots of times." This inclination to mock the hubris of male power in fact provides a through-line for Tomlin's work, and Tomlin's unwavering feminism has been a staple of her public appearances. As many profiles about the comedian repeat, she bravely walked off the set of *The Dick Cavett Show* in 1972, when actor Chad Everett referred to his wife as his "property"—along with his horse and dog. Speaking to *Lesbian News* in 2003, Tomlin commented, "I think the basic, real premise of feminism . . . is really humanism, to me."[41] As this comment suggests, feminist ideals underpin Tomlin's oeuvre.

This commitment is perhaps nowhere more blatantly expressed than in the 1980 film *9 to 5*, which Tomlin stars in with Jane Fonda (another feminist icon) and Dolly Parton. While *9 to 5* disperses its points of female identification amongst three characters (instead of having Tomlin play all the roles), the film nevertheless employs the same sort of large-scale critique evidenced in Tomlin's one-woman shows. As Karen Hollinger observes, "The film's female characters represent three different types of working-class women,"[42] characters that include Violet (Tomlin), a widow and a mother of four who is immensely professionally competent and efficient, yet whose talents are exploited; Doralee (Parton), a buxom, earnest secretary continually rebuffing her boss's lecherous advances; and Judy (Fonda), a timid and inexperienced housewife suddenly left by her husband and now forced to earn her own paycheck.

A paean to fighting gender discrimination, the film focuses on the trio as mistreated office workers who deliciously avenge the sexist injustices perpetuated by their chauvinistic male boss, Hart (Dabney Coleman). Hart's outrageous behavior violates all three women.

He sexually harasses Doralee, asks her to retrieve fallen pencils as an excuse for looking down her blouse, constantly propositions her, and even grabs and attempts to seduce her. He belittles Judy and repeatedly humiliates her in the office. Finally, he takes advantage of and takes credit for Violet's work, claiming that her business plans are his own, and then refuses her a promotion, choosing instead a less competent man who Hart claims "has a family" (as if Violet did not). 9 to 5 clearly expresses its loyalty to and sympathy for its female characters, inviting audiences to recognize multiple forms of workplace discrimination and to consider their material effects. Violet's plotline, where she is repeatedly denied credit for the work she does, speaks particularly eloquently to women's professional marginalization and the very real economic consequences that ensue as a result. In an elaborate fantasy sequence, the film prompts us to share the women's comic but fitting daydreams of revenge, in line with the different injustices they suffer. Doralee imagines, for instance, hog-tying Hart, a visual representation of the sort of physical constriction to which he subjects her.

Pointing to a solution to what might seem like intractable problems, the film suggests that placing women at the helm of corporate cultures is a necessary first step. Thanks to a series of mishaps, and in a caper-like fashion, the three women confine Hart to his home while they take over the running of his formerly dictatorial office, where they make a series of progressive changes to the workplace. These include instituting flex-time and job sharing, initiating a program for hiring people with disabilities, and offering onsite childcare, alterations that in turn improve office productivity and morale. Commenting on this film in 2006, Tomlin offers a direct connection between the sort of humanistic feminism that she values and the fact that treating women well makes basic economic sense: "9 to 5 made people aware of equal pay for equal work. It hasn't really happened, but it has come closer. We're aware of sexual harassment, and of course, there are very few companies that have daycare centers, which seems to me would be the most humane, positive thing to do for a worker. The worker would be more loyal, they'd be more productive. It's so crazy not to do the human thing. It seems to me to be much more profitable to do the human thing."[43] 9 to 5, importantly, makes a very similar argument.

Though the women are estranged at the beginning of the film, recognition of their shared harassment and discrimination ultimately bonds Violet, Doralee, and Judy. Their friendship in turn services their insistence on an equitable work environment, a reality that highlights how collective action can lead to progressive change. Such details confirm *9 to 5*'s cultural significance as a last gasp of a strong popular feminism. Released at the moment when women's presence in corporate America was gaining increased cultural visibility, the film acknowledged and highlighted the fact that women were frequently unwelcome and mistreated in those spaces. The film also stands at the cusp of an incipient postfeminism, since recognitions of the sort of sexism that *9 to 5* skewers would soon give way to backlash portrayals of barracuda woman bosses, such as the one found in *Working Girl* (1988), where corporate injustice is personified by a selfish woman. Subsequent to *9 to 5* and the final defeat of the ERA in 1982, the predominant cultural image of the working woman is that she risks sacrificing marriage and family in the name of professionalization, a theme that has, in the twenty-first century, served as a hallmark of postfeminist thought. Even publications that acknowledge women's marginalization in the workforce, such as Sheryl Sandberg's bestselling 2013 advice manual *Lean In*, tend to situate corporate executive women as spokeswomen rather than featuring the sort of relatable working-class women that *9 to 5* so warmly depicts.

Some twenty-five years after the release of *9 to 5*, Tomlin remains a figurehead for the triumph of feminist principles and values, commitments that continue to register in her narrative work. This observation was confirmed as recently as 2015, when Tomlin starred in *Grandma*, in which she plays the titular character, a cranky centenarian who helps her teenage granddaughter secure the funds to procure an abortion. This is also one of the first times that Tomlin played a confirmed lesbian, and she is simultaneously mourning the death of her lifetime partner in the film. The same year, Netflix released the web series *Grace and Frankie* (2015–), a comedy starring Tomlin and Fonda, who portray two nemeses who learn that their husbands have fallen in love and who bond over the desertion. In addition to inviting Tomlin into yet another media market—Netflix has been credited with revolutionizing delivery systems when it began producing original streaming content—the production clearly calls on the women's iconic collaboration in its reprisal of *9 to 5*'s emphasis on female solidarity.

Feminist ideas are indeed a staple foundation of all of Tomlin's comedy. In a glowing *Ms.* magazine review of *The Search for Signs of*

Intelligent Life in the Universe, Marilyn French offers this tribute: it is "the first work that I know of that simply takes it as a given that a mass audience will accept feminist attitudes, that proceeds on the assumption these attitudes are shared and that therefore does not lecture, hector, or even underline."[44] Tomlin's willingness to presume feminist ideas marks her comedy, though it is important to recognize that few of her characters are feminist per se. As Suzanne Lavin cogently articulates, Tomlin's personalities can be categorized according to their willingness to challenge received gendered hierarchies. Lavin offers the following heuristic: "Those who have identified most closely with the patriarchy (Ernestine, Mrs. Beasley, Suzie Sorority) are the most damaged. By contrast, those characters who break from the patriarchy into a freer individuality, like Tess, Crystal, and Sister Boogie Woman, offer alternative roles for women in their independence of thought and spirit."[45] Tomlin's willingness to state the unpopular makes it clear that she too identifies with the latter grouping, an affinity that circumscribes her professional work. In all, Tomlin can be said to have introduced and maintained a feminist presence in key comedic sites—variety and stand-up shows, solo performances, mainstream films, and television roles—and her exposure and visibility have ensured the wide and varied reach of her progressive ideals.

NOTES

1. Suzanne Lavin, *Women and Comedy in Solo Performance* (New York: Routledge, 2004), 34.

2. Bob Smith, "Lily Tomlin's Take on Customer Service," *Management Review*, July 1994, 17.

3. "Lily . . . Ernestine . . . Tess . . . Lupe . . . Edith Ann . . . ," *Time*, Mar. 28, 1977, 68.

4. Quoted in Lavin, *Women and Comedy*, 37.

5. Jeff Sorensen, *Lily Tomlin: Woman of a Thousand Faces* (New York: St Martin's, 1989), 3.

6. Quoted in Sorensen, *Lily Tomlin*, 5.

7. Quoted in ibid., 5–6.

8. Quoted in ibid., 54.

9. "This Is a Record," LP, accessed at youtube.com/watch?v=G0l9fE2RAj8.

10. Quoted in Sorensen, *Lily Tomlin*, 33–34.

11. *Saturday Night Live* transcript from Sept. 18, 1976, http://snltranscripts .jt.org/76/76a.phtml.

12. Quoted in Lavin, *Women and Comedy*, 33.

13. "Lily . . . Ernestine," 68.

14. Ibid.

15. One of the few sketches of this character that is readily accessible in the public domain, the skit can be viewed at www.youtube.com/watch?v=s_lmeFOWyzI.

16. Patricia Nelson, "Character Crossings: Sexuality and Intersectional Comedy in Lily Tomlin's Early Variety Specials," paper delivered at the SCMS annual conference, Seattle, Mar. 2014.

17. Tomlin's send-up of the housewife role likewise echoes a sketch by fellow feminist comedian Carol Burnett, where Burnett is attacked and eventually killed by household cleaning products, as if to suggest the suffocating nature of her domestic position.

18. Elizabeth Spelman, "Anger and Insubordination," in *Women, Knowledge, and Reality: Explorations in Feminist Philosophy*, ed. Ann Garry and Marilyn Pearsall (Boston: Unwin Hyman, 1989), 270.

19. Chadwick Roberts, "Lily 'White': Commodity Racism and the Construction of Female Domesticity in *The Incredible Shrinking Woman*," *Journal of Popular Culture* 43, no. 4 (2010): 815.

20. Ibid., 804.

21. Sara Hosey, "Canaries and Coalmines: Toxic Discourse in *The Incredible Shrinking Woman* and *Safe*," *Feminist Formations* 23, no. 2 (Summer 2011): 85.

22. Ibid., 35.

23. Quoted in Sorensen, *Lily Tomlin*, 128.

24. John Esther, "The Incredible Never-Shrinking Lily Tomlin," *Lesbian News*, 28, no. 12 (July 2003): 26.

25. Tomlin continues to work in the documentary form. She appears in the twenty-fifth-anniversary edition of the documentary *Stonewall: The Making of a Gay and Lesbian Community* (2010), offering a tribute to Vito Russo. She also narrates and served as an executive producer on the activist documentary *An Apology to Elephants* (2013) about the brutal treatment of elephants in zoos and circuses. Partner Jane Wagner wrote the film's narration.

26. Alonso Duralde, "Thoroughly Modern Lily," *Advocate*, Mar. 15, 2005, 56.

27. Tomlin did, however, appear on the cover of *Time* in 1977, thanks not to her sexuality but rather to her wide popularity; the cover proclaims her the "new queen of comedy."

28. Duralde, "Thoroughly Modern Lily," 57. Tomlin admits in this interview that she has never been able to corroborate her recollection of the *Time* offer.

29. Jennifer Reed, "Lily: Sold Out!: The Queer Feminism of Lily Tomlin," *Genders* 49 (2009); n.p., www.colorado.edu/gendersarchive1998-2013/2009/04/01/lily-sold-out-queer-feminism-lily-tomlin.

30. Jennifer Reed, *The Queer Cultural Work of Lily Tomlin and Jane Wagner* (New York: Palgrave Macmillan, 2013), 23.

31. Jennifer Reed, "Lily Tomlin's *Appearing Nitely*: Performing Difference Before Difference Was Cool," *Journal of Popular Culture* 37, no. 3 (2004): 437.

32. Reed, "Lily: Sold Out!"

33. Quoted in Lavin, *Women and Comedy*, 46.

34. Quoted in Reed, "Tomlin's *Appearing Nitely*," 446.

35. Lavin, *Women and Comedy*, 45.

36. Quoted in Sorensen, *Lily Tomlin*, 99.

37. Jill Dolan, "'Finding Our Feet in the Shoes of (One An) Other': Multiple Character Solo Performers and Utopian Performatives," *Modern Drama* 45, no. 4 (Winter 2002): 501.

38. Reed, *Queer Cultural Work*, 71, 73.

39. Nelson, "Character Crossings," n.p.

40. Ibid.

41. Quoted in Esther, "Incredible Never-Shrinking," 27.

42. Karen Hollinger, *In the Company of Women: Contemporary Female Friendship Films* (Minneapolis: University of Minnesota Press, 1998), 107.

43. Randy Shulman, "Interview with Lily Tomlin," *MetroWeekly*, Apr. 26, 2006.

44. Quoted in Sorenson, *Lily Tomlin*, 161.

45. Lavin, *Women and Comedy*, 50.

CHAPTER 8

MOMS MABLEY AND WANDA SYKES: "I'MA BE ME"

BAMBI HAGGINS

"YOU'D BETTER RECOGNIZE" is a phrase often used to make folks understand exactly with whom and what they are dealing—a black vernacular form of "Don't you know who I am?" conflated with "Can't you understand the point here?" A statement rather than a rhetorical question, it embodies a sense of authority and empowerment in the speaker—almost regardless of the situation—and encompasses the authenticity of "keeping it 100." Keeping it 100 percent real, as in genuine and honest, has always been a part of marginalized people's humor, whether through sly signification or by more overt means. When considering how comics have used stand-up as a means of saying, "You'd better recognize"—regarding issues of identities, politics, and other social foibles—two comics from very different eras come to mind: Jackie "Moms" Mabley and Wanda Sykes. The comedic lineage of Wanda Sykes can undoubtedly be traced back to Moms Mabley, the "alpha" of stand-up comics, who began her career on the boards of the Chitlin Circuit and broke the color line to gain mainstream acclaim late in her career.

Both comics critique the politics and mores of their day from a commonsense perspective, both are known for their sexual candor, and both speak to and across cultural and racial boundaries. One must also consider that Mabley and Sykes are triple threats—they're black, they're gay, and they're women. Although Mabley was not closeted in her personal life (her compatriots on the circuit have said they were well aware of her sexual orientation), she performed heterosexuality onstage through a paradoxically desexualized hypersexuality, made possible by her use of old-lady drag. From the 1920s to the 1970s, Mabley used her bawdy but comforting comic persona of "Moms" to speak truth to power—with a maternal yet mischie-

8.1. Already a seasoned performer, Moms Mabley was taking Harlem by storm in 1948.

vous smile. In a very different political climate, Sykes was already an established stand-up comic, comedy writer, and a go-to BBF ("black best friend") on the big and small screens when she publicly came out in response to the passing of California's Proposition 8 in 2008. The annunciation of her sexuality was folded into the autobiographical mix of her act. Her style did not change; it was simply enriched by a more expansive and inclusive sense of Sykes's identity. After coming out, Sykes seamlessly incorporated her sexual orientation into the sociopolitical discourse of her stand-up—whether performing at a gay pride event, on her HBO special, or at the White House Correspondents' Dinner.

I have a recollection of seeing Moms Mabley on *The Ed Sullivan Show* (CBS 1948–1971) in 1969 and of laughing at her crazy outfit and her funny, gravelly voice. Although my parents weren't fans of the "party albums"—their comic tastes were far from blue (they preferred the squeaky-clean, universalist riffs of a young Bill Cosby or Richard Pryor)—I can remember us watching Moms on *Ed Sullivan* as a family. While it was becoming more common to see black folks on television (*I-Spy* [NBC 1965–1968], *Julia* [NBC 1968–1971], *Mission: Impossible* [CBS 1966–1973], *The Flip Wilson Show* [NBC 1970–1974]), in the late sixties and early seventies, it still had a special-events feel to it. It was not until decades later, while doing research on black stand-up comedy, that I realized that the woman I had thought of as just a funny old lady had played a significant role in setting the trajectory for stand-up comedy as sociopolitical discourse—a lineage that has not been acknowledged nearly enough.

The first time I remember seeing Wanda Sykes was as the incredibly candid and disgruntled employee in the skit "Wanda in the White House Mailroom" on *The Chris Rock Show* (HBO 1997–2000). As though speaking for all those who are at the bottom of the bureaucratic food chain, Sykes's character gave an outsider's insider view of "what's really going on" at that big house on Pennsylvania Avenue. In her Comedy Central special *Wanda Sykes: Tongue Untied* (2003), she brought that same kind of no-holds-barred critique to matters personal and political. Sykes's comic persona, with its candid, conversational tone and contentious sociocultural critique, has the edginess of Chris Rock but shows an ease of delivery that is remi-

8.2. Wanda Sykes causes a stir at the first White House Correspondents' Dinner of the Obama administration, 2009.

niscent of Moms Mabley when she takes on the role of storyteller as truth teller. Capturing the nuances and inflections of black vernacular speech, Sykes's voice, often brassy and a bit curt, speaks across cultural boundaries without seeming to make an effort to do so.

Although I've written about both Wanda and Moms before, in relationship to my analysis of another groundbreaking comic, Whoopi Goldberg (in *Laughing Mad: The Black Comic Persona in Post-Soul America*), this chapter celebrates the way two singular black voices use comic social discourse to say some very real things in two very different eras.[1] And, to be honest, there were nuances in both their comedy and the construction of their personae that I simply did not appreciate the first time around; thus, there is the need to make scholarly amends. Previously, I had used the terms "revolutionary mammy" or "revisionist mammy" to describe Mabley. Now, I don't feel that those modifiers go far enough in terms of distancing Moms's strategically self-deprecatory performance from the self-denigrating norms of minstrelsy's mammies. As Arsenio Hall states, "Maybe not having the teeth, the way she dressed, the hat, the presentation, was the 'okey doke.' It was almost like she was hiding how bright she was and sneaking a message in the backdoor at the same time."[2] Furthermore, I now believe that Sykes's comic voice may in some ways be bolder and more daring than the comic to whom she is most often compared, Chris Rock, with a more consistently left-leaning social and political bent.

This chapter's title, "I'ma Be Me," is borrowed from Sykes's 2009 HBO special. The phrase is an ideological bookend to "You'd better recognize," and together they provide the comic modus operandi for Mabley and Sykes. Both phrases are inextricably tied to the women's comedic work and also speak to their ability to master the media at hand—the comedy records of the mid-twentieth century and the comedy specials of the new millennium, respectively. These two remarkable women were after a very specific endgame: giving voice to their individual and yet shared perspectives of being black, a woman, and a sexual being, in times (past and present) when identities are still not viewed in intersectional terms but rather are posited in a way that only one form of Otherness can be privileged. This chapter seeks to examine how the personal and political are enunciated in the construction of their personae and their comic discourse as well as how they used the microphone to both assert their agency and enact their own unique brands of activism. Throughout their careers and within their acts, the "You'd better recognize" was often stated, but it was *always* implied.

BECOMING MOMS: ORIGIN STORY

In some ways, A-list comics are like superheroes: they have innate gifts that allow them to win the hearts and minds of the people/their audience; there is a division between their secret identities (as people) and their crusading characters/personae; and there are not a lot of black women in either camp. In order to understand the arc of the superhero, you need to know his origin story; the same is true for understanding how a comic's persona is formed and how her comic trajectory is set. Moreover, in the case of Mabley, too few understand how many comedy "firsts" should be attributed to her. Although their origin stories differ greatly, for both Mabley and Sykes their lived experiences inform the groundbreaking style and content of their comedy. Their superpower is speaking their truth to power with sly smiles.

> I married too young, fifteen years old. When I come along, your parents picked who you were to marry. And my daddy picked this old man. Old man. Older than dirt. My daddy liked him. My daddy shoulda married him.
>
> MOMS MABLEY, *WHOOPI GOLDBERG PRESENTS MOMS MABLEY*

In describing the trajectory of a career spanning more than five decades, one could easily opine that her comic voice was seasoned by hardships: powerlessness in the face of patriarchal power early in her life, the ongoing trials of living and working under Jim Crow, and the negotiation between her identities and the persona that she constructed. However, as Whoopi Goldberg said in her documentary on Mabley, Moms's story is much like the story of black folks in America—"There's a lot that is not there."[3] There are many stories about Mabley's youth. They are stories of loss, of rape, of forced marriage, of her flight to freedom, and of finding her salvation and her voice on the stage. Moms Mabley was the "granny" as griot, whose heart, hipness, humor, and honesty shone through in her slyly subversive storytelling. If comedy is tragedy plus time, Mabley truly earned the title of "The Funniest Woman in the World."

Born Loretta Mary Aiken in Brevard, North Carolina, in 1897 (although that date is disputed), she was one of twelve children in a family of black, Irish, and Cherokee descent. She lost both parents before she was out of her teens—her father died in a car crash when she was eleven, and less than two years later her mother, who had remarried, was hit by a truck and killed. Mabley was raised primarily by her grandmother, who was her strength and later her inspiration.

Mabley's childhood was far from idyllic: her innocence was taken when she was very young, when, as she once stated, "I was raped and everything else." It is believed that she was twice the victim of sexual assault—first at the age of eleven by an older black man and then again two years later by her town's white sheriff. Both rapes resulted in pregnancies and twice she bore children who were given up for adoption. When her stepfather, acting as her legal guardian, forced her to marry a much older man, Mabley fled the loveless match and North Carolina with the encouragement and blessing of her grandmother. In 1911 Loretta Mary Aiken hitched a ride with a traveling minstrel show going to Cleveland, Ohio.[4] Leaving everyone behind—for better and for worse—she was on her way to becoming Moms. Throughout her career, Mabley's "old-man" material was both an act of rebellion and an assertion of agency: "Somebody asked me, 'What is it like being married to an old man?' I said, 'Honey. I don't know what to say. The best I can explain it, it's just like trying to push a car up a hill with a rope.'"

Moms's decision to go into show business was practical: "I was pretty and didn't want to become a prostitute." She could sing and dance, but comedy was her gift: her impeccable timing and quick wit made her an asset to any of the traveling productions working on the Theater Owners Booking Association circuit (TOBA). From 1912 to 1920 she honed her skills, combining song and dance with a growing dose of comedy. For Moms, life on "Toby Time" (also known as the Chitlin Circuit) meant playing multiple shows daily for low pay, staying in whatever space Jim Crow allowed, and performing to black audiences in segregated second-tier clubs and theaters across the Midwest and Northeast, with a majority of the venues in the South. As the story goes, it was during this time that Loretta Mary Aiken became Jackie Mabley in response to the actions of a man: her fellow performer and, for a short time, first boyfriend, Jack Mabley, who, she said, "took a lot off me and the least I could do was take his name."[5] The nickname "Moms" was given to her because of the maternal streak that endeared her to fellow performers on the TOBA circuit and beyond.

The transformation into the Moms persona we know came easily to her. Channeling her own grandmother (and donning frumpy, mismatched clothing, floppy hat, and shoes), Mabley, then a lovely young woman in her twenties, adopted appearance and speech that subverted the construction of the sassy mammy. Yet "[h]er rubbery-faced mugging, gravel-voiced delivery, and desexualized appearance did not diminish the liberatory potential of her comedic discourse": in fact, that ruse made the revolutionary part possible.[6] In crediting her grandmother for her "hipness," Moms spoke with candor about how black women have handed down commonsense wisdom detailing how to survive and thrive in a world that was all-too-often hostile.

> I never will forget my granny. . . . You know who hipped me, my great-grandmother. Her name was Harriet Smith; she lived in Brevard, North Carolina. This is the truth! She lived to be 118 years old. And you wonder why Moms is hip today? Granny hipped me. She said, "They lied to the rest of them, but I'm not gonna let you be dumb. I'm gonna tell you the truth." In fact when they'd tell me them fairy lies, Granny'd tell me the truth about it. One day she's sitting out on the porch and I said, "Granny, how old does a woman get before she don't want no more boyfriends?" She was around 106 then. She said, "I don't know, honey, you'll have to ask somebody older than me."

Thus, in amongst the "dahlins" and the "chilluns," Mabley dispensed her downhome wisdom, and she spoke the truth.

In 1921 Mabley was "discovered" by Jodie and Susan Edwards, better known as the husband-and-wife song-and-dance team of Butterbeans and Susie. Known for their bawdy act filled with double entendres, marital squabbling, and risqué comedy songs (including "I Want a Hot Dog for My Roll"), the couple took Moms under their wings, eventually bringing her to New York at the height of the Harlem Renaissance. Mabley went from earning fourteen dollars a week to taking home over ninety.

By following the trajectory of Mabley's career, you can trace the development of black comedy from the waning days of the minstrel show to the civil rights era and beyond. She followed the Chitlin Circuit to New York City. By 1923 she was appearing regularly at Connie's Inn, the Cotton Club, and the Savoy Ballroom, where she shared the stage with the likes of Pigmeat Markham, Bill "Bojangles" Robinson, and the bands of Louis Armstrong and Cab Calloway. The character of "Moms" became fully formed during the glorious years of the Harlem Renaissance. While performing in "colored revues" all over

New York City, Mabley made more than one foray onto the Great White Way. The skits, which Moms cowrote and performed with Zora Neale Hurston, provided some of the few highlights in *Fast and Furious: A Colored Revue in 37 Scenes* (1931). While *New York Times* theater reviewer J. Brooks Atkinson arguably might have had issues with more than the "New Negro Revue," describing, with disdain, "the animalism of Negro entertainment," even the reviewer for the *New Amsterdam News* confessed, "This is not a great show. . . . Jackie [Moms] Mabley, sans cork, is at her best in the Revue."[7] Broadway audiences were not ready for the very ethnic and slightly blue comedy of Moms and other "Toby Time" vets, including Pigmeat Markham. However, black audiences were more than ready for Moms. In 1939 Moms began performing at the venue that would become her home away from home and the ultimate stage for black performers, the Apollo Theater in Harlem. Mabley was the first female comic to play at the Apollo and quickly became an audience favorite. As a regular at the Apollo, Moms would often play for fifteen-week stints—starring with a new act each week. By the 1950s Mabley was at the top of the bill on her tours, and at the Apollo, she was their biggest star. At the height of her career, she was earning ten thousand dollars a week for her Apollo gigs . . . and "Moms ruled the Apollo."[8]

Although the large helpings of "randy granny" in Mabley's humor were her comedic staples, she continued to be relevant for decades because the maternal wit and wisdom that informed the very core of her act assured her "children" that she was telling them the truth.

LEARNING FROM MOTHER AND MOMS: BECOMING WANDA

When I was growing up, my mother, she wouldn't even let us dance in the car. A good song would come on the radio and (we'd dance). . . . She would stop the car. "Uh, do you wanna dance or do you wanna ride. Cuz you ain't dancing in my car. . . . White people are looking at you." [She turns to look.] What? Oh damn. She was right.
WANDA SYKES, *I'MA BE ME*

While Moms Mabley broke down barriers that allowed Wanda Sykes to find a place in the world of stand-up comedy, the self-determination imbedded in Sykes's upbringing helped to shape her comic persona—as did her mother's brand of respectability politics, which can be understood as "White people are looking at you." As Sykes noted in a 2010 interview, "My mom grew up in rural Virginia, so it was about

:rception. It was about don't let white people think you're—they lready have these awful names and things that they call us. Don't e that."[9] I cannot help but identify with how she internalized her nother's pragmatic object lesson on race relations.

Sykes, like many a "post-soul" baby (born between the March on Washington [1963] and the *Regents of the University of California vs. Bakke* [1978] Supreme Court decision), came of age after the height of the civil rights movement; life with her father, Lucas, an Army colonel, her mother, Olivia, who worked at the National Security Agency Credit Union, and her brother, Harry, was decidedly middle class.[10] As a post-soul baby myself (from a blue- rather than a white-collar upbringing), the same message passed along by Sykes's mother was articulated a little differently in my house: "Don't be typical," my mother would say; the directive being don't act like what "they" (read: white folks) think of as typical, or more aptly, stereotypical. In both instances, the relationship between the white looks and black bodies speaks to W. E. B. Du Bois's concept of "double consciousness": a "sense of always looking at one's self through the eyes of others, of measuring one's soul by the tape of a world that looks on in amused contempt and pity."[11] Early in her life and career, Sykes asserted, "I'ma be me."

Sykes has a swagger onstage that is often associated with "street smarts from life in the 'hood," when, in fact, she grew up in Gambrills, Maryland, a suburb of Annapolis. Although close to both Charm City and Chocolate City (Baltimore and Washington, D.C., respectively), Sykes did not have the "it's crazy out there on the streets" experience of many comics coming out of the Washington, D.C., area in the 1980s and 1990s. As Sykes stated:

> I think with me, it's the way I carry myself. . . . People just assume I had to fight my way through the hard life and the streets to get to where I am and that's where my personality comes from. But hey, I was born in Virginia, raised in Maryland, and it's not like everything was great. There was still racism and all where we grew up.[12]

Indeed, one must remember, while it was the suburban South, it was still the South. Sykes agrees that she has a certain "toughness" and "streetwise sensibility"; she adds, "You need that not just to survive the 'hood—you need that to survive, you know, the guys who wear the white hood."[13]

From an early age, Sykes pulled few punches: she was the child

who loved to relay opinions expressed by her parents in private conversations at inopportune times. Sykes admitted, "I was very outspoken, and it got to the point that whenever they had guests over,
they would send me off to my grandmother's because they had no
idea what was going to come out of my mouth. . . . If I heard them say
something about someone, or if someone owed them money, I had no
problems bringing it up to that person. So it was just best for them
to keep their friends and send me off for the evening."[14] Although always considered funny by her peers and teachers alike, Sykes went
on to study marketing at Hampton University in Virginia after high
school. After graduation, she returned to Maryland and went into the
family business: the government. She secured a job at the NSA as a
contracting specialist, "which meant I shopped, but instead of buying shoes, I bought spy equipment."[15] However, life as a Washington bureaucrat, albeit one with top-secret clearance, did not satisfy
Sykes, even though she held the position for five years. In the fall of
1987, Sykes trusted the words of all those who in the past had told
her, "You're so funny. You should be onstage." Her first gig was at a
Coors Light Super Talent Showcase in northern Virginia. According
to Sykes, "I didn't know what I was doing, never been to a comedy
club, had no idea that it could go horribly wrong. I was just so oblivious. . . . I wasn't nervous or anything. Just got up and told jokes because that's how I saw people do it on TV and people would laugh.
And that's what happened."[16]

Although she continued to work at the NSA at the beginning—using comp time, nights, and weekends to hone her craft at the Comedy
Café, Garvin's, and clubs all over the greater D.C. area—Wanda Sykes
had found her place: onstage with a microphone in her hand.

After leaving the NSA and moving to New York in 1992, Sykes's
first big break came when she opened for Chris Rock at Caroline's
Comedy Club. In 1997 Sykes became a writer (and cast member) on
The Chris Rock Show, and in 1999 she received an Emmy Award
as part of the creative team. Her early association with Rock positioned her within a black comedy elite, thus providing Sykes with
a degree of cultural cachet and legitimacy that garnered black fans
as well as drawing the attention of mainstream audiences. Early in
her career, Sykes's comedy was a mixture of the personal (relationship humor) and the political (as well as sociocultural critique); by
the time her second HBO special aired, *Wanda Sykes: I'ma Be Me*,
her act had naturally evolved, and it showed very clearly how the personal is political.

TRUTH TO POWER: THE MESSAGE THROUGH THE MEDIUM

Much could be said about how Mabley and Sykes engaged with the Hollywood mainstream. After all, between Moms's early appearances in filmed versions of "colored" revues like *Boarding House Blues* and *Killer Diller* (both directed by Josh Binney, 1948), her guest spot in the Isley Brothers independently produced soul concert film *It's Your Thing* (Mike Gargiulo 1970), and her starring role in the fable of political agency in the late civil rights era, *Amazing Grace* (Stan Lathan 1974), life and comedy had changed for black folks. So too could we discuss Sykes's starring roles in two short-lived series: the sitcom *Wanda at Large* (Fox 2003) and the panel talk show (think *Politically Incorrect* crossed with *Conan*) *The Wanda Sykes Show* (Fox 2009–2010), as well as her later venture, *Wanda Sykes Presents Herlarious* (OWN 2013–2014), a showcase for women comics. Indeed, Sykes's roles as the BBF on the big and small screens brought more complexity and spirit to what was rapidly becoming a tired trope. She played the acerbic (and sassy) assistant to Jane Fonda in *Monster-in-Law* (Robert Luketic 2005); had a recurring role as a fictionalized version of herself and friend to Cheryl Hines's long-suffering wife of Larry David on *Curb Your Enthusiasm* (HBO 2001–2011); and appeared as Barb, the sarcastic but supportive friend and business partner to Julia Louis-Dreyfuss on *The New Adventures of Old Christine* (CBS 2006–2010). These roles have all been discussed more thoroughly in the chapter on Sykes in Linda Mizejewski's *Pretty/Funny: Women Comedians and Body Politics* and, in a more elliptical way, in *Laughing Mad*. However, for the purposes of this chapter, the focus will be on Mabley's and Sykes's performances as stand-up comics—whether onstage, on vinyl, on network television, or on Comedy Central and HBO. Furthermore, I seek to make the connections between their backstories and the stories they tell us through their comedy routines.

COMMONSENSE SOCIAL DISCOURSE

You think you're gonna hear some jokes? Well, Moms don't know none. Moms don't know no jokes. . . . but I can tell you some facts.
MOMS MABLEY

Both Moms and Wanda excelled in live performance, but both also utilized the medium at hand to expand the reach of their comedy: for

Mabley, access to even larger audiences began with her recording career, and for Sykes, it was the (cable) televised version of her stand-up act. Mom's debut album was the 1956 Vanguard Records release *A Night at the Apollo*, which featured Mabley playing to her most dedicated fans. Like one of the comics to whom she had been "mom" and mentor, Redd Foxx, Moms made comedy albums that became known as "party records," so named for their raucously blue, adults-only content. (Although much of the material considered blue back then would probably now not earn an R rating on film and would warrant only a TVMA label on basic cable.) Moms signed with Chess in 1960 and recorded *The Funniest Woman Alive* before a live audience in Chicago. The album sold over one million copies and earned Moms a gold record. Riding the comedy-record boom of the early 1960s, Moms had incredible success, recording over twenty albums. This boom was a boon for Moms and helped the veteran performer to cross over, gaining her "overnight success" in the entertainment mainstream.

Mabley was a pioneer of comedic social discourse. Although decrying the prowess of old men and praising the virtues of young ones remained comedy gold for Mabley throughout her career, her "conversations" with presidents, first ladies, and world leaders at the United Nations became progressively more central to her act in the late 1950s and the 1960s, in both live performances and on vinyl. By calling these political heavyweights by their first names or nicknames, Moms literally spoke truth to power, saying what many wanted to say but could not. Moms, as the feisty and kindly revolutionary granny, used folk wisdom, commonsense pragmatism, and her keen eye for hypocrisy to weigh in on issues as diverse as the Cold War, racism, sexism, and the defense of the younger generation's calls for social change. Mabley's commentary on her comedy albums, especially *Moms Mabley at the "UN"* (1961) and *Moms Mabley at the Geneva Conference* (1962), was on the cutting edge of comedy as social and political discourse. The content of her comedy challenged audiences, even as her persona and delivery soothed them: on *Live at the Playboy Club* (1961), at first you can hear the hesitancy of the white Chicago audience to laugh at material on race. However, Moms circles around the subject and takes another approach—by the end of the performance, she has them. A veteran of both the Chitlin Circuit and the overt discrimination and racism its performers experienced, Moms knew how to work an audience and did so skillfully—adjusting, without editing, her material and the points she wanted to get across while also keeping the humor as the driving force. As Elsie Williams notes, "With the integrated audiences of the sixties and seventies, the comedian continued to perform, basically, the same kind of folk humor that she had developed on the earlier 'chitlin' circuit,' where the boundary of segregation made the question of boundary practically irrelevant."[17]

In her commentaries on civil rights, Mabley's adherence to the revolutionary directives of the movement was unequivocal. Her observations about both racial violence and the struggles of black activists were encased in vaudevillian-style joke series, which provided pointed critiques within the guise of old-fashioned entertainment:

> Colored fellow down home died. Pulled up to the gate. St. Peter look at him, say, "What do you want?" "Hey man, you know me. Hey, Jack, you know me. I'm old Sam Jones. Old Sam Jones, man, you know me. Used to be with the NAACP, you know, CORE and all that stuff, man, marches, remember me? Oh, man, you know me." He just broke down there, "You know me." He looked in his book. "Sam Jones," he say, "No, no you ain't here, no Sam Jones." He said, "Oh, man, yes, I am; look there. You know me. I'm the cat that married that white girl on the capitol steps of Jackson, Mississippi." He said, "How long ago has that been?" He said, "About five minutes ago."

There is also inherent defiance in Mabley's stand-up, whether on vinyl, in person, or on television—the "You'd better recognize" is there, whether commenting on her own status or making clear the status of another. Performing in the South, after a substantial hiatus, Mabley remarked on how far they (the white South) had not come and how far she had:

> Baby, it's rough down there. . . . I swear them people still think we have y'know . . . we have to mind them. Do what they say do! Some old Klan come talkin' about, "Mammy." I said, "No damn 'Mammy!' Moms!" I don't know nothing about no log cabin. I never seen no log cabin. Split level in the suburbs, baby!

Her insistence that her name is "Moms," not "Mammy," is a powerful statement about the significance of naming and the refusal to allow the false image of happy subservience to be hoisted upon her in elision of the history of abuse, oppression, and violence that, like many black women, Moms had experienced at the hands of white men. Her claim to "no log cabin" but rather a "split level in the suburbs" speaks to what she, as a black woman, has attained. This also presents a moment of rupture when the gap between the person and the persona becomes visible, while it also lambasts both racism and classism. One could argue that there is a spiritual kinship between this assertion of black success and a running gag that she used throughout the sixties and early seventies: Moms would come onstage in her full frumpy costume with an ermine coat draped around her shoulders and a handsome young man on her arm. As he removed her ermine and prepared to leave, Moms would say, "Just throw that thing anywhere. I love to throw them around, don't you know." Giving the audience a glimpse of the other Moms, the one who "offstage . . . is a striking figure in tailored slacks, matching sports shirt, Italian shoes, horn-rimmed glasses—and teeth," Mabley winked at her audiences—some of whom got the liberatory element in the joke and then implied, "See how good I am at this *act*."[18]

Moms made her television debut at the age of seventy-three in the Harry Belafonte–produced *A Time for Laughter* (ABC 1967), starring with numerous black stars, including Godfrey Cambridge, Dick Gregory, and Diana Sands. This guest spot led to more appearances: *The Ed Sullivan Show* (CBS 1948–1971), *The Flip Wilson Show* (NBC 1970–1974), *The Bill Cosby Show* (NBC 1969–1971), and *The Smothers Brothers Comedy Hour* (CBS 1967–1969), to name a few. This exposure finally brought Moms into *all* of America's living rooms—and you could never quite predict what she was going to say.[19] An example of this can be seen when, during a 1969 appearance on *The Merv Griffin Show*, Mabley talked about going back to the South and being given a "nickname."

> MOMS: What's that man got that horse in pictures . . . that Western man.
> GRIFFIN: Roy Rogers?
> MOMS: They name me Roy Rogers's horse.
> GRIFFIN: Trigger?
> MOMS: Yeah, everywhere I go, they're, "Hello, Trigger. What you saying, Trigger?" (Innocently) At least I think that's what they say.

An excellent example of Mabley speaking truth, very politely and directly, to power can be found on her 1970 album *Moms Mabley:*

Live at Sing Sing. Without much fanfare, Mabley had been performing for the inmates at Sing Sing, the notorious maximum security
prison, for years. In the waning years of her career, Moms continued
to visit her incarcerated children, and this album captured her last
performance at Sing Sing. The beginning of the show makes clear
where Moms's allegiance lies as she comes onto a maximum security stage:

> Hello, dahlings! I want to thank this wonderful man who made it
> possible for Moms to be up here today—and that's Warden Lehman.
> Warden, Come out here a minute, son. (*Audience cheers*) Come on
> out, baby! Thank so much for bringing Moms here. All of these are
> Moms' children. And I brought something for you: two of Mom's lat-
> est albums. One's called "Abraham, Martin, and John," and the other
> one is called, "What Generation Gap?" Now you just *go home* and
> put them on your machine and laugh yourself to death, 'cause they're
> funny.

As theater director Ellen Sebastian Chang puts it so aptly, "When
[Moms] frames it, she's saying, 'All right motherfucker, go home.
Cause you know they don't like you, go home and die. Die laughing,
but make sure you die.' She got it. She got the tension and she understood what a pressure cooker it was. She was able to culturally release
some of that tension, let some of the steam out."[20] In strolled Moms,
expressing her solidarity with her children in the nicest way possible to a man, Warden Lehman, who was, arguably, hated by the prison
population. She did it at a time when prison conditions and racial
tensions were coalescing across the country and making for a volatile
atmosphere—before the riots at Attica and the boom of the prison-in-
dustrial complex. There was a fearlessness in Moms that informed
her comedy, and when she had somethin' to say she'd say it—whether
at Sing Sing or in Carnegie Hall.

COMEDIC CANDOR: SOCIAL DISCOURSE WITH CONFIDENCE

One can see a similar fearlessness in Wanda Sykes—and also an impressive air of confidence when she takes the stage. In her half-hour
show for *Comedy Central Presents* (1998, as Wanda Sykes-Hall), her
first lines are, "You all look good. Not as good as me, but you look
good." Over the course of her career, Sykes has crafted a distinct

comic persona that has the potential to reach and appeal to multiple audiences without contorting her voice or diluting the content of the comedy. However, even early in her career she was not above lampooning those who are seen to be in her ideological camp when she thinks they are taking themselves—not their issues—too seriously. In the half hour, Sykes recounted doing a benefit for a feminist organization with Gloria Steinem in the audience. "Now, benefit means no money, so I should be able to say what I want to say. I figured if I piss them off who cares. What are they gonna do, get mad and pay me?" Embracing the "what-the-hell" attitude of that moment, she "went onstage and said, 'I can't stay out here with you broads too long 'cause I've got to go home and cook my man a nice hot dinner, and he likes oral sex by 9:45.' I'm glad y'all laughed; they didn't."[21]

In contemporary comedy, getting "your hour" (an hour-long stand-up special) is a pivotal moment in your career; it usually signifies that you've crossed over from being a headliner on the road to playing theaters and other venues where the audience is specifically paying to see you. In her first hour-long special, *Wanda Sykes: Tongue Untied* (Comedy Central 2003), Sykes's persona and her voice were carefully crafted to allow her to direct her ire not only at the absurdities in culture and politics but also at the entertainment industry's racial politics as well.

> You know, my agent would call and say, "Wanda, you don't even want to hear this." I was like, "No, tell me. What is it?" [*Incredulous tone in her voice*] She's like, "All right, they want you to play a maid and you win the lottery. But you love working for this family so much you continue to be their maid." [*Defiantly*] I said, "Set it up. I want to meet these people so I can slap that dumb-ass idea right out of they head." What makes you think that people want to work for you like that? That's ridiculous. I'm gonna tell you right now, if somebody walked in and told me I just won the lottery, I would walk out in the middle of this joke.

Without belaboring the point, she clearly alludes to the problematic representational history of black women on television stretching back to the ultimate happy darky domestic, Beulah, from the 1950s domestic comedy of the same name. However, as a key element of Sykes's persona, she does not shy away from confrontation in order to make someone see that they are not acting right. Sykes's act combines an easy self-assurance and constitutional intensity that shows no sign of either self-deprecation or self-denigration. She is neither too grateful to be in front of an audience nor too haughty to play to the crowd. However, the fact that she does not suffer fools kindly seems quite evident.

Her political fare pulls no punches, and she often points out the correlations between institutional actions and racial bias. In her discussion of Homeland Security and random searches (read: racial profiling), she states, "There is nothing random about it. When you get to the gate, and they're standing there with a Sherman Williams paint chart, if your ass is darker than khaki, you're getting searched."[22]

Sykes's commentary is straightforward and pragmatic, and she is not afraid to ideologically embody another "L" word: left. Similar to her comic contemporary Dave Chappelle (also from D.C.), who uses song titles to describe his and the black American condition ("Killin' Them Softly" and "For What It's Worth"), Sykes makes a homage to two significant black figures in her titles: the artist and filmmaker Marlon Riggs, whose documentary *Tongues Untied* (1989) gave voice to the silenced black gay experience; and voting rights and civil rights activist Fannie Lou Hamer, who famously stated, "I'm sick and tired of being sick and tired."

While comic critique of President George W. Bush became standard fuel for stand-up by the mid-2000s, Sykes was on that train fairly early, and her dismissal of the job being done by Bush is equally candid and biting.

> What did the president know before 9/11? He didn't know a damn thing. Remember, he didn't get smart until after 9/11. . . . [Bush has] a 70 percent approval rating [meaning that] a majority of us were satisfied with the job the president was doing. Which makes sense to me, because he pretty much did everything I expected him to do: the economy is in the toilet, we're at war, and everything's on fire. He's met all my expectations. (*Tongue Untied*)

In her first HBO special, *Sick and Tired* (2006), Sykes takes on the social conservatism of the Bush agenda. In *Sick and Tired*, she announces that, in response to the assault on women's rights during the Bush presidency, she had two abortions on the way to the performance "to stock up." With both comic barrels directed at sexism and political policies aimed at regulating sexuality, the defiant stance of this joke is emblematic of the explicitly feminist impulse in Sykes's humor. However, as illustrated in the earlier reference to the chilly reception she received at the feminist fundraiser, her act also reflects a wariness about how (or whether) feminism and its problematic whiteness speaks to and for women of color.

As an outspoken supporter of President Obama in 2008, she freely explored the joys of "Change" (Obama's campaign motto), while calling both sides of respectability politics into question in *I'ma Be Me*.

> First black President. I'm so happy because now I can relax a little bit. You know, I can loosen up. Don't have to be so black all the time. Don't have to be so dignified because we did it. Black folks, we always have to be so dignified because we know if we fuck up, we set everybody back a couple of years. We shoulda killed Flavor Flav like ten years ago.

Resonating with the notion that "white people are looking at you," Sykes's joke that Flavor Flav and other black performers of the reality television ilk should be eliminated suggests how the behaviors of one person of color can and do have ramifications for another in twenty-first-century America. She also recognizes the ways in which black folks can internalize racialized expectations—to recall our mothers' black desires about not wanting to be seen as "typical" and Du Bois's description of the impact of white surveillance. In the same act, Sykes explores the implications of a "postracial" nation with her satirical assertion that black stereotypes no longer have weight following the election of Obama. Throwing respectability politics to the wind, she defiantly states,

> I can buy whole watermelons now. I no longer have to grow them in my closet under my weed lamp. Before I would go in the grocery store and look at the whole watermelons . . . look at all these white people looking at me. Get my dignified ass over to the salad bar. . . . [Now] Whole watermelon on my shoulder, "Yeah, Obama, bitch." I hope he gets a second term, then I'm going to Popeye's.

While one would characterize Sykes's act in *I'ma Be Me* as extremely topical, she manages to make some ideological assertions that pay off with sociopolitical profundity, as exemplified in her routine on the difficult confirmation hearings for Supreme Court Justice Sonia Sotomayor.

> When a minority or another race gets a little power, it makes them [white men] nervous, cause they're scared that race is gonna do to them what they did to that race. They get nervous, so they start screaming "reverse racism!" Now, wait a minute. Isn't reverse racism when a racist is nice to somebody else? That's reverse racism. What you're afraid of is called karma.

However, for Sykes, the fact that times they are a changin' only goes so far: the night that Obama was elected was bittersweet for her and for millions of other Californians when Proposition 8 passed, thus banning gay marriage in the state. The passage of Proposition 8 prompted Sykes to come out publicly, although she had been out privately for some time.

> I had to come out. I had to say something, because I was so hurt and so fucking pissed. . . . You know, that night was crazy. Black president—yay! Oh, Prop 8 passed—oh shit! Now, I'm a second-class citizen—what the fuck? I was up here, and now I'm back down here. Actually, I'm lower . . . as a gay black woman—uh-uh, even lower.

That night in November 2008 revealed the conflict and the conflation of progressive and regressive impulses within American society in general, and within the black community as well. As a result, Sykes became an outspoken advocate for her community, the LGBTQ community.

THE PERSONAL IS POLITICAL: LIVING INTERSECTIONALITY

The comedy and the personae of Mabley and Sykes speak to and of their experiences living while black, female, and gay in the twentieth and twenty-first centuries. Returning to the notion that they are triple threats (black, gay, and women), it is not surprising that the womens' comic discourses demonstrate the intersectionality of their identities and their personae. In an interview with *Perspectives* magazine in 2004, Kimberle Crenshaw, who is often credited for coining the term "intersectionality," gave a commonsense explanation of this vital concept regarding minority women who are harmed or discriminated against: "Intersectionality simply came from the idea that if you're standing in the path of multiple forms of exclusion, you are likely to get hit by both. These women are injured, but when the race ambulance and the gender ambulance arrive at the scene, they see these women of color lying in the intersection and they say, 'Well, we can't figure out if this was just race or just sex discrimination. And unless they can show us which one it was, we can't help them.'"[23] The comedy of Mabley and Sykes, like that of so many others who use humor as a means of sociopolitical commentary, is positioned at the aforementioned collision, where it endures the crashes between ideology, culture, and politics. The personal and the political are always intermingled.

During Mabley's comic coming-of-age amidst the Harlem Renaissance, she came out as lesbian at the age of twenty-seven in 1924, a fact that was accepted by her comrades on the boards because "it was nobody's business." As Norma Miller, who was a dancer at the Apollo during its salad days, matter-of-factly states:

> Onstage she was Moms and she was always after the great Cab Calloway but you never saw her with a young man. You saw her with a young girl. There was no question. . . . We never called Moms a "homosexual." That word never fit her. We never called her gay. We called her Mr. Moms.[24]

Like many bisexual and lesbian black women, including Bessie Smith, Gladys Bently, and Gertrude "Ma" Rainey, Moms found show business hospitable to her sexual orientation during the Roaring Twenties and beyond. Though Moms was not in the closet per se, some of her fans never knew her sexual orientation; while she was outspokenly heterosexual onstage in her granny grab-bag-chic garb, offstage Moms preferred tailored suits, slacks, and women. Moms annunciated female pleasure in her act with its double entendre–filled, libidinous nature (often on the merits of young men and the deficiencies of the old). Her "rubbery-faced mugging, gravel-voiced delivery," and unorthodox couture combined to create a nonthreatening and liberatory space within her comedic discourse. When onstage, Mabley could be seen with handsome young men in tow; offstage the lovely young things were female. Yet, by switching the genders of her sexual objects of desire in her act, which was done out of necessity during

and ═══

JACKIE
MABLEY

Funniest Woman in America

HARLEM'S HIGH SPOT
APOLLO
WORLD'S GREATEST COLORED SHOWS
125ᵗʰ ST. near 8ᵗʰ Ave. · Tel. UNiversity 4-4490

8.3. "Mister Moms" in publicity materials for her gigs at the Apollo.

most of her career, Moms still managed to subvert gender norms in a celebration of her sexual agency and feminine desire: "My husband died four years ago. 'But you have a three year old daughter.' I said my husband died, I didn't." Furthermore, Moms was a comic pioneer in that she tested and broke the boundaries for what a woman could say onstage. Mabley used her seemingly benign persona to say whatever she wanted—and, often, what she wanted was replete with sly significations and colored in various shades of blue. Decades before Andrew Dice Clay supplied R-rated versions of nursery rhymes,[25] Mabley did it with a bit more panache: "Mary ain't had no little lamb; Mary had a little sheep; she put it in her bed to sleep; and the sheep turned out to be a ram. Now Mary has a little lamb."

By foregrounding her sexual agency, candor, and autonomy against what had to be seen as a highly marginalized position, Mabley forwarded a commonsense feminist agenda, "allow[ing] for public discussion of the female's sexual needs and . . . focus[ing] on the inadequacy of the [usually old] male to fulfill such needs, both off-limits as subjects in comedy routines by women until very recently."[26] However, because Mabley's annunciation of sexual agency was transmitted through the lens of the randy granny, the audience is allowed to choose how they read the assertion of autonomy within some of her bluer comic discourse. Wanda Sykes does not give the audience that choice.

Throughout her career, Sykes has emitted a comfortable sexuality that does not go to the physically and verbally explicit comedic extremes of other black women comics, such as two of the "Queens of Comedy," Sommore and Mo'Nique. Rather, she uses the shock of sexually explicit material to underscore a larger sociopolitical issue as illustrated in her most recent HBO special, *I'ma Be Me*:

> Being gay is not a choice. If you believe that, then you're saying that straight people are straight because they chose not to be gay, right? And I'm sure a lot of straight guys in here, you know what I'm talking about. I'm sure there are several occasions where you probably think, "You know, I think I'm gonna suck a dick today. Nah, I choose not to."

Sykes's point here isn't nuanced—she calls out the absurdity of thinking that sexual orientation is a choice. While the public reaction to her coming out was fundamentally positive, the private process had not been as pain free. Later in the same special, Sykes substitutes race for sexual orientation and explains what it would be like to come out "black" to her parents:

> . . . Mom, I'm black. "Oh no, Lord Jesus! Not black, Father God! Oh, not black, Lord! Anything but black, Jesus! Give her cancer, Lord! . . . Anything but black, Lord." . . . Mom, I'm black. That's just how it is. "No, you know what? You've been hanging around black people. You've been hanging around black people. And they got you thinking you black. They twisted your mind."

In this story, Sykes hits on many of the devastating responses faced by those coming out to socially conservative (and sometimes religious) parents. In a joke series reflecting on the seemingly nonsensical nature of questioning something as innate as race, Sykes offers a skillful rebuttal to those who think sexual orientation is a choice.

This story, however, has its roots in Sykes's lived experience—on several levels.[27] At the age of forty, Sykes, who had previously been married to David Hall (a record producer whom she had divorced

8.4. Wanda Sykes: *I'ma Be Me* (2009) was the comic's premium cable coming-out performance.

more than a decade earlier), was preparing for an upcoming surgery; her mother and her sister-in-law were set to come out to support her.

> And I said, "Mom, let me just explain something to you. You know I'm living with so-and-so; I just want you to know that we're not just roommates. . . . She's my girlfriend. . . ." She was like, "What do you mean?" I was like, "Mom, come on, you have to have known this. . . . I just want to make sure we're clear on this." She just fell apart, fell apart and ended up not coming out here for my surgery.[28]

A period of estrangement followed, and neither of her parents attended her wedding to her partner, Alex Sykes (formerly Alex Niedbalski), which preceded Sykes's public coming out by only a month. Sykes has since reconciled with her parents; in 2013 she said, "We're in a great place right now, my parents are wonderful. . . . They weren't at my wedding, but they were at the kids' last birthday party."[29]

In different but spiritually similar ways, Moms Mabley and Wanda Sykes used their lived experiences of being marginalized on three different axes of Otherness to speak truth to power—whether to TV viewers from the stage of *The Ed Sullivan Show* or to audiences in Middle America in the 1960s or to the Washington and Hollywood elite at the White House Correspondents' Dinner in the first decade

8.5. Whoopi Goldberg's directorial debut, *Whoopi Goldberg Presents Moms Mabley* (2013), is a long-overdue tribute to the comic legend.

of the new millennium. As they've moved through their careers, the wholeness and ideological unity of their comic storytelling and truth telling becomes progressively more apparent—and much more difficult to dismiss as just being funny.

In her book *Black Looks*, bell hooks outlines directives for the radical empowerment of black women.

> When black women relate to our bodies, our sexuality, in ways that place erotic recognition, desire, pleasure, and fulfillment at the center of our efforts to create radical black subjectivity, we can make new and different representations of ourselves. . . . To do so we must be willing to transgress traditional boundaries . . . [and] no longer shy away from the critical project of openly interrogating and exploring representations of black female sexuality as they appear everywhere, especially in popular culture.[30]

The comic discourse of Moms Mabley and Wanda Sykes has done and is doing that important work through its inherently subversive nature: speaking their truths and communicating so much through their comedy that folks can't help but learn as they laugh. On May 23,

1975, Jackie "Moms" Mabley died at the age of eighty-one: the first woman comic to play at the Apollo and its all-time record holder for appearances, the young woman who grew old playing the granny and the sage, the comedian who had experienced and seen the travails of being black and a woman and a lesbian and the Funniest Woman in the World. When fellow comic pioneer Dick Gregory spoke of the exceptional nature of her talent in his eulogy for Moms, he stated simply, "Had she been white, she'd have been known fifty years ago." In 2016 Wanda Sykes is at the top of her comic game and continues to be a presence on television screens and theater stages, while she lends her voice to helping the youth of the next generation: whether as benefactor to those in Detroit's Ruth Ellis Center for Homeless LGBTQ Youth or as mother, with Alex, to her fraternal twins, Olivia and Lucas. Undoubtedly, Sykes's world would have seemed unfathomable to Mabley. And without Mabley, who would have blazed the trail for Sykes? Their contributions to comedy, spoken from the intersections of race, gender, and sexual orientation, continue to inspire others and to model how laughter can be transgressive and transformative. And that we'd better recognize.

NOTES

1. Bambi Haggins, *Laughing Mad: The Black Comic Persona in Post-Soul America* (New Brunswick, NJ: Rutgers UP, 2007). See chapter 4, "Crossover Diva: Whoopi Goldberg and Persona Politics," 132–177.

2. *Whoopi Goldberg Presents Moms Mabley* (Dir. Whoopi Goldberg; Whoop/One Ho Productions 2013). DVD. Note that a number of the jokes cited in this chapter from Mabley's comedy routines and certain specific factual statements regarding her background and the significance of her work are references to material provided for this documentary, for which I was a historical consultant.

3. Ibid.

4. Kliph Nesteroff, "Moms Mabley—Agitation in Moderation," *WEMU's Beware of the Blog*, Aug. 26, 2007, http://blog.wfmu.org/freeform/2007/08/moms-mabley---a.html.

5. Ibid.

6. Haggins, *Laughing Mad*, 149.

7. J. Brooks Atkinson, "The Play," *New York Times*, Sept. 16, 1931; and "Lewis Sees 'Fast And Furious' Here: Figures It Is Worth the Price, as Shown at Lafayette," *New York Amsterdam News*, Oct. 7, 1931, 10.

8. *Whoopi Goldberg Presents Moms Mabley*.

9. Lee Michael Katz, "Funny Girl," *Washingtonian*, "People and Politics," June 11, 2010, www.washingtonian.com/articles/people/funny-girl.

10. The term "post-soul baby" combines the notion of the "soul baby" and the concept of "post-soul America," terms that come from cultural critics Mark Anthony Neal and Nelson George.

11. W. E. B. Du Bois, quoted in Linda Mizejewski, *Pretty/Funny: Women Comedians and Body Politics* (Austin: University of Texas Press, 2014), 159.

12. Katz, "Funny Girl."

13. Ibid.

14. Ibid.

15. Ibid.

16. Ibid.

17. Elsie A. Williams, *The Humor of Jackie "Moms" Mabley: An African American Comedy Tradition* (New York: Garland, 1995), 78.

18. "Behind the Laughter of Jackie 'Moms' Mabley," *Ebony*, Aug. 1962, 89–91.

19. After 1969 she would eulogize President Kennedy and Dr. King with Dion's "Abraham, Martin, and John," which in Moms's version includes JFK's slain brother Robert Kennedy. The song hit number thirty-five on the Billboard charts in the summer of 1969, making Moms the oldest person ever to have a U.S. Top 40 hit.

20. *Whoopi Goldberg Presents Moms Mabley*.

21. The anecdote would later be used as the inspiration for an episode during the first season of *Wanda at Large*.

22. *Tongue Untied*.

23. Kimberle Crenshaw, "Intersectionality: The Double Bind of Race and Gender," interview by Sheila Thomas, *Perspectives*, Spring 2004, 2.

24. *Whoopi Goldberg Presents Moms Mabley*.

25. Andrew Dice Clay, whose humor often bordered on misogyny, had his signature version of a certain nursery rhyme: "Jack and Jill went up the hill, both with a buck and a quarter. Jill came down with $2.50. Ohhhh."

26. Williams, *Humor of "Moms,"* 81.

27. In 2011, during National Breast Cancer Awareness Month, Sykes revealed on *The Ellen Degeneres Show* that when she went in for a breast reduction surgery, it was discovered that she had DCIS (ductal carcinoma in situ) in her left breast. Sykes, who has a history of breast cancer in her family, opted to have a bilateral mastectomy. The comic was initially hesitant to reveal her story, saying, "I'm black, then lesbian. I can't be the poster child for everything." *The Ellen Degeneres Show*, Sept. 26, 2011.

28. "Wanda Sykes Fell Out with Parents after 'Coming Out,'" *Express*, Oct. 28, 2013, www.express.co.uk/news/showbiz/439668/Wanda-Sykes-fell-out-with-parents-after-coming-out.

29. Ibid.

30. bell hooks, *Black Looks* (Boston: South End Press, 1992), 76.

CHAPTER 9

ROSEANNE BARR: REMEMBERING *ROSEANNE*

ROSIE WHITE

ON SEPTEMBER 14, 2013, British journalist Lucy Mangan paid homage to *Roseanne* (ABC 1988–1997) in her regular Saturday *Guardian* column. Mangan was working her way through the box set in preparation for the twenty-fifth anniversary of the show's debut in October 1988.

> Watching *Roseanne* now, though, generates some sober reflections amid the laughter. The neat formulas and resolutions of most sits and their coms are revealed. As is the fact that the space, literally and metaphorically, that women occupy in television has not expanded but contracted.[1]

This comment offers a twenty-first-century perspective on *Roseanne*, since the show was originally produced and broadcast in the late eighties and early nineties. How does *Roseanne* look to a contemporary viewer? Like Mangan, I watched the series on British television when it was first broadcast, and re-viewing it in the twenty-first century takes me back to a particular era in my life when I was a poverty-stricken postgraduate in a small northwestern English city. In the late 1980s and early 1990s *Roseanne* was a standout show; there was nothing like it on network television, and, more specifically, there was no one like Roseanne Conner. That depiction of an embattled working-class family revolving around an overweight, sexy, cynical woman, has never really been bested. In September 1989 the *Ladies Home Journal* described Roseanne Conner as "the champion of sass-warfare, a true-blue collar heroine who takes no lip from her boss, her spouse or her kids."[2] The show was a number-one ratings success that propelled its star and creator into the Hollywood firmament while depicting a messy account of working-class family life. It is difficult to watch *Roseanne* now without nostalgia, and Mangan goes on to compare *Roseanne* with the more privileged milieu of Lena Dunham's *Girls* (HBO 2012–2017), the feminist comedy *du jour*. Much has been written in the popular and academic press regarding the recent upsurge of female comedy stars and showrunners.[3] Shows such as *30 Rock* (NBC 2006–2013), *Parks and Recreation* (NBC 2009–2015), *New Girl* (Fox 2011–), and *Girls* appear to signal a promising trend in American television comedy, showcasing women writers and producers as well as star performers. As the hit shows listed above indicate, however, this trend privileges a particular on-screen version of femininity: white, middle-class, heterosexual "adorkable" women—which makes this a timely moment to remember *Roseanne*.

That hit sitcom ground to a halt in 1997 after a disastrous final season that saw it fall from fifth to thirty-fourth in the Nielsen ratings.[4] As the final episode was about to air, writer David Plotz slated Roseanne Barr "as a parody of celebrity, indulging in every whim of the Hollywood overclass"; he argued that the show did not help to raise the standard of American sitcoms or to open that genre to a new rush of working-class characters but merely demonstrated that a stand-up comedian could front a television comedy series.[5] More recent press, however, has acknowledged the extent to which *Roseanne* did open the door for other series featuring eccentric blue-collar families, such as *Grace Under Fire* (ABC 1993–1998), *Malcolm in the Middle* (Fox 2000–2006), and *The Middle* (ABC 2009–).[6] Both Eileen Heisler and DeAnn Heline, creators of *The Middle*, worked on *Roseanne*, as did Amy Sherman-Palladino and Joss Whedon. Plotz's diatribe, however, was consonant with contemporary readings of the sitcom and its star as *Roseanne* came to an end. Barr was seen as the sole cause of the show's demise, as a woman who was "imploding," "losing the plot," or "out of control."[7]

This negative account of Roseanne Barr is part of the media narrative of her celebrity: the tabloid focus on her behavior, body, private life, and fashion choices.[8] Such popular accounts play to the schadenfreude of Barr's fall from primetime grace and chime with academic work that cites *Roseanne*'s demise and Barr's subsequent career as an example of the ways in which a "counter-ideological sitcom" and performer can be expelled from network schedules.[9] Twenty-first century work on *Roseanne* must inevitably refer to Kathleen Rowe Karlyn's landmark analysis of *Roseanne* and Barr herself as an "unruly woman." Rowe Karlyn proposes Barr as an example of comedy that "opens up space for the expression of anger," addressing the character of Roseanne Conner in the sitcom and Roseanne Barr's extradiegetic star persona as resistant to the demands of Hollywood media through their age, size, and class identities.[10] Re-viewing *Roseanne* in the light of these debates invites nostalgia not only for a more overtly political form of television but also for a less complex political landscape that perhaps only the passing of time affords. Such nostalgia positions *Roseanne* and Barr herself as representing a second-wave feminism that has allegedly disappeared from the network schedules, if not from Western politics.

Yet Barr is not an unproblematic feminist heroine; rather, she is a canny survivor in a complex and competitive multiplatform media culture that does not often suffer older, working-class, Jewish women. Part of that survival strategy is undoubtedly endurance; Barr, like Roseanne Conner, refuses to shut up and go away. She is outrageously productive—compulsively blogging, tweeting, and writing—and in this sense appears eminently suited to contemporary convergence culture. Rather like that multiplatform environment, her voice is provocative but not securely wedded to a particular politics. She is authentically inauthentic, a feminist with a postfeminist sensibility. What do I mean by this? One of the most powerful aspects of Barr's star cachet is her "realness," a quality predicated on her background and authenticity. As Roberta Mock notes, however: "Roseanne's staged 'realness' . . . has always been a contestable site, hybrid and fragmented."[11] Nowhere is this contestability more evident than in commentary about Barr's cosmetic surgery.[12] If Barr's feminist unruliness is located in her body—Rowe Karlyn conflates the excess and "looseness" of her body with that of her subversive speech[13]—plastic surgery cuts to the heart of feminist debates about whether such choices demonstrate the potential to remodel one's identity in a postmodern setting or whether the denial of one's history conforms to societal norms regarding what constitutes "beauty." Stephanie Genz proposes that such debate extends a longstanding feminist discussion regarding the hegemony of western beauty myths.[14] For many radical feminists of the second wave, feminine beauty is, as Audre Lorde argues, a "patriarchal invitation to power," denoting a refusal of feminist ideals in its conformist endorsement of middle-class, straight, white femininity and its consequent betrayal of women of color, working-class women, and lesbians. [15] Fat, in these terms, is indeed a feminist issue. Yet Genz notes that with the advent of popular post-feminism and its discourses of individual "empowerment," plastic surgery problematizes the notion of authenticity:

> In effect authenticity emerges as a new discursive ideal in postfem-inist media culture that stresses the possibility of self-realization in the absence of essentialist conceptualizations of the self. . . . Au-thenticity comes to acquire a range of different meanings, being at once an indicator of individual agency and choice while also becom-ing linked to consumerist ideologies and a postmodern visuality that privileges surface over interiority.[16]

Barr embraces this new version of authenticity; even as her writing, comedy, and interviews repeatedly call upon second-wave radical feminist ideals and arguments, her postfeminist celebrity persona si-multaneously calls into question that political ontology. And perhaps that is what it takes to survive in a postfeminist era, within a me-dia environment where feminist and antifeminist discourses are en-tangled in such complex and unrelenting ways.[17] Barr is radical *and* conformist, marginal *and* mainstream. As Mock states (regarding Barr's Jewish identity): "Roseanne's is the voice of a not-quite-white, not-quite-heterosexual, unnaturally 'real,' multiple, hysterical, mas-culine, all-consuming woman fashioned through consumption."[18] Even as Barr claims to contradict the mores of bourgeois culture, she simultaneously aligns herself with bourgeois values. In her sec-ond autobiography, Barr describes her move to plastic surgery as a re-sponse to incest and sexual abuse, a rationale that fits the script of bourgeois narratives of self. Beverley Skeggs notes the strategic power of the "reflexive self" in late western modernity:

> The logic of this experimental individualism (the prosthetic self) for those who can tool themselves up is that disembedding, de-racination, de-gendering and de-classing is possible, even at a time when such classifications are becoming more acute for those at the extreme ends of the social scale.[19]

Barr's public persona engages with such reflexive "prosthetic" indi-vidualism through her adventures in plastic surgery, as in her autobi-ographical narrative (both self-authored and in interviews). Yet in doing so she compulsively references her race, class, and gender. Rather than "disembedding" herself, Barr deploys aspects of her identity— as feminist, as Jewish, as working class—in strategic terms, more and less successfully. As has been evident throughout her career, she will not shut up. In 1993 she commented on her reception in the press: "I'd like it to be about my body of work, not just my body."[20] Yet she made this statement in an article in *Playboy*, at a time when Barr was already adapting her body with breast reductions, a stomach tuck, and a nose job.[21] Again, this paradox can be understood as the voice of a postfeminist celebrity with a feminist sensibility, living all the contradictions that juxtaposition implies. While Barr and *Roseanne* may be figured as resistant to the discourses of mainstream media culture, they are also lodged firmly at its heart. By the 1990s popular culture was adept at incorporating feminist debates to sell consumer products via the commodification of feminism and female agency, deploying discourses of class, race, and gender while tacitly denying that such differences *really* matter.[22]

Such contradictions are evident in Barr's writing, as in this account of her mission on *Roseanne*:

> TV is a language all its own, a land of one dimensional stereotypes that destroys culture, not adds to it. TV is anti-art, a reflection of consumerism that serves the power structure. TV is about demographics. Demographics are about women who buy products. Women have been made prisoners of TV—the more they watch, the more products they buy. Why, then, if TV is largely a medium for and about women, are most of the women on TV being raped, murdered, humiliated, degraded, reduced to their body parts and verbally attacked? The more power we are told we don't have, the more power we are willing to concede.
>
> In *my* show, the Woman is no longer a victim, but in control of her own mind. I wanted to make family sitcoms as we know them obsolete.
>
> I wanted to make television that is not a tool of corporate America, television that is instead in direct opposition to corporate thinking altogether.[23]

This is a remarkable statement, demonstrating both a keen understanding of the corporate regime of network television and a desire to change it from within through sheer force of personality: "In *my* show . . ." The desire to produce a countercultural discourse within a deeply conservative medium is laudable if somewhat naïve, calling on an oppositional model of feminist politics that is no longer feasible—if it ever was. "TV" in this passage is constituted as a coherent body: "*a* language . . . *a* land . . . *a* medium . . . *a* tool of corporate America" (my emphases). TV is undoubtedly all of these things, but it is also part of an overarching system that Barr continues to operate within. Media culture is adept at incorporating subversion and opposition, at deploying "radical" ideas and images to sell us more stuff, and feminism is often reconstituted in popular discourse as both common sense and repudiated other.[24] This is the power of postfeminist incorporation. Yet Barr's statement raises a tantalizing question: What would "television that is . . . in direct opposition to corporate thinking" look like? Television-as-antitelevision is hard to imagine, but the much-derided final season of *Roseanne* may be understood as an attempt to achieve this ambition.

Before the final season aired, Myra Macdonald noted how *Roseanne* addressed difficult questions about the family, the housewife, and heterosexuality, but due to the constraints of the sitcom format, the series never fully developed those tensions.[25] The ninth and final season surpasses those limitations by exploding the generic logic that kept the Conners in check. As such, it is an example of television-as-antitelevision that sets out to deconstruct the family sitcom by breaking open the narrative certainties of *Roseanne*. The season opens with a disturbing rift in the relationship between Roseanne and Dan Conner (John Goodman); in a precredit scene, she calls him fat and he retaliates, instigating a separation that undermines the security of their eight-season on-screen marriage ("Call Waiting," season 9, episode 1). As Roseanne and Dan agonize over their relationship, she finds herself watching television and, in a series of dream sequences, walks us through a history of women in American sitcoms on the three major networks. Roseanne sees herself in parodies of *That Girl* (ABC 1966–1971), *I Dream of Jeannie* (NBC 1965–1970), and *The Mary Tyler Moore Show* (CBS 1970–1977), a fantasy montage that cites *Roseanne*'s television heritage. The antirealist style of this first episode sets the agenda for the final season, in which *Roseanne* turns the camera on television itself and attacks some of the fictions it sustains. Although the ninth season has been widely panned, it presents an acidic parody of popular television, celebrity culture, and postfeminism. This does not make it good. The scripts and performances are at times clunky, "jumping the shark" in so many ways that the affectionate realism of earlier seasons is shattered. And perhaps this is the point. By 1997 *Roseanne* had been outstripped in the ratings by *The Simpsons* (Fox 1989–), a series about another working-class family that has proved extremely resilient. *The Simpsons* is cheap to produce and highly satirical—but it is animation. It has no stars. Barr's celebrity persona is as much the subject of the final season of *Roseanne* as the Conner family itself.

The ninth season's storyline, like the fantasy sequences it introduces, turns the American dream of wealth into a series of scenarios that often border on nightmare. When the Conners hear that they have won the Illinois State Lottery with a jackpot of $108 million, they go crazy. Roseanne states that she is "going to get me a ton of plastic surgery" ("Millions from Heaven," episode 2), referencing Barr's well-publicized elective procedures. Roseanne's boss, Leon, says their win is his "worst nightmare," echoing Barr's widely reported comment following her marriage to Tom Arnold in 1990: "We're America's worst nightmare: white trash with money."[26] Subsequent episodes depict the culture clash of upper-middle-class hotels, health spas, and high society when faced with the "white trash" behavior of the Conners and their entourage. This makes David Plotz's claim that Barr became "a parody of celebrity, indulging in every whim of the Hollywood overclass" moot, as the ninth season self-consciously parodies such indulgent celebrity lifestyles, and Barr herself is frequently the butt of the joke.[27] "Pampered to a Pulp" (episode 6), for example, lampoons the now-standard narrative of makeover television. Shows such as *The Swan* (Fox 2004–2005), *American Princess* (WeTV 2005–2007), and *What Not to Wear* (Discovery 2003–) all follow the standard program format of "reveal and heal," which involves initial humiliation followed by a redemptive makeover process and the final tearful "reveal" in front of friends and family. As Gareth Palmer notes in his critique of *What Not to Wear*: "Any amount of bullying and abuse is necessary for the individual to be improved."[28] Such shows claim to overcome or eradicate class distinctions but in fact work to enforce "desirable" class and national identities through their demonstrations of how appropriate cultural capital should be performed.[29]

In "Pampered to a Pulp," Roseanne and Jackie go to an upmarket hotel and health spa where they are checked in and inspected so that the staff can "reveal and heal" them; Roseanne is bluntly told by sev-

9.1. Carol (Moon Unit Zappa) evaluates Roseanne (Roseanne Barr) and Jackie (Laurie Metcalf) in "Pampered to a Pulp," *Roseanne* (1997).

eral of the staff that she is "unpleasantly fat." A number of sequences parody the rituals of women's health and beauty: while Roseanne is pilloried for her girth, Jackie is abused for her small breasts and inappropriate body hair. Laurie Metcalf, as Jackie, delivers a remarkable performance, physically contorting herself as she apologizes for her alleged shortcomings or becoming entangled in a static cycling machine as she tries to follow the new regime. The spa staff guide Jackie and Roseanne through a series of humiliating processes; they are put into therapeutic seaweed wraps so tight that they cannot move or breathe and are subjected to violent Thai massage, painful waxing, and derogatory facials. Finally, in search of a less agonizing treatment, Roseanne agrees to go through past-life regression therapy, featuring Ahmet and Moon Unit Zappa as ridiculous New Age practitioners, and she "regresses" to become Xena. In a subsequent session about how to dress, she challenges the fashion designer Todd Oldham (playing himself) about the size of women's clothing in haute couture, and when he patronizes her with the advice that she has "a pretty face," she knees him in the groin. The final scene depicts Roseanne and Jackie dressed in outrageous "designer" outfits, parading through the spa foyer to gasps of amazement (or horror) from the staff and Oldham.

"Pampered to a Pulp" exposes the extent to which the "reveal" of makeover shows is predicated on middle-class ideals regarding straight white femininity. Staff at the spa are cruel and rude, and the processes that Roseanne and Jackie are subject to are neither relaxing nor scientific. Both Barr and Metcalfe demonstrate, via clownish physical comedy, the discomfort of the treatments and the g-string leotards they have to wear. Their final "reveal" in outrageous outfits merely confirms the whole process as ridiculous. In its closing scenes the episode features Tammy Faye Bakker (playing herself) teaching a make-up class. Bakker states, "Let your face tell its own story," only then turning to face the camera and reveal the grotesque distortions of plastic surgery. This disturbing combination of a visual punch line and a parody of the "reveal" effectively announces that the humor in this episode—as in the whole final season—is designed to be neither subtle nor nuanced; this is comedy as polemic.

Subsequent episodes enact a similar satire on high society. In "Satan, Darling" (episode 7) their old friend Nancy Bartlett (Sandra Bernhard) takes Roseanne and Jackie to a New York charity event. Everyone is dressed in black, and Roseanne and Jackie are tutored in the rules of their new society—"spas are out . . . bragging's in"—while Nancy's friend Astrid (Mo Gaffney) points out ridiculously named socialites. Although Roseanne and Jackie are agog at their new surroundings, the New York scene clearly offers a distorted milieu where the most desirable body size is cited as "two pounds above organ failure." Most tellingly, Roseanne repeatedly eyeballs a mannequin-like woman who stands alone at the party, holding a martini glass that she never drinks from. This static figure resembles Jackie Onassis and represents a commentary on privileged forms of femininity; thin, white, immobile, and silent.

The episode also features guest appearances from Jennifer Saunders and Joanna Lumley as Edina Monsoon and Patsy Stone, in a bizarre mash-up of *Roseanne* and *Absolutely Fabulous* (BBC 1992–2012).[30] Edie and Patsy chase after the money from the lottery win by plying Roseanne and Jackie with alcohol and drugs. Hallucinating, Roseanne steps through a rotating door in the wall of the ladies toilet to find a group of society witches (including Marlo Thomas, star of *That Girl*, and Arianna Huffington) and then enters another fantasy sequence where Darlene (Sara Gilbert) is pregnant in a parody of *Rosemary's Baby* (1968). During an attempt to rescue the baby, Roseanne is confronted by the "devil's advocate," played by Barr her-

9.2. Roseanne eyeballs the silent Jackie Onassis lookalike in "Satan, Darling," *Roseanne* (1997).

self, who announces, "You have become a have in a world of have-nots." The subsequent episode continues the class theme as Astrid invites the Conners to stay with her dysfunctional upper-class family on Martha's Vineyard. The show addresses the amorality of privileged classes by employing lines such as "We don't start wars, we just profit from them" ("Hoi Polloi Meets Hoity-Toity," episode 8).

This critique of the beauty myth and of upper-class society sits oddly with the fantasy sequences; in any case, as we are told in the final, two-part episode, this is all a dream. It does, however, appear to be a dream (or a nightmare) that is primarily concerned with gender, class, and identity. There is a strong sense of doubleness throughout, as Barr satirizes her own celebrity while also playing Roseanne Conner. When Barr as "devil's advocate" reminds Roseanne that she has "become a have in a world of have-nots," it is not clear whether Barr or the character "Roseanne" is being addressed. More than anything else, these sequences appear to openly reference Barr's "staged 'realness.'" Even the working-class authenticity of the sitcom's central character is addressed. Roseanne Conner still claims to be rooted in her working-class identity, despite her sudden wealth. In a later episode Dan returns home for Christmas after visiting his mother—a trip funded by the lottery win, which prompts him to want to move her to a better hospital—and it emerges that he has become involved with his mother's nurse. When Dan tells Roseanne, she is devastated, refusing to be comforted by his assertion that nothing significant had happened. Roseanne pointedly states: "I'm not Rose Kennedy. I'm working class. I see the world in black and white; no amount of money will get me to see grey" ("Say It Ain't So," episode 13). Roseanne hereby claims her working-class identity as affect, in a scene that harks back to the more realist style of earlier seasons. *Roseanne* addressed class identity throughout its run, speaking to it, parodying it, representing it. The ninth season brings that process to a logical conclusion by highlighting the media focus on Barr's life outside the show. The Conners are suddenly at large, engaging in high-end consumption and mixing with high society. They are looking outwards, and *Roseanne*'s final season attends to the contradictions of an increasingly mediatized landscape at the close of the twentieth century. The show and its star work against the grain of popular television and celebrity media culture, which attempt either to efface class identity or to fetishize it as a stereotype, as something that represents a particular position. Instead the working-class Conners and their entourage offer a commentary on celebrity lifestyles, anticipating the effect of celebrity news streams and online blogs in the twenty-first century.

As season 9 draws to a close, comedy becomes drama; the tone of each episode is increasingly elegiac, working towards the final episode where the tragic "reality" of Roseanne's life emerges. Roseanne and Dan struggle to resume their relationship ("Hit the Road, Jack," episode 14; "The War Room," episode 15; "A Second Chance," episode 18), Darlene gives birth to a premature baby ("The Miracle," episode 19), and Roseanne's mother Bev (Estelle Parsons) comes out to *her* mother (Shelley Winters) and acquires a girlfriend ("Mothers and Other Strangers," episode 11; "Roseanne Feld," episode 20). The commentary on Barr's success and celebrity continues as she encounters Landford's elite and agrees to invest in local business, turning the factory she once worked in over to the workers to save it from closure ("Landford's Elite," episode 16; "Some Enchanted Merger," episode 17). Most pointedly, when Roseanne's life story becomes the subject of a bidding war between cable and network television companies, the executives want to either sanitize or sensationalize it ("The Truth Be Told," episode 21). The last two episodes constitute an elegy for the series as a whole, signaled by a pointed reference to the

9.3. Roseanne writes her own story in "Into That Good Night, Part 2," *Roseanne* (1997).

first episode of the first season, in which Roseanne was called in to see Darlene's teacher because her daughter had been barking in class.

In a remarkable closing sequence, the storyline of this ninth and final season is completely exploded. In "Into That Good Night, Part 2" (episode 24), the Conners sit around a table eating Chinese takeout as the camera moves around them, echoing the show's famous title sequence, and Roseanne in voiceover begins to describe her inspiration for the show. Barr's prosthetic self is to the fore in this mash-up of her performance as Roseanne Conner, her star persona, and the sitcom series she created. The line between performer and character is irrevocably blurred; it is unclear whether the voice we are hearing is that of Roseanne Conner or Roseanne Barr, producing a disorienting profusion of metatexts. Regarding her mother (in the show), Roseanne says that she made her gay so that she would "have some sense of herself as a unit"; and notes that her sister *is* gay (as Barr's sister Geraldine is) and that "she's been my rock." When the camera reaches Dan, Roseanne reveals that she "lost him last year when he had his heart attack," and the screen goes dark with Dan's voice distantly heard calling, "Rosie?" The scene cuts to Roseanne sitting alone in the basement, which has become her writing room. She has made the whole lottery story up as a means of coping with the grimmer realities of her "real" storyline. Dan is dead, and as Roseanne sits at her desk, reading and writing, her voiceover delivers a monologue that rewrites that final season as a fantasy created by its central character.

This "it was all a dream" finale is more than a shark-jumping peccadillo; what it delivers is an extraordinary moment in popular television, as a star character suddenly steps out of the frame and reflects upon her narrative. It is also extraordinary in its refusal to support the medium's imperative for visual spectacle. There is no action here, just a woman sitting at a desk, looking at a pile of papers and occasionally making a note or a correction. Writing is the least visually exciting activity; when television or film addresses the life or work of a writer, it is often intercut with flashbacks, extradiegetic soundtracks, or visual depictions of what is being written. None of that is employed here; instead we are cast into a more brutal theatrical milieu, with Roseanne in mid-shot thinking about her life. The voiceover "tells" us what she is thinking, but it is not decorated with cutaway scenes or music; this is television as antitelevision in a sequence which lasts several minutes:

When you're a blue-collar woman and your husband dies it takes away your whole sense of security. So I began writing about having all the money in the world, and I imagined myself going to spas and swanky New York parties just like the people on TV, where nobody has any real problems and everything's solved within thirty minutes. I tried to imagine myself as Mary Richards, Jeannie, *That Girl*. But I was so angry I was more like a female Steven Segal wanting to fight the whole world. For a while I lost myself in food and a depression so deep that I couldn't even get out of bed till I saw that my family needed me to pull through so that they could pull through. One day, I actually imagined being with another man. But then I felt so guilty I had to pretend it was for some altruistic reason. And then Darlene had the baby, and it almost died. I snapped out of the mourning immediately, and all of my life energy turned into choosing life. In choosing life, I realized that my dreams of being a writer wouldn't just come true; I had to do the work. And as I wrote about my life, I relived it, and whatever I didn't like, I rearranged. I made a commitment to finish my story even if I had to write in the basement in the middle of the night while everyone else was asleep. But the more I wrote, the more I understood myself and why I had made the choices I made, and that was the real jackpot. I learned that dreams don't work without action; I learned that no one could stop me but me. I learned that love is stronger than hate. And most important, I learned that God does exist. He and/or She is right inside you, underneath the pain, the sorrow, and the shame. I think I'll be a lot better now that this book is done. ("Into That Good Night: Part 2," episode 24)

As the credits roll Roseanne leaves the basement and goes to sit on the shabby sofa in the old living room, switching on the TV and flicking through the channels alone. We hear Roseanne's anarchic laughter for a final time, the riotous sound that started each episode, but now it is a rough-edged cackle that echoes in a silent room.

In this series finale Barr does indeed unpack the family sitcom format; her monologue addresses women, power, and television. She has destroyed the family sitcom by destroying the central tenet of the heterosexual couple (through Dan's death) and by removing the comedy. This is not a funny ending to a very funny show; it is rather a deadly serious commentary on the preceding season (if not on the series as a whole). "Into That Good Night, Part 2" is remarkable television—a pyrrhic conclusion to a hit show. By removing the comedy and exposing the trauma and conflict that underlie Roseanne's wisecracking persona, Barr also ensures that she cannot go back, because she does not go gently. Barr thus deploys her authentically inauthentic star persona to deconstruct the format that made her famous. It is a revolutionary act.

If the final season of *Roseanne* offers a critical commentary on the history of women and television sitcoms, what has happened to Barr since *Roseanne* is equally significant. She has taken to the online world with a vengeance, while television networks evidently find it difficult to place her. In the years since *Roseanne*, Barr has hosted a talk show (*The Roseanne Show*, CBS 1998–2000); a cookery show, *Domestic Goddess*, produced by her son, Jake Pentland; and a reality show about making that cookery show, *The Real Roseanne Show* (ABC 2003).[31] In July 2011 *Roseanne's Nuts*, a reality show set on Barr's macadamia nut farm in Hawaii and featuring her son and partner, aired on Lifetime but was cancelled by September.[32] As Barr broke news of the cancellation on Twitter, she was already in talks with Fox about a new scripted sitcom, *Downwardly Mobile* (NBC 2012), and had announced that she was running for political office.[33] The series made it to pilot stage with NBC but was not picked up. In 2013 NBC announced that they were working with Barr on another new comedy series.[34]

Television production and broadcasting have changed beyond imagining since *Roseanne*'s last episode in 1997, and the new generation of television comedies written, produced by, or starring women occupy a very different landscape. As the résumé above indicates, Barr continues to work on television, albeit often in short-lived productions. Barr's post-*Roseanne* career demonstrates television's Darwinian environment, a corporate system like any other, constantly searching for faster and cheaper ways to profit in a global consumer market. Barr's latest venture into sitcom territory will reportedly take advantage of a new *modus operandi* that exploits the industry's "magic number" of one hundred episodes produced before a show is sold into syndication. The production company Debmar-Mercury was the first to deploy this new strategy; rather than waiting for the one-hundredth episode to emerge at the usual industry pace of production, they shoot one hundred episodes in one go, air them at a gallop on one network, and thus go straight to syndication. This is achieved by doubling the rate of production—two episodes a week are filmed rather than the standard one—and by cutting corners at every turn. It is a post-Fordist approach to sitcom production that produces material with an eye on the rerun market for comedy shows and explicitly prioritizes profit over quality. The sting in the tail is how that profit is gendered:

> Not only do these shows sign up already bankable stars such as [Charlie] Sheen, George Lopez, and *Frazier*'s Kelsey Grammer— tempting them by offering a big chunk of the eventual profits—but they try to follow the formulas of syndicated sitcom hits. "We will only do male-led sitcoms" [Debmar-Mercury president] Bernstein says, explaining why his company doesn't sign up female stars, "because that's what repeats."[35]

Barr is an exception to this focus on male stars, primarily because of the continuing success of *Roseanne* in syndication; as of June 2013, she was working with *Nurse Jackie* (Showtime 2009–) cocreator and former showrunner Linda Wallem on scripts for the new series.[36]

Looking back on the final season of *Roseanne*, it now appears remarkably prescient in its critique of postfeminist sensibility. If contemporary media culture offers a contradictory postfeminism that represents second-wave feminism as both "common sense" and repudiated other, *Roseanne* is a reminder that feminist arguments continue to be relevant, important, and necessary.[37] Angela McRobbie argues that in postfeminist popular culture: "The new female subject is, despite her freedom, called upon to be silent, to withhold critique, to count as a modern sophisticated girl."[38] Barr, a woman rather than a "girl," refuses that "modern, sophisticated," and silent complicity. Her political positions may be diverse—as evidenced by her online activities—but she remains committed to a second-wave model of engaged activism, stating in a recent Tweet: "Feminism devoid of any economic or class analysis is fema nism."[39] Barr has embraced cyberactivism and the access it provides to diverse publics and institutions.[40] The raucous laughter that introduced each episode of *Roseanne* is thus unconfined. Barr continues to land television spots, such as her current stint as a judge on NBC's *Last Comic Standing* (2003–) and work on Investigation Discovery's *Momsters: Moms Gone Bad* (2014–), but they attest to her marginal position in relation to the major networks. Her online output, as with her work with Investigation Discovery, is indicative of her continuing relation to and refusal of the corporate regime of networked sitcoms. In a recent PBS documentary, Barr reflected on *Roseanne*: "Just to throw some mud in the eye of the beast was fun."[41] One can only hope that some of the current crop of women working in popular television comedy will be able to say the same.

NOTES

1. Lucy Mangan, "Roseanne Barr Got Working Women; Lena Dunham's *Girls* Doesn't Come Close," *Guardian Weekend*, Sept. 14, 2013.

2. Cited in Janet Lee, "Subversive Sitcoms: *Roseanne* as Inspiration for Feminist Resistance," in *Gender, Race, and Class in Media: A Text-Reader*, eds. Gail Dines and Jean M. Humez (London: Sage, 1995), 470.

3. See, for example, Erika Engstrom, "'Knope We Can!': Primetime Feminist Strategies in NBC's *Parks and Recreation*," *Media Report to Women* 41, no. 4 (Fall 2013): 6–21; Lesley Goldberg, "TCA: Lena Dunham Says HBO's *Girls* Isn't *Sex and the City*," *Hollywood Reporter*, Jan. 13, 2012, www.hollywoodreporter.com/live-feed/tca-hbo-girls-lena-dunham-judd-apatow-281483; Lisa W. Kelly, "For Us, By Us? Gender, Privilege and Race in HBO's *Girls*," *CST Online*, 2013, http://cstonline.tv/for-us-by-us-gender-privilege-race; Martha Lauzen, "The Funny Business of Being Tina Fey: Constructing a (Feminist) Comedy Icon," *Feminist Media Studies* 14, no. 1 (2014): 106–117; Linda Mizejewski, "Feminism, Postfeminism, Liz Lemonism: Comedy and Gender Politics on *30 Rock*," *Genders* 55 (Spring 2012): n.p., www.genders.org/g55/g55_mizejewski.html.

4. Joanne Morreale, "Television in the 1990s and Beyond," in *Critiquing the*

Sitcom: A Reader, ed. Joanne Morreale (New York: Syracuse University Press, 2003), 247.

5. David Plotz, "Domestic Goddess Dethroned: How Roseanne Lost It," *Slate*, May 18, 1997, www.slate.com/articles/news_and_politics/assessment/1997/05/domestic_goddess_dethroned.html.

6. Tanner Stransky, "20 Years Ago This Week . . . Roseanne Marries Tom Arnold," *Entertainment Weekly*, Jan. 29, 2010, 8.

7. Alessandra Senzani, "Class and Gender as a Laughing Matter? The Case of *Roseanne*," *Humor* 23 no. 2 (2010): 245.

8. Ibid., 241–246.

9. Rosanne Freed, "The Gripes of Wrath: Roseanne's Bitter Comedy of Class," *Television Quarterly* 30, no. 2 (Fall 1999): 90–99; Elizabeth Arveda Kissling, "On the Rag on Screen: Menarche in Film and Television," *Sex Roles* 46, no. 1/2 (Jan. 2002): 10–11.

10. Kathleen Rowe (Karlyn), *The Unruly Woman: Gender and the Genres of Laughter* (Austin: University of Texas Press, 1995), 67. Also see Kathleen Rowe Karlyn, "Roseanne: Unruly Woman as Domestic Goddess," in Joanne Morreale, *Critiquing the Sitcom*, 251–261.

11. Roberta Mock, *Jewish Women on Stage, Film, and Television* (Basingstoke, UK: Palgrave Macmillan, 2007), 136.

12. For an examination of the deployment of explicit discussion about surgical interventions as a comedic strategy, see Roberta Mock's essay "Stand-up Comedy and the Legacy of the Mature Vagina," *Women and Performance* 22, no. 1 (2012), 9–28.

13. Rowe Karlyn, "Roseanne," 256.

14. Stephanie Genz, "Under the Knife: Feminism and Cosmetic Surgery in Contemporary Culture," in *Women on Screen: Feminism and Femininity in Visual Culture*, ed. Melanie Waters (Basingstoke, UK: Palgrave Macmillan, 2011): 123–135.

15. Cited in ibid., 124.

16. Ibid., 125.

17. Rosalind Gill and Christina Scharff, introduction to *New Femininities: Postfeminism, Neoliberalism, and Subjectivity*, ed. Rosalind Gill and Christina Scharff (London: Palgrave Macmillan, 2011), 4.

18. Mock, *Jewish Women*, 138.

19. Beverley Skeggs, *Class, Self, Culture* (London: Routledge, 2004), 133.

20. Quoted in Joanne R. Gilbert, *Performing Marginality: Humor, Gender, and Cultural Critique* (Detroit: Wayne State University Press, 2004), 143.

21. John Lahr, "Dealing with Roseanne," *New Yorker*, July 17, 1995, 48.

22. Rosalind Gill, *Gender and the Media* (Cambridge, UK: Polity Press, 2007), 84; Kimberly Springer, "Divas, Evil Black Bitches, and Bitter Black Women: African American Women in Postfeminist and Post-Civil-Rights Popular Culture," in *Interrogating Postfeminism: Gender and the Politics of Popular Culture*, ed. Yvonne Tasker and Diane Negra (Durham, NC: Duke University Press, 2007), 249–276.

23. Roseanne Arnold, *Roseanne: My Lives* (London: Century, 1994), 234–235.

24. Gill, *Gender and the Media*.

25. Myra Macdonald, *Representing Women: Myths of Femininity in the Popular Media* (London: Edward Arnold, 1995), 144–145.

26. Stransky, "20 Years Ago," 8.

27. Plotz, "Domestic Goddess Dethroned."

28. Gareth Palmer, "'The New You': Class and Transformation in Lifestyle Television," in *Understanding Reality Television*, ed. Su Holmes and Deborah Jermyn (London: Routledge, 2004), 182.

29. Palmer, "'The New You'"; Martin Roberts, "The Fashion Police: Governing the Self in *What Not to Wear*," in Tasker and Negra, *Interrogating Postfeminism*, 227–248; Brenda Weber, "Imperialist Projections: Manners, Makeovers, and Models of Nationality," in Waters, *Women on Screen*, 136–152.

30. Barr had won the rights to coproduce an American version of *Absolutely Fabulous* with Warner Bros.; see Lahr, "Dealing with Roseanne," 44.

31. John Leland, "A Roseanne Wrapped in an Enigma," *New York Times*, July 27, 2003.

32. Lesley Goldberg, "Lifetime Cancels *Roseanne's Nuts*," *Hollywood Reporter*, Sept. 21, 2011, www.hollywoodreporter.com/live-feed/lifetime-cancels-roseannes-nuts-238847.

33. Lacey Rose, "Roseanne Barr Preps Comeback Sitcom 'Downwardly Mobile' for 20th Television (Exclusive)," *Hollywood Reporter*, Aug. 10, 2011, www.hollywoodreporter.com/news/roseanne-barr-preps-comeback-sitcom-221143.

34. Cynthia Littleton, "Pilot Picture Clearer," *Daily Variety*, May 7, 2012, 4, 16; Cynthia Littleton, "NBC Raises Barr Again," *Daily Variety*, Feb. 1, 2013, 6.

35. Jaime J. Weinman, "Fast-forward to the Reruns," *Maclean's*, July 29, 2013, 1.

36. Nellie Andreeva, "NBC Eyes 10/90 Order for Roseanne Barr Comedy Co-Written by Linda Wallem," *Deadline Hollywood*, June 28, 2013, www.deadline.com/2013/06/roseanne-barr-comedy-series-order-near-nbc-linda-wallem.

37. Gill, *Gender and the Media*, 1.

38. Angela McRobbie, "Post-Feminism and Popular Culture," *Feminist Media Studies* 4, no. 3 (2004): 260.

39. @therealroseanne, May 28, 2014.

40. See, for example, http://paper.li/TheRealRoseanne/1354942269; and https://twitter.com/therealroseanne.

41. "The Independent Woman," *United States of Television: America in Primetime* (BBC 2013), season 1, episode 3.

CHAPTER 10

WHOOPI GOLDBERG IN HOLLYWOOD:
QUEERING COMIC GENRE GENEALOGIES

REBECCA WANZO

It's not what you call me, but what I answer to.
AFRICAN PROVERB THAT SERVES AS THE EPIGRAPH TO
WHOOPI GOLDBERG'S *BOOK*

IN A COLUMN ASKING, "Does Whoopi Always Associate With Flops?," Robert Bianco wrote, "It's not easy to write a starring role for Ms. Goldberg, who is hardly your typical romantic lead. . . . For whatever reason, seldom has Hollywood used a major talent so poorly, or has a major talent squandered her abilities on so many terrible projects."[1] While Goldberg's performances in her one-woman show, *The Spook Show* (1984), and its (Broadway) iteration, *Whoopi Goldberg* (1984), are universally understood as tours de force, many people agree, as Goldberg has stated herself, that nobody in Hollywood knew what to do with her.[2] But the discourse of failure and stereotype replication risks ignoring Goldberg's legacy as the first African American woman to get multiple lead roles in mainstream Hollywood films and as the most financially successful African American film actress in the twentieth century.[3] Her "fit" in Hollywood, however awkward, might tell us something about how different types of performers and consumers who "do not fit" might engage with cultural fantasies produced and circulated by the American film industry.

The tension between Goldberg's incongruity within Hollywood and her ability to fit within various genres is an important part of her legacy as a comic actress. Many philosophers and theorists have argued that humor is produced by incongruity, and in the western imagination black people are inherently incongruous. In one of the most famous texts about humor, Henri Bergson's *Laughter: An Essay on the Meaning of the Comic*, Bergson asks, "Why does one laugh at the negro?"[4] For Bergson, operating with a western understanding of black people as always out of place, black people seem to be whites in disguise. But Goldberg's performances in comedy make hypervisible the ways in which idealized bodies are the masks all performers must wear to fit in the Hollywood imaginary. Goldberg's play with "not fitting in" and performing the other badly is a means of simultaneously disrupting identity categories and affirming her ability to belong.

In this chapter I argue that while Goldberg was often characterized early in her career as an actress Hollywood did not "know what to do with," the alleged dissonance created by her presence in Hollywood films demonstrates some of the tensions inherent to comedic genres, tensions produced by racialized, gendered, and normative sexual frameworks those genres both depend upon and constantly disrupt. The discourse of Goldberg "not fitting" actually reflects the narrow reading of black women in broader cultural narratives.[5] A number of scholars have argued that many of Goldberg's performances are mammy roles, but such reductive readings risk missing how her performances situate black women into other generic genealogies. Like Mia Mask, I agree that in many of her films she "menaces the dominant discourses of womanhood, femininity, nuclear family, and class boundaries."[6] Mask argues that Goldberg performs a "carnivalesque rebelliousness," borrowing the term from Mikhail Bakhtin. In examining how the actress uses masquerade and drag, she highlights Goldberg's disruption of gender performance. However, her reading only tells half the story of Whoopi's comedic performances. Her early films were not just about disruption. If all of us who grew up watching Hollywood fantasies are somewhat interpellated by them, her performances also demonstrate how we may approach these fantastic ideals with not only resistance but also love, longing, and attachment to the narrative pleasures of fulfillment and closure offered in Hollywood film.

The term "genre" describes narratives with similar elements, and if we preserve the taxonomic understanding of "genre" as genus, family, and relationality, even people who are treated as cultural outliers are still a part of the family. Narratives about heroes, lovers, and other saviors are what most of us were raised with in the United States, and creators understood as outside of the mainstream often recraft genres to make room for the specificity of their cultural experiences. I want to make a case here for rereading Goldberg's work as demonstrating how outliers rework scripts of national belonging. Her choice of film roles shows her investment in producing performances that are part of various traditions of comedy or drama. These genres, for Goldberg, belong as much to her as they do to others. She articulates her sense of American belonging most explicitly in her first collection of essays, *Book*.

> I'm not an African American. . . . I'm a mutt. There's a whole lot of historical adventure that belongs to me, and I refuse to let our cultural demagogues rob me of what's mine. George Washington belongs to me. Lou Gehrig belongs to me. Jackie Robinson belongs to me. Nathan's hot dogs belong to me. . . . The Lower East Side is mine. The amber waves of fucking grain? Mine. I'm as American as Chevrolet.[7]

"American-ness" is myth, shared history, and what Benedict Anderson has termed "imagined community," and the myths of American identity are omnipresent in film genres.[8] Goldberg's performances highlight the ways in which she does have a place in these genealogies, albeit one that constantly calls attention to how her inherent incongruity in American protagonist frameworks as a racialized subject merges with gender incongruity to highlight how integral fitting by "not fitting" is to not only comic genealogies, but some discourses of Americanness itself. As Rick Altman argues, "Neither genre nor nation is a single coherent concept referring to a single coherent referent. The very notion of genre and nation depend on constant conflict among multiple competing but related notions, based on diverse user need and varied parameters."[9] Because genre depends on "constant conflict," the dissonance some critics have detected in her films may be instrumental in telling us what kinds of bodies and performances these genres resist *and* accommodate.

This chapter tracks Goldberg's play with belonging in comedy through incongruence—largely through expansive use of what I would describe as drag—in pivotal performances in the first part of her career. From her articulation of the role ideal bodies play in cultural value in her one-woman show to playing with the notion of varied kinds of drag in *Sister Act*, *The Associate*, *Ghost*, and *Corinna, Corinna*, Goldberg both disrupts idealized constructions and naturalizes a black female presence in genres that are consistently situated in Hollywood as inappropriate for black women stars. While both popular critics and scholars all too easily read Goldberg as a mammy, such readings force Goldberg into normative readings of black female bodies when so many of her performances contest normative readings of black women and queer race and gendered representations in classic generic formulas. If "queer" can refer to, as Eve Sedgwick argues, "the open mesh of possibilities, gaps, overlaps, dissonances and resonances, lapses and excesses of meaning when the constituent elements of anyone's gender, of anyone's sexuality, aren't made (or can't be made) to signify monolithically," then a number of Goldberg's comedic starring roles disrupt monolithic readings of gender and sexuality in Hollywood genre.[10] In showing that Goldberg functions as a queer figure in the first decade of her career, I am not suggesting that Goldberg has never embraced heteronormative plots, or that she provides a radical disruption of the pleasures of genre. On the contrary, part of what makes Goldberg an interesting figure as a star is the negotiation of her relationship between the normative and queer, the fantasy and the real, belonging and outsider status.

WHOOPI AND DRAG

Drag performance lies at the tension between reassertion and subversion of gender categories. Such performances can be a subject's assertion of an identity that does not match gender assignment, a hyperrepresentation of naturalized gender performances and norms, or both. In this chapter I am not looking at the kind of drag performances that do the work of articulating gender identity and serve in creating productive queer community. Instead, I focus on a comedic tradition of drag that is not interrelational. Drag highlights the racialized nature of gender presentation. Thus drag performances have a relationship to minstrelsy and what I would more generally term "race-face" performances. Comedians have long made use of drag—usually men performing as women—but understanding Goldberg as also working within this tradition can help us see how many of her comedic performances call attention to the racialized nature of gender performances and the fantasies that circulate around idealized bodies.

Whoopi Goldberg's play with gender presentation was immediately apparent in the one-woman show that first brought her national attention, *The Spook Show* and its Broadway version, *Whoopi Goldberg*. Sporting dreadlocks before the style became widely popular with African American women, and loose-fitting shirts and pants that do not call attention to her body, Goldberg's aesthetic choices bore a relationship to one of Goldberg's most profound influences, Jackie "Moms" Mabley.[11] Although a lesbian, Mabley made jokes on-stage about her desire for young men, and she critiqued racism through the charade of being a harmless, cantankerous grandmother. Mabley was black and female, but her black female performance was nonetheless a masquerade. And she used this masquerade to tell comedic stories that critique racism and sexism.

Goldberg performs a variety of male and female characters in her one-woman show. Bambi Haggins argues that the male character Fontaine represents the "truest indication of Goldberg's actual comic voice" at the time the character was first performed.[12] Informed by Goldberg's own experience as a heroin addict, Fontaine is a drug addict with a witty, black radical political voice who "stays high" so he "don't get mad." Producing the longest monologue in the show, Fontaine would take center stage in the show *Fontaine: Why Am I Straight?* (1988), and some version of that critical voice would be seen in Goldberg's stand-up, in various film performances, and in the public persona she exhibits in interviews and role as a host on the talk show *The View* (ABC 1997–).

However, while Fontaine is clearly an important part of Goldberg's comic identity, the voices in "Little Girl with Blonde Hair" and "Crippled Lady" are equally important to understanding Goldberg's comic career and the ways in which she calls attention to feminine performance by women who do not possess ideal bodies. In the monologue, "Little Girl with Blonde Hair," Whoopi adopts the persona of an African American six-year-old girl with a long, pale shirt hanging from her head. She smiles sweetly at the audience and introduces herself with the line, "This is my long, luxurious blonde hair. Ain't it pretty?" This is a comic version of the affect described in the Kenneth and Mamie Clark experiments with black dolls that would be important in the *Brown v. Board of Education* case and in the story of Pecola Breedlove in Toni Morrison's *The Bluest Eye*, in which a young black girl associates blue eyes with love and escape from emotional abuse.[13] Although born in the allegedly "post"–civil rights era, Goldberg's young character still associates blonde hair and blue eyes with possibility.

She says she will have "blonde hair and blue eyes" and "be white," which would enable her to have a "dream house, and dream car, and dream candy" and live with Malibu Barbie and Ken. If you are white you can "go somewhere exciting," and her evidence for this is tele-

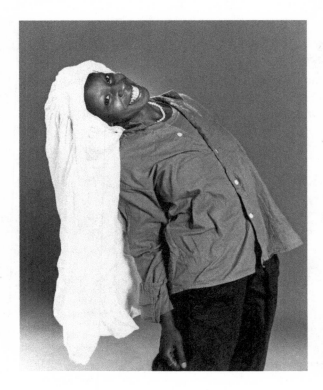

10.1. Whoopi Goldberg as "Little Girl with Blonde Hair." Photofest.

vision consumption: "You gotta have long hair to be on *The Love Boat.*" Her (black) mother, in contrast, "work all the time" and "don't even know nobody exciting and nobody exciting know her." Since her mother "doesn't even look like nobody on TV, not even in the *Justice League*—not even on *The Smurfs,*" her lack of value and importance is transparent to a young girl already schooled in racialized hierarchies of value.

The artificiality of affluent white femininity is often an object of humor, but part of the poignant humor is the six-year-old girl's failed performance of that brand of femininity. Goldberg also performed white femininity in the skit "Surfer Girl" to a different end—fully embodying the oft-derided valley girl until she shocks (and slightly indicts) the laughing audience with the reveal that she is thirteen, homeless, and infertile because of a coat-hanger abortion, but the skit of the six-year-old depends on the black girl not being able to pass as white. Her hair "don't do nothing," and when she says, "I want some other kind of hair that do something else," she is clearly also desiring to be some other kind of person who can do (and be) more. She interacts with black people in the audience and approaches them in puzzlement: "Why you don't have your shirt on? You came outside without it and nobody said nothin?" Since "nobody on TV" looks like them, the message she absorbs is that whiteness—an excess of whiteness—is what makes someone visible and valuable.

Goldberg's Little Girl character makes whiteness hypervisible as something that people other than African Americans may struggle to embody. How many white people look like Barbie or Ken and have a dream house? As Richard Dyer has argued, whiteness has been associated with beauty, particularly with women. At the same time, "Whiteness, really white whiteness, is unattainable. Its ideal forms are impossible."[14] The actual hue of whiteness in skin is something even "white" people must aspire to. "The most celebrated blondes" in Hollywood were not truly blonde (and blondeness is overrepresented in media in relationship to its occurrence in nature)—Jean Harlow, Marilyn Monroe, and Bridget Bardot used peroxide to attain their blondeness, a sign of perfect whiteness. Goldberg's skit thus calls attention to the performative nature of whiteness as pure, virginal, and ideal. But if there is also an "aspirational structure" in whiteness, we can see how Goldberg's calling attention to the black child's desire for whiteness gestures to both the performativity in whiteness and its emptiness, a thing that the western subject must pass through to arrive at the "dream house" and "go somewhere exciting." Whiteness here becomes play in a way that both mimics and profoundly disrupts the tradition of cross-racial performance in U.S. culture most commonly known through minstrelsy. Minstrelsy, as Eric Lott has explained, is white performance of imagined black practices for purposes of institutional control, obscuring the realities of black life.[15] Here, the presence of Goldberg's blackness is never supposed to be invisible, and it makes visible the workings of whiteness in order to attack institutions that limit mobility.

Goldberg's "Crippled Lady" performance also recognizes the role that fantasy bodies play in our idea of social mobility and happiness, although her critique of discourses about disability is troubling. From her position as a privileged, temporarily abled body, she performs as a woman who has a physical disability—most likely cerebral palsy, although she never tells the audience.[16] Her movement is limited and speech slightly delayed and slurred. She describes being startled by a man who finds her foxy and allows herself to do things like dance and have an intimate partnership, dreams that she had abandoned. This relationship helps her fantasize about being able bodied, and Goldberg presents her limbs as straightening and her voice transforming to "normal." In her "cripface" performance, we see a replication of a narrative logic that people of color have often critiqued in stories about discrimination—that the person unburdened with "otherness," here able-bodiedness, teaches the other a path to transformation and liberty.

But read in relationship to the long history of Goldberg's play with various kinds of drag, this disability drag should also be understood as an example of her experimenting with trying on "other" and "ideal" bodies as a path to discovering the self. Understanding the politics of transformation in these performances calls attention to a broader trajectory of Whoopi performances that interrogate and complicate the ways in which whiteness and other kinds of ideality make it possible "to do something." Her consistent engagement with this idea helps us to reread the early part of her movie career in which she had starring roles and to connect some performative tropes. Just as the voice of the angry Fontaine confronting racism emerges in various films, the voice of longing that treats impersonation or fantasy as the thing that enables possibility is important in her work as well, although the unfulfilled desire created by her incongruousness is the operative key to the fantasy. In other words, *unsuccessfully* playing others is often what enables Goldberg's characters to be, or become, more themselves.

THE NUN FILM: PURITY DRAG

Whoopi's interest in fantasy bodies and drag as means to transformation is not idiosyncratic in terms of Hollywood film. As the origins of her hit film *Sister Act* (1992) demonstrate, it was a film premised on the idea of drag. Writer Paul Rudnick explains how he came up with the idea for the screenplay:

> I was lying on my couch one afternoon in the late nineteen-eighties, trying to come up with an idea for a screenplay, and I began thinking about drag. Why is a guy in a gown, I wondered, funnier than a woman in a three-piece suit? I tried to imagine a disguise or transformation that might be more fun for a female star, and my thoughts turned to nuns. Nuns can be dictatorial, sexually repressed, and scary—and therefore, entertaining.[17]

10.2. Whoopi with white nuns as backup singers in *Sister Act* (1992). Buena Vista Pictures/Photofest. © Buena Vista Pictures.

Women who are nuns can have a variety of character traits, but Rudnick focuses on nuns as fantastic bodies—nonhuman, a cipher of church pathologies and platitudes. Spectacular nuns who are not quite human are omnipresent in film and television, from the saintlike and stunningly beautiful Ingrid Bergman in *The Bells of St. Mary's* (1945) to the supernatural flying nun. Rudnick explains that he wanted to "subvert" the "prissy uplift" of nun films like *The Sound of Music* (1965), *The Trouble with Angels* (1966), and *The Song of Bernadette* (1943) with a disruptive showgirl heroine who would embody "raunch, sex, and the unstoppable gospel of cheap showbiz." Ultimately he saw himself as making a movie—a Disney movie no less—that would try "to subvert the Catholic Church."[18]

In the end, *Sister Act* would be well within the uplift tradition of the nun film, and after many rewrites Rudnick would take his name off the final version.[19] But some of Rudnick's original intent remains in the film. If the nuns' habit is a form of drag in Hollywood, a gendered performance of excess that transforms the character's relationship to others, Goldberg's drag as a fantastic nun body works within her general project of inhabiting the other as a route to the self. Goldberg's "Little Girl" character functions as an interesting touchstone for some of her other performances, because *Sister Act* again demonstrates that performing the other *badly* is often an important part of her comedy.

An interesting aspect of Goldberg's persona is that she often sings or lip-syncs in films, but she is not a good singer. She has very little range, which isn't compensated for with an interesting singing voice. *Sister Act* was initially a vehicle for Bette Midler, an actress who became famous with a cabaret act, and if she had made the film it would have been a film that showcased her singing talent.[20] Thus part of what is often striking about Whoopi's singing performances is that she inhabits a role people expect black women to play, but she does not do it well. When we first meet her character, Delores, she is singing to an empty lounge, but Goldberg's value as a black performer is clearly not defined through one of the traditional black film roles, that of a singer. She can be a *bad* black singer and still be a star.

This is just the first role that the character Delores does not—or is not expected to—perform well. She is a bad singer, and then she enters her primary disguise in the film, and the performance that the audience is cued to expect her to perform badly, as nun. Goldberg's performance of Delores as someone who does things badly allows us to read *Sister Act* as a film that takes as much pleasure in subverting expectations of sincerity and authenticity as it does in upholding them. If the nun film traditionally ends with closures of moral uplift, then the revision of these ends disrupts naturalized constructions of deserving characters getting their just rewards.

The nun film either begins with purity or treats transformation into the ideal nun as a desired end. In a film like *The Trouble with Angels*, many of the film's pleasures derive from the unruliness of a teenage Hayley Mills chafing at the bonds of a Catholic school and the rule of the mother superior, played by Rosalind Russell, an actress who in her youth portrayed her share of unruly women. At the end of the film, the teenager receives a "call" to the church, and her liveliness is contained. *Sister Act*, in contrast, plays with transformation. When Delores witnesses a crime and goes into hiding as a nun, she eventually receives the job of directing the choir. Delores is so successful she brings people back to the church and invites the attention of the pope, who wants to see the nuns perform. The transformation of Delores hinges on her forming a bond with the nuns, but we do not actually see some radical transformation of character. In fact, the nuns seem to change more—they can reach the community and find their voices through the choir. In the credits we see that Delores becomes famous for her ordeal and produces albums with nuns (or women in nun drag) as backup singers. She commercializes the experience, profiting from the brief *performance* of transformation. In a reversal of the history of white singers making use of (often better) black backup singers, she utilizes nuns as (better) background singers to become successful. But the traditional forms of intimacy—moral uplift or the mammy who saves—are undercut by the ways Delores succeeds by pretending (and badly) to be something she is not.

WHITE MALE DRAG

Goldberg's most straightforward drag performance is in *The Associate* (1996), another film organized around pretending badly. The story of *The Associate* highlights how the idealized, white male upper-class persona can offer both rewards and injury. While previous iterations of the story featured male actors, Goldberg's black femaleness makes affluent white masculinity more visible as a troubling ideal. The origin of the film is a Chilean novel, *El socio*, by Jenaro Prieto. Since its publication in 1928, it has had eight film and television adaptations in multiple countries. *El socio* tells the story of Julian Pardo, who is struggling financially and invents a British man, Walter Davis, to be his partner; the myth of him builds so that people begin to follow the imaginary man's financial choices. Eventually, Pardo appears to have developed a dissociative disorder, believing that Davis has become real. He has a final confrontation with his partner that results in his suicide, which the authorities decide was a murder by the fictional Davis.

Part of what Prieto and the adaptions play with is the knowledge of how idealized white, wealthy, male bodies are fantastic ideals that can nonetheless mobilize success for people far from that subject position. Published during a period of irresponsible stock speculation that would be a factor in the Great Depression, the novel speaks to a deep distrust of the fictions and games that can produce and replicate wealth. At the same time, a stable factor in wealth accumulation is the prestige of people who have the right credentials, credentials so standardized that they often do not have to be spoken to be imagined, and so distant from everyday people that the wall between success and failure can seem insurmountable if everyday people attempt to climb it. We are never told what Pardo lacks, but his fiction becomes more real than he is. In the final confrontation, he imagines

Oscar Wilde joining Davis in condemning Pardo to irrelevance and obscurity. Wilde's book actually speaks, quoting his Socratic essay, "The Decay of Lying": "The only real beings are those which have never existed."[21]

Thus part of what makes this story travel are the material possibilities offered by non-real bodies, as well as the inevitable failure of less-privileged subjects to truly coopt the value of them. Pardo attempts to utilize the fantasy body for his own ends, but the power of the fantasy would prove more "real" to others than he would. Traveling across time and national borders, we can see that the "little girl with luxurious blonde hair" possesses this same knowledge. In order to do exciting things and have "dream" possessions, idealized bodies are important. In the original version, the British-European other stands for the obviously more privileged subject. But in moving the story to the United States, Whoopi's black and female body highlights the kinds of obstacles to success that U.S. discourses of meritocracy resist.

While Pardo is unlikable, and by most indications a less than gifted businessman, in *The Associate* Goldberg plays a brilliant Wall Street analyst who quits her job after her less accomplished colleague Frank takes credit for her work and is promoted. Like the French version *L'Associé* (1979) that preceded it, *The Associate* is a comedy. But Goldberg largely plays this role "straight," as we need to believe in her professionalism as a businesswoman, and she only shifts to broad comedy when she is forced into drag to impersonate her fictional white male partner, Robert S. Cutty. But Goldberg is also an impossible body in this film—other characters cannot seem to imagine that an African American woman could be a brilliant financial analyst.

There is humor in the contortions she undergoes to seek business after she leaves to start her new firm, but the affective register is mostly one of pathos as a parade of white men tell her that their partners would not be interested in her proposals. We see a close relationship between her dramatic and comic roles here—while initially outraged when her colleague outmaneuvers her, the subdued resignation resulting from discrimination is something Goldberg has often been called on to perform in her career in both comedies and dramas. But once she gets her foot in the door with the lie, it becomes somewhat of a buddy comedy as we watch Goldberg and her assistant Sally (played by Dianne Wiest) attempt to carry out a con on the white male power brokers who consistently underestimate them.

10.3. Whoopi playing it straight and out of place in *The Associate* (1996). Buena Vista Pictures/Photofest. © Buena Vista Pictures.

When she finally dons drag with a Marlon Brando mask, Goldberg's comedic performance does not capitalize on her specific gifts, as it is more characteristic of what Jack Halberstam has described as a white male nonperformative performance.[22] Part of what has made comic performances of an upper-class white masculinity work is the disconnect between the body performing that affect and the imagined stiffness of real white masculine subjects, something that African American comics such as Eddie Murphy and Richard Pryor have famously utilized in their comedy.[23] But here the comedy does not emerge from Goldberg's gift for impersonation; the humor is from the constraint and discomfort in the mask, suit, and gloves. Only her eyes—anxiety filled, but sometimes enraged—give a glimpse of the black woman beneath the masquerade.

The fantasy reward of the film is the drag reveal. Goldberg reappears as Cutty one final time at an all-male club and removes her mask, condemning the exclusivity that resulted in her need for drag. Women are relegated to the lobby, and black men are only servants. The outliers—black men and white women—begin clapping for her, and the white financiers implausibly follow with a standing ovation. Of course, this is not a film about realism. In reality, the network of finance is built by a history of shared schools, work experiences, and pleasures that would make it impossible for a mythical man to succeed. The film also features fairly offensive representations of young white women in finance—the two we see emphasize that their only power springs from using their sexuality. Goldberg is the only female financial analyst who does not believe in trading sex for power. Her race and age seem to have removed her from the erotics of the workplace, but when she accepts "Cutty's" award and thanks the club for admitting their first woman, she neglects to mention blackness, although the nod to the role of race is that there appear to be no black men in the club other than as servants. Goldberg struggles to pass as Cutty, but only by playing with the fictions of ideal whiteness is she allowed to become successful. Blackness and femaleness make the logic of the invisible partner plot hypervisible, demonstrating how idealized identity fictions function as currency.

ROMANCE DRAG

Both of these films lack a love interest, something that usually would have occurred with a white actress. In other versions of *El socio* one of the primary conflicts that emerges is how the wife or girlfriend develops an attachment to the invisible partner. Goldberg explicitly rejects romance when a tenant chides her for not having a life. *Sister Act* also forgoes a romantic plot that was initially included in the script. Producers cast an African American actor as the detective who places her in hiding, but the script does not focus on that relationship in the film. The absence of this relationship gestures toward Whoopi's relationship to romantic comedy traditions. The screwball comedy genre traditionally depicts affluent women played by glamorous white stars running rings around befuddled men in whacky courtship plots, and Goldberg could easily fit into a revision of the screwball comedy. At her core, the screwball heroine is quirky and disruptive of the space around her, with a larger-than-life charm, and Goldberg is perfectly capable of playing such a character. She tries on what I term "romance drag" in a variety of films, wearing various conventional romantic-heroine masks in subgenres such as the screwball comedy, romantic thriller, and employer-employee romance. In romance drag, actors or actresses make hypervisible all the excesses of the romance plot through their complicated fit in the genre, and while a romantic coupling is achieved, the affective pleasures of the film lie elsewhere.

The forced compulsory heterosexuality of the narrative is a sleight of hand in relationship to most important affective connections in the film. Thus I see the "obligatory romance plot," often criticized as an add-on in many Hollywood films, as a kind of drag in which the ill-fit of conventional gender performance is an avenue to more complex identity expression.[24]

In *Jumpin' Jack Flash* (1986), Goldberg's first film after *The Color Purple* (1985), she tries on the screwball comedy and romantic thriller heroine role. She plays a frumpy but talented computer analyst, covering up her body with bulky clothes, who is introduced to the audience with images of her in an apartment filled with mystery and spy novels and film posters. Predictably, the film gives her a chance to live the fantasy, and she helps a spy she briefly talks to electronically. The true screwball relationship in the film, however, is her connection with the prototypical befuddled romantic lead—a handsome, stuffy new coworker who we learn later is an American spy. He doubts her unruly way of doing things in the office and drags her away when she mouths off to the police, and in many scripts the pair might have become the central romantic relationship. Worth noting is that at this point in her career, Goldberg had a very conventionally attractive, slim, and toned body. When she dons a sequined blue evening gown and blonde wig in order to crash a British embassy party, she lip-syncs "You Can't Hurry Love" in order to pass as the entertainment, and she is charismatic enough that a man abandons his wife to escort her in. This episode in the film classically combines screwball comedy and sex, as she shows a great deal of leg and skin, almost losing her dress as it gets caught in a shredder. But her sexuality is also somewhat contained by the screwball comedic performance. The tape recorder at her side, which she utilizes to pass as the singer (emphasizing again that Goldberg cannot pass as the conventional black singer in films), and her display of discomfort in the strapless dress she keeps adjusting both signify her awkwardness and disrupt a sexualized focus on her body.

This makeover reveals her ability to look glamorous, and as Linda Mizejewski argues, the makeover is essential to the romance genre, demonstrating the heroine's suitability for courtship even as African American women's makeovers are often insufficient for winning the male protagonist.[25] But the ill fit of Goldberg's makeovers in films illustrates a more complicated relationship the actress has to conventional gendered performance and representation. While both scholars and reviewers have often criticized how she dresses in films, Goldberg has clearly often chosen to dress in baggy clothes that do not call attention to her shape. In her one-woman show, dressing in an ungendered way enables a variety of personae, and in *Flash* she presents a ragamuffin look that marks her as the quirky heroine who sleeps in a hat and dons fuzzy penguin slippers. In the comedy action film *Fatal Beauty* (1987), as an undercover cop she frequently dons ill-fitting wigs and women's clothes to present different kinds of feminine performance, or as Mask argues, "femininity as masquerade."[26] Because the attire so poorly adheres to her frame, the fact that she is putting on different kinds of femininity—as a prostitute or an innocent church-going woman new to the city—is highlighted. She pulls at the sexy dress in *Flash*, the ill-fitting disguises in *Beauty*, the nun's collar in *Sister Act*—and the discomfort she displays in different kinds of feminine garb is not an accident or coincidence.

Her transparent discomfort with normative feminine performance is the sign of lack of fit, and in conventional romantic comedy the quirkiness would be the thing that endears the normative hero to her. But with the notable exception of *Made in America* (1993), Goldberg rarely gets the guy in Hollywood film.[27] While critics—and Goldberg herself—have criticized how hard she has had to fight to have romance included in her films, the abundance of other kinds of chemistry she has in nonheterosexual romance plots places pressure on the push for heteronormativity as the idealized plot structure for women performers. Rather than see Goldberg fail as a romantic lead, I would look at how the failed or unconvincing romance plot highlights the primacy and pleasures of other kinds of relationships in people's lives.

The best example of romance drag being a mechanism for addressing the pleasures of another kind of relationship is *Corrina, Corrina* (1994). As in *Fatal Beauty*, Goldberg lacks chemistry with the film's male lead. Her real connection is with the child in the film. But because of the history of black women being read as mammies, part of what the romance drag does is transform the mammy narrative. Goldberg is most often read as performing a mammy. Bambi Haggins sees many of her film roles as "revisionist mammies": the Jamaican housekeeper in *Clara's Heart* (1988); the maid participating in the bus boycott in *The Long Walk Home* (1990); the maid/babysitter who transforms the lives of a grieving widower and his daughter in *Corrina, Corrina*; the lesbian caregiver of a woman dying from

AIDS in *Boys on the Side* (1995); the medium helping lovers separated by death in *Ghost* (1990); and the nun on the run in *Sister Act*.[28]

The problem with a tendency to see all these performances as mammies—even revised ones—is that it capitulates to reductive readings of African American representation despite complexities in script or performance. These readings risk ignoring other genealogies or thematic concerns that Goldberg's black female performances subtly transform. The mammy body is a fantasy body too, as well as a drag performance. The mammy discourse emerged most strongly after the Civil War as a way to construct a narrative of racial reconciliation between blacks and whites—black caregivers who loved their charges without ambivalence.[29] But if many of the fantasy bodies I discuss above are completely other from Goldberg because the identity seems too far from her own, the mammy is other because it is the character that overdetermines readings of her performances and creates a narrative she struggles to escape. If we frame Goldberg's characters and performances in different genealogies, we can see the ways in which she disrupts genres.

As Mia Mask argues, Goldberg does a great deal to try to disrupt the mammy narrative.[30] Writer and director Jessie Nelson lost her mother when she was young and, inattentive to the obstacles posed by age and race, she fantasized as a child that a caregiver would marry her father. She brings that ethos to the screenplay, eliminating the age difference and constructing, nevertheless, a fantasy. *Corrina, Corrina* is less of a mammy narrative than a nanny romance.

The genre formula of the nanny romance, most prominently on display in *Jane Eyre* and *The Sound of Music*, has appeared in many book, television, and film romances. Children are not always necessary, because the maid of the house, indicating class difference, often performs the same function. In this fantasy the emotionally distant father (man of the house) needs help dealing with his children and other aspects of his life. The nanny brings knowledge, liveliness, and love into the cold household that was incomplete before her arrival.

If we place *Corrina, Corrina* within this other genealogy, we can see how the black caregiver is never imagined as a real mother (or in the case of domestic melodramas, as possible competition for the white woman attempting to garner the attention of the male love interest). The film immediately attempts to disrupt this when Goldberg is introduced. As she steps off the bus the camera lands on her stylish foot, shod in a high heel, crushing a cigarette. The camera-tilt up from her feet to her body is reserved for attractive women, so with this shot the film signifies her relationship to other alluring women. When she arrives at the house for her interview, she attempts to tell the white father, Manny (Ray Liotta), what she wants with an assertiveness that leads to her rejection. But when he sees her interacting with his daughter Molly (Tina Majarino) in a way that draws her out of her silence, she receives the job.

We soon learn that Corrina is educated and very knowledgeable about music—something that connects her to Molly's father, a musician who writes jingles. Her career goal would be to write liner notes for albums. He is, of course, surprised by her knowledge and the fact that he enjoys her company—another feature of the nanny romance genre. But the racial difference makes hypervisible a problem of the genre: namely, that structural inequality places women in roles where they are not expected to be seen as equals. While one of the pleasures of the employer/maid romance in a film like *The Farmer's Daughter* (1947) is the maid's rise to Congress and her equality with her employer, often the end goal of the narrative is romantic love and parenting. Here, Manny is aided by Corinna's musical skills, and her partnership with a less interesting and less talented man does not feel like an ideal end.

The real chemistry lies between Corrina and Molly, as she also brings Molly into her life—work, family, and church. Subverting narratives that treat black women as appendages in white households, as women who lack a life away from domestic work, Corrina's world is where Molly feels at home. And it is she who is sometimes made to feel like an outsider. Given the history of black women as vulnerable to sexual assault when working in households—and the erasure of the black female caregiver as a romantic rival to white women in the nanny romance plot—this film attempts to position black women in a generic history that performs multiple erasures to reinforce the idea that black women are not viable as ideal mothers or wives. Both black women and white women can have salvific functions in Hollywood narratives, but by placing Goldberg in a role traditionally held by a white woman, *Corrina Corrina* disrupts both the mammy and nanny romance formulas.

Goldberg's ability to build chemistry with other performers also disrupts the primacy of the romantic plot in *Ghost*, a film illustrative of the generic tensions that Goldberg can successfully bring to a film.

It begins as a straightforward dramatic thriller. We are introduced to a lovely young yuppie couple, Sam (Patrick Swayze) and Molly (Demi Moore). After Sam is shot and killed by a mugger, his ghost discovers his death was not random and that Molly is at risk. He seeks out a medium and finds Oda Mae Brown, played by Goldberg, and the film suddenly begins alternating between being a romantic thriller and an interracial buddy comedy. While *Ghost* would energize the careers of all three performers, Goldberg, as reviewer Janet Maslin notes, is "the one performer here who seems to have a clear idea of what she's up to."[31] Another reviewer wrote that while Swayze and Moore are "very competent . . . the best screen work comes from Goldberg."[32] Goldberg would win a best supporting actress Oscar for the part, a win that has often been attributed to her adherence to a stereotypical black role. Although she is playing what is often called the "black helper role" and the "magical negro," what Mia Mask terms her "comedic charisma" is apparent in the film.[33] *Ghost* is a successful tearjerker, although nothing about Swayze or Moore's performances is distinctive, and *Ghost* is no marker of what a Swayze or Moore film should do. In contrast, Goldberg's ability to blend broad physical comedy, a black commonsense voice, and a dramatic performance shapes many of her performances. Donald Bogle argues that in *Ghost*, Goldberg is simply an updated version of Willie Best, an African American actor who portrayed a slow-speaking, wide-eyed, easily frightened black servant in a few early comic horror films.[34] I am not entirely sure what the least stereotypical reaction to encountering a ghost might be, but Goldberg's initial puzzlement when her con game is disrupted by the supernatural is followed by fear and then friendship with Swayze, and she does not replicate Best, whose roles never threatened to steal the film from the leads.

In arguing that Goldberg's character disrupts the primacy of the heterosexual romance plot, I am complicating the common criticism of the film's refusal to produce a homoerotic moment between Goldberg and Moore. An often-discussed failure of the film in terms of imagining interracial and queer intimacy is a moment when Sam inhabits Oda Mae in order to touch and kiss Molly again.[35] Director Jerry Zucker chose to show a ghostly Sam instead of the real Oda Mae's body. This moment undoubtedly shies away from any possibility of queerness and lesbian desire, but I would also point out how much of Goldberg's star persona—despite the fact that she is a gifted mimic—has involved performing an other badly. Just as with the "Little Girl Narrative" and as a "nun," Whoopi's performances call attention to her inability to pass, even momentarily, for someone other. In one moment in the film, after other spirits have learned about her gifts, an African American man inhabits her body in order to speak to his widow; after he speaks briefly to her, Oda Mae casts him out. The traditional representation of the spirit medium in films is of an odd, sensitive soul who allows something other to really transform her. Not only does Oda Mae's character refuse this, Goldberg's star presence in *Ghost* is such that she would never be convincing as someone else.

ROUGHLY A DECADE AFTER her emergence as a star in *The Color Purple*, Goldberg would cease to have starring roles in Hollywood films. She would continue to play a variety of parts in television and film, but if she had a significant part in a theatrical release, it was more likely to be as a black matriarch. Donald Bogle argues that the problem with Goldberg's films is that she was never placed in a "cultural context with which a black audience could identify."[36] On the contrary, films for black audiences in which she had supporting roles, such as *How Stella Got Her Groove Back* (1998), *Kingdom Come* (2001), the film adaptation of *For Colored Girls* (2010), or the television films *Good Fences* (2003) and *A Day Late and a Dollar Short* (2014), fail to make use of her comic potential. The "adventure" that was Whoopi Goldberg's first decade in Hollywood may not have produced the most perfect films, but it did produce films that placed pressure on normative generic frameworks about black women. Moreover, Goldberg's constant play with racialized and gendered drag performance made visible the erasures and pleasures in Hollywood fantasies of belonging.

NOTES

1. Robert Bianco, "Does Whoopi Always Associate with Flops?," *Star News*, Apr. 18, 1987, 8D.

2. Kam Williams, "Whoopi Goldberg: The Kingdom Come Interview," *Washington Informer*, Apr. 18, 2001, 21.

3. Oprah Winfrey is the most financially successful black entertainer by far, but her success was garnered as a talk show host and producer, not from starring film roles.

4. Henri Bergson, *Laughter: An Essay on the Meaning of the Comic*, trans. Cloudesley Brereton and Fred Rothwell (Boston: IndyPublish, 2008), 19.

5. See Rebecca Wanzo, "Beyond a 'Just Syntax': Black Actresses, Hollywood,

and Complex Personhood," *Women and Performance: A Journal of Feminist Theory* 16, no. 1 (2006): 135–152. I argue that analyses of popular black performances can rely on what I term a "just syntax," suggesting that performances can be reduced to 'just' being a mammy, a coon, or a sexualized black woman. But I also argue that black performers often negotiate the tension between stereotype and complex personhood, reflexively gesturing toward constraints placed on black performances created by Hollywood genres (137).

6. Mia Mask, *Divas on Screen: Black Women in American Film* (Urbana: University of Illinois Press, 2009), 107.

7. Whoopi Goldberg, *Book* (New York: Weisbach Books, 1997), 106. See also Lisa Pertillar Brevard, *Whoopi Goldberg on Stage and Screen* (Jefferson, NC: McFarland), 3–19. Brevard talks about Goldberg's rejection of the term African American and her "determined understanding, pursuit, and application of the American Dream" (3).

8. Benedict Anderson, *Imagined Communities: Reflections on the Origin and Spread of Nationalism*, rev. ed. (London: Verso, 2006), 50. Anderson argues that nations are imagined "regardless of inequality and exploitation that may prevail in each. . . . [They are] always conceived as a deep horizontal comradeship."

9. Rick Altman, *Film Genre* (London: BFI Publishing, 1999), 205.

10. Eve Kosofsky Sedgwick, *Tendencies* (Durham, NC: Duke University Press), 8.

11. Bambi Haggins, *Laughing Mad: The Black Comic Persona in Post-Soul America* (New Brunswick, NJ: Rutgers University Press, 2007), and Brevard, *Whoopi Goldberg*, discuss Mabley's influence on Goldberg, and Goldberg discusses Mabley herself in the HBO documentary she produced, *Whoopi Goldberg Presents Moms Mabley* (2013).

12. Haggins, *Laughing Mad*, 139.

13. James T. Patterson, *Brown v. Board of Education: A Civil Rights Milestone and Its Troubled Legacy* (New York: Oxford University Press, 2001): 42–45; Toni Morrison, *The Bluest Eye* (1970; reprinted New York: Pocket Books, 1972).

14. Richard Dyer, *White* (London: Routledge, 1997), 78.

15. Eric Lott, *Love and Theft: Blackface Minstrelsy and the American Working Class* (New York: Oxford University Press, 1993).

16. I borrow the idea of "temporarily abled" from disability scholars, who point out that people move in and out of disability over the course of their lives.

17. Paul Rudnick, "Fun with Nuns," *New Yorker*, www.newyorker.com/magazine/2009/07/20/fun-with-nuns.

18. Ibid.

19. Ibid.

20. Ibid.

21. Jenaro Prieto, *The Partner*, trans. Blanca de Roig and Guy Dowler (London: Thornton Butterworth, 1931), 253.

22. Judith Halberstam, *Female Masculinity* (Durham, NC: Duke University Press, 1998), 234.

23. See, for example, Eddie Murphy, *Raw* (1987), and Richard Pryor *Live and Smokin'* (1971).

24. Suspense and action films often fulfill the terms of romance drag, tack-

ing on a romantic subplot when romance is not the most important relationship. In the film *Miss Congeniality* (2000), Sandra Bullock plays a frumpy agent who is transformed into a contestant in a beauty pageant. Bullock is very conventionally beautiful, but the excesses of beauty pageant femininity call attention to the excesses of gendered makeovers. And while she does "get the guy," a fellow agent played by Benjamin Bratt, the affective logic of the film is not about the romantic resolution: it is about her connection with the other women in the pageant and the embrace of these feminine excesses in forming the community she lacks in her predominantly masculine workplace.

25. Linda Mizejewski, "Queen Latifah, Unruly Women, and the Bodies of Romantic Comedy," *Genders* 46 (2007): n.p., www.genders.org/g46/g46_mizejewski .html.

26. Mask, *Divas*, 133.

27. She does get the guy in a television film in which she plays competitive billiards (*Kiss Shot*, 1989).

28. Haggins, *Laughing Mad*, 153.

29. See Kimberly Wallace-Sanders, *Mammy: A Century of Race, Gender, and Southern Memory* (Ann Arbor: University of Michigan Press, 2008).

30. Mask, *Divas*, 107.

31. Janet Maslin, "Looking to the Dead for Mirth and Inspiration," *New York Times*, July 13, 1990.

32. Desson Howe, *Ghost*, July 14, 1990, www.washingtonpost.com/wp-srv /style/longterm/movies/videos/ghostpg13howe_a0b28d.htm.

33. Mask, *Divas*, 105–140.

34. Donald Bogle, *Toms, Coons, Mulattoes, Mammies, and Bucks: An Interpretative History of Blacks in American Films*, 3rd ed. (London: Continuum, 1994), 329.

35. Chris Holmlund, *Impossible Bodies: Femininity and Masculinity at the Movies* (London: Routledge, 2002), 133; Mask, *Divas*, 107.

36. Bogle, *Toms, Coons, Mulattoes*, 297.

CHAPTER 11

MARGARET CHO'S ARMY: "WE ARE THE BADDEST MOTHERFUCKERS ON THE BLOCK"

REBECCA KREFTING

The underrepresented, unvoiced, ignored part of our population, the great many people who make up the Cho Army, are something you are unaware of, and they're pretty much the gang not to fuck with. We are the baddest motherfuckers on the block.

MARGARET CHO, *I HAVE CHOSEN TO STAY AND FIGHT* (2005)

SOUTH KOREAN AMERICAN COMIC Margaret Cho will be the first one to tell you that she is not an authority on all things Asian or even Korean, but that does not stop people from asking her to weigh in as a comic spokesperson on matters concerning the Orient. But she also identifies as queer, as a fag hag, as a feminist, as an activist, and as a recovering alcoholic, among many other identities. While the media has a narrow vision regarding the matters upon which Cho can comment (i.e., race/ethnicity), her fans understand that she is *both/and*. She is both Korean and American; she is both queer and married to a man; she is both a feminist and a femme bottom. The reality of our lives is far messier than the organized and clearly defined identity camps served up in televisual representations. Stand-up comedy offers space to speak to the complexity of our identities; indeed, communications scholar Judith Yaross Lee argues that Cho's politicized content and comedy style—her attention to social issues relevant to women, LGBTQ folks, Asian Americans, and people of color and her adroit shifts into accents and characters representing these groups—allows her to perform "in ways that resist classification within any group."[1] This kind of border crossing expands the tribes loyal to Cho, ensuring an ever-widening audience for her charged humor aimed at illumining social inequality and injustice. Cho is among one of the savviest purveyors of charged humor, a kind of humor that intentionally educates and mobilizes audiences, creates community, and offers strategies for social change.[2]

Interestingly, Cho defies classification even as she claims membership to all minority groups; in other words, because she enjoys honorary membership to all minority groups, she troubles the tendency to "silo" minority groups, instead performing in ways that unite multiple marginalized communities. As she puts it: "Because I am like the members of so many different minorities, it sort of gives me carte blanche . . . to comment on things and not worry so much about any kind of repercussions like 'oh you're not supposed to say that because you're not one of us.' But I am, you know. Because I'm always going to be 'one of us,' *we're always going to be 'one of us,'* because I just have that kind of membership in every club" (my emphasis).[3] This subversive rhetorical maneuver conveys the need to recognize our similarities *as oppressed* subjects, even as minority groups experience subordination in different ways. As this chapter's opening quote conveys, her "we" references folks based not on social identity (e.g., race, sexuality, or ability) but rather on shared experiences of being "underrepresented, unvoiced, ignored." One joke at a time, this is one of the ways Cho builds her army—a ragtag, motley crew of die-hard fans who hail from every identity camp imaginable, many of them sharing her experiences of being cast as an "Other."

Over the course of a twenty-five-year career in stand-up comedy, Margaret Cho has demonstrated a keen ability to maximize her visibility and exposure so that she can broadcast worldviews lauding social justice and embracing difference. This chapter will track Cho's career over the past quarter of a century, attending to three important dimensions that combine to inform an understanding of Cho's position as a comic diva and icon: the substance of her charged comedy (i.e., analyses of performances and writings); the cultural economy in which she crafts her art and the modes of distribution used to disseminate that art; and audience composition—the many marginalized communities that embrace her and constitute the "Cho Army." I model this multiperspectival approach to Cho's work on the work of cultural studies scholar Douglas Kellner, who champions a tripartite analysis of material and visual culture that focuses on the "production and political economy of culture, cultural texts, and the audience reception of those texts and their effects."[4] This approach avoids focusing too narrowly on any one aspect of a cultural artifact and si-

11.1. Margaret Cho (2010).
Photograph courtesy of
"photognome" on Flickr.com.

multaneously recognizes that these perspectives—cultural economy,
the text itself, and audience reception—are coconstitutive. For example, political and cultural events shape the content of Cho's comic
material, as when she rails against Sarah Palin for proudly declaring that she "tolerates gays"; or when she bemoans the media's obses-
sion with longtime coma patient Terri Schiavo (which she considered
a distraction from wars in Iraq and Afghanistan); or when she vocal-
izes support for the Dixie Chicks, who were subject to critical oppro-
brium for saying they were ashamed to share lineage to Texas with
George W. Bush.[5] Cho uses charged humor, a style of comedy with
a social justice orientation, to counter dominant myths and replace
cultural fictions with (her personal) truths about minorities—sexual,
racial, gender, and otherwise. Her activist sensibilities inform her approach to performing comedy; in other words, the substance of her
comedy seeks to mobilize those she identifies in the chapter epigraph
as "the underrepresented, unvoiced, ignored part of our population."
For her, the revolution begins in unifying America's many tribes that
feel disparaged, invisible, or maligned by mainstream media, political institutions, and society. Her comic content, as with any stand-

up comic, informs audience composition. So pro-gay, feminist, liberal humor arising from a woman of color attracts fans who share Cho's social identities and/or worldviews. Furthermore, the content/text together with modes of production and distribution inform, if not altogether determine, the kinds of audiences Cho's comedy could reach at various points in her career.

The Immigration and Nationality Act of 1965 effectively ended an antiquated and overtly racist national-origin quota system for U.S. immigrants that had been in place since lawmakers passed the Emergency Quota Act in 1921. Alongside other previous immigration policy successes—such as the repeal of the Chinese Exclusion Act (1943) and the Luce-Heller Act of 1946 (which was signed by President Harry Truman and allowed southeast Indians and Filipinos to emigrate to the United States, albeit in very small numbers)—the 1965 act paved the way for the Korean-born couple Young-Hie and Seung-Hoon Cho to settle in the United States in 1964. The new arrivals' status as citizens was still in flux when Moran (now Margaret) was born on December 5, 1968, at San Francisco's Children's Hospital. With a comedy writer for a father (he wrote joke books in Korea) and a mother who is just plain funny, Cho was born with comedy in the blood and on the brain. Her father left for Korea only three days after her birth and spent several years working on immigration matters. Her mother sent an infant Margaret over to Korea, where her aunt (her father's sister) cared for her for almost three years. Reunited with her mother by the time she was three years old, Margaret Cho and her family would spend the rest of her early childhood and youth living in ethnically and sexually diverse neighborhoods in San Francisco. For a time, her parents ran a snack bar in the Japantown Bowling Alley; later they bought and operated a bookstore called Paperback Traffic on Polk Street in a famously gay neighborhood. And thus began Cho's long-standing love affair with gay men—she cites gay men first as curious objects of interest and later as best friends, confidants, and loyal fans.[6]

As a teenager, a natural aptitude for performance secured Cho's entrance into the San Francisco School of the Arts, even as she flunked out of her other high school. For Cho, stand-up comedy was an accessible form of performance, allowing her to capitalize on her sense of humor to work through anxieties of being a young, Asian American, female misfit. Plus, stand-up comedy was all the rage in the 1980s, and there were numerous venues in San Francisco where she could hone her craft. Gifted comic performances got her a spot on the then-popular *Star Search* (1983–1995), a talent showcase hosted by Ed McMahon featuring dancers, singers, and stand-up comics. Talent agents selected Cho to perform on the international version of *Star Search*, wherein Cho represented the nation of Korea, despite being an American citizen. This would be the first of many slights Cho would suffer at the hands of television producers over the next couple decades. While performing comedy in the Bay Area (before she could subsist entirely on profits from her stand-up shows), Margaret Cho worked in her parents' bookstore, recorded phone sex messages, dressed up as Raggedy Ann for FAO Schwartz, and (wo)manned the counter at a boutique called Stormy Leather.[7] Good press and exposure early on catapulted Margaret Cho to feature-comic status, which meant she began getting gigs at national comedy-club chains to open for the headliner as well as touring on the college comedy circuit. By 1993, at the impossibly young age of twenty-four, she was already in conversation with ABC executives about using her life as the basis for a sitcom, a popular and profitable pattern for stand-up comics like Bill Cosby, Jerry Seinfeld, Roseanne Barr, Tim Allen, Brett Butler, and Martin Lawrence. In 1994 *All-American Girl*, the first Asian American sitcom, fell flat with audiences, including Asian Americans, for a variety of reasons and was not renewed for a second season. Afterwards, feeling dejected, ugly, and generally miserable, Margaret Cho continued performing stand-up comedy, writing screenplays, and making TV appearances during the next few years. In 1999, after she got sober and decided to channel her anger and frustration into her art, she set off on a national tour with the show *I'm the One That I Want*, opening at Westbeth Theatre Center in New York City. A book by the same name would follow a year after the release of her first concert film in 2000. Since the turn of the millennium, she has released seven concert films and continues to tour the nation, showcasing her stand-up comedy. She wrote, produced, and starred in her own film *Bam Bam and Celeste* (2005), capitalized on the reality TV craze with her own show (*The Cho Show*, VH1 2008), spent six seasons as a cast member of *Drop Dead Diva* (Lifetime 2009–2014), and cohosts *Monsters of Talk*, a weekly podcast that first aired in January 2013. All the while she writes: books, forewords and introductions to edited volumes, screenplays, performances, and blogs. Not everyone is fond of Margaret Cho—a tattooed avenger of civil liberties—but most people know who she is. Over the course of a career spanning nearly three decades, she has made an indelible impression on the American public and garnered an eclectic and diverse fan base.

For the first decade of her career, Cho pursued traditional avenues for garnering mainstream success, dutifully working the college circuit and performing in national comedy-club chains. To be clear, for a comedian mainstream success implies a few things: appearances on late-night TV talk shows, feature and headliner status in national comedy-club chains, and an hour comedy special (or more). Having achieved mainstream recognition and visibility by the late 1990s, Cho used her fame and amassed capital to take control of the means of production for her future comedy performances. Emergent technologies, such as social media platforms, proved useful to staying connected with an ever-growing fan base, offering Cho potentially successful ways of bypassing traditional pathways to branding and evading reliance on major media outlets for exposure. Social media platforms have proven a successful tool for self-promotion, and comics use a variety of them, and liberally so, to generate funny material while also promoting shows and merchandise to fans. Delighted at the prospect of circumventing media sources that routinely denigrate her, Cho cleverly shifted her approaches to promoting her work to capitalize on innovations in new media in order to maintain public visibility and continue to circulate her brand of charged humor. While these approaches are still in some ways pregnable to social and industry pressures and are supported by profit-seeking models, they offer greater freedom for comic artists to create and distribute their material. Not incidentally, Margaret Cho was the first person I followed when I created a Twitter account. About two minutes later, Margaret Cho was also my first follower. Savvy ways of cultivating connections with her fan base ensure that her ideas—radical notions of self-love, social equality, and an emphasis on shared humanity—continue to gain traction.

THE 1990S: GETTING MAINSTREAMED

The 1990s were characterized by the rise of new media like the internet and an ever-expanding cable television palette. Entertainment corporations launched channels devoted exclusively to delivering comedy to the American public. The Comedy Channel (1989) and Ha! (1990) merged in 1991 to form Comedy Central, which featured sketch comedy shows, stand-up comedy specials and showcases, and comedy films. Having a plethora of opportunities to perform stand-up comedy on television and in the hundreds of comedy clubs that arose during the comedy boom of the 1980s meant more work and the promise of a living wage for professional comics. What might have appeared to be Edenic conditions for comics were sullied by the heavy-handed editing and censorship exercised against comic material. Television censors focused on removing not just expletives or sexually explicit content but also charged humor that confronted viewers with hard truths about social injustice. Many Americans were convinced that legislative changes during previous decades had all but ended social inequality for people of color, the differently abled, and women. Humor oriented towards social justice, such as charged humor, belied this faulty optimism, making it less profitable or appealing during this time. Television producers sought safe comedy that would not jeopardize advertising revenue, and, in general, the mostly white, middle-class patrons of comedy clubs did not want to pay to feel guilty about something they believed was effectively outmoded.[8] For someone like Margaret Cho, whose life experiences attested to the persistence of racism, sexism, and homophobia, stand-up comedy offered a forum to voice discontent, but Cho was not trafficking in much charged humor during those years. Her early comedy was autobiographical, a little raunchy and rebellious, but definitely not the biting sociopolitical commentary that punctuates later concert films. Reflecting on those days, Cho admits that back then she "never thought about the overreaching kinds of things like race and identity."[9] Whether she was aware of it or not, this was a smart choice, given that her audiences were composed mainly of white, middle-class suburbanites and their college-age offspring. Mimicry of her immigrant Korean mother proved especially popular with industry gatekeepers, college audiences, and comedy-club patrons alike. Cho spent the better part of this decade working diligently to craft a likeable stage persona in order to build a following and achieve mainstream status.

It is unlikely that Margaret Cho would have the massive fan base she has today had she not followed conventional routes for success in stand-up comedy. She began performing stand-up as a teenager in San Francisco in the very late 1980s when she made her way from local open-mic comedy shows to larger commercial venues like Holy City Zoo and Punchline. At the age of twenty, she made her first television appearance on VH1's wildly popular *Stand-Up Spotlight* (1988–), hosted by a depoliticized Rosie O'Donnell. She impressed the owner of St. James Club, a gay bar in San Jose, who liked her sexual frankness and ruminations on being the daughter of immigrants and bet that his gay male clientele would too. He was right, and she made her own discovery—she loved performing for gay audiences. In the early 1990s she managed to nab a few appearances on MTV, told jokes on ABC's ½ Hour Comedy Hour (1991), and began doing regular shows at Josie's Juice Joint in the Castro district, where many queer comics came to perform. She felt at home in these clubs and in retrospect, writes:

> Working for a predominantly queer crowd taught me a lot about how to be a good comic. I found the audiences at Josie's were smarter, more political, more compassionate. Josie's didn't serve alcohol, so they were way more awake too. In straight clubs back then, the late night shows where the patrons were so drunk they could barely get through a full joke without screaming were way more like baby-sitting than actually performing. I am forever grateful to my wonderful audiences back then, people who told me when I was funny and forgave me when I wasn't. Like all great divas, I owe everything to the kindness of gay men.[10]

From 1991–1994 Cho traveled throughout California and the country performing at comedy clubs and colleges and universities. During this time, young and adventurous amateur performers like Janeane Garofalo, David Cross, Kathy Griffin, and Laura Kightlinger sought to resuscitate comedy from what they saw as a national comedy scene saturated with hacky, predictable jokes. Alternative comedy—characterized by improvised, anecdotal, stream-of-consciousness humor—cropped up on the West Coast and lured in comics desiring to try something different on stage. In an interview with Yael Kohen, Cho addresses her relationship to alternative comedy, noting: "I always stayed firmly within the conventional comedy clubs—I never left. I didn't have the luxury of just being an alternative comic. . . . It wasn't where I learned to do comedy."[11] This did not mean that she wasn't impressed by the work of these comic pioneers; rather, it was not a style of comedy that worked well for the audiences she had already committed to entertain in national comedy-club chains or Midwestern university towns. She continues:

> I think it [alternative comedy] gave me a lot of freedom to expand on what I was doing, and it gave me a lot more confidence, but I had to

modify it too. You couldn't just take that into the mainstream comedy rooms at the time; you still had to have jokes. That was really important. I had to make money, which I was doing at the time, but I still wanted to be hanging out. You never make any money in alternative groups, so you would go to the alternative groups for hanging out, and go to the rest of the gigs for making money.[12]

Her need to earn a decent wage and her choice to perform in traditional comedy venues won her the attention of booking agents for late-night television talk shows and later of ABC producers. She won the 1994 American Comedy Award for Female Comedian and soon after landed TV appearances on shows like *The Arsenio Hall Show* (1989–1994) as well as a coveted spot in the all-lady lineup on *Bob Hope Presents the Ladies of Laughter* (1992). It was not long before producers approached her about starring in her own sitcom.

Though it seemed like a good investment—Margaret Cho was an award-winning comic and had made numerous television appearances and lapped the country several times over performing to TV's most desired demographics in comedy clubs and colleges—*All-American Girl* lasted a mere one season, leaving producers dismayed and puzzled. Audiences loved her impressions of her Korean mother on stage, so why wouldn't viewers similarly appreciate a sitcom where conflicts arose between the immigrant parents with strange customs and their Americanized children? After all, in either performance scenario otherness becomes the source of laughter. Michelle Woo, writer for *KoreAm Journal* (an online monthly magazine delivering Korean American news) recalled that the show "faded in and out faster than a thumbprint on a Hypercolor T-shirt," but on the upside, it "was the first network sitcom to feature a predominantly Asian American cast—a milestone that brought tempered hope for a group that had for decades been reduced to kung fu fighters, dragon ladies and kooky bucktoothed neighbors in mainstream media portrayals."[13] Calling it a failure, as some critics did, overlooks the monumental importance signified by a show with an entirely Asian American cast.[14] With no creative control and little say in the writing process, Cho watched as the network treated her ethnicity as a gimmick and trotted out stereotypes about Asians to draw in viewers. In a promotional image for the show, posted on her Facebook page twenty-two years later, she points out the inclusion of chopsticks used to underline the title, a gimmicky and insulting visual signifier of Asian American-ness.

11.2. Post on official Margaret Cho Facebook page (2016).

Such narrow, if not altogether erroneous, representations and ideas about what it means to be Asian American were all part of the network's attempt to deliver an authentic picture of an Asian American family. For Cho, attempting to achieve "an accurate Asian family" is highly problematic because "there is no such thing. . . . Another way of being racist is to ask for authenticity."[15] The problems that arose during production of *All-American Girl*, among other things, politicized Cho.

Although her sitcom was short-lived, Margaret Cho benefitted from the exposure. The public flocked to the comedy clubs where she had now achieved headliner status. More income (from the sitcom and from stand-up) meant she could pursue other creative projects, like writing screenplays and forming a sketch comedy troupe called The People Tree; more visibility meant additional offers for film roles and television appearances, adding bulk to an already bulging bank account. Her stand-up comedy during this time does not have the same edge, clear message points, or charged quality that her later concert films would have. Though she establishes herself as a fag hag and an ally to the gay community, this is barely a blip in *Drunk with Power* (1996). Instead, she talks more about dating fiascos with men, fears of becoming fat, and her work in the entertainment industry. Racism does come up a couple times, like when she quips:

Also when you're an Asian American actress working, it's hard to get work because whenever they have an Asian in a movie they always have to justify our existence. You know, you can't just be there. You have to be there for some reason, like you have to be either a computer expert [*laughter*], or some kind of Tai Chi master [*laughter*], or an exchange student [*laughter*].[16]

Early seeds of charged jokes told in future concert films exist, but the overall performance lacks the context necessary to situate Cho as antiracist, feminist, and pro-gay. She makes a good point about Asian stock characters, but there is simply no audience affirmation for that message. Notice that there is no audience response for the statements prefacing the recitation of those stock characters; in contrast, in specials filmed in the next decade the audience cheers, whistles, and claps when she makes similar points. Instead, when she tells this joke in *Drunk with Power*, the audience guffaws at the mention of each stock character (computer expert, Tai Chi master, and exchange student), and it is difficult to tell why they are laughing. Is it merely mutual recognition of those stock characters—that kind of chuckle often coupled with turning to your friend and smiling as if to say, "So true." The fact is we never really know, because humor is subjective. But comics who make charged humor a mainstay in their routines, like Cho would do in the twenty-first century, educate audiences early on as to where they stand on matters of social justice and equality. This kind of clarity of voice and perspective means that viewers will not be confused about the nature of the joke and what or who is under attack.

Stand-up comedy allows for greater control of self-presentation, but that does not mean that what we as audience members see and hear is *the* truth; rather, it is a version of the truth. Importantly, it is Margaret Cho's version of the truth, but it is also carefully constructed, edited, and choreographed to stoke interest and loyalty from others who have felt similar social pressures and likewise have felt the sting of oppression.[17] Cho personally attests to carefully deliberating which stories she will relay (and how), which social issues she chooses to confront, and which portions of her life she opts to make public.[18] For instance, despite speaking frankly about her sexual forays with many, many, many people, Cho does not include material about her husband of many years, Al Ridenour, a comic performance artist. Cho constructs a stage persona that, while bearing verisimilitude to her life, is still carefully crafted and re-presented to audiences in order to entertain and educate. Her books and many performances offer two modes of storytelling, presenting congruent content that "demonstrates how it is not the story itself that is of utmost importance, it is *the way that story is told*."[19] Thus, a failed sitcom is not a product of Cho's shortcomings as a performer but of her inability to attain an impossible white beauty ideal or conform to stereotypes about Asian Americans. And a rejected screenplay is less a matter of poor craftsmanship and more a result of refusing the unwanted sexual advances of a handsy producer with the capital and connections to produce the film. (Yes, that really happened.) What may look like someone candidly sharing hilarious stories is actually the product of a conscientious wordsmith.

Careful rhetorical footwork on stage in the 1990s reduced the likelihood of alienating mainly white, heterosexual audiences while also signaling identification with and membership to the Asian American and LGBTQ communities. In *Drunk with Power*, she reassures heterosexual male audience members that she enjoys giving blowjobs; moreover, she says that she is straight and sexually available. She makes stereotypically gendered jokes about feeling fat, and the entire set is punctuated with stereotypes about Asian Americans, lesbians, and people of size. These generate the loudest guffaws of affirmation.[20] Constructing this persona was a successful strategy for getting mainstreamed, and it ultimately conferred the name recognition and financial independence necessary for Cho to leave comedy clubs and migrate to larger performance halls and theatres. This does not mean that she does mainstream comedy now (by "mainstream" I mean comedy that would play well to the dominant culture); rather, it signifies that the mainstream status she achieved in the 1990s allowed her to delve into commercially risky material that would appeal to new fan bases. In her analysis of Cho's body of work, gender and sexuality studies scholar Linda Mizejewski writes: "By 2010 Cho enjoyed a decidedly 'niche stardom' comprised of mainstream recognition and popularity centered in the LGBTQ community."[21] Were it not for the sitcom or her due diligence performing hundreds of shows in comedy clubs across America and internationally, Cho would not have been able to pursue the creative projects she undertook in the twenty-first century—movies, TV shows, comedy tours, variety shows, books, blogs, music videos, and a clothing line—nor would she have had the fan base to support the biting, socially conscious, charged humor that she became known for in *I'm the One That I Want*. Enjoying mainstream status and visibility, Cho was finally in a financial position to control the production and distribution of her stand-up comedy. The bio on her website attests to this: "After her experience with *All-American Girl*, Margaret wanted to make sure she would only have to answer to herself, making sure she was responsible for the distribution and sales of her film, taking a page from what music artist Ani DiFranco did with her Righteous Babe Records."[22] This was a game changer for the composition and growth of Cho's Army as she became increasingly vocal about social ills in ways that made minorities feel accepted and safe at comedy performances, places where we traditionally brace ourselves for attack.

THE TWENTY-FIRST CENTURY: BUILDING AN EMPIRE

The internet didn't feel new by the turn of the century, but innovations in new media—for example, blogging and wiki platforms, MOOs (online, text-based, multiplayer gaming), interactive computer and video games, and social networking sites like MySpace, Facebook, Twitter, Tumblr, and YouTube—became increasingly popular, luring people away from print media and television sets. Wireless communication technology obviated the need for a home phone altogether, and by 2008, 52 percent of the world's population were wireless phone subscribers. Spanish sociologist Manuel Castells summarizes these shifts as "evolv[ing] from a predominantly homogenous mass communication medium, anchored around national television and radio networks, to a diverse media system combining broadcasting with narrowcasting to niche audiences."[23] Astutely aware of the internet's potential to connect her to fans without mediation or interference, Margaret Cho established a webpage, began blogging, and climbed on board when young entrepreneurs launched social networking sites. Confident in her ability to fill large performance venues, she took to the road on a series of self-funded and produced stand-up comedy tours with material that was decidedly charged. Comedy performed in the twenty-first century enlisted the support of the have-nots and the downtrodden. And existing fans were in for a bit of a surprise; compared to her older material (heard in comedy clubs, on television, and on her audio recordings), Cho's independently produced performances and publications (online and print) clearly established her as a queer ally (and later as queer), a champion of civil liberties, and a

11.3. Cho on cover of *Ms.* magazine spring issue (2003). Photograph courtesy of *Ms.* magazine.

staunch feminist. She became a woman on a mission to fight misrepresentations of Asian Americans, unhealthy and impossible standards of beauty, and homophobia—and now she had the capital to spread the word far and wide.

During the filming of her concert show *Revolution* (2004) at the Wiltern Theatre in Los Angeles, Cho proceeded to peel off articles of clothing: a jewel-laden crownlike head covering, her stylized ladyboots, and a wig she criticizes as being too "chinky." Doffing material signifiers of Asian-ness and femininity, Cho plays with her presentation of self, unmasking the work we all do as part of our daily performances of gender, ethnicity, class, and sexuality. Subversion of social norms and expectations via dress, comportment, speech, and behavior reveals the terrain of culture as a powerful site upon which social change can be enacted. Statements made during her show acknowledge this: "I think if racial minorities, sexual minorities, feminists, both male and female, hell all liberals, if we all got together . . . that would equal power. And that power would equal change. And that change would equal a revolution [*cheering and clapping*]."[24] Using the exceedingly popular cultural form of stand-up comedy, Cho plays Pied Piper to a ragtag bevy of social outcasts. And like many charged comics before her (e.g., Dick Gregory, Robin Tyler, Richard Pryor, and Kate Clinton), she trusts that comedy can challenge social inequality, that revolutions can begin in entertainment venues.

Scholars analyzing the corpus of Cho's work recognize her commitment to social justice, without calling it charged humor.[25] A genre of humor that has been around as long as comedians have been cracking jokes, charged humor stokes community, advocates equality for all, and offers solutions for social redress. This humor is carefully crafted by the comic to unmask and challenge the cultural fictions circulating about minority groups "with specific intentions to promote unity and equality or to create a safe and accepting space for people from all walks of life."[26] After taking control of the means of comedy production, Cho punctuates her comedy with jokes that advocate self-efficacy and social agency, advice she sees as essential in a society that renders inferior anybody who is not a straight, white, able-bodied man. The power and subversiveness of self-love and the reclamation of personal beauty for social misfits are running themes in her concert film *Beautiful* (2009).

I'm really into complimenting myself and you should do the same. . . . We gotta compliment ourselves because we get enough shit in the world. Like I did this radio show and the deejay asked me: "What if you woke up tomorrow and you were beautiful?" [*Audience laughs as she makes a shocked face*] What do you mean, what if? [*Laughter*] He said: "What if you woke up and you were blonde and had blue eyes and you were 5'11" and weighed a hundred pounds and you were beautiful? What would you do?" And I said: "Well, I probably wouldn't get up because I would be too weak to stand." [*Laughter*] And I felt very sorry for him because if that's the only kind of person you think is beautiful, you wouldn't see very much beauty at all in the world [*cheering and clapping*]. And I think everybody is beautiful. . . . I think it's very important to feel beautiful. I think it's very political to feel beautiful, especially if you're queer, because if you're queer you have to take on the world every single day of your life. So you have to feel beautiful [*clapping begins*] to survive [*clapping swells and the audience cheers*].[27]

This joke locates people of color, queer folks, and women who do not fit the description of beauty proffered by the deejay as the groups most commonly subjected to unattainable social norms and ideals— a distanciation that results in self-loathing, body dysmorphia, and, at its extreme, suicide. Cho cleverly makes each of us the sole determinant of beauty, wresting that power from the media and placing it back in our hands, empowering us to not only feel beautiful ourselves but to reject dominant beauty ideals as a matter of survival. In this way, her charged humor uses personal experience to reveal the logics of social subordination and construct new ways of interpreting the world around us.

Intentions to foment social change are a critical component of charged humor. It signals the author's desire for more than just a laugh and makes the performer's objectives clear to audiences (and scholars), which helps circumvent the penchant to attribute resistance to performers whose motives are not congruent with interpretations of the performance text (for instance, if I tried to argue that misogynist comedy is feminist). Scholars studying the body of Cho's work vary in their approach to and readings of her performances. These studies range from examinations of Cho's autobiographical mode of storytelling, to rhetorical constructions of Asian American identity, to the way beauty and the body factor into the experiences of women comics; yet, at the heart of these analyses lies a shared admission that Cho intends to use comedy to advocate on behalf of minorities in the service of social change.[28] In a phone interview with Gary Kramer, author of *Independent Queer Cinema: Reviews and Interviews*, Margaret Cho describes her comedy as "a kind of myth-making and myth-breaking" that is "very political and motivational in its own way."[29] She goes on:

> It's about being a woman of color and stepping into power—wearing my greatness on my shoulders and being ostentatious and outrageous. . . . To step into our political power is essential. . . . I realized that I had the ability to combine my need to be funny with my desire to help people. And by that, also help myself. I think it was just

discovering the ability to combine the two that made me the artist I am now.[30]

Not only does this intentionality show up in her performances but also in writing projects like her two autobiographies: *I'm the One That I Want* (2001) and *I Have Chosen to Stay and Fight* (2005), which Linda Mizejewski describes as "follow[ing] the pattern of consciousness-raising narratives that rally readers and audiences toward social change."[31] Furthermore, in keeping with a black feminist epistemology advanced by Patricia Hill Collins, Cho's writings use personal experience to advance cultural critique, emphasize the importance of dialogue and action, champion empathy to create intercommunity coalitions, and encourage individual accountability for our actions and beliefs.[32] Cho writes: "We have no idea how powerful we actually are. We were never considered part of the general, 'respectable' population. This land is your land, but this land isn't my land—that is what so many of us thought. This second-class citizenship has sunk in so deeply that we have barely any awareness of it. We had no idea that this is the enemy we are truly fighting."[33] The enemy lies without and within, according to Cho, making it a battle waged against oppressive forces both external (e.g., government, media, religion, education) and internal (e.g., the ways in which we view and treat ourselves). Stoking social equality through authorial intent, fostering cultural citizenship among minorities, and using humor to unite and mobilize minority communities are all the core ingredients of charged humor.

It is not enough to offer cultural critique exposing social ills. Charged humor goes further and offers possible solutions to those ills—something Margaret Cho does in her stand-up comedy, blogs, and published writings. In her second book, *I Have Chosen to Stay and Fight*, an autobiographical call-to-arms to the repressed and oppressed, Cho peppers the pages with action-oriented directives: "We need to wake up. It's time to start some shit. Alarm clock = Revolution"; "What is needed now is action, not hopelessness"; and "It is time to hold fast to our beliefs, to create new standards for our elected officials, to continue to commit our acts of civil disobedience."[34] This manifesto includes suggestions like descending on city hall and demanding marriage licenses for gay unions, unseating politicians who interfere with women's reproductive rights, and exercising empowerment by being selfish at times—in other words, attending to your own needs, desires, and dreams can be a wholly radical act for minorities. She expounds on this latter point in her concert film *Notorious C.H.O.* (2002):

> And if you are a woman; if you are a person of color; if you are gay, lesbian, bisexual, transgender; if you're a person of size; if you're a person of intelligence; if you're a person of integrity, then you are considered a minority in this world [*cheering and clapping*]. And it's going to be really hard to find messages of self-love and support anywhere, especially women's and gay men's culture. It's all about having to look a certain way or you're worthless. . . . When you don't have self-esteem, you will hesitate before you do anything in your life. You will hesitate to go for the job you really want to go for. You will hesitate to ask for a raise. You will hesitate to call yourself an American. You will hesitate to report a rape. You will hesitate to defend yourself when you are discriminated against because of your race, your sexuality, your size, your gender. You will hesitate to vote. You will hesitate to dream. For us to have self-esteem is truly an act of revolution and our revolution is long overdue [*cheering and clapping*]. I urge you all today, especially today in these times of terrorism and chaos, to love yourselves without reservation and to love each other without restraint, unless you're into leather [*laughter*] then by all means, use restraints.[35]

For minorities, the lack of economic resources, cultural capital, and political access is compounded by internalized oppression that leads to self-contempt and complacency, a documented psychological state that makes people believe that any supposed inferiority is biological or natural and ultimately results in underperformance. Social psychologist Claude Steele studied this phenomenon, for which he coined the term "stereotype threat," and conducted a series of social experiments among college students that demonstrated the grave impact such beliefs have on the success of women and racial/ethnic minorities in education, athletics, job performance, and other social interactions.[36] Without a call to action and a clear path of action, charged humor might simply be mistaken for satire or sociopolitical commentary.[37] This also happens to be the characteristic of charged humor that makes people the most uneasy, particularly those comfortable with and benefitting from America's current social order.

Greater artistic freedom came when Margaret Cho produced and distributed *I'm the One That I Want* and, two years later, *Notorious C.H.O.* (The latter was also distributed as an independent film.) According to her bio, "Both films were acquired by Showtime Cable Networks, and produced by Margaret's production company, a testament to the success of Margaret's bold business model."[38] It breaks down like this: Cho's production company finances each stand-up tour and the filming of the associated concert film, thus earning tour proceeds and owning the rights to distribute the film as desired. Premium network channels like Showtime must pay to air the special, usually a fee for the first airing of the film and residuals each time the film repeats. This model continued with future concert films like *Revolution* (2004), *Assassin* (2005), *Beautiful* (2009), *Cho Dependent* (2011), and *PsyCHO* (2015). It eliminates payouts to industry producers and networks who otherwise control creative content and distribution. (They determine whether and where to sell the rights, not the performer.) The performer walks away with a flat fee for services rendered—no residuals, no royalties, no difference in pay if the special airs one time or a thousand times. It also means that the owner of that content determines what gets included or cut prior to airing or distribution. To avoid these issues, Cho joined forces with Karen Taussig to create Cho Taussig Productions Inc., and both women became executive producers for the concert films distributed. In an interview, Karen Taussig remarks: "Everybody is owned by something and there's only so far they can go. And maybe if Margaret was also owned by a corporation we'd be cutting stuff out or whatever, but she's not."[39] Even powerful and provocative comedy performers like Stepehn Colbert and Bill Maher can only go so far because they are still subject to network producers kowtowing to advertisers. Strategic professional moves like creating a production company, writing books, and using blogging and other social networking to communicate with fans sans outside interference means that Cho arbitrates the messages and material she brings to the public; as a result she can exercise self-determination in making appeals to particular niche audiences.

Margaret Cho's writings published during the early aughts mirror the charged comedy she disseminated during the same time. Following the release of *I'm the One That I Want* (the concert film), Cho published a book by the same name that expands on the autobiographical material she delivers in the former. Her second book, *I Have Chosen to Stay and Fight* (2005), compiles blog posts (and some new writing) into a politicized feminist manifesto, a call-to-arms to the disenfranchised. For example, she writes:

> I am fighting when I'm sleeping. In my dreams, I must slay the dragon of European heterosexual male society, then I wake up in the morning and must be an activist. I have to watch the news and movies about the people who I am not, then translate my struggle in order to make it palatable for those people who don't have to march but are sympathetic to my voice. This is a major part of my audience, an easy ear to bend—yet I still must bend that ear myself. I make the effort and that makes the difference, and this is what I'd like a break from. What if I didn't have to bend anyone's ear? What if the playing field really was level? I'd love to see how far I could go. What if all I had to show off were my mad skills? Wouldn't I really be able to fly then?[40]

If it was not already clear who Cho targets for her army, the book is divided into chapters that address specific social identities to which she belongs/identifies/allies herself; these are: LGBTQ folks, women/feminists, liberal Christians, Korean Americans, sexual "deviants" (specifically those into bondage and sadomasochism), antiracists, and Democrats.[41] Ian Harvie, a transmale comic who went on the road with Cho for a stint in the early aughts, described their audiences in the following way: "The people who would come to see her big shows were largely GLBTQ folks and extreme liberals. These were basically the same people I was performing for back in Boston . . . : wildly diverse, liberal, and queer."[42] Cho's writings published and comedy performed during this time brought the clarity of purpose and context lacking in her earlier stand-up comedy, though it is highly doubtful that she could have become a household name in the 1990s performing and writing in ways that challenged social inequality, condemned bigots, and mobilized minority communities. No longer subject to regulation, her control of the means of production and distribution gave Cho carte blanche to speak truth to power.

Blogs (a shortened term for weblogs) rose in popularity in the late 1990s alongside the creation of new blog tools like Open Diary and SlashDot and social networking programs that housed blogs and connected bloggers to each other. Such programs allowed for proliferation of commentary on culture and politics without the requisite pedigree expected of journalists, reporters, and pundits. On one hand, readers may discount such commentary or information as lacking credibility, but on the other it gives voice and visibility to the people because "the global digital communication system, while reflecting power relationships, is not based on the top-down diffusion of one dominant culture."[43] Put differently, bloggers can disrupt the traditional production and flow of information that privileges white masculinist perspectives and works on behalf of powerful multinational corporations that heavily influence governance. As a regular contributor to *Huffington Post* and *xoJane* as well as maintaining her own public blog on her webpage, Margaret Cho invests a great deal of time in blogging. Blog posts offer periodic updates about her work (upcoming shows, podcasts, benefits) and share photos of her in addition to personal reflection and commentary on her own experiences (living in Los Angeles, vacations, etc.) and social commentary on popular culture and politics. It proves a surefire way to communicate with her fan base without heavy mediation and is more expedient than writing a book, which can take years from pen to press. According to her, it is also subversive in the following ways:

> Bloggers have altered the way we view the news. Censorship and propaganda cannot go undetected in the blogosphere. Through the steady devotion of bloggers to tell the truth, to make their stories known, to communicate, to exist, loud and clear, we are blessed with an entirely new way to experience media. The news sources we relied on, the ones we feared would betray us with lies to protect their corporate allies, are no longer needed. . . . Without freedom of information, we have no freedom. Without access to the truth, we are powerless. . . .
> I trust the bloggers more than the nightly news because even though everyone has an agenda, theirs are closer to mine. In these times, we must just try to get closer to ourselves, get back to who we are. Identifying ourselves in the unrelenting storm of false information is one way bloggers can help. Protecting the truth by becoming bloggers ourselves, instead of retreating into lies and twisted political posturing, needs to become our way of life. Choosing to stay and fight for ourselves is the only way we can survive.[44]

Activist in their orientation, Cho's blogging efforts mirror the messages she includes in her stand-up comedy and epitomize the famous feminist dictum: "the personal is political." For example, during a visit to Aroma Spa and Sports in Los Angeles, where clothing is optional, spa attendants asked Cho to cover up her tattooed body because it offended some of the older Korean/Korean American female patrons. Reflecting on the experience, she vents her frustrations, writing:

> Their intolerance viewing my nakedness—as if it was some kind of an assault on their senses, like my ass was a weapon—made me furious in a way I can't really even express with words—and that for me is quite impressive. This bitch always has some shit to say. I guess it comes down to this—I deserve better. I brought the first Korean American family to television. I have influenced a generation of Asian American comedians, artists, musicians, actors, authors— many, many people to do what they dreamed of doing, not letting their race and the lack of Asian Americans in the media stop them. If anything, I understand Korean culture better than most, because I have had to fight against much of its homophobia, sexism, racism— all the while trying to maintain my fierce ethnic pride.[45]

In this instance, Cho turns rejection and public shaming into an opportunity to illustrate that she can be both Korean American, and a proponent of gay rights, and a champion of racial equality, and accepting of differences whatever they may be. These positions and identities are not and do not have to be mutually exclusive. It is credo and mantra in defense of alterity, and blog posts like this one not only remind existing and potential fans that she exists to rally on their behalf but that subordination takes many forms and affects many groups, not just their own. Racism should matter to the LGBTQ community and likewise homophobia should matter to communities of color, because as the saying goes: no one is free when others are oppressed. The same activist mentality that informs Cho's blog posts governs her regular usage of other social media platforms, while her command of such platforms ensures consistent contact and engagement with a diverse fan base.

A savvy user of social media, Margaret Cho stays connected with her fans by maintaining accounts on Twitter, Facebook, Instagram, YouTube, and Pinterest. She syncs many of these accounts—meaning that a contribution to Instagram will show up on Twitter and Facebook—and by doing so can appeal to various networks/groups, including family, friends, acquaintances, fellow comics and artists, and the many fans that constitute the Cho Army. Not content to sim-

"There's 17 million Asian-Americans in this country, and there's 17 million Italian Americans. They have The Godfather, Goodfellas, The Sopranos. We've got Long Duk Dong."

- Alan Yang

11.4. Margaret Cho Twitter post (2016).

ply tweet about her professional projects, Cho frequently (as in daily) retweets numerous messages to support and boost turnout for her fellow comics, to share information about her favorite entertainers and bands, and to endorse causes like animal adoption and helping the homeless. Always attentive to her fans, you can witness Cho bantering back and forth with them on Twitter—retweeting accolades of her work, favoriting their tweets, and even responding directly to them. Posting on Twitter, Instagram, and Facebook is relatively quick and painless; however, YouTube requires more work in order to film, edit, and then upload to this online video-sharing site. Undeterred by the greater time commitment, Cho used YouTube to stoke interest and enthusiasm for her MOTHER! Tour (the U.S. portion of the tour began in Atlanta and Athens, Georgia, in August 2013), which she describes as "an untraditional look at motherhood and how we look at maternal figures and strong women in queer culture."[46] As she made her way across the United States (again), she uploaded video updates from various performance destinations across the country (e.g., St. Louis, Denver, San Francisco, Austin, Boston, and D.C.). There are a dozen such updates wherein Cho, dressed casually and usually without makeup, talks to the camera (that is, her fans) about her stay in that city, much like she is talking to an old friend. She details her fish egg birthday dinner in San Diego, shows everyone her new boots bought in Dallas, and reminisces about the last time she performed in San Francisco's Nob Hill Masonic Theatre. But she is still promoting her shows. The brief videos (one to two minutes each) show clips of her singing her original hit "Fat Pussy," introducing musical guests that rotate in and out of her tour, and urging fans to come out for a great show. This combination of the personal and professional employed on social media platforms collapses traditional hierarchies and boundaries between fans and celebrities and maintains a public image of Cho as "one of us." Such maneuvers align with Cho's personal worldviews of shared humanity and signal mutual allegiance between Cho and her fans. It is a win-win situation. Fans support Cho's work and in return she advocates on their behalf, championing civil rights in political and cultural spheres.

On an episode of HBO's *The Green Room with Paul Provenza*, fellow funnyman Jeffrey Ross calls Cho's comedy "the outsider's act," and on her website bio Cho acknowledges that many "people who come to my shows don't necessarily consider themselves traditional comedy fans. I seem to be a safe alternative for people who don't think they're being represented in society."[47] Cho does not just offer a safe alternative for the underrepresented; she also provides a safe space to laugh without fear of being made the butt of the joke. Going to comedy clubs or shows can be a scary thing for many of the groups drawn to Cho's comedy—you never know if you or the communities to which you belong will be thrown under the proverbial bus, targeted in a way that forecloses certain identities as inferior, as in Henny Youngman's famous one-liner, "Take my wife . . . please!" Margaret Cho elaborates on this:

> As a queer Asian American feminist, I am always at risk, as my existence, or whatever, is perceived to be some kind of fodder for bad jokes from hack comedians. The homophobia, racism, and sexism I hear and feel constantly is taken as trivial. I have been told time and time again, it's just a joke. Who cares? Well, I care, and it hurts me. It dehumanizes me and adds to the invisibility I already feel, which also doesn't make sense. How can being singled out and abused make you feel like you aren't even there? In the alchemy of bigotry, it does. Safety is important to people like me, and my shows are where people can truly feel safe and visible and real and I am grateful I can do that. It's better than magic. It's relief. The burdens of race, sexuality and gender are lifted. It's OK to be you and me when we are together.[48]

Attending one of her shows offers respite in an otherwise inhospitable culture, and this is clearly intentional. Cho's performances—what Ernesto Javier Martinez calls "faggot pageantry," because she identifies with gay male subcultures and often invokes gay mimicry in her stand-up—are "unique instantiations of bearing faithful witness to queerness, not because she claims to represent gay men accurately or in their full complexity and diversity, but because she highlights the fractured (compromised) locus from within which gay men negotiate active subjectivities, and from which she herself negotiates survival as a racialized, queer woman."[49] In her charged comedy and writing, valuation of the complexity of identity and group heterogeneity functions as a clarion call for her fans to do the same; in this way she embraces her audience for *all* of who they are and enjoins fans to reject reductive representations of Others. By using multiple mediums to distribute her comic material—performances, books, blogs, and social media—she has been able to capture the adoration of an extensive fan base. She routinely sells out shows in venues that seat thousands, and her books have been national bestsellers. And with nearly half a million Twitter followers, four hundred thousand Facebook friends, and over a hundred thousand Instagram followers, it is clear that a loyal army of admirers have elevated Margaret Cho to status of comedy icon. She curries favor among the disenfranchised, celebrates their shared humanity, and then reminds them they have work to do as members of the Cho Army.

CONCLUSION

The media transmits representations of various social identities—gender, race/ethnicity, sexuality, ability—continuously on television, on film, and in the glossies beckoning us as we check out of stores. It is a formidable challenge to ignore what mainstream media says we should look like, how we should act, what we should buy, and what/ whom we should believe. The struggle for self-definition collides and often competes with the constant barrage of information and images that constitute our culture, making it a battleground where identity formation plays out.[50] It is true that exclusion from the political process—whether by force, wealth, or circumstances—and lack of financial clout present major obstacles to individuals and communities seeking to create social change. But if we are produced through culture (in other words, if our identities are shaped by music, literature, performance, film, and fine arts) then this also becomes a valuable site to contest misrepresentations and protest relegation to second-class citizens. Margaret Cho's stand-up comedy is a cultural form she

11.5. Margaret Cho in her music video "I Wanna Kill My Rapist" (2015).

can use to set the record queer about who she is as an American citizen, a woman, a feminist, a Korean American, and a member of the queer community.[51] Unlike television producers, writers, or reporters, when Cho authors her life experiences—whether through comedy, books, blogs, or tweets—she disrupts the ways she herself has been shaped and mediated by the media. This reimagining of the self points toward the ludic possibilities for future reimaginings of minority communities. If we can see Cho as a dynamic, complex, and even contradictory woman, we begin to reject gross generalizations and stereotypes about any single person or community.

There is no doubt that Margaret Cho is a busy lady. Whether she is touring with Cyndi Lauper to raise money for the Human Rights Campaign, accepting a "Korean of the Year" award, strutting her stuff on *Dancing with the Stars* (ABC season 11), canoodling with the cast of *30 Rock* as a gender-bending Kim Jung Il, performing in "Weird Al" Yankovic's music video "Tacky" (a remake of Pharrell Williams's "Happy"), making cameo appearances at the Golden Globe Awards, or a contestant on *@midnight*—Chris Hardwick's popular game show centered around social media—you can be sure that these are only side projects that take a backseat to self-funded creative ventures like mounting new comedy tours, cohosting *Monsters of Talk*, and writing. She worked hard in the 1990s in order to be in a financial position to exercise control over the production and distribution of her work, bringing a social justice sensibility to her twenty-first-century creative projects, from blogs to books to comedy to acting. On seeing Cho perform, humorist Emily Levine gushed:

When I first saw Margaret Cho—with all credit to Sandra Bernhard—I was like, "Oh my God. This is like the quote from Muriel Rukeyser, the poet: 'What would happen if one woman told the truth about her life? The world would split open.'" To have that kind of bravery and just put it all out there. I was blown away. I still am.[52]

Levine's reaction is not uncommon, particularly among the minorities and allies to whom Cho targets her charged comedy. During Cho's 2004 Assassin Tour, her chauffer, an African American woman named Kewana, said: "When I see her, I see myself. I see another aspect of a person of color that, you know, I didn't realize." During the same tour, black filmmaker and assistant professor at Temple University Michelle Parkerson extolled the values of Cho's humor: "It is heartening. It lets you know you're not alone. It lets you know that someone speaks the same language as you."[53] For minorities or anyone who sympathizes with those experiencing social and political exclusion, Cho's performances offer assurance that they are not alone or crazy and provide a safe space in which to celebrate diversity and difference—theirs and others. After all, if it is a numbers game, the members of Cho's Army—all the sexual deviants, the unfavorably complected, the poor, the cult members, the disposable people, the bitches and gender truants, the evil-doers, the undocumented, the foreigners and the freaks—would certainly win.

NOTES

1. Judith Yaross Lee, *Twain's Brand: Humor in Contemporary American Culture* (Jackson: University Press of Mississippi, 2012), 47.

2. For further explication of charged humor and the socially conscious comics who perform charged humor, see Rebecca Krefting, *All Joking Aside: American Humor and Its Discontents* (Baltimore: Johns Hopkins University Press, 2014).

3. *Margaret Cho: Assassin*, directed by Kerry Asmussen (Cho Taussig Productions, 2005), video.

4. Douglas Kellner, "Cultural Studies, Multiculturalism, and Media Culture," in *Gender, Race, and Class in Media: A Critical Reader*, ed. Gail Dines and Jean M. Humez (Thousand Oaks, CA: Sage, 2011), 10.

5. These references come from the following concert films (respectively): *Margaret Cho: Beautiful*, directed by Lorene Machado (Clownery Productions, 2009), video; *Margaret Cho: Assassin*; *Margaret Cho: Revolution*, directed by Lorene Machado (Wellspring Media, 2004), video.

6. Margaret Cho, *I'm the One That I Want* (New York: Ballantine Books, 2001).

7. Ibid.

8. Further information and evidence supporting these claims regarding censorship and shifting public sentiment during this time can be found in chapter 2 of Krefting, *All Joking Aside*.

9. Michelle Woo, "20 Years Later Margaret Cho Looks Back on 'All-American Girl,'" *KoreAm Journal*, Sept. 15, 2014, http://iamkoream.com/20-years-later-margaret-cho-looks-back-on-all-american-girl.

10. Margaret Cho, "The Kindness of Gay Men," introduction to *Out on the Edge: America's Rebel Comics*, ed. Mike Player (New York: Alyson Books, 2008), 2.

11. Yael Kohen, *We Killed: The Rise of Women in American Comedy* (New York: Sarah Crichton Books, 2012), 221.

12. Ibid., 234–235.

13. Woo, "20 Years Later."

14. *Fresh Off the Boat* (ABC 2015–) is the first Asian American sitcom since *All-American Girl* premiered twenty years ago.

15. "Margaret Cho, Jeffrey Ross, Richard Lewis, and Kamail Nanjiani," *The Green Room with Paul Provenza*, season 2, episode 5, Aug. 11, 2011, www.youtube.com/watch?v=bmr1khDeah4.

16. *Margaret Cho: Drunk with Power* (San Francisco: Uproar, 1996), audio recording.

17. Performance studies scholar Dan Bacalzo writes, "By taking control of the production of truth through autobiographical performance, Cho positions herself as being able to intervene in existing discourses around representation." Bacalzo, "The One That She Wants: Margaret Cho, Mediatization, and Autobiographical Performance," in *Embodying Asian American Sexualities*, ed. Gina Masequesmay and Sean Metzger (Lanham, MD: Lexington Books, 2009), 44.

18. See her personal interview in the bonus features included on *Margaret Cho: Assassin*.

19. Bacalzo, "The One That She Wants," 48.

20. *Margaret Cho: Drunk with Power*.

21. Linda Mizejewski, *Pretty/Funny: Women Comedians and Body Politics* (Austin: University of Texas Press, 2014),130.

22. "Margaret Cho: Bio," http://margaretcho.com/bio, accessed June 12, 2014.

23. Manuel Castells, *Communication Power* (Oxford: Oxford University Press, 2009), 62, 127.

24. *Margaret Cho: Revolution*.

25. Jeffrey Carroll describes Cho's performances as a "hot-voiced look at inequality and prejudice that is overcome through a rhetoric of self-delineation and pride"; and Michaela Meyer argues that "Cho's rhetorical subtext challenges dominant ideological constructs that proliferate racial, ethnic, and sexual oppression in American society." See Jeffrey Carroll, "Margaret Cho, Jake Shimabukuro, and Rhetorics in a Minor Key," in *Representations: Doing Asian American Rhetoric*, ed. LuMing Mao and Morris Young (Logan: Utah State University Press, 2008), 269; and Michaela Meyer, "'Maybe I Could Play a Hooker in Something!': Asian American Identity, Gender, and Comedy in the Rhetoric of Margaret Cho," in Mao and Morris, *Representations*, 279.

26. Krefting, *All Joking Aside*, 2.

27. *Margaret Cho: Beautiful.*

28. Interestingly, the scholarship on Margaret Cho focuses on stand-up comedy performed in the twenty-first century, and scholars neither cite nor mention the comedy albums released in the 1990s. I suspect that the incongruity between the content of her performances in the 1990s and those self-produced in the twenty-first century would trouble some of the arguments made in those publications.

29. Gary M. Kramer, ed., *Independent Queer Cinema: Reviews and Interviews* (New York: Harrington Park Press, 2006), 109.

30. Ibid., 108–110.

31. Mizejewski, *Pretty/Funny*, 131.

32. Patricia Hill Collins, *Black Feminist Thought: Knowledge, Consciousness, and the Politics of Empowerment* (New York: Routledge, 2000), 251–271.

33. Margaret Cho, *I Have Chosen to Stay and Fight* (New York: Penguin, 2005), 154.

34. Ibid., 18, 153.

35. *Margaret Cho: Notorious C.H.O.*, directed by Lorene Machado (Wellspring Media, 2002), video.

36. Claude M. Steele, *Whistling Vivaldi and Other Clues to How Stereotypes Affect Us* (New York: Norton, 2010).

37. For a lengthier discussion on the characteristics of charged humor and the ways charged humor can be distinguished from satire, see Krefting, *All Joking Aside*, 25–35.

38. "Margaret Cho: Bio."

39. *Margaret Cho: Assassin.*

40. Cho, *I Have Chosen*, 43.

41. Ibid., n.p.

42. Ian Harvie, "Funny Boi," in *Out on the Edge: America's Rebel Comics*, ed. Mike Player (New York: Alyson Books, 2008), 279.

43. Castells, *Communication Power*, 136.

44. Cho, *I Have Chosen*, 237.

45. "Aroma Smells Like Bigotry," *Margaret Cho* (blog), Mar. 25, 2013, http://margaretcho.com/2013/03/25/aroma-smells-like-bigotry.

46. "Margaret Cho: Bio."

47. "Margaret Cho, Jeffrey Ross, Richard Lewis"; "Margaret Cho: Bio."

48. Margaret Cho, "Margaret Cho Talks about Her Pride in Being Called a 'Queer Icon' in Light of Michelle Shocked's Anti-gay Rant," *xoJane*, Mar. 21, 2013, www.xojane.com/issues/margaret-cho-talks-about-her-pride-in-being-called-a-queer-icon-in-light-of-michelle-shockeds-anti-gay-rant.

49. Ernesto Javier Martinez, *On Making Sense: Queer Race Narratives of Intelligibility* (Stanford, CA: Stanford University Press, 2012), 138.

50. Recognizing culture as a key site for negotiating identity, Americanist scholar Lisa Lowe writes: "Struggles for empowerment are often exclusively understood within the frameworks of legal, political, and economic institutions. . . . Yet an important link in this relation is the *production of individual and collective subjectivities through cultural forms*" (my emphasis). See Lowe, *Immi-*

grant Acts: On Asian American Cultural Politics (Durham, NC: Duke University Press, 1996), 155.

51. According to Lowe, these kinds of personal testimonies evident in stand-up comedy work to "connect subjects to social relations"; thus, "culture is the medium through which alternatives to liberal citizenship in the political sphere are narrated, where critical subjects and collectivities can be reproduced in new configurations, with new coherences." Ibid., 156.

52. Emily Levine, quoted in Kohen, *We Killed*, 234.

53. *Margaret Cho: Assassin.*

CHAPTER 12

ELLEN DEGENERES'S INCORPORATE BODY:
THE POLITICS OF AUTHENTICITY

BRENDA R. WEBER AND JOSELYN K. LEIMBACH

Ellen is like the epitome of a feminist. She refused to wear a dress for the Academy Awards. She is so authentic!

STUDENT IN G404, GENDER AND CELEBRITY, AT INDIANA UNIVERSITY, FALL 2013

Oprah is very business minded. . . . I'm just not that way. I'm happy my show is successful. But I am also content just to be me.

ELLEN DEGENERES, *NEW YORK TIMES*, JANUARY 17, 2014

"Being able to be free—literally—and to express herself in a way that she can be 100 percent truthful with the audience has allowed them to fall in love with her," says Winfrey, who guest-starred as DeGeneres's therapist in that infamous [coming out] episode of Ellen. *"Honest-to-God truth: I don't believe she would have been as successful as she has become had she not come out."*

OPRAH WINFREY, *HOLLYWOOD REPORTER*, AUGUST 22, 2012

IN 2008 ELLEN DEGENERES opened her talk show with a humorous monologue about her wife Portia de Rossi, saying, "Last night, Portia and I were sitting in our living room, on the sofa, and Portia opened up a book. And right away I started to worry. I thought, oh, the television's broken [*laughter*]. But she was studying; she said she was studying for her U.S. citizenship test. And I said, 'Where the hell are you from?' [*stronger laughter*] Turns out she's from Australia. I didn't even know it. A beautiful country famous for its strudel [*giggles*]." DeGeneres goes on to quiz the audience about some of the questions that Portia must field on the citizenship exam, only to suggest that potential citizens need to be tested on a few more topics that are actually much more relevant to U.S. citizenship. "You should exercise your right to vote. Otherwise, your favorite singer on *American Idol* may be sent home! [*robust laughter and applause*] And then they should teach about driving, that should be on the test for sure. If you pull up to a gas station, don't be one of those people that stops at the first pump; pull forward, go all the way forward! [*cheers, applause, and laughter*]" In many respects this moment is unremarkable, since in tone and content it resembles so much of Ellen's comedy and celebrity. She has made a career out of being nice and funny, of taking the everyday moments of life and turning them into humor. But as this snippet of her monologue also shows, she is equally skilled at taking flashes of the exceptional, in this case her marriage with de Rossi, and turning them into the humorous and the everyday, inviting her audiences into their domestic world without actually violating their privacy.

As the epigraphs that start this chapter indicate, Ellen DeGeneres is not famous for being famous. She is famous for being herself. Or at least, as we will argue, for conveying authenticity under the banner of a comedic Ellen-ness in which her perceived genuineness functions as the mortar that holds the house of Ellen together. This is not to say that Ellen DeGeneres—as a comedian, a person, a celebrity, or a brand—is either duplicitous or disingenuous in the construction of her star text. Instead, we believe that the chief defining element of her Ellen-ness, her perceived authenticity, gives rise to a likeability that seemingly cannot be produced (and so therefore presumably cannot be faked). This authenticity builds a foundation for her humorous performances and simultaneously, and perhaps consequently, makes her irresistibly popular across media markets.

Ellen's particular brand of comedy, at once naively childlike and potently perceptive, disarms her audience with her playfulness and challenges them with her thought-provoking insights. This combination of youthful innocence and cultural savvy, which functions behind the protective armor of comedy, positions Ellen in an in-between space that blurs identity-based boundaries and creates productive and acceptable combinations that shift her signature comedic moments from potentially threatening transgression to guileless play.

As our first epigraph indicates, Ellen's transgression of gendered and sexual norms reinforces audience investments and readings of her as genuine and unmediated. Remarkably, her refusal to wear a dress at the 2006 Oscars, the swankiest of Hollywood glamour-fests, was perceived by our students as a gesture not only of authenticity but also of feminism because, for them, it indicated she was "true" to herself (and therefore a strong woman). Read through the lens of gender as representative of a deeper interior truth, this rejection of a feminine gendered performance at an event so fully meant to display hyperfemininity reaffirmed Ellen's perceived bravery, which, in turn, bolstered her authenticity credentials.

Given this, it's more than ironic that one of the funniest moments in her 2014 turn as the host of the Academy Awards occurred when she donned a glittery pink ball gown so that she might look like an awkward Glinda the Good Witch from *The Wizard of Oz*. The surface humor relied on a perceived incongruity between Ellen's standard masculinized gender appearance and the excessive femininity of the frilly pink dress. Dressing as Glinda further allowed Ellen to make use of a gay sign system. As Glinda, she was a FOD (Friend of Dorothy), a euphemism to identify same-sex desiring people. Ellen's Glinda moment also demonstrated that this public lesbian, so tied to codes of authenticity, knows a thing or two about camp or theatrical moments when expected gender displays (generally, but not always, associated with the sexed body) can be subverted through a performed excess that has the potential to disrupt naturalized understandings of sex/gender relations. Indeed, donning a dress (and this pink sparkly one in particular) allowed Ellen to transcend the sexual mainstream/subculture divide, creating an opportunity for humor that can speak to a variety of audiences on multiple levels. Ellen's play with seemingly contradictory performances (as between butch female masculinity and hyperfemininity) is the cornerstone of her comedic engagement with gender and sexual norms. Yet rather than undermining her particular brand of authenticity, these inconsistencies reinforce the "truth" of the person behind the celebrity persona. In fact, the juxtaposition makes her more funny.

The sexual economy of Ellen is critical to her authenticity quotient. In many ways, she is America's public lesbian, and her controversial outing as a lesbian (character and actor) on primetime television, once so deleterious to her career, now serves as the bedrock moment that established her bid to authenticity. She is an unpretentious and seemingly genuinely nice and funny person who fought (and fights) bravely against bigotry, hand in hand with her wife, Portia de Rossi, and her mother, Betty DeGeneres, who both often appear proudly on the sidelines, cheering her to greatness. Yet Ellen's emphasis on emotional support as a means to overcome discrimination leaves larger oppressions virtually invisible, potentially disassociating her activism from the realm of politics and channeling it towards the impact on the individual. Thus her own politics are often concealed, and her heterosexual fans are granted honorary liberal status by virtue of their admiration for her. As Lacey Rose writes in the *Hollywood Reporter*,

> The exuberance and ease that DeGeneres brings to daytime—even in the midst of the increasingly rancorous national debate on same-sex marriage—can make anxious moms and tired housewives feel as if a friend is in their living room (or, thanks to segments that appear regularly on Yahoo, on their computer screen). "For an hour each day, Ellen makes you forget your troubles and feel good," says Hilary Estey McLoughlin, president of Warner Bros.–owned Telepictures. "She's an antidote for the times."[1]

Rather than seeing Ellen DeGeneres as an antidote for the times, however, we perceive her as an emblem of them, precisely because she engages in political battles sparingly and with equal parts humor and savvy. There is perhaps no person more deserving of the "slash" that denotes the flexible labor of the personal/professional than Ellen DeGeneres: actor/comedian/talk-show host/award-show host/cover girl/record-label owner/author/television producer/celebrity endorser/occasional talent-show judge/social media maven. Her career is a testament not only to her talent and perseverance but also to the cross-platform hybridity of media in a twenty-first-century context, where traditional forms, such as television and film, are augmented by new media and social media outlets such as YouTube, Facebook, and Twitter.[2] As the number of subscribers to Ellen's YouTube channel and Facebook page clearly indicates, Ellen has mastered social media. As further evidence, we need look no further than the "selfie that broke the Internet," when DeGeneres, as host of the 2014 Oscars ceremony, live-tweeted a photo of herself and a gaggle of her celebrity friends (including Meryl Streep, Bradley Cooper, Julia Roberts, and Kevin Spacey). The image was retweeted so often that circuits overloaded, thus crashing transmission possibilities and becoming what AP television writer David Bauder termed a "landmark media moment."[3]

Our epigraphs also suggest an important relation between Ellen's produced authenticity and audience readings that verify this performance, demonstrating the degree to which such claims to authenticity point to the possibilities that an entertainer might function, as a celebrity and a person, outside of commercialized and political spheres. For example, in the second epigraph, Ellen distances herself from the commercialism she associates with Oprah's brand, suggesting that she finds contentment in just being herself (as if that Ellenness is separate from self-branding). In reaffirming the distinction between herself and Oprah, she posits Oprah's performance of self as a highly mediated product dependent upon achieving maximum exposure and financial success. Positioning herself as the counter- (if not the anti-) Oprah, Ellen constructs a persona rooted in "realness" and distanced from demands of the financial marketplace. The promotion of an authentic self-as-separate-from-celebrity is emphasized in the second epigraph, a *New York Times* interview in which Ellen prioritizes self-fulfillment and happiness over professional and financial success.[4] Yet even as Ellen disassociates herself from the business realm, she is deeply enmeshed within it. In fact, this consistent characterization of self has resulted in excessive economic and professional success, a point made clear in our third epigraph, Oprah Winfrey's statement to the *Hollywood Reporter*.

We argue that Ellen DeGeneres is able to appeal to so many audiences, across so many mediated platforms, and over so many systems of meaning because of the perceived authenticity of what we are calling her incorporate body. We use the term to indicate a specific fashioning of self that combines and fuses together hybridities of desire and identity under a single sign of authenticity, using her nonthreatening accessibility and perceived realness to fuel her performance. The significance of Ellen's sexual identity is critical to her incorporate body. Ellen's hybrid performance reasserts mainstream tolerances and neutralizes the threat of her sexual difference through authenticity and familiarity. That's rather serious stuff for such a funny person.

In the many iterations of her celebrity comedic persona, Ellen acts as sign and symbol of exuberant, even juvenile, everydayness, as can be seen in a wide array of sites on her talk show, from her performances of physical comedy and her daily somewhat awkward dance intros to pranks and games (like hiding in bathrooms to scare celebrity guests, catching it all on hidden camera, or doing trivia quizzes with audience members where wrong answers earn them a drop through a hole in the floor). Though she is a media mogul worth a reported $200 million and is on intimate terms with Hollywood's A-list, these excesses are recalibrated through an ethos of authenticity named simply as Ellen. Thus her "incorporate" body both references business practices aligned with the construction and commodification of her star text and alludes to the incorporation of multiple (seemingly contradictory) aspects of personality, all fused together under the Ellen brand.

WHAT YOU SEE IS WHAT YOU GET

In the twenty years since Ellen DeGeneres's primetime appearance on her eponymous sit-com *Ellen* (ABC 1994–1998), the woman who first entered public consciousness as a stand-up comedian has cultivated her stardom and blossomed into an intermedial superstar known for her consistent success in modeling, authorship, voice acting, and, of course, hosting a daytime talk show. She is one of those few superstars who is widely known by her first name alone, a fact we will capitalize on throughout this chapter. The politics of naming suggest that the use of a first name diminishes power. Yet in this instance, Ellen's recognition challenges this discourse, since she has built such recognition for herself that her first name, as common as it is, cannot be disassociated from her persona. With the notable exception of her role as Dory in Pixar's *Finding Nemo* (2003) and *Finding Dory* (2016), much of Ellen's fame comes from portraying characters named Ellen who are theoretically herself (though Dory's goofy sense of humor is clearly cast in the Ellen mold). The crossover between her public persona and private life has contributed to making Ellen a person seemingly knowable and known to audiences, her life and loves on full display. Her apparent transcendence of the public/private distinction characterizes the ways she disrupts other oppositional binaries through a hybridity that integrates two seemingly contradictory concepts.

For instance, as we have noted, Ellen performs a very public lesbianism and is vocal about her marriage to Portia de Rossi, yet on her daytime talk show her most over-the-top flirtations occur with her male guests (and for the benefit of her seemingly straight female audience). Even as she performs female masculinity on mainstream American television, she obtained a contract with the makeup company CoverGirl, a traditionally heterofeminine concern and company.

12.1. Ellen DeGeneres as CoverGirl model (2011).

Indeed, she wears a full face of makeup in most of her on-screen performances. This media convention is not limited to female bodied or feminine-presenting individuals. In fact, it is not unusual for masculine male bodies to engage in similar, if less explicit, practices. CoverGirl's decision to employ Ellen as a representative falls within a growing trend in which, according to Danae Clark, "the advertising industry is playing upon a material and ideological tension that simultaneously appropriates aspects of lesbian subculture and positions lesbian reading practices in relation to consumerism."[5] Thus Ellen's connection to CoverGirl denotes the makeup industry's recognition of a growing market for lesbians with increasing amounts of disposable income as an untapped consumer base. This trend goes hand in hand with cultural revisions of a lesbian identity that has transitioned from an imagined blue-collar, working-class position to that of white-collar, middle- and upper-middle-class status, as well as exploiting the heightened visibility of feminine-presenting "lipstick" lesbians. These shifts presumably call for alternative class and gendered conventions regarding appearance and the use of/desire for makeup by this population. Yet the CoverGirl ads do not only inter-pellate a lesbian consumer, tied as they are to the "girl-next-door" quality of Ellen's friendly appeal.

Additionally, Ellen's body meets normative conventions of attrac-tiveness through her able-bodied, slim figure and her promotion of healthy diet and exercise practices. Her seemingly universal appeal highlights her desirability as spokesperson who has the ability to attract the attention of women on a wide spectrum of sexual iden-tities. Importantly, Ellen's use of makeup, at least for our students, doesn't seem to count as artifice and thus does not detract from ei-ther her perceived authenticity or her feminism. Ellen's fusion of self-as-celebrity functions across different media formats while troubling ideologically asserted binaries through a hybridity that challenges di-chotomous constructs. As Linda Mizejewski asserts, "The multiple and often contradictory effects of . . . [Ellen's] visibility and later ce-lebrity" show a career that is "characterized by its own leakiness, to borrow the Bakhtinian term, its slippages out of categories and defi-nitions."[6] Mizejewski further notes that Ellen's sexual and gendered difference is mediated by her blonde, blue-eyed whiteness as well as her advocacy for generosity and kindness, two thoroughly feminine traits that reify her female sex even as her masculine gender display troubles conventional expectations. Her emphases on consumption, evidenced in her role as spokesperson for CoverGirl and JC Penney (as well as the numerous product placements in her talk show), insert her into a consumer-driven neoliberal logic that ensures her inclu-sion within and support of capitalist free-market economic systems.

In fact, Ellen's success in spite of, or perhaps due to, her lesbian identity epitomizes neoliberal proclamations of a postoppression era, and her renewed success following the backlash of her initial outing points to neoliberal logics of self-determination. Ellen's tacit support of these larger ideological systems allows her the freedom to engage in hybrid performances that trouble gendered and sexual constructs. Further, the systems themselves are bolstered by her inclusion, re-affirming the foundation of "tolerance" that justifies diminishing governmental safety nets. Even as she engages in philanthropic work, Ellen emphasizes a neoliberal individualism that takes the place of state-supported structures, such as welfare, and maintains the invis-ibility of enduring systems of oppression. When her show highlights the financial difficulties of some of her "deserving" but struggling audience members (often rewarding them with new cars or piles of cash made possible by corporate sponsors eager to use generosity as a form of product placement on and through her show), Ellen and her corporate sponsors' "kindness" reinforces the redundancy of government interventions in a free-market economy. Individual struggles are seemingly "solved" through a large check from a named sponsor or with a new car (never addressing the increased insurance costs and taxes associated with this gift), and all of these acts fall under Ellen's admonition at the end of each show to "be kind to one another!" These compassionate interventions and admonitions for kindness became all the more urgent with the rising popular tide of nationalism and the presidential shift from Obama to Trump.

Ellen epitomizes tenets of both conspicuous consumption, in her role as spokesperson, and selflessness, through her philanthropic efforts, even as the generous acts recenter her own privilege through choices about what kind of suffering is worthy of receiving assistance and what products contribute to a "livable" life. Her continued membership within prevailing economic structures legitimizes Ellen's enactment of an "incorporate body," wherein she blurs the boundaries between multiple (seemingly contradictory) aspects of personality and disrupts naturalized identity-based hierarchies and characteristics. Thus, Ellen's incorporation of seemingly incommensurate categories and her service to corporate/capitalist demands fuse the star-as-person and the star-as-brand—an amalgamation that ultimately maintains her mainstream appeal. As such, Ellen serves as a model for the contemporary relationship between life and work. In *Media Work*, Mark Deuze argues that "the modern categories of life and work at the beginning of the twenty-first century must be seen as spilling over, converging, making each of these key aspects of our human condition subject to the conditions of the other."[7] Ellen's blending of self/brand and private/public, all while maintaining an air of unquestioned veracity, exemplifies contemporary demands for the flexible worker in an age of advanced capitalism.

Ellen's involvement in a wide range of media formats and business endeavors further exemplifies contemporary demands for the flexible worker. According to Emily Martin, the flexible worker is "able to learn new abilities continuously and take up new functions as the market dictates."[8] Ellen's ability to transcend the initial public and corporate resistance to her open lesbianism relies upon her ability to construct a palatable personality whose sexual orientation is merely incidental to her bubbly and good-spirited attitude. The combination of her lesbian-yet-desexualized lifestyle and her disavowal of the threat of her lesbianism (and its politics) facilitates her audience's claims to being "progressive," allowing them to rest easily with a homonormativity that never threatens to slide into the queer.[9]

Ellen's foray into multiple mediated arenas, as comedian, actress, spokesmodel, talk-show host, and so on, showcases her diverse interests yet maintains the consistency of the Ellen brand. Rather than dividing her persona into multiple forms, each role builds on and bolsters a notion of Ellen's sincerity, since each is positioned as an outgrowth of her energy rather than as evidence of her ego. Her presence in film, on television, in advertisements, in magazines, on the internet, and in social media makes access to Ellen a regular occurrence, creating a pseudorelationship between her self and her audience. In this vein, Deuze argues, "We apply to mediated experiences the same rules and conventions as to face-to-face or otherwise 'real' experiences";[10] thus we expect that our familiarity with her brand constitutes an intimacy with her person. Through Ellen's media saturation and blurring of the public/private binary, she is positioned (and often positions herself) as a trusted and loved friend rather than a performer whose fictional performances and publicity-driven appearances promote themselves and their cultural product as commodities.

In doing so, the Economy of Ellen uses social media to exquisite ends: she (or her team) scours Facebook pages for funny moments; the show often includes forms of "amateur mediation" like hilarious autocorrect texts or awkward video vines; and she has a particularly intense relationship with YouTube, often inviting people who have posted impressive videos to perform on her show and in one case offering a "found" musical talent a record contract through her own label (eleveneleven). If the sign of true intimacy is the gaze of recognition and appreciation from the Beloved, these everyday "personal" interactions close the loop of affection, in the process securing Ellen's appeal as a person (rather than a product) with whom audience members might create bonds of attachment and affection.

Ellen's embodiment, particularly in relation to gender, is central to her persona and performed authenticity. In her skinny jeans, canvas sneakers, blazers, and thin ties, she is coded as a variant of the butch lesbian—who also happens to be a cover girl for a major cosmetics company. In like manner, she also troubles conventional understandings of sexuality, proclaiming herself an out gay women but regularly refusing same-sex erotics. As one case in point, when *Friends* star Matthew Perry visited Ellen's show, he and she put together an on-air comedic bit where they called a topless maid company in Los Angeles. Asking for more details about the services topless maids might perform, Perry at one point asks dryly, "From our voices, which of us do you think is more interested in your services?" The receptionist answered, "Um, Ellen?," to which Ellen herself quickly rebuked, "Oh no, not at all."

Quite often her marriage becomes the very marker of her absence from same-sex erotics, as she erases her interest in other women simply by reasserting, "I'm married!" This disavowal also occurs through her often physically contained interactions with female guests. In one particular interaction with fellow CoverGirl spokesmodel Sofia Vergara, Ellen has the actress read a prepared script for an unofficial CoverGirl commercial while Ellen stands behind her and "applies" her makeup.[11] The comedy of the sketch is rooted in the disruption of Vergara's unquestioned beauty when the makeup application goes inevitably and hilariously awry. During her reading, Ellen's hands, symbolically functioning as Vergara's, cup her breasts and later insert makeup into her cleavage.

Although Ellen engages in these sexualized behaviors, she is disassociated from the action by virtue of her invisibility behind Vergara. This moment highlights Ellen's childlike humor through her inept makeup application, positioning her outside of mature femininity and reaffirming her desexualization. The sexual interactions are further diminished through the reiteration of Vergara's heterosexuality, both in discussions of her fiancé and in the recurring appearance of young, physically fit, half-naked male bodies that, as we will later discuss, exist for the pleasure of Ellen's presumably heterosexual female audience. Further, the comedic interactions between the two women often occur at Vergara's expense. Although Vergara is a willing participant, a reoccurring theme in their interactions privileges Anglo-American English, positioning Vergara's Colombian accent as not just foreign but unintelligible.

This trope is repeatedly exercised not only on Ellen's show but also in the official CoverGirl commercial in which the women appear. By emphasizing Vergara's otherness, Ellen's "playful" teasing rehashes the children's game of repetition (or telephone), but with a difference. When Ellen dressed as Vergara for Halloween in 2012, she not only (poorly) imitated Vergara's accent, but her attempts to repeat Spanish phrases inevitably failed, which, in turn, reasserted her white privilege through humor.[12] This emphasis further removes her from the threat of her own lesbian desire through cultural constructions of children as asexual. While Ellen's interactions with Vergara balanced the presupposed sexual desirability of Vergara and Ellen's denial of her position as a desiring lesbian subject, she also accomplishes this disavowal by flirting, sometimes outrageously, with her male guests.

Ellen's 1997 outing remains a groundbreaking moment for queer visibility, even as her sexuality remains confined to a palatable portrayal that seemingly caters to mainstream audiences through a personal politics that reiterate domesticated and apolitical homonormative patterns that bolster the heteronormative logics of her show. According to Candace Moore, within the context of Ellen's daily talk show, "straight desire is always the point-of-reference."[13] Ellen's consistent allusions to her married status emphasize her adherence to sexual conventions that vindicate normative sexual demands and concomitantly convey her lesbianism as the "same" as heterosexual desires. This ideological interplay ensures that she remains unthreatening to her audience of presumably white, heterosexual, middle-class mothers by reaffirming the normativity and presumption of heterosexuality through interactions with guests that highlight romantic milestones (like engagements and marriages) and the birth of children. Even when engaging with issues that directly address her lesbianism, Ellen disavows political discourse by highlighting her relationship to consumption and distancing the discussion from broader LGBTQ concerns, focusing instead upon the personal nature of homophobic attacks. By way of asserting these points more clearly, in the remainder of this chapter we turn to two interactions that demonstrate Ellen's balance between the heteronormativity of her show and her strategically political, individualized, and consumption-driven engagement with homophobia. We perceive these dynamics as central to the incorporate body.

IT WAS ONLY A KISS . . .

For a talk show fronted by "America's most-famous lesbian," *The Ellen DeGeneres Show* (*TEDS*, NBC 2003–) contains a surprising amount of comedic (even slapstick) male beefcake, served up for the pleasures and delights of a decidedly middle-aged and presumably heterosexual female audience (never a hint of gay male desire in the air). If someone didn't know better, Ellen/*TEDS* could well be read as "in" on the heterosexual game, offering her studio and at-home audiences (both groups positioned as being middle-aged, middle-class, female, and straight) a viewing pleasure through copious amounts of visual access to young, muscled, famous men in various states of undress. One of the tacit promises Ellen makes to her largely female audiences is that she will contrive reasons to compel ripped men to take off their clothes—from fake massage sessions for David Beckham to dunking tanks for Derek Hough, both scenarios requiring that male bodies be stripped and six packs be exposed.[14] We would go so far as to argue that under the guise of her good-natured and "decent" humor, the exposed male body is a staple of her offering, a point made readily when the gag of *Ellen*'s season 9 premiere was Ashton Kutcher's naked body. With the success of his new role on *Two and a Half Men* (CBS 2003–2015)—which also makes use of his muscled, unclothed body—Kutcher claimed that all of his future appearances would be in the nude, starting with Ellen's show.

The talk show's gags on occasion ask other famous men, who are less, shall we say, Adonis-like, to expose their bodies: for instance, the chubby comedian Jack Black. But by and large, the comedic bits put on display a vast array of athletic, slim, youthful, muscled men (of all races), who seem more than happy to play along with the joke, gyrate at Ellen's command, or allow blindfolded audience members to guess their identities by feel. Just as giving away cars to needy people functions as a form of "being kind to one another," these moments where young, male Hollywood celebrities happily, and even eagerly, expose their chiseled chests to Ellen and her giggling audiences further a sense of both her sexual difference and her good-natured kindness. We are meant to understand that as a lesbian, she could never be interested in seeing these men strip, and since they do so readily at her request, their bare forms can only serve to amuse her feminized audiences rather than benefit her own interests.

We would not go so far as to say that Ellen as a presence is absent any kind of erotic energy. The queerness of her show's environment emerges in many contexts, particularly her interactions with (presumably close) male friends. One example occurred during her fawning interaction with Jared Leto after his 2014 Oscar win, in which Ellen not only congratulated him for winning "most beautiful last night," but showed a clip from his acceptance speech whittled down to simply repeat his proclamation "I love you, Ellen."[15] Ellen's teasing flirtations can also be seen in her 2013 interview with Steve Harvey, in which he joked about her "tak[ing] a handful of butt" during a photo shoot. Later in the clip, Harvey expressed concern that his shirt was too open, stating, "That's way too sexy for daytime TV." In response, Ellen promptly leaned over and unbuttoned his shirt further to reveal his bare chest. Although Harvey played along, he joked, "I don't know why I come on your show and let you do what you do to me."[16]

Ellen flirts with her male guests in a manner unimaginable were the roles reversed, either with Ellen as a male host or with her male guests as females. The sexual dynamics with her female guests are often conspicuously absent this kind of playful bawdiness, with the notable exception of Vergara, whose ethnic difference and "excess" sexuality mediate and facilitate the on-screen flirtations. Distancing herself from same-sex physical contact and desire, no matter how innocuous, maintains Ellen's particular brand of lifestyle lesbianism that disassociates identity from desire, thus reinforcing homonormative mandates by comedically performing a model of desexualized lesbianism. The sexualized dynamics in her interactions with men suggest that the play between the (presumably) heterosexual man and Ellen's distinctly lesbian sexuality creates a space that both reinforces and destabilizes sexual conventions. Ellen's same-sex desire permits a kind of sexual aggression and display towards her (seemingly) heterosexual male counterparts that alters the sexual dynamics between men and women generally conveyed in mainstream media.

As case in point, consider an episode of her talk show that aired on April 8, 2014, when Ellen invited Rob Lowe to the set to celebrate his fiftieth birthday and the release of his new celebrity memoir, *Love Life*. Ellen's questions begin by emphasizing Lowe's masculine desirability and power, highlighted in his book by an almost-hookup with Madonna, herself an icon of female sexual empowerment. Yet Lowe's sexual "failures" are also emphasized when he tells the story of Jewel Kilcher's rejection during their filming of the short-lived television show *Lyon's Den* (NBC 2003–2004). Basically, when the script called for Lowe's character to kiss Jewel's, her lack of amorous response became obvious to the point of humiliation.[17] In order to fully convey the depths of his failure, Lowe enlists Ellen to reenact his interaction with Jewel. With Ellen cast in the role of Lowe and Lowe portray-

ellen

12.2. Ellen DeGeneres
kisses Rob Lowe, *The Ellen
DeGeneres Show* (2014).

ing Jewel, Ellen moves in to kiss Lowe. He awkwardly pulls away
and attempts to avoid the kiss. This, in turn, seems to fuel Ellen's insistence, as she moves her body in a position of caricatured physical
dominance to Lowe's and he slowly accedes to her passion. The whole
comedic vignette recreates visually and humorously more than one
clichéd heterosexual romance trope of the man who overpowers the
woman with sexual need and desire (Rhett and Scarlet having so successfully imprinted the pattern in *Gone With the Wind*).

In retelling and reenacting the initial moment of failure, Lowe,
in some sense, enacts a heterosexual fantasy of lesbian accessibility.
Tasked with facilitating the reenactment of Lowe's story, Ellen momentarily transitions to play the man, reinforcing heterosexual "nat-
uralness" even amidst her audience's titters and amusement for her
performance; yet as we've noted, the dual generic frames of humor
and talk show work in tandem to "right" this moment, making it
less about sexualized rupture or performative desire and more about
Ellen's code of brave comedy. (She will even kiss a man for a laugh.)

Fittingly, there is an alternative reading of this moment. Let us
start with the presumption that the roles performed by both Ellen
and Lowe could not be reversed. Only in exaggerating his own understanding of Jewel's motives, where he interprets her reaction to the
kiss as a moment of disgust, can Lowe depict the humorous indignity
of it. There may very well be something queer in the highlighting of
Ellen's masculinity in the face of Lowe's lack of masculine prowess.
Yet the question remains, what is it about Ellen that facilitates this

interaction and leads to such a memorable kiss, which is more hilarious than hot? Could we imagine a similar performance between Lowe and Jimmy Fallon? Or Lowe and Chelsea Handler? Or Ellen and Chelsea Handler? Our sense is that Ellen's married lesbianism creates a safe space for Lowe's married, heterosexual performance of a kiss that can function as both sexualized play and asexual comedy. This, in turn, contributes to an incorporate body that unifies hybridities (of motive, of desire, of behavior) under the sign of comedy.

Ellen's sometimes over-the-top heterosexual flirtations and open lesbianism combine to "play" heterosexuality for an appreciative crowd, who are insiders to the joke of the interaction. Because the underlying sexual tensions are presumably nonexistent, Ellen is permitted sexual leeway in her engagements with her male guests that are unimaginable in other circumstances. The awkwardness of the heterosexual interaction further evidences the "truth" of Ellen's lesbianism, thus reinforcing an authenticity that stands at the heart of her incorporate body. The ever-present specter of Ellen's lesbianism positions the moment as comedic, and Lowe's reaction (he states in a daze, "That was insane!") denotes the exceptional nature of the kiss/joke.

MY HATERS ARE MY MOTIVATORS

Perhaps in response to the difficulties Ellen faced following her coming out, her professional identity/brand rarely ventures into the realm of the political. She may be an out lesbian, she may be a masculine-presenting woman, but these aspects of her life, particularly her marriage to de Rossi, toe the line of conventional gender relations. She does not hide her same-sex relationship, and her transparency further reiterates the authenticity of her brand, yet her lesbianism remains staunchly within the realm of a homonormativity that emphasizes a version of the lesbian and gay community that is domesticated and desexualized. The depolitical nature of and proclamations for sameness associated with homonormative rhetorics thus undermine the potential threat of sexual otherness.

In the rare moments where Ellen's personal ethics overlap with politically relevant concerns, she couches her views in the language of individualism. As an example, during one segment from her talk show where she addressed the murder of a young boy, killed (according to Ellen) because of his gayness, she proclaimed, "I don't want to be political. I'm not a political person, but this is personal to me."[18]

Given her construction as an individual who prioritizes fun and lightheartedness, when Ellen does engage in overtly political activism, she must reframe the terms of the conversation to disavow the politics of her perspective, instead asserting the individual and, in this instance, the personal. In so doing, Ellen reinforces the effects of individuals on other individuals and avoids critiques of systemic oppressions. Only when the cultural politics of the moment contrasts with the ethics she performs on her show are systemic oppressions granted visibility. Ellen's "family friendly" show and persona generally take up gay and lesbian concerns around two modes of gayness: the impact of homophobia upon LGBTQ youth and the matter of same-sex marriage.[19] Both modes of activism reside within the realm of homonormative values that reinforce the centrality of the family and normative sexual performances.

Yet even with Ellen's "apolitical" stance, she has not escaped controversy. In early 2012, One Million Moms, a subgroup of the American Family Association (listed as a hate group by the Southern Poverty Law Center), protested JC Penney's decision to "get in bed" with Ellen as the company's spokesmodel, a protest based solely on the fact of her gayness. The controversy that arose out of Ellen's role as the face of JC Penney created an instance in which the values she ubiquitously performs were tested. The One Million Moms fight became as much about a protest against Ellen as it was about homophobia. By positioning Ellen as the figurehead of the debate, One Million Moms (which could also, ironically, be the name of Ellen's fan base) became the embodiment of a nameless and faceless homophobia in the life of an innocent individual, even as, through the lens of the conservative Christian organization, Ellen's gayness functioned as the embodiment of an attack on "traditional values."

In her February 7, 2012, response to the protests, Ellen used the platform of her talk show to directly address the controversy, ending her monologue by contrasting the message of hate with her own belief system: "I stand for honesty, equality, kindness, compassion, treating people the way you want to be treated, and helping those in need. To me those are traditional values, and that's what I stand for."[20] According to Scott Wooledge, an editorialist for the *Huffington Post*'s "Gay Voices" section, most of the visibility for the protest arose from publicity generated by the Gay and Lesbian Alliance Against Defamation (GLAAD), which used the controversy in an attempt to emphasize the lack of employment protections for LGBTQ populations. While GLAAD fought to use the issue to put a face on a larger concern about bullying and systemic injustice, Ellen's response centralized herself as the core figure of the controversy. In effect, her engagement with the One Million Moms protest positioned Ellen as the sole victim of their mass bullying, thus putting a decidedly neoliberal spin on these matters through an emphasis on individualism rather than systemic oppression, all played out in a marketplace of both ideas and commerce.

Comedy, of course, is central to this entire dynamic. After announcing JC Penney's decision to keep her as their spokesperson, Ellen joked, "It's great news for me since I need some new crew socks." Indeed, comedy both defused the tension around the situation and offered her the upper hand in its spin, since Ellen could use her celebrity to expose the Million Mom's antiprogressive stance on LGBTQ persons. "This organization doesn't think I should be the spokesperson because I'm gay. For those of you tuning in for the first time, it's true, I'm gay. I hope you were sitting down." Perhaps more than any other, this "d'uh" moment—greeted with laughs and cheers from her audience—reinforces a social zone where her public gayness is accepted as a knowledge so obvious as to be commonplace, in turn reinforcing Ellen's impact on the cultural landscape and invoking a soupçon of queerness in a sea of homonormative banality. Moore asserts that Ellen "present[s] the out-of-the-ordinary repeatedly until its very performance, occurring daily, becomes un-alarming and even infectiously celebratory."[21] Ellen's willingness to unapologetically "be herself" in the face of homophobia reasserts her authenticity and positions her same-sex desire within the realm of normality, wherein this moment of "coming out" moves beyond an exceptional event into public knowledge and common sense.

Ellen's message to her One Million Moms detractors mirrors her neoliberal and homonormative ideologies and is firmly rooted in the principles of gay rights, the promotion of equality, the prioritization of the individual, and the privilege of consumption. If Facebook and blog posts are to be believed, JC Penney received a slight increase in revenue after the publicity of the protest from customers who used their power as citizen-consumers to support Ellen and JC Penney's decision to stand with her. Given that the actual numbers of people involved in One Million Moms was reportedly closer to forty thousand (compared to the 3.6 million viewers who, at the time, tuned in to watch the show),[22] Ellen decidedly overrode the group's claim to majority status, even pointing to the numerical disparity of its name versus its membership as well as the messages of support for Ellen and JC Penney on the group's now-inoperative Facebook page. Ellen's victory in this arena, as with her interaction with Rob Lowe, reinforced her own authenticity. Whereas the kiss with Lowe affirmed her same-sex desire even as she mimed heterosexual behaviors, her confrontation with One Million Moms emphasized her personal ethics rather that critiquing systemic oppressions. In this instance, Ellen countered hate speech with an ethos of love and kindness.

CONCLUSION

Ellen DeGeneres's ability to balance seemingly incompatible personality traits—homonormative queerness, asexual lesbianism, apolitical/individualized/commercial politics, masculine femininity—has translated to success and visibility previously unseen in out LGBTQ celebrities and comedians. Although Ellen is not the first famous individual to come out of the closet, her 1997 outing, the subsequent public reaction, and her prosperous reemergence have arguably made her the (laughing) face of lesbianism at a time when gay politics has gained increasing traction in mainstream forums. Ellen's skill at negotiating the boundaries between normative conventions and her sexual and gendered marginalization, most apparent in her performance of the private as public, models contemporary relationships between the individual and labor by creating productive hybridities that blur the boundaries between seemingly oppositional qualities that define personality.

The ever-present shadow of Ellen's lesbianism and masculine gender display is both eclipsed and bolstered by the spotlight placed on the "authenticity" of her brand. Ellen employs her private life, particularly her lesbianism and relationship with de Rossi, to highlight the "truth" of her childlike, "genuine" professional persona enacting the public/private overlap required from flexible workers in advanced capitalism. Her "incorporate body" disrupts oppositional binaries in lieu of unified hybridities, all in service to her corporate comedic brand: the Economy of Ellen maintains her inclusion within hegemonic cultural constraints, even as she expands the limits of "acceptability." As evidenced in her kiss with Lowe, Ellen's lesbianism reinforces heteronormative mandates. Her performance queers sexual and gendered conventions even as she undermines the threat of excessive homosexuality. In so doing, she disrupts conventional deployments of sexual desire in the context of intimate interaction. These moments reassert the primacy of her lesbian sexuality and trouble conventions of sexualized engagements through the "performance" and denaturalization of stripped heterosexual men and a desiring (but not of the men) lesbian woman.

Importantly, Ellen's incorporate body distances her sexual identity from queer politics and activist engagement in service to the mainstream palatability of her star text. In addressing conservative homophobia as a concern of the individual rather than as representative of a broader phenomenon affecting a marginalized community, Ellen effectively reinforces the mandates of a postoppression culture that focuses on the power of the individual expressed through her role as consumer-citizen. Rather than positioning the conservative rhetorics in relation to systemic oppressions, Ellen's analysis of the One Million Moms protest reasserts the consumption-driven apoliticality of her lesbian lifestyle.

Ellen's place within the system is perhaps most apparent in her role as spokesmodel to various companies, wherein her sexuality and gender performance incite increased publicity and read as liberal for the companies for whom she stands. Although Ellen's lesbianism could be read as a challenge to hegemonic sexual mandates, the professional success she has garnered ensures a built-in customer base that presumably bridges both the heterosexual women targeted by her daily talk show and the LGBTQ communities she claims membership in. Yet Ellen's bid for individual "authenticity" distances her personality and brand from the taint of corporatization by asserting the neoliberal values of individual happiness and personal truth. Ultimately, we believe Ellen's comedic performance of an "incorporate body" gives the illusion of challenging hegemonic logics through her open disavowal of gender and sexual conventions, even as she upholds the foundations on which these structures are built.

NOTES

1. Lacey Rose, "The Booming Business of Ellen DeGeneres: From Broke and Banished to Daytime's Top Earner," *Hollywood Reporter*, Aug. 22, 2012, www.hollywoodreporter.com/news/ellen-degeneres-show-oprah-winfrey-jay-leno-364373.

2. We are not arguing here that intermediality (multiple forms of media working in a culture at the same time) is new. We argue instead that this particular moment is marked by what can more aptly be termed transmedia—the idea

that media products are not coherent unto themselves but work in symbiotic relation and, sometimes, in resistance to one another in ways both diachronic and synchronic.

3. David Bauder, "Ellen's Oscar Celeb Selfie a Landmark Media Moment," *Associated Press*, Mar. 3, 2014, http://bigstory.ap.org/article/ellens-oscar-celeb-selfie -landmark-media-moment.

4. Brooks Barnes, "Easy, Breezy, Trending: Ellen DeGeneres, TV and Twitter Hit, Ready to Host Oscars," *New York Times*, Jan. 17, 2014, www.nytimes .com/2014/01/19/arts/television/ellen-degeneres-tv-and-twitter-hit-ready-to-host -oscars.html?_r=0.

5. Danae Clark, "Commodity Lesbianism," in *The Lesbian and Gay Studies Reader*, eds. Henry Abelove, Michèle Aina Barale, and David M. Halperin (New York: Routledge, 1993), 191.

6. Linda Mizejewski, "Ellen DeGeneres: Pretty Funny Butch as Girl Next Door," chapter 6 in *Pretty/Funny: Women Comedians and Body Politic* (Austin: University of Texas Press, 2014), 197.

7. Mark Deuze, *Media Work* (Malden, MA: Polity Press, 2007), 42.

8. Emily Martin, *Flexible Bodies: Tracking Immunity in American Culture—From the Days of Polio to the Age of AIDS* (Boston: Beacon Press, 1994), 152.

9. According to Lisa Duggan, homonormativity is "a politics that does not contest dominant heteronormative assumptions and institutions, but upholds and sustains them, while promising the possibility of a demobilized gay constituency and a privatized, depoliticized gay culture anchored in domesticity and consumption." In other words, homonormativity plays according to the "just like you" script, where LGBTQ people are positioned as acting, desiring, and behaving like "everybody else." Queer identity, by contrast, refutes categories and boundaries, finding belonging in counter-normative identities, sexualities, and lives. Lisa Duggan, *The Twilight of Equality? Neoliberalism, Cultural Politics, and the Attack on Democracy* (New York: Beacon, 2003), 50.

10. Deuze, *Media Work*, ix.

11. "Ellen and Sofia Vergara Are CoverGirls," *TEDS*, Jan. 16, 2012.

12. "Ellen and Sofia Vergara on the Ellen Show," *TEDS*, Oct. 31, 2012.

13. Candace Moore, "Resisting, Reiterating, and Dancing Through: The Swinging Closet Doors of Ellen DeGeneres's Televised Personalities," in *Televising Queer Women: A Reader*, ed. Rebecca Beirne (New York: Palgrave Macmillan, 2008), 26.

14. Ibid., 27.

15. "Jared Leto Wins Best Supporting Actor," *TEDS*, Mar. 3, 2014.

16. "Steve Harvey Gets Personal," *TEDS*, May 24, 2013.

17. Jewel Kilcher is another example of a female celebrity whose fame, perhaps more so than Ellen's, is reliant upon her first-name recognition. Her initial foray into the realm of popular culture occurred as a singer/songwriter in the mid-90s, at which time she dropped her last name.

18. Larry King was a California high school student who was murdered by a fellow student in 2008. Ellen remained silent, as did much of the mainstream media, about the overlap between Larry King's sexual orientation and his gendered nonconformity. The conflation of homophobia and cisgenderism renders

the experiences of those on the trans spectrum invisible and prioritizes sexuality over gender performance. In so doing, individuals who conform to expected gender display are recentralized by LGBTQ rhetorics, and their experiences of gayness are positioned as universal. "Ellen DeGeneres on Fifteen-Year-Old Boy, Larry King, Killed for Being Gay," *TEDS*, Feb. 28, 2008.

19. In addition to her brief discussion of the Larry King murder, Ellen was also extraordinarily vocal during the bullying "crisis" of 2012.

20. "Ellen Addresses Her Critics," *TEDS*, Feb. 7, 2012.

21. Moore, "Resisting, Reiterating," 20.

22. Robert Seidman, "Syndicated TV Ratings: 'Wheel of Fortune' Edges 'Big Bang,' 'Judge Judy' for Top Honors; 'Dr. Phil' Remains #1 Talk Show," *TV by the Numbers*, Feb. 23, 2012, www.tvbythenumbers.zap2it.com.

CHAPTER 13

SARAH SILVERMAN: CUTENESS AS SUBVERSION

ANTHONY P. MCINTYRE

SARAH SILVERMAN HAS BEEN one of the most controversial and celebrated comedians (irrespective of gender) in the United States since her emergence on the stand-up scene in the 1990s. Silverman came to prominence in 2005 with her comedy special *Jesus Is Magic* after having a varied career in which she combined acting and comedy writing with her stand-up work. She reportedly had a difficult time working as a staff writer on the 1993–1994 season of *Saturday Night Live* (NBC 1975–), an experience later parodied in an episode of *The Larry Sanders Show* (HBO 1992–1998), in which she played a new staff writer struggling to have her jokes chosen by a head writer who favors the material of male writers. Silverman also appeared in numerous television shows, including *Seinfeld* (NBC 1989–1998), *Star Trek: Voyager* (UPN 1995–2001), and *Mr. Show with Bob and David* (HBO 1995–1998). Silverman's movie roles, particularly in *School of Rock* (2003), confirmed the comedian's comments in interviews about the restricted roles offered females in the entertainment industry and reinforced her determination to refuse roles she couldn't control.[1] It is in Silverman's stand-up comedy, her television series *The Sarah Silverman Program* (Comedy Central 2007–2010), and the various short-form videos she increasingly distributes on YouTube that her comedic vision is most clearly expressed.

The disjuncture between Silverman's looks—her prettiness and cute appearance—and her taboo-breaking comedy material has drawn attention to the comedian, but it also forms the foundation on which her entire comedic persona trades. Critics often stress the transgressive nature of Silverman's work, with its interrogations of prevailing norms of sexuality, race, and identity. Silverman's subversive treatment of normative femininity and her emphasis on the body are central to her humor, as is her ambivalent articulation of contemporary Jewish identity.[2] In one of Silverman's best-known controversial jokes, she quips, "I was raped by a doctor, which is a bittersweet experience for a Jewish girl." This joke succinctly highlights the intersection of cultural Jewishness and sexual content that the comedian's material can encompass. Silverman's humor situates her as part of a broader trend that has emerged since the mid-1990s, in which empowered Jewish identities are articulated in a comedic register, a trend commonly associated with male performers such as Adam Sandler and Seth Rogen. However, as Linda Mizejewski has noted, Silverman's particular deployment of such material typically activates charged discourses of ethnicity and race, a key factor in the performer's perceived "edginess."[3]

My focus on cuteness in Silverman's work elucidates aspects of the actress's life and comedy that have become more prominent as she has aged, and as a result I primarily analyze material from the second decade of the twenty-first century. I begin by defining "cuteness" and theorizing its connections to both vulnerability and the grotesque: key terms that inform the remainder of the essay. An analysis of texts such as Silverman's 2010 memoir *The Bedwetter*, as well as her role as the voice of Vanellope in the Disney animation *Wreck-It Ralph* (2012), illustrates the ways in which both vulnerability and a proximity to the grotesque are crucial to the unruliness characteristic of this performer. The following section interrogates cuteness's key role in contemporary interspecies relationships as I examine the mediated relationship between Silverman and her dog, Duck, during the pet's illness and eventual death in 2013. Silverman's relationship with Duck demonstrates not only the affective instability of cuteness as it comes close to its border with sadness, but also how invocations of vulnerability foreground the ethical dimension of the entangled relationship of care.

This chapter's final two sections deal with cuteness in relation to gender. As Silverman has increasingly come under public scrutiny owing to her perceived failure to comply with societal expectations for women (e.g., marriage, motherhood, political passivity), in both her life and her work, the aesthetic of cuteness emerges as a means through which she articulates and interrogates such gendered norms. Examining first how Silverman has often been framed in media reports in terms of "abject singlehood" and childlessness, I go on to demonstrate how in a variety of different media the comedian demonstrates an ambivalent "maternal proximity" that can highlight both the appeal of cuteness and the melancholic feelings such yearning for (often thwarted) attachment can compel.

CUTENESS, VULNERABILITY, AND THE GROTESQUE

"Cute" content has been increasingly visible across a variety of media since the turn of the millennium and is capable of delivering a powerful affective hit. Although by no means a new aesthetic, cuteness is now a prominent presence in contemporary screen culture, with videos such as "sneezing panda" topping the most-viewed charts on YouTube for years (and at the time of writing it has over two hundred million views); the sharing of cute online videos has become a daily ritual for many net users, and they even show up, occasionally, on American nightly news shows. One defining feature of the cute is that it depicts something vulnerable, and this factor is key to the emotional response it evokes. Thus, the baby panda (or kitten or human child) provokes a response inextricably connected with a highly asymmetrical power dynamic: watching a vulnerable object. The helplessness of the cute object is key to the current prevalence of this trend and, as I shall argue, appeals to the viewer who suffers the pervasive sense of precarity and powerlessness that increasingly characterizes life in the new millennium.[4]

Cuteness's affective charge is highly ambivalent, indexing feelings of powerlessness and mastery, manipulation and aggression. Indeed, Sianne Ngai suggests that it is more akin to a dialectic than an aesthetic due to the vacillation of the emotional response it compels.[5] For instance, we can develop an attachment to cute objects, yet such feelings may also turn to aversion as a result of what is sometimes perceived as the overt manipulation of emotions that this aesthetic trades in. Such antipathy many times results in a backlash against the initial cute object.[6] Indeed, it is my contention that this aspect of cuteness, its ability to compel contradictory responses and reactions, is key to its ability to unleash its subversive potential. Cuteness can also be subversive in its engagement with vulnerability, a condition that has seen significant critical reappraisal within feminist philosophy of late. Building on Judith Butler's work on precarity, for instance, Erinn Gilson contests reductive negative definitions of vulnerability and argues for a more ambivalent formulation that recognizes the potential for "positive manifestations and value [such as] enabling the development of empathy, compassion, and community."[7] Such alternate formulations are necessary, she argues, to contest what she sees as a cultural valorization of invulnerability (notable, for instance, in the current proliferation of cinematic superheroes), a trend that leads to an ethical closure of the self.

One further significant aspect of vulnerability is the way in which such feelings can be subject to political manipulation. Writing on the links between melodrama and contemporary politics, Elisabeth Anker convincingly argues that a set of conditions that increasingly characterize the contemporary neoliberal moment—political disenchantment, widespread financial precarity, and "tightening norms for individual behavior"—have led to a "generalized and often ineffable sense of helplessness and vulnerability." Anker traces how in the wake of the terrorist attacks of 9/11 such a pervasive sense of vulnerability across the population was displaced onto the newly perceived terrorist threat, creating the ideal conditions whereby what she terms "melodramatic political discourse" could marshal such feelings of powerlessness into "deepening [citizens'] identification with state power."[8]

Cuteness is central to Silverman's work, although she habitually deploys it in a manner that pushes the aesthetic toward grotesquery. In fact, the actress's performative style is predicated on a liminality that highlights the instabilities inherent to fixed categorizations, often through grotesque tropes. Kathleen Rowe, building on the work of Mary Russo, argues that "the unruly woman dwells close to the grotesque" due to her associations with "both beauty and monstrosity."[9] One central feature of the grotesque is its traversal of fixed boundaries such as "inside/outside" and "high/low." Silverman's trademark scatological humor and use of tropes of hybridity (such as her self-description as "half-monkey, half-Jew") are clearly identifiable as grotesque. The connection between cuteness and grotesquery has been identified by Daniel Harris, who points out that cute dolls are often "anatomical disasters" with wildly disproportionate features. Furthermore, Lori Merish has traced a genealogy of cuteness from nineteenth-century freak shows and figures such as General Tom Thumb (Charles Stratton), a hugely popular dwarf performer, in whose person the categories of child/adult become intertwined.[10] We can think of children's beauty pageants, with their conflation of the adult and the child (a subject dealt with in *The Sarah Silverman Program*) as a contemporary arena where the cute and the grotesque meet. Mer-

13.1. Silverman's *Saturday Night Live* publicity image from the episode she hosted in October 2014 destabilizes the cuteness of the teddy bear.

ish argues that cuteness can function as a marker of erotic regulation enforcing the containment of childhood sexuality, yet this border is unstable and evocations of cuteness are instrumental to its transgression. This can be seen in a film such as *Ted* (2012) and its depiction of the eponymous teddy bear who comes to life upon a boy's wish only to grow into a lascivious adult while retaining his original appearance. The humor of a cute, cuddly bear soliciting prostitutes and simulating masturbation by squirting hand soap on his face clearly encapsulates the border between the cute and the grotesque.[11] In an October 2014 *Saturday Night Live* episode Silverman hosted, one of the promotional pictures used between advertisements draws on similar tropes in its depiction of the actress being spanked by a life-size teddy bear. The image, which features Silverman dressed in typically girlish attire and gazing provocatively at the camera, simultaneously invokes and contests fixed categorizations of "child/adult" and "human/animal" with its overt equalization, a tactic evident across a wide variety of the performer's work.

Silverman's signature look (one that has remained consistent throughout her comedy career) heavily utilizes features of girlishness—for instance, her hair is often in pigtails or a ponytail—yet the actress's work (particularly of late) frequently registers the anxieties of aging femininity, as I discuss below. In addition, Silverman commonly invokes childhood with her material; for example, almost half of her autobiography *The Bedwetter: Tales of Courage, Redemption, and Pee* (2010) is focused on it. The book itself inspired the producers of the animated film *Wreck-It Ralph* to develop the role of the diminutive and feisty Vanellope von Schweetz specifically for the performer.

The ease with which Silverman's trademark humor is transposed onto a Disney character confirms the centrality of childhood to her star persona. Also significant is the physical representation of Vanellope, which was modified to look more like Silverman as the production progressed. Just as Stephen Jay Gould identified the evolution towards cuteness of an initially spiky Mickey Mouse, a character that became rounder, softer, and more wide-eyed as the twentieth century progressed,[12] we see some of Silverman's features adapted similarly in the figure of Vanellope. While still recognizable from her long dark hair, eye color, and smile, the eyes are noticeably larger and rounder, the nose smaller and softer, and the character altogether more diminutive: key features of the cute aesthetic. This juvenation of the actress through cute aesthetics does raise some problematic questions regarding representation, however. As Elizabeth Bell has argued, female Disney characters are "somatic, cinematic, and cultural codes, that attempt to align audience sympathies and allegiance with the beginning and end of the feminine life cycle, marking the middle as a dangerous, consumptive, and transgressive realm."[13] The policing and elision of middle-aged women evident in such tropes (aided, as we have seen, by a recourse to cute aesthetics in popular cultural texts) is further exemplified in the intensification of public criticism Silverman has faced since entering her forties, an aspect of her stardom I deal with in further detail later.

The helplessness that is a defining feature of cuteness is central to both *The Bedwetter* and *Wreck-It Ralph*: the titular bedwetting of the autobiography and Vanellope's status as a "glitch" in the movie—that is, the character displays malfunctioning tendencies within her videogame world that effect her social exclusion. While such demonstrations of helplessness may constitute something as being cute, her stories of childhood bedwetting move Silverman's material towards the border of cute/grotesque due to an increased association with what Mikhail Bakhtin termed the "material bodily lower stratum."[14] That is, once we see the "inside/outside" border of the body being trans-

13.2. *Wreck-It Ralph*'s (2012) Vanellope von Schweet: a "cutified" and juvenated version of Silverman.

gressed through bodily fluid (urine), our pity moves towards revulsion. In *Wreck-It Ralph*, similar associations are foregrounded in Vanellope's first meeting with Ralph (voiced by John C. Reilly), when she intentionally misinterprets the war-based videogame he told her he just escaped from as "Call of Doody" (rather than Duty). Thus we see even in a highly mediated animated role the abjection Mizejewski identifies as central to the comedian, as well as the element of the grotesque emerging that is central to the cute aesthetic.[15]

Silverman was chosen for the part of Vanellope after *Wreck-It Ralph* director Rich Moore read her autobiography.[16] Indeed, in press engagements promoting the animated film, Silverman stresses the similarities between Vanellope and herself:

She's got this glitch, and in the end she learns that her biggest shame can become her superpower. And for me, I was a bed-wetter growing up, and it did become sort of my superpower, because in doing standup I had nothing to lose: I had already experienced humiliation that bombing in front of strangers could not compare to.[17]

Thus we see the strength that Gilson argues can emerge from vulnerability,[18] which is central to the positive outcomes of both *Wreck-It Ralph* and *The Bedwetter*.

Silverman's humor sometimes deploys cuteness as part of her relentless transgression of linguistic, political, and identity boundaries, particularly regarding her femininity and her Jewishness. Consider the following section from her stand-up special *Jesus Is Magic*:

> You know who has a tiny vagina? Barbie. Not Klaus Barbie, the infamous Nazi. Nazis are a-holes, and I'll be the first one to say it—because I'm edgy. Nazis are motherfucking asshole wipes. Dicks. Oh, they're cute when they're little, I will give them that. They're so cute: Why can't they stay small?

In the linguistic leap from Barbie (the doll) to the notorious war criminal, we see the tethering of the world of childhood to that of the very adult realm of twentieth-century atrocities, which provokes a destabilization of register. The gravity with which the treatment of Jews in Nazi Germany is commonly invoked is reversed by way of a doll's "tiny vagina" and the associated trivialization of Klaus Barbie. In addition, Silverman's use of expletives is also characteristic of childhood: "a-holes" and "asshole wipes" are terms we would associate with adolescents taking faltering steps toward an adult language.

The final part of the joke is the coup de grâce, in which cuteness is invoked. As Ngai notes, "The cute object seems to have the power to infantilize the language of its infantilizer."[19] Silverman's slight lapse into "baby talk" in the last line ("Why can't they stay small?") and her accompanying arm gestures mimicking an infant in the cot concisely capture the affective response that cute objects compel from their spectators. This manipulation of our emotions through an evocation of helplessness neatly demonstrates the complex reversal of power relations that cute objects can obtain. Yet through her use of cuteness in this instance, Silverman subverts the power of historical discourses and notions of victimhood and oppression. In this way she utilizes cuteness in compliance with a broader cultural turn toward

empowered Jewish identities, which actively engage with the Holocaust through various modes such as abrasive comedy and revenge
fantasies.[20]

If, in the routine above, we can see cuteness deployed in a way that
destabilizes historical constructions of ethnic identities, through her
Twitter feed and other material Silverman also complicates the notion of human/animal bonding, a standard trope of cuteness. Both
animal companionship and child-adult relationships feature consistently in Silverman's star text, often portrayed through a frame of
cuteness. Through such representations, Silverman at times articulates an identity outside restrictive heteronormative ideals. In particular, through Silverman's mediation of her relationship with her diminutive dog, Duck, we see cuteness and the emotional comfort it
offers to many both celebrated and questioned.

In the second season of *The Sarah Silverman Program*, two episodes humorously interrogated such human-animal bonds, focusing
on Silverman's relationship with Duck—named "Doug" in the series.
In "Vow Wow," (season 2, episode 16) Silverman, playing a version of
herself, attempts to marry Doug, while "Joan of Arf" (season 2, episode 2) sees her arrested for engaging in an "unlawful interspecies relationship" with her pet when she is witnessed licking its anus. Displaying the grotesque traits that typically characterize the series,
both episodes nevertheless highlight in different ways the vulnerability and interdependence of owner and pet. One scene in "Joan of
Arf," where a repentant Silverman visits the dog in prison, subverts
the common cute trope of animal cross-dressing, as we see the dog
wearing pants "for his own protection" while a guard monitors the
visit to ensure there is no petting "below the waist." Interestingly,
the vows Silverman delivers to Doug in her marriage ceremony (prior
to his running off to chase a skateboarder) echo the sentiments she
articulated in her sincere obituary for the dog upon his death.

In 2013 Silverman's Twitter feed narrated a transition along the
cute/sad continuum as Duck's health deteriorated and the animal
was eventually euthanized. This liminal terrain between cuteness
and sadness raises questions of obligation and the emotional vicissi-
tude that such a relation of care entails, questions usually elided in

standard iterations of cuteness. That is, when the inherent vulnerability of the cute object reaches such a level that feelings of helplessness are transferred to the spectator, it loses its cute status.

Star texts encompass many aspects beyond the actual self of the star/celebrity. The presence of Duck/Doug in Silverman's star text attests to what Donna Haraway terms a relation of "torque": she notes that "where biographies and categories twine in conflicting trajectories, there is torque."[21] While, as noted, Silverman's dog was a regular presence on *The Sarah Silverman Program*, it is perhaps on Twitter that Duck has been a more prominent fixture. Silverman commonly tweeted cute pictures of the diminutive canine, many times when he was sleeping or in "cute" positions such as having a sock on his head. As mentioned above, the illness and eventual death of her dog in 2013 constituted a period in which the actress frequently tweeted about the relationship she had with Duck. The narrative of decline presented via Twitter attested to the "torqued" relationship between the pair, which went beyond a simple owner/pet classification, a relationship that has become increasingly common in contemporary society.[22] Perhaps the clearest and most poignant encapsulation of this existence in "several, braided categories at once"[23] comes in a tweet from 2013: "I just realized that my dog WANTS to be on the leash b/c I keep him from walking into walls. I'm a seeing eye person."[24] By inverting the position of the "seeing eye" dog, the tweet shows the relationship between Silverman and Duck to have evolved into a relationship of both emotional and physical dependence.

As Haraway notes, changes in terminology can signal important mutations in the character of interspecies relationships. Both in the satirical treatment of Silverman's relationship with "Doug" in *The Sarah Silverman Program* and in the performer's joking reference to herself as a "seeing eye person," the shifting nature of human/canine interdependence becomes clear. Arguably, this growing trend of human/animal intertwined relations of care challenges the valorization of independence and self-sufficiency in contemporary culture and helps refute the questionable ideal of an invulnerable subject.

Silverman's tweets demonstrably reject such reductive formulations. One of Silverman's social media postings about Duck shows a picture of some blood on a T-shirt and states, "Yes, that is blood from my dog's asshole."[25] A single interpretation of this is far from simple. As a comedian who trades in "edginess," did Silverman tweet this to evoke a dark laugh—scatological humor taken to its ultimate end

13.3. Silverman and her late dog Duck in the image she added alongside the "obituary type thing" she posted on her Whosay social media page (2013).

point—or did she write it to evoke sympathy from her followers? The comedian herself seems unsure of this point and indeed uses the incident where she took the picture as material in the stand-up special *We Are Miracles* (2013), in which it gains a laugh. Yet the evolution from cute to sad is evident in this and a number of other tweets from the time with the affective instability of the cute/grotesque foregrounded throughout. Silverman seems instinctively to want to jolt us out of the soporific spell that cuteness can cast over its consumers, and her deployment of this aesthetic rarely comes without an attendant aspect of critique.

The following lines with which Silverman ended an "obituary type thing" posted on social media site Whosay poignantly reveal the intimate nature of her relationship with her dog: "14 years./My longest relationship./My only experience of maternal love./My constant companion./My best friend./Duck."[26] By forcing us to look beyond a cute exterior and acknowledge the vulnerability that this aesthetic can encapsulate, such new media narratives can make visible changing norms in contemporary relationalities. Silverman's language attests to Duck being more than a pet, framing the relationship in language more common to human kinship structures ("maternal love," "best friend," "constant companion"). By sharing an account of her dog's declining health in real time over social media, the comedian, in her highly visible position as a celebrity, also highlights the emotional precarity that such human-animal relationships often serve to attenuate, as well as the vulnerability on both sides of the relationship—a narrative that tends to be elided in contemporary popular culture.

ABJECT SINGLEHOOD AS CONTEXT FOR SUBVERSIVE CUTENESS

Through her overt invocation of the maternal in relation to her recently departed pet, Silverman is also broaching two topics that increasingly frame media reportage of the comedian: maternity and ageing. As Kirsty Fairclough has noted, "Female celebrities have become the chief site upon which contemporary tensions and anxieties surrounding femininity, motherhood, body image, cosmetic surgery, marriage and ageing are played out."[27] I contend that Silverman's subversive usage of cuteness at times is predicated upon the centrality of maternal longing to the affective appeal of this aesthetic. Further, the ways in which cuteness is rigidly structured in relation to specific age brackets (very old or very young, usually) mean her usage of this aesthetic engages directly with the other anxieties and tensions related to female ageing. The remainder of this section highlights the very public ways in which such discourses cohere around Silverman, in preparation for an analysis of how they emerge within her work.

Since entering her forties, Silverman has been increasingly under scrutiny with regard to her age. One remarkable instance of this critical surveillance was an open letter written by Rabbi Yaakov Rosenblatt to the Jewish Press in October 2012 in response to Silverman's political YouTube video, "Let My People Vote." Taking offence at Silverman's supposed framing of her argument in biblical language as well as what he sees as her "sickening" and "vulgar" comedy, the rabbi strongly attacks Silverman's choices in her "private" life. The letter is worth quoting at length in order to demonstrate the extent of such scrutiny:

> You will soon turn 42 and your destiny, as you stated, will not include children. You blame it on your depression, saying you don't want to pass it on to another generation. . . . Surely you appreciate being alive and surely, if the wonder of your womb were afflicted with your weaknesses and blessed with your strengths, it would be happy to be alive, too. You said you wouldn't get married until gay people can. Now they can. And you still haven't married. I think, Sarah, that marriage and childrearing are not in the cards for you because

you can't focus on building life when you spend your days and nights tearing it down.[28]

The fact that such intimate topics as Silverman's decision to not have children, her history of mental illness, or her marital plans are considered fair game for a religious figure to comment on in the press indicates the extent to which non-normative female subjectivities are exposed to policing in contemporary postfeminist culture. As Diane Negra and Su Holmes have argued, within contemporary popular culture "motherhood can be figured as a redemptive (as well as punitive) discursive framework," and Rosenblatt's letter portrays Silverman as having explicitly chosen to reject any possibility of redemption.[29]

A further example of such attitudes was evident at the November 2013 *Comedy Central Roast of James Franco* in which Silverman was a participant. (Indeed, Silverman is often the female exception at such events and has a form of comedy that is particularly popular among males, a fact she is reluctant to be drawn on in interviews.)[30] Silverman's criticism of some of the ageist and sexist jokes made at her expense at the roast was widely reported.[31] Actor Jonah Hill's comments are characteristic: "Sarah is a role model for every little girl out there. I mean every little girl dreams of being a single, fifty-eight-year-old stand-up comedian, with no romantic prospects on the horizon." The fact that a generic "little girl" is invoked to hammer home the critique here is telling of this figure's significant cultural purchase, and Silverman herself invokes girlhood to articulate the anxieties of ageing, as shall be seen in the video *Fête des Pets*, analyzed in a later section. Nevertheless, Silverman's childlessness seems the unspoken accusation here. As Negra argues, an increased pathologization of single women as "abject" figures who have "[drifted] off course" and are coded as desperate is endemic in contemporary popular culture.[32] That Silverman is not in fact single tends to be lost in media reportage on the comedian, which instead focuses on her age and, frequently, on her publicly expressed decision not to have children.

As Mizejewski notes, women's comedy has increasingly served as a platform of resistance to contemporary conservative discourse about traditional roles for women, and specifically to the cultural mandate of motherhood. Despite her political work promoting female reproductive rights, Silverman is not as vociferously critical of the motherhood mandate as comedians such as Kathy Griffin.[33] In fact, as I have shown, a number of elements in Silverman's star text are predicated on a close association with childhood and exhibit a degree of maternal ambivalence. The following section demonstrates that Silverman typically uses cuteness in a way that registers such ambivalence, drawing out the pleasurable and melancholic aspects of maternal attachment.

CUTENESS AND MATERNAL PROXIMITY

Through associations with childhood that are proximate to the maternal, Silverman contributes to the increased cultural visibility of middle-class women with no children who have both emotional and financial capital to spare. This grouping has found expression recently with the emergence of the acronym PANK, describing professional aunties with no kids.[34] Melanie Notkin, who coined the term, has also written the bestseller *Savvy Auntie: The Ultimate Guide for Cool Aunts, Great Aunts, Godmothers, and All Women Who Love Kids* (2011), the title indicating that this advice book is squarely aimed at those with a proximate attachment to another's child. Significantly, in a postfeminist culture in which women's visibility is increasingly defined by their consumer power, Notkin frames her argument for the importance of this demographic that "society overlooks" in starkly economic terms. She notes that "childless aunts are a sizeable segment of younger women with disposable income, dynamic influence, and a digitally connected lifestyle who are extraordinarily generous with the children in their lives, those children's parents, and our communities at large."[35]

Silverman's PANK status (with the inherent bonds of attachment the name implies) allies her with "maternalized" consumers of cuteness due to similarities between the emotional connections that link both groups to the objects of their affection (aunties to their nieces or nephews, consumers to their cute products). As mentioned above, a defining characteristic of the PANK demographic is its economic power, detailed in the oft-cited statistic that PANKs spend on average $387 a year on each child in their lives. Similarly, Merish notes how cuteness "graft(s) commodity desire onto a middle-class structure of familial, expressly maternal emotion."[36] Thus, we see how both cuteness and the PANK demographic are further bound together due to the centrality of consumerism to both.

While not always relating to her actual nieces and nephews, Silverman regularly invokes her relationships with children in her interviews and stand-up routines. In *We Are Miracles*, Silverman talks about material she has developed specifically for girls aged between three and nine years old. The crux of the joke is that she tells the child that she is actually a princess but that the girl can't tell anyone "because I want to be treated normal." Silverman then reports on the girl's wide-eyed amazement and the fact that the child spends the rest of the visit spying on her. Silverman elaborates on this story in a radio interview:

> I went really far with it with my friends Sam and Nicky's daughter. I did that whole thing where I say, "I'm a princess; don't tell anybody." And then I say, "When I come visit you in New York, I have some of my old princess stuff. It doesn't fit me anymore, would you be interested in it?" [The girl replies] "Yes, yes, I would." So I came to New York and there's this huge Halloween store on 4th and Broadway . . . and I bought a bunch of three-year-old, size three, little girl princess stuff, and I took it out of the package and mussed it up and put it into a trash bag and brought it over. Ah, it's the little pleasures![37]

The conflation of spending power and the "cool aunt" savvy that Notkin identifies as central to PANK status is evident here. In utilizing the figure of a princess, however, we see one of the (frequent) contradictions of Silverman's positioning. As Mizejewski notes, Silverman courts ambivalence with her own beauty, notably in a 2007 *Maxim* cover where she appears as half-woman, half-gorilla hybrid.[38] Yet with her persistent invocation of princesshood (a recurring trope, as we shall see), Silverman reinforces a powerful marketing phenomenon that glorifies "feminine exemplars of inherited wealth and (spending) power"[39] and that, in contrast to much of her work, reinforces hegemonic norms of race and gender.

With the release of "Uncle Sarah's Playtime App" in 2012, we again see Silverman returning to childhood in her material. Indeed, take the advertising copy's direction: "Next time you need someone to watch your little ones, put Uncle Sarah into the hands of your kids!"[40] The statement articulates the proximate relationality that I see as inherent to Silverman's star text. Silverman's discursive refusal of the term "aunt" suggests a lack of comfort on the part of the comedian with the prescriptive gender roles inherent in such terms, and it is reflective of the "queering" of normative attitudes that

13.4. Silverman's Uncle Sarah App, which she devised specifically for children (2012).

much of her cute-inflected material achieves. However, outside of her stand-up material, Silverman is notably conventional in her attitude towards culturally (but not religiously) Jewish family values. For instance, an interview in the *Guardian* newspaper in the United Kingdom featured both Silverman and her father talking about their close relationship, and the comedian has appeared alongside her reformist rabbi sister Susan at Q&A sessions at universities; the pair has also had a profile written about them.[41]

The "Uncle Sarah" app provides a number of different activities, such as peek-a-boo, story time, and going through your ABCs. Adults expecting humor similar to the popular *Go the F**k to Sleep* (2011) storybook, which sends up the trials and tribulations of bedtime, will no doubt have been disappointed. The app is altogether gentler in its comedic register and, unlike the book, is actually meant to entertain young children (and no doubt the adults in their lives as well). The peek-a-boo feature is just that: a game in which Silverman appears from behind a tartan blanket saying the phrase. During story time, Silverman relates a series of banal events from her life, such as going to the shop to find it didn't have her favorite brand of coconut water. However, she tells each story (mostly) in the third person, as though it happened to the "princess" and not to her. This is followed by an opportunity for the toddler to tell a story while Uncle Sarah listens, nodding and occasionally making attentive comments like "Really?"

While there are occasional nods to the parents, such as a country-music style rendition of the ABC song (a reference most infants would miss), the remarkable thing about the app is its commitment to entertaining toddlers and the centrality of cuteness and babies in general to the comedian's work in the second decade of the twenty-first century.

The routines discussed below from *We Are Miracles* attest to this, but they go much further in their interrogation of the ambiguities of cuteness. As indicated earlier, Silverman has been increasingly framed in media accounts in terms of her relationship to motherhood. Tackling head on the issue of maternity in the joke below, Silverman states:

I want a baby. The thing with me is, the caveat is, I don't want a ten-year-old in ten years, you know what I mean? I want a *baby*. I figured out a solution that I think works for me. I'm not preaching it to anyone, but, uhm, I think I'm going to adopt, like, terminally ill babies . . . every six months to two years–ish.

Immediately registering a disturbed reaction from the audience, Silverman adopts her trademark faux naïf style, asking, "Are you thinking what kind of person would look to adopt a dying baby? *I think an amazing person.*" In this routine the comedian plays on the internal instability of the cute aesthetic by stressing its dialectic of power and powerlessness and its proximity to the grotesque and the morbid. The joke takes the audience from identification, liking babies, through to its end point, a woman loving babies so much she doesn't want them to grow up, the maternal impulse at its most abject.

In *Fête des Pets (Fart Party)*, many of the elements aligned with cuteness in Silverman's material are evident. This short video from 2013 was made for the YouTube channel Jash, which Silverman started along with a number of other comedy figures. The video is a pastiche of European art cinema tropes; filmed in black and white, it features a French voice-over and English subtitles. In it Silverman, dressed in a chic and glamorous Parisian manner, is shown going through an emotional break up with her boyfriend, violently arguing with him and jealously watching as he finds affection with another to whom she finally loses him. However, the twist of the piece is that both her "boyfriend" and his new partner are around six years old.

The film, which she describes as a "French film noir," can be read

13.5. Silverman and "boyfriend" enjoying happier times in the short film *Fête des Pets* (2013).

as a display of the anxieties over ageing and maternity that Diane Negra has termed a "time crisis," characteristic of a "postfeminist lifecycle."[42] We can see the protean nature of the cute aesthetic at work in its complex rendering of this phenomenon. What is enacted in *Fête des Pets* is a conflation between the "maternal desire" Merish identifies as central to cuteness and romantic love.[43] Answering an interview question about whether she wants children, Silverman admits the powerful emotional pull of children: "I love children. I'm embarrassingly baby-crazy. I could be in the middle of any intense conversation and if somebody walks by with a baby, I'm gone."[44] Yet in *Fête des Pets* the ambivalent nature of such a maternal longing is foregrounded, and Silverman purposefully inverts the affective register, playing on the double meaning of cute, with its possible suggestion of sexual attraction in tension with the more common meaning. Through having the male in the relationship inhabit the role of the cute one based on age and costume—as Merish and others have noted, the rendering of children as adults is a staple of cute genres—the traditional positioning of the female as bearer of the cute in a romantic relationship is reversed and destabilized. The power of the cute object (in this case the boy) over Silverman's character grows stronger as he becomes more despondent in his unhappiness with the relationship, and again Silverman treads close to cuteness's liminal border with sadness.

Additionally, Silverman's love rival in *Fête des Pets* is a little girl of a similar age to the boy, lampooning competition between females at a time when, as sociologist Eva Illouz has noted, changes in romantic/sexual ecology have resulted in men gaining a significant advantage compared to women in their ability to find a (frequently younger) partner, because "the samples from which men can choose are much larger than they are for women."[45] Silverman in this piece deploys cuteness at a nexus of tensions regarding ageing femininity; one of the notable features of this aesthetic is that it can encapsulate contradictory notions at the same time. Thus in *Fête des Pets*, maternal desire and sexual desire are conflated, and societal shifts that shape our patterns of intimacy come to the fore. The short film itself is balanced delicately between comedy and tragedy, and the film articulates the vulnerability and yearning for attachment that can be seen as central to so many contemporary subjectivities.

CONCLUSION

Silverman, as I have shown, is able to harness cuteness in a way that causes us to question more closely the aspects of vulnerability that are a pervasive feature of our emotional landscape. Whether due to aggravating factors such as uncertainties of employment; national security concerns; the erosion of borders between public and private spheres that disrupts our conceptions of leisure; an increased lack of faith in collective democracy; or ever-more-constrictive behavioral norms that are frequently highly gendered, many authors have highlighted emotional precarity as a key feature of twenty-first-century life.[46] In tandem with such developments has been the rise in the popularity of cute content across a wide variety of media, not least the huge number of cute animal pictures and videos that get shared every day on the internet.

In this context we can see what is at stake politically in our increased consumption of cute images. My contention is that cuteness has an inherent tendency to be politically neutralizing: it commonly creates an intimate public that affords respite from the sense of helplessness that pervades contemporary life by (ironically) providing pleasure in aesthetically consuming vulnerability in others.[47] The value of Silverman's articulation of cuteness is that it stretches the aesthetic to the point that its liminality with the grotesque, the sad, and the vulnerable becomes apparent, and in so doing she not only articulates narratives of emotional precarity in a fresh and engaging way but disrupts the uncritical consumption of cuteness, calling into question the unstated power relations that comprise this aesthetic.

NOTES

1. Will Leitch, "Animal Magnetism," *NYMag.com*, Apr. 11, 2010, http://ny mag.com/arts/books/features/65351.

2. Sam Anderson, "Irony Maiden: How Sarah Silverman Is Raping American Comedy," *Slate*, Nov. 10, 2005, www.slate.com/articles/arts/culturebox/2005/11 /irony_maiden.html; Paul Lewis, "Beyond Empathy: Sarah Silverman and the Limits of Comedy," *Tikkun* 22, no. 5 (2007), 88–89; Linda Mizejewski, *Pretty/ Funny: Women Comedians and Body Politics* (Austin: University of Texas Press, 2014); Aaron Tillman, "'Through the Rube Goldberg Crazy Straw': Ethnic Mobility and Narcissistic Fantasy in *Sarah Silverman: Jesus Is Magic*," *Studies in American Humor* 3, no. 20 (2009): 54–84.

3. Mizejewski, *Pretty/Funny*, 110.

4. For a more detailed definition and examination of contemporary manifestations of cuteness than is possible here, see Joshua Paul Dale et al., "The Aesthetics and Affects of Cuteness," in *The Aesthetics and Affects of Cuteness*, ed. Joshua Paul Dale et al. (New York: Routledge, 2017), 1–34.

5. Sianne Ngai, *Our Aesthetic Categories: Zany, Cute, Interesting* (Cambridge, MA: Harvard University Press, 2012), 98.

6. Christine Yano traces the backlash against the Hello Kitty illustrated character in her book on the subject and elsewhere. I have also analyzed the backlash against singer and actress Zooey Deschanel's overtly cute star image. See Christine Yano, *Pink Globalization: Hello Kitty's Trek across the Pacific* (Durham, NC: Duke University Press, 2013), 163–198; Anthony P. McIntyre, "Isn't She Adorkable! Cuteness as Political Neutralization in the Star-Text of Zooey Deschanel," *Television and New Media* 16, no. 5 (2015): 422–438.

7. Judith Butler, *Precarious Life: The Powers of Mourning and Violence* (London: Verso, 2004); Erinn Gilson, *The Ethics of Vulnerability: A Feminist Analysis of Social Life and Practice* (New York: Routledge, 2014), 8.

8. Elisabeth R. Anker, *Orgies of Feeling: Melodrama and the Politics of Freedom* (Durham, NC: Duke University Press, 2014), 16, 29.

9. Kathleen Rowe (Karlyn), *The Unruly Woman: Gender and the Genres of Laughter* (Austin: University of Texas Press, 1995), 11; Mary Russo, *The Female Grotesque: Risk, Excess, and Modernity* (New York: Routledge, 1995).

10. Daniel Harris, *Cute, Quaint, Hungry, and Romantic: The Aesthetics of Consumerism* (New York: Basic, 2000), 3; Lori Merish, "Cuteness and Commodity Aesthetics: Tom Thumb and Shirley Temple," in *Freakery: Cultural Spectacles of the Extraordinary Body*, ed. Rosemarie Garland-Thomson (New York: New York University Press, 1996), 187.

11. For a more detailed analysis of the connections between cuteness, the grotesque, and overt sexualization, see Anthony P. McIntyre, "*Ted, Wilfred*, and the Guys: Twenty-First-Century Masculinities, Raunch Culture, and the Affective

Ambivalences of Cuteness," in Dale et al., *Aesthetics and Affects of Cuteness*, 274–294.

12. Stephen J. Gould, quoted in Ngai, *Our Aesthetic Categories*, 82.

13. Elizabeth Bell, "Somatexts at the Disney Shop: Constructing the Pentimentos of Women's Animated Bodies," in *From Mouse to Mermaid: The Politics of Film, Gender, and Culture*, ed. Elizabeth Bell, Lynda Haas, and Laura Sells (Bloomington: Indiana University Press, 1995), 109.

14. Quoted in Mizejewski, *Pretty/Funny*, 95.

15. Harris, *Cute, Quaint*, 8; Mizejewski, *Pretty/Funny*.

16. Frank Lovece, "Sarah Silverman Gives Voice to Disney Girl in 'Wreck-It Ralph,'" *Newsday*, Oct. 24, 2012, www.newsday.com/entertainment/movies/sarah-silverman-gives-voice-to-disney-girl-in-wreck-it-ralph-1.4145392.

17. Ibid.

18. Erinn Gilson, "Vulnerability, Ignorance, and Oppression," *Hypatia* 26, no. 2 (2011): 310.

19. Ngai, *Our Aesthetic Categories*, 87.

20. Examples of this trend are evident in a variety of media, from major Hollywood movies like *Inglourious Basterds* (2009) and *Munich* (2005), which articulate revenge fantasies, to publications such as *Heeb* magazine that provocatively approach the Holocaust in their content.

21. Donna Jeane Haraway, *When Species Meet* (Minneapolis: University of Minnesota Press, 2008), 134.

22. A number of facts attest to this changing relationality: ownership of dogs and cats has increased fourfold since the mid-1960s, with more than 90 percent of people considering these animals "a family member"; 83 percent of owners refer to themselves as their animal's "mom" or "dad"; spending on pets amounted to \$55 billion in the United States in 2013; during the Great Recession (2007–2012) pet spending increased 28 percent. See David Grimm, *Citizen Canine: Our Evolving Relationship with Cats and Dogs* (New York: Public Affairs, 2014), 12.

23. Haraway, *When Species Meet*, 135.

24. Sarah Silverman, Twitter, July 9, 2013, https://twitter.com/SarahKSilverman/status/354496589433282561.

25. Sarah Silverman, Whosay, Aug. 30, 2013, www.whosay.com/status/sarahsilverman/716298.

26. Ibid., Sept. 4, 2013, www.whosay.com/status/sarahsilverman/720768?wsref=tw&code=rQm6EXB.

27. Kirsty Fairclough, "Nothing Less Than Perfect: Female Celebrity, Ageing, and Hyper-scrutiny in the Gossip Industry," *Celebrity Studies* 3, no. 1 (2012): 90.

28. Yaakov Rosenblatt, "An Open Letter to Sarah Silverman," *Jewish Press*, Oct. 11, 2012, www.jewishpress.com/indepth/opinions/dear-sarah-silverman/2012/10/11.

29. Diane Negra and Su Holmes, "Going Cheap? Female Celebrity in the Reality, Tabloid, and Scandal Genres," *Genders* 48 (2008): n.p., www.genders.org/g48/g48_negraholmes.html.

30. See Leitch, "Animal Magnetism."

31. Silverman was widely quoted across a number of media platforms as saying, "I feel like it's a part of, as soon as a woman gets to an age where she has

opinions and she's vital and she's strong, she's systematically shamed into hiding under a rock." However, she later acknowledged the importance of freedom of speech to comedians when asked about her initial response. See, for instance, Andrew Ryan, "The One Thing You Can't Make Fun of Sarah Silverman For," *Globe and Mail*, Sept. 18, 2013, www.theglobeandmail.com/life/the-hot-button/the-one-thing-you-cant-make-fun-of-sarah-silverman-for/article14394326.

32. Diane Negra, *What a Girl Wants? Fantasizing the Reclamation of Self in Postfeminism* (London: Routledge, 2009), 61.

33. Mizejewski, *Pretty/Funny*, 24–25.

34. Melanie Notkin, "Study Uncovers 23 Million Generous Women Society Overlooks," *Psychology Today*, Dec. 1, 2012, www.psychologytoday.com/blog/savvy-auntie/201212/study-uncovers-23-million-generous-women-society-overlooks.

35. Ibid.

36. Merish, "Cuteness and Commodity Aesthetics," 187.

37. Terry Gross, "Sarah Silverman: Turning Ignorance into Comedy," *Fresh Air* (NPR, July 15, 2011).

38. Mizejewski, *Pretty/Funny*, 109.

39. Negra, *What a Girl Wants?*, 48–49.

40. "Uncle Sarah iPhone App," MEDL Mobile, Inc., last updated Nov. 12, 2012, www.medlmobile.com/apps/iphone/uncle-sarah.

41. Hadley Freeman, "Comedians and Their Parents: Sarah Silverman and Father Donald," *Guardian*, Dec. 14, 2013, www.theguardian.com/culture/2013/dec/14/sarah-silverman-father-comedian-background; Kevin Fallon, "Sarah and Susan Silverman: Comedian and Rabbi Are Perfect Sisters," *Daily Beast*, Mar. 31, 2014, www.thedailybeast.com/articles/2014/03/31/sarah-and-susan-silverman-comedian-and-rabbi-are-perfect-sisters.html.

42. Negra, *What a Girl Wants?*, 47.

43. Merish, "Cuteness and Commodity Aesthetics," 185.

44. Gross, "Sarah Silverman."

45. Eva Illouz, *Why Love Hurts: A Sociological Explanation* (Cambridge, UK: Polity, 2012), 243.

46. See, for example, Lauren Gail Berlant, *Cruel Optimism* (Durham, NC: Duke University Press, 2011); and Guy Standing, *The Precariat: A New Dangerous Class* (London: Bloomsbury Academic Press, 2011).

47. For a more detailed articulation of this argument, see McIntyre, "Isn't She Adorkable!," as well as Dale et al., "Aesthetics and Affects of Cuteness"; and Alison Page, "'This Baby Sloth Will Inspire You to Keep Going': Capital, Labor and the Affective Power of Cute Animal Videos," in Dale et al., *Aesthetics and Affects of Cuteness*, 75–94.

CHAPTER 14

TINA FEY: "QUALITY" COMEDY AND THE BODY OF THE FEMALE COMEDY AUTHOR

JULIA HAVAS

IN 2003 THE *NEW YORKER* published a profile of Tina Fey, then head writer of American television's comedy institution *Saturday Night Live*. The piece quotes comedian and *SNL* peer Amy Poehler describing Fey's work ethic as "monastic"; Poehler adds, "She's not the first girl to belly-flop into the pool at the pool party. She watches everybody else's flops and then writes a play about it."[1] Still on the cusp of becoming a household name as the go-to female producer and performer of "quality" comedy and "Hollywood's token feminist" of the 2000s, Fey is already portrayed here as a brilliant writer of observational comedy but not as a *performing* star. Under the tutelage of creator and executive producer Lorne Michaels, she worked as head writer at *SNL* from 1999 to 2006 and reformed the quality and previous "frat-boy" tone of the show to establish a sharper and more women-friendly mode of comedy. This, and her quick-witted persona as *SNL*'s "Weekend Update" news anchor, had already started to shape her reputation as arbiter of a new era of female-authored and female-centered comedy, marked by a foregrounding of gender-based humor.

So Fey's public image has from its early days been configured as that of the comedy *writer*, and her importance for women's comedy has been located in the discursive dichotomy between the writer versus the performer. That is, unlike most female comedians discussed in this book, her public image rests on a carefully constructed, and often self-deprecating, contrast between her reputation as an *author* of comedy versus other comedians (usually her fellow *SNL* players) who excel as *performers* of comedy. As a comic star, Fey initially became known for her writing talent, her creative support of other (mostly female) comedians, and her knack for gendered social observations—but not for a versatility of comedy performance. This image continued to determine the novelty of her later celebrity as a comedy performer, as a female author of quality television comedy, and as a satirist. Rather than apply an aesthetic evaluation of this constructed dichotomy in Fey's star text (i.e., whether there is any empirical truth to the "better writer than performer" claim), I investigate in this chapter its ramifications for her position in American comedy culture. My primary focus is on the gender politics and media discourses around popular feminism that govern the shaping of this image.

This chapter draws on the combined methods of star studies, reception studies, and textual and performance analysis to examine how the feminism associated with Fey's comedy and star text became complicated throughout her career by the discourses of authorship, genre, and "quality television." While the latter concept is weighted down with gendered expectations and conventions, no less weighty are the expectations of "quality feminism" exhibited by Fey's feminist critics, especially in response to the increasingly grotesque physical comedy she performs in the role of Liz Lemon on the NBC sitcom *30 Rock* (2006–2013). This series is Fey's most widely recognized platform to date for exploring feminist issues in popular culture, while, crucially, it is also renowned as a singular-authored TV text with considerable cultural cachet. *30 Rock* strikingly demonstrates the tensions between the contemporary ideal of "feminist" quality comedy and female body-based comedy, as seen in the series' textual features and the media debates about the feminist credentials of both the series and its protagonist, Liz Lemon. In contrast, as my conclusion argues, Fey's next major writing and production project, the Netflix series *Unbreakable Kimmy Schmidt* (2015–), has been understood as more unequivocally aligned with popular feminism than *30 Rock*'s gender politics had been.

FEY AS SERIOUSLY COMIC

The high-profile Fey-Poehler friendship plays out the writer–performer contrast that defines Fey's celebrity, given that Poehler first garnered kudos for her versatile impersonation skills and comic characters on *SNL* and is generally held in high regard as a female comedy performer.[2] Crucially, this distinction has also bled into the ways in which the two have been associated with feminist politics in their star texts and through their comedy on their respective sitcoms, Fey in *30 Rock* and Poehler in *Parks and Recreation* (NBC 2009–2015). In their contrasting public personas, Fey is configured as an observer/analyst of gender politics, articulated mostly through her comedy rather than through involvement with feminist activism, while Poehler embodies the no-nonsense feminist, outspoken about her politics and affiliated with a number of organizations supporting girls and women.[3] Handily, it is Fey who has perhaps most succinctly characterized Poehler's assertive attitude about feminism *and* comedy performance in her autobiography *Bossypants*.[4] In a widely circulated anecdote, Fey describes an incident at an *SNL* meeting when Poehler improvised a raunchy and loud comedy bit that a male colleague complained about, saying he did not like it because it was "not cute." Poehler promptly snapped: "I don't fucking care if you like it!"[5]—a sentiment that, according to Fey, is a generally applicable comeback to opponents of women's comedy.[6] Of course, sharing the anecdote reinforces Fey's own public persona as a feminist comedian, but tellingly, she conveys this via the description of someone else's comeback, rather than by using her own example. This detail again feeds into Fey's primary image as the socially observant feminist comedy auteur, configured in the discursive contrast between the writer (Fey's anecdote) and performer (Poehler's raunchy comedy and retort).[7]

Entangled in the female writer/performer dichotomy is what Linda Mizejewski calls "the dynamic of pretty versus funny" in her account of contemporary American female comedians. For Mizejewski the history of women's comedy is inevitably bound up in a negotiation of sexual difference in relation to masculinized comedy norms. These traditions (re)produce the notion of the female comedian as an anomaly, able to articulate funniness only by sidestepping traditional conventions about the female body, sexuality, and femininity.[8] In Fey's case, her reputation as a writer and sober observer of gender relations is tied to her negotiation of, capitalization on, and occasional rejection of the moniker "the thinking man's sex symbol."[9] On the one hand, this moniker foregrounds Fey's position as "a comic who is being taken seriously," as Mizejewski demonstrates.[10] Her star text as primarily a writer and astute observer of feminist issues gives her high standing as a female comedian because it is the kind of funny that foregrounds its "serious" (political) implications. On the other hand, the moniker also lays bare comedy's historic gender dynamics by positing heterosexual male audience members as the primary recipients of Fey's wit, confirming their own intelligence and allowing them to enjoy her sexual appeal.

Mizejewski also shows that the pretty-versus-funny dichotomy is particularly pertinent in the postfeminist cultural paradigm, according to which second-wave feminism's political aim of empowering "all" women has been realized. Postfeminism locates female empowerment in sexual agency and desirability as proof of feminism's success and links this empowerment to consumer culture's logic of marketability. Given the ubiquity of the postfeminist ethos and its relentless focus on women's body image and sexuality, today's female comedians are especially bound up in the "pretty versus funny" issue, since postfeminism both informs their star texts and is often the target of their comic material.[11] Thus Fey's feminist agenda has been closely connected to her parody of postfeminist femininities, but these femininities nonetheless shape the trajectory of her own celebrity. The media struggles to make sense of her image as a witty and critical female comedian by presenting her as a glamorous cover girl, a practice that provides further fodder for her comedy.[12] Eleanor Patterson claims this dynamic dominates Fey's star text, which the comedian navigates (for instance, in her memoir *Bossypants*) by stressing the constructed nature of female glamour and her preference for unglamorous femininity: "Her confession that she 'secretly' prefers to be ugly, unglamorous Tina Fey should not be taken at face value as avowal of any authentic truth, but rather, an awareness of how her star text circulates, and an effort to manage it."[13]

A double negation then is at work in Fey's centrality in American comedy culture, in terms of the humor she represents and in her star text; both are founded on the female comic's insistence that she is not, or at least *does not act*, pretty—a trait that allows her to be a female comedian. Her humor and star text also convey that she is not a good performer, making her culturally imaginable as a good writer. Writing and performing comedy are both seen traditionally as "unfeminine," or, in Kathleen Rowe Karlyn's influential term, "unruly" qualities for women,[14] since they position the female comedian in a role that allows for a transgressive treatment of gender politics. This double negation allows Fey to occupy a position in popular culture as an auteur of quality comedy whose work focuses on gender politics. Further, because her comedy also frequently satirizes gender in relation to a number of other social issues, such as race, politics, sexuality, nationhood, television culture, capitalism, feminism, or consum-

14.1 Tina Fey on the "Weekend Update" segment of *Saturday Night Live* (2004).

erism, it can be interpreted by critics as having greater significance than a "merely" gender-focused commentary, allowing her entry into the league of prestigious ("to-be-taken-seriously") author-comedians.

Fey's oeuvre since leaving *SNL* demonstrates how her satirical humor is used for feminist commentary and is calculated to maintain her reputation as cerebral observer of gender relations. Because she started her on-camera career as the female anchor on "Weekend Update," this persona had initially dominated her media images: the feminist with a biting wit and castrating smile, sporting a dark suit and dark-rimmed glasses (soon spotlighted by journalists as a fetish object and symbol of her observant cleverness).

This persona informs her character in the 2004 hit teen comedy *Mean Girls*, widely regarded as a landmark of high school comedies for its sociological take on teenage girls' experience of school as a universe of hierarchal cliques. Fey had written the screenplay while still at *SNL*, and she cast herself in the film in a supporting role as math teacher Ms. Norbury, who functions as a moral compass for confused protagonist Cady (Lindsay Lohan) and eventually for the school's whole cohort of girls engaged in petty fights and slut-shaming. The film's emblematic scene has Ms. Norbury gathering the girls around to take part in a group confession and giving them a gentle lecture on female solidarity. The scene functions as feminist advice and consciousness raising: "You all have got to stop calling each other sluts and whores. It just makes it okay for guys to call you sluts and whores."

The sequence is symptomatic of the way the film further situates Fey's star text as that of observer and commentator. Rather than performing feminist comedy, Fey performs as the character who offers the moral/feminist commentary for the other characters. Consider, in contrast, the comedy sketches and stand-up routines of Lily Tomlin, Margaret Cho, Amy Poehler, or Tig Notaro, comedians whose feminist reputations are linked to highly skilled performances and politically charged command of body and space and are mobilized to contradict and criticize assumptions about women's roles in society and in comedy. Instead, Fey usually performs a version of herself—a semi-fictional feminist *subject* as the source of satirical humor: "Tina Fey" of the "Weekend Update" news desk, Ms. Norbury of *Mean Girls*, or her self-presentation in her autobiography *Bossypants*, in which she shares tips on how to negotiate being a mother and a woman in the workplace. Elsewhere I have written about the ways in which her small supporting role in the second season of *Unbreakable Kimmy Schmidt* as psychiatrist Andrea Bayden functions in a similar capacity: Dr. Bayden gives crucial therapeutic advice to the helpless protagonist even as the role also reconfirms Fey's discursive authorship over the fictional text.[15]

As comic performer, Fey's two most prominent platforms so far have been the sitcom *30 Rock* and her infamous impersonation on *SNL* of Republican vice presidential candidate Sarah Palin during the 2008 presidential campaign. Perhaps to reconcile the Palin parodies with the existing "better writer than performer" image, Fey interpreted the parodies in numerous interviews and in *Bossypants* as a happy accident owing to the physical resemblance between herself and Palin, which Fey had initially been reluctant to admit.[16] While the Palin parodies worked as political feminist humor on more than one level (not just as satire of party politics but also of media treatments of female politicians), they also helped Fey to incorporate the comedy performer into her public image. Given that her performance of bumbling comic heroine and thinly veiled alter ego Liz Lemon on *30 Rock* has been ambiguously embraced by critics (as shown below) and was often the target of her own self-deprecating remarks,[17] the

Palin parodies were essential for configuring her comedy as not just an observation of gender relations but also as an enactment of them.

The writer-versus-performer tension in Fey's stardom is so widely acknowledged that it was part of her opening monologue in her first *SNL* hosting gig after she had left the show.[18] This monologue aired February 23, 2008, shortly after the end of the 2007–2008 television writers' strike, in which Fey had participated as a picketer. She devotes the first half of the monologue to the strike, explaining its significance for television writers and sarcastically celebrating its success by providing a lengthy, numbers-heavy outline of the final agreement between the studios and the Writers Guild of America. Referring to TV writers throughout as "we," and subtly criticizing the agreement by discussing its fine details, she reinforces her public identity as a "writer first" intellectual. She then mocks her perception of herself as "more of a writer than . . . a performer" by having revered *SNL* alumnus Steve Martin (another writer turned comedy star) show up to "help" Fey prepare for the role of performer on the show. Their comic enactment of a tutor-student situation involves both physical comedy and impersonations. Martin advises her that "a writer lives up here" (touching her head) but "a performer works from the gut," putting his hand on Fey's stomach. He recoils, having felt her Spanx. "What, you got bike shorts there?" he asks, to which Fey snaps, "Don't worry about it." He keeps slapping Fey across the face for her lack of self-esteem and gives her comically impossible prompts for her lines, which she follows with perfect timing and mimicry. In all, the skit showcases Fey's mimicry skills and undermines the perception that she can't be both a performer and a writer; she clearly needs no coaching in comedy performance from an established male comic, though this is the bit's main premise. The Spanx joke is, at this point in her career, a fairly typical example of her use of female physicality and its uncomfortable/unglamorous aspects: devised to be a shocking discovery for the male comic, it mocks the gendered implications of the performer/writer dichotomy as a version of the traditional body/mind dualism, in which women are associated with the body and men with the mind. Considering that Fey wrote the monologue, it pithily satirizes the perception that she can't be both a writer and a performer. And it plays with the assumption that her comedy performance needs a male comic's approval, since Martin's very appearance in the monologue is subject to Fey's authorly control.

14.2. Tina Fey and Steve Martin on *Saturday Night Live* (2008).

Fey left *SNL* in 2006 to produce *30 Rock* for NBC. The series' narrative hook is its metafictional and semi-autobiographical nature; as a fictionalized re-creation of Fey's time as head writer at *SNL*, it revolves around the week-to-week production of an *SNL*-like variety show named *The Girlie Show* with head writer Liz Lemon at the helm, played by Fey. The main cast includes conservative executive boss Jack Donaghy (Alec Baldwin), and vain TV stars Jenna Maroney (Jane Krakowski) and Tracy Jordan (Tracy Morgan), the latter hired in the pilot episode to add black masculinity to the fictional show's dynamic. From this premise emerged a series that mined hot and controversial topics in American culture and politics throughout its run, in the process hybridizing a number of comic genres and traditions (and thus providing multiple interpretations for critics). The show was part backstage and workplace comedy, part satire of the American entertainment industries, part women's comedy (for its female lead and creator), and part an engagement with issues of race, class, and power. Its multidimensional nature, and also the exceptionally fast-paced and self-referential dialogue, quickly landed the sitcom in the contemporary cohort of quality television comedy for both scholars and critics.

The term "quality comedy" is couched in contemporary discourses that surround the overarching category of quality television. Since *30 Rock* is conceived as part of the postnetwork trend of quality comedy and Fey is understood as its prime author, it is useful to point out the term's gendered implications. Television scholarship has shown that categorizing a program as "quality" establishes a strategic distinction from earlier TV traditions, which are seen as "low" cultural entertainment; the term is consequently bound up in anxieties about television's past as a dated and feminine/feminizing source of pleasures, also associated with a classed ("mass") and consumerist culture. In their comprehensive study, Michael Newman and Elana Levine give a detailed account of the ways in which current discourses around quality television seek to establish its relative higher standing in cultural hierarchy by associating it with cultural pleasures inherently coded as masculine.[19] Among others, these include the invocation of a cinematic aesthetic and the valorization of "high concept" and character-focused serialized narratives (deemed more complex than the episodic narrative or soap opera's open-ended structure).[20] Also, and central to my analysis, this discourse celebrates the singular (inherently male) "author" of the quality TV text, a concept borrowed from cinema studies' tradition of auteur theory and contrasted with "regular" television as nonauthored and produced by a team of nameless collaborators. In this context, Fey's establishment as a female author of a sitcom of high cultural standing is treated as something of an anomaly in itself and has important repercussions for the significance of her work and her celebrity. Furthermore, "female authorship" complicates the meanings produced within the comedy as enacted in the figure of Liz Lemon, including its consistent commentary on issues of genre traditions, female performance, and body politics.[21]

30 ROCK, FEMALE AUTHORSHIP, AND QUALITY TELEVISION

Diane Negra's project on female-authored celebrity memoirs of the post-2008 recession era demonstrates that a majority of such texts aim to "claim feminism" at a time when the word has once again gained some cultural cachet.[22] The autobiographies she examines, including Fey's *Bossypants*, are shown to perform ambiguous cultural work in their advocacy of a "common-sense feminist" relation to female labor. Spearheaded by such books as Sheryl Sandberg's *Lean In*, they "espouse an ever-expanding program of self-discipline rather than structural reform" in the recessionary economy by emphasizing a postfeminist ("feminine") relationship to work.[23] Crucially, the latter is manifested in these autobiographies as a (continued) valorization of emotional self-work and self-governance instead of social consciousness and awareness of class privilege. In this biological, essentialist notion of femininity, the nuclear family and motherhood are foregrounded as narratives configuring feminized relationships to labor.[24]

This is certainly evident in the way Fey's *Bossypants* deals with her authorship of *30 Rock* in maternalized and "feminized" terms. In a somewhat paradoxical turn, given the masculinist associations of quality television, she promotes *female* authorship by establishing that the "quality" label of the series lies in its novel female tone. This speaks to the brand requirement of quality TV for novelty, which here is partly achieved by the author's gender. Both Fey and media discourses about the show contribute to the dominant reading of *30 Rock* as originating singularly from Fey herself. While also emphasizing in *Bossypants* the contributions of other writers and producers (especially showrunner Robert Carlock), Fey often refers to the series as her "baby," drawing out this metaphor into an overarching analogy that dominates the discussion. She juxtaposes motherhood and creative labor in an array of jokes and puns; for example, her account of the conception and early production history of *30 Rock* runs parallel with that of her first daughter's birth: "In September, my daughter was born. (For the record: epidural, vaginal delivery, did not poop on the table.)" Several pages later, she writes: "In March, the first season of *30 Rock* was complete. (For the record: no epidural, group vaginal delivery, did not poop on the table.)"[25] While the parallel between authorship and giving birth is an age-old theme in romanticized discussions of creative work (as the double meaning of the word "labor" demonstrates), Fey deromanticizes it and then twists the metaphor into a sarcastic pro-life allegory:

> Now, I know I'm not saying anything that hasn't been said hundreds of times, but *30 Rock* is the perfect symbol for the pro-life movement in America. Here's this little show that no one thought would make it. I'm sure NBC considered getting rid of it, but by the time we won the Emmy, they were too far along.
>
> As the mother of this now five-year-old show, would I still rather have a big, strong *Two and a Half Men* than our sickly little program? No, I would not, because I love my weird little show. I think this show was put on earth to teach me patience and compassion.[26]

In short, *Bossypants* positions *30 Rock* in the paternalistic tradition of single-authored works of art (complete with quality television's reputation as sophisticated but unpopular entertainment), but as the above quotations suggest, Fey's rhetoric around motherhood throws this trope into a dubious light by insistently emphasizing less-talked-about and idealized aspects of childbirth and childrearing.[27]

Given that *30 Rock* is a metafictional text about television, the series goes to great lengths to acknowledge and investigate the contradictions of female authorship in the medium. The series' importance for women's comedy is precisely this centralization (and "taking seriously") of a female/feminized point of view in the face of masculinist cultural values. In *30 Rock*'s acidic tone, network TV is portrayed as both feminine (female-targeted) and masculine (in its production traditions) while also being hopelessly passé: Lemon's job is habitually ridiculed, and her variety show *The Girlie Show* is apparently in need of masculinization in order to reach the desired male audiences.

Gender politics is a running theme on the series, and the pilot episode immediately makes clear its self-consciousness about this. The pilot also acknowledges *30 Rock*'s own stakes in breaking away from associations with the derided traditions of feminine entertainment in the era of quality comedy. In one of the first scenes of the episode, Kenneth the NBC page (Jack McBrayer) describes *The Girlie Show* as "a real fun ladies' comedy show for ladies" to a group of visitors on the NBC studio tour (and thus to the TV audience). At this moment, Liz Lemon steps out of the elevator in front of the group, and Kenneth proudly presents her as the creative mind behind the series. Cut to an onlooking kid releasing a loud burp with an unimpressed face ("Pilot"). The whole of the episode (and also of the series) consistently stresses that network programming, especially the kind targeted at women, is by definition inferior. In a subsequent scene, the newly appointed NBC executive Jack Donaghy criticizes *The Girlie Show*'s ratings demographics, which show, from Donaghy's perspective, the lowly status of *TGS*'s audience: the show's current stars are "popular with women and older gays . . . but you're missing men between eighteen and forty-nine." Liz responds, "I'm not *missing* them, they're just not there." Jack insists it's a problem that needs to be fixed, implying that television as a source of feminine pleasures needs redressing in the new cultural climate. Jack Donaghy's aggressive capitalist masculinity underlines this; he enters the pilot episode by literally (and unnecessarily) kicking down an office door and penetrating the feminized world of television as Liz Lemon knows it.

As a show-within-a-show sitcom, *30 Rock* is open about its legacy of female-centered TV comedy. In this sense, quality comedy's rejection of its historic predecessor, the multicamera sitcom, is more complicated here than theorists of the contemporary "comedy of distinction" generally have it,[28] and this has everything to do with female authorship and gender politics. There is a distinction to be made, though, in the ways *30 Rock* associates itself with television's history of female-led quality programming. On the one hand, Fey's series cites prominent examples of female-centered sitcoms like *Murphy Brown* (CBS 1988–1998) and even more emphatically *The Mary Tyler Moore Show* (CBS 1970–1977), which was a blueprint of the MTM-era quality comedy.[29] On the other hand, *30 Rock* also cites and lampoons *Sex and the City* (HBO 1998–2004), the postnetwork era's premier example of postfeminist quality television. These references are unsurprising given *30 Rock*'s similar focus on the single career woman's work and romantic life in the big city: beginning with the pilot, the series pays homage to *The Mary Tyler Moore Show* while ironically twisting the earlier show's conventions, as the production team and TV critics often noted.[30]

However, *30 Rock* uses *Sex and the City* in more complicated ways. For feminist cultural critics, *Sex and the City* exemplifies how recent female-targeted quality television embraces postfeminist ideals via the sexual empowerment of a narrowly defined female subject (white, heterosexual, upper-class) who is closely associated with a feminized and fetishized consumer culture.[31] Moreover, *Sex and the City* is a landmark series in generic terms as well, popularizing the (mostly) half-hour dramedy form. Its hybridization of the romantic comedy and melodrama resulted in a new formula for the expression of women's stories, but that formula also continued to limit those stories to crises about romance and domestic life.[32] Challenging the low cultural status of the romantic comedy and melodrama genres, feminist media scholars have long argued for their feminist and political (as opposed to aesthetic) value, given their focus on female subjectivity.[33] *Sex and the City*'s success signifies a certain new prestige for "women's genres," even as it ensures a relative lower standing in relation to the revered hour-long quality dramas thought by some television scholars to have revolutionized the aesthetics and cultural status of television's "tired" forms.[34]

Throughout its run, *30 Rock* explicitly invoked and parodied the template of *Sex and the City* to satirize Liz's love life, establishing the "failed femininity" that she represents.[35] As opposed to *Sex and the City*'s "successful" and glamorous femininities, *30 Rock*'s early seasons posit a more "realistic" working woman in Liz Lemon, whose disinterest in girliness, commitment to work, and obsessions with food provide the basis for comedy but also for points of identification in the politics of representation. As *Salon* journalist Molly Marie Griffin put it, in contrasting Liz Lemon with *Sex and the City*'s Carrie Bradshaw (Sarah Jessica Parker): "We wanted to be Carrie; Liz Lemon is who we feel like in comparison. . . . We love her because she's one of us, but we love her even more because she's even grosser, weirder and more awkward than we are."[36] *30 Rock* offers up this distancing from "fantasy" and move towards "reality" quite openly. In a scene in the first season, Liz, Jenna, and Jack's girlfriend Phoebe (Emily Mortimer) are sitting in a restaurant; after some chat about boyfriends, Jenna remarks: "How *Sex and the City* are we right now? I'm Samantha, you [Phoebe] are Charlotte, and you [Liz] are the lady at home who watches it" ("Cleveland").

In interviews Fey repeatedly confirms *30 Rock*'s self-positioning against *Sex and the City*, especially regarding her show's disdain of romance narratives and her character's avoidance of sexual situations. "I wanted to write her that way because I didn't want to film those scenes," she told a journalist in 2010. "I wanted to be able to have a show where I didn't have to be cute and I didn't have to sit on top of anyone in a bra—that was important to me as a writer-performer. So as a character, her attitude about sex came from that. I liked it because it was not something I had seen before that."[37] *Sex and the City* is a recurring reference for Fey's comedy even outside of the context of *30 Rock*. For instance, on the audio commentary of the movie *Baby Mama* (2008), in which she starred alongside Amy Poehler, the two comment on a scene's low-key treatment of female bonding. To Poehler's joke, "This is like the poor man's *Sex and the City*," Fey quips, "This is 'Dry-humping and the Outer Boroughs.'"[38] The remark works well to distance her and Poehler's comedy from postfeminist sexuality and to suggest their liminal position in this dynamic. These textual and extratextual comments about *Sex and the City* overtly criticize and dismiss that series' glamorous female subjects, empowered mostly by their sexuality, which had been celebrated as a groundbreaking media portrayal of women.

Fey's preference for being "funny" over being "pretty" is key to *30 Rock*'s rejection of dramedy and postfeminist romance in favor of the more prestigious and traditionally masculine genres of satirical workplace and comedian comedy (i.e., comedy structured around the performance of an individual star). In fact, *30 Rock*'s generic construction as a female-led quality comedy relies heavily on its parodic and satirical treatment of the postfeminist dramedy, and this is connected to the discourse of gendered authorship around its comic star. In turn, the "writerly" or "authorly" aspect of Fey's image circles back and incorporates comedy *performance* into her star text: over the course of *30 Rock*'s run, Fey develops Liz Lemon into the central character of a comedian comedy that is not rooted in romance or traditionally feminine, domestic narratives. Fey's image as "bad" performer (as opposed to "good" writer) is transposed to Liz Lemon's "bad" performances of femininity and romance but "good" (prominent) performances of parodic comedy. The open discussions of gender politics and feminism on *30 Rock* gain their cultural value from these distinctions about genre, authorship, and performance. The series centralizes gender politics and feminism in a way that the culturally derided genres of dramedy, romance, and melodrama cannot— namely it provides them with cultural status due to the "superior" aesthetics of satire, parody, and comedian comedy.

At the same time, *30 Rock* continues the ambiguous cultural work of keeping "feminine" genres firmly in their place. A key element in the ambiguous treatment of these genres and their gender politics is Fey's performance of Liz Lemon's infamous "failed femininity" as female grotesquery. Yet if *30 Rock* strives to mine quality comedy from the derided postfeminist romance, this performance of the female grotesque sits uncomfortably with the female/feminist comedian's "cerebral" reputation, already entangled in discourses about quality. This tension is discussed in detail in the next section.

BODY POLITICS, GENRE, AND FEMINISM ON *30 ROCK*

30 Rock's cultural work as metacommentary on American media and gender fits well with Fey's star image as the cerebral and observant female comedian who comments on body politics but does not engage much in bodily humor herself.[39] During the run of the series however, a shift gradually took place in its portrayal of Liz Lemon, which complicated this image. This happened simultaneously with

Fey's growing prominence in American media discourses and with the construction of her "cover girl" image, which softened her reputation as a "brainy" (read: masculine) comedian. Mizejewski notes that the *30 Rock* episode "Mamma Mia" (season 3, episode 21) satirizes Fey's star image by having her appear on a magazine cover in a grotesque ("funny") pose instead of a glamorous one. "Neither Tina Fey nor her character Liz Lemon is generally associated with bawdy, grotesque comedy," she concludes, "but the cover-girl episode of *30 Rock* strongly suggests that for both of them, gender expectations about being pretty are rich comic material."[40] Here I want to challenge this assessment by demonstrating that both Fey and Liz Lemon gradually did become associated with a grotesque and increasingly physical parody of femininity on the series, an association perhaps most vividly realized in the "Mamma Mia" episode.

The feminist blogosphere's debates over the meanings of Liz Lemon's portrayal of female grotesquery and its negative implications for feminism suggest just how prominent this feature became in the final seasons of the series.[41] These debates originated in the ambiguous interpretations of the portrayal's effect on Fey's image: in earlier seasons, Lemon/Fey had been declared ideal feminist role models due to the perceived realism in Fey's depiction of the character. The "Tina Fey backlash" (as termed by journalist Rebecca Traister) started once the portrayal cranked up the cartoonesque and corporeal aspects of her "failed femininity" as a parody of media-created femininity.[42] Given that physical humor carries the taint of low cultural entertainment, this trajectory also threatened to corrupt the show's status as quality or "grown-up" entertainment in a medium otherwise seen as hopelessly infantile.[43]

A representative example of the "Fey backlash" is journalist Sadie Doyle's verdict: "The character of Liz Lemon is played by beautiful, successful, smart, funny, apparently happy person Tina Fey, and is meant to be unattractive, only semi-successful, smart, funny, and unhappy. It's interesting that 'smart' and 'funny' get to stay in the picture, as long as the looks, the success, and the happiness are toned down; it tells you something about who you're allowed to like."[44] The characteristic for which Lemon became a celebrated point of identification in her early media reception, namely her "deeply flawed" femininity, was recognized in the backlash years by critics as becoming too exaggerated to be feminist. Similarly, Linda Holmes's and Sam Adams's criticisms of the Lemon character in the series' later seasons express this in terms of physical excess (of visual representation and of behavior): for both, the show departs from earlier "realistic" representations of urban womanhood by exaggerating Lemon's cartoonesque features, which infantilize the character and the show's comedy.[45] Considering that quality television is often celebrated as grown-up entertainment, this lament directly connects the show's gender politics to the discursive requirements of cultural value on TV. Adams likens the Liz of later seasons to "dumbass Homer Simpson," and gives as an example the character's "wearing a Duane Reade bag as underwear"; still, though, "There's something genuinely transgressive about a TV heroine who keeps her tampons in the fridge and looks like she pulled her outfits from the dirty clothes hamper."[46] Nonetheless, he finds that these portrayals of female slovenliness ultimately endanger the comedy's aesthetic values.

Examples of these transgressions abound in the show's later seasons, in which Liz Lemon increasingly plays the carnivalesque grotesque "spectacle" that Rowe Karlyn describes in relation to the unruly woman. In addition to her eating habits, which provide recurring gags, many of the "cringe" elements of 30 Rock emerge from jokes about her bowel movements. She gets diarrhea on a date with her handsome neighbor Drew (Jon Hamm), and he sees her sitting on the toilet while a foul smell wafts from her direction ("St. Valentine's Day," season 3, episode 11). She gets food poisoning from a dodgy sandwich on a road trip and is repeatedly shown hugging the toilet ("Stone Mountain," season 4, episode 3). The episode "Reaganing" (season 5, episode 5) has a flashback scene in which Lemon chattily shares with Jack an embarrassing anecdote: "I'd been on the toilet so long my legs had fallen asleep, so when I tried to stand I just fell into my throw up." Jokes about menstruation similarly recur in later seasons (e.g., "Standards and Practices," season 6, episode 11), and these abject aspects of her female body, be it bad breath, sweating, or hairiness, are usually framed by Jack's disgust. In these examples, Liz's female body functions as the manifestation of the "lower stratum" in Rowe Karlyn's account of the Bakhtinian grotesque.

These portrayals certainly work against the high-tone aesthetics of quality comedy. They also work against feminist concepts of how female grotesquery can be used for progressive ends. The latter becomes clearer in light of Jane Arthurs's concepts of feminism and the female grotesque in comedy, which draws on Mary Russo's work.[47] Arthurs differentiates between two characteristic extremes of female grotesques in popular culture. One is the "'stunted' body who transgresses in her being." This is the body of Roseanne Barr or Melissa McCarthy, marginalized for her fatness and excessiveness, with feminist potential because she is "the passive repository of all that is denied by the sleek and prosperous bourgeois." On the other end of the spectrum are bodies that are not excessive but become so by "embracing the ambivalent possibilities of carnival through masculinisation."[48] These are the active, "stunting" bodies of acrobatic slapstick performers such as Fay Tincher, as described in chapter 2, who are conventionally attractive, even hyperfeminine, but who express female agency by foregrounding "funny" physicality. If these two types, both with feminist potential, characterize the female grotesque of contemporary media, then Lemon and Fey pose a problem that might account for the intense controversy around their reputed feminism. Nominally, Fey the postfeminist cover girl is incongruous with Lemon the "stunted" grotesque: the ugly and frumpy TV writer with the large buttocks, pigeon-toed walk, and nasty eating habits. Further, Lemon/Fey hardly fit the mold of the "stunting" physical comedian who expresses feminist unruliness by combining traditional feminine looks with masculine behavior. This mode of grotesquery needs a desirable body as a reference point for it to make sense (like Patsy Stone [Joanna Lumley] as a parody of bourgeois hyperfemininity in *Absolutely Fabulous* [BBC 1992–2012]).[49] Fey's portrayal of Lemon does not work like this. Even though Fey's extratextual stardom positions her as the attractive cover girl, within the text of *30 Rock* her character Liz Lemon is positioned as physically unattractive. My point is that Lemon's ambiguous status as female grotesque is an overdetermined result of the series' and its star's position in discourses concerning both quality and postfeminist desirability.

The show's production team repeatedly explained the turn towards physical comedy in terms of genre, distancing the show from romantic comedy in favor of comedian comedy and satire. At a panel discussion after the series' end, Fey and writer Robert Carlock discussed a first-season scene in which Jenna and Liz have a "typical" girls' chat over cake about "boys 'n' stuff" which seemed "boring" and "not our show . . . not what these characters should be doing."[50] But as I have previously argued, this distancing from the romance narrative (and specifically the postfeminist romance of *Sex and the City*) continues to carry, somewhat obsessively, the rejected predecessor as *30 Rock*'s point of reference. Further, this quotation implies that the generic rejection (romance is "boring") occurs on the basis of gender politics (women chatting about boys is unfunny), suggesting the show's ambiguous relationship to feminine-coded entertainment.

While Fey often portrays Liz Lemon as a female grotesque—unfeminine and sexless—in a parody of postfeminist femininity, in most cases this is carefully offset with a confirmation of personal agency and a self-conscious rejection of the romance narrative, including the text's constant play with and metatextual refusal of a Jack-Liz romance. In the most overt instances, as in the "Mamma Mia" episode, Lemon *initiates* many of these gross performances, and they often function both as culmination and resolution of plot. In the episode "Black Light Attack!" (season 4, episode 10), she lets her moustache, nicknamed Tom Selleck, grow out to help Jenna compensate for her anxieties about aging publicly. In the scene where she presents Tom to the world, both Liz's subjectivity and the staff's horror are showcased as she walks down the corridor in slow motion. The moustache itself is more of a Frida Kahlo than an actual Selleck, signaling a more "realistic" image of female facial hair as opposed to comic exaggeration, but the upheaval it causes *is* hyperbolically comic and enhanced precisely because of the moustache's "realness." Lemon has a blast being hairy while publicly eating, drinking (milk, nonetheless), and laughing with a full and open mouth at a male writer who retches at the sight of her. The scene is counterpointed with a shocked Jack, who is in the background watching and trying to convince an employee that he is in love with Lemon. Thus, Lemon's "unruly" excess as female agency is balanced out with, and in fact does not work without, social disgust at her body and attitude; the comedy emerges from this contrast.

Other examples abound. In "The Tuxedo Begins" (season 6, episode 7), Lemon dresses up as an over-the-top mixture of a smelly bag lady and Heath Ledger's Joker character from *The Dark Knight* (2008), spending the whole episode in the costume to prove a point to Jack about the misery of urban living and again reveling in the performance of "repulsive" female physicality. In "Apollo, Apollo" (season 3, episode 16), she allows the staff to see an embarrassing video of her acting in a 1990s TV advertisement for phone sex that includes a close-up image of Lemon and another woman trying to be sexy while eating a greasy slice of pizza. Countering the staff's raucous laughter, Lemon resignedly comments: "I remember that girl. She cried all day." Overwhelmingly, these instances show her enjoying or at least

14.3. Left to right: Judah Friedlander, Tina Fey, and Keith Powell in the episode "Black Light Attack!," *30 Rock* (2010).

owning up to social revulsion over her gross body or bodily performance, be it a Chaplinesque waddle due to a bunion surgery ("Aunt Phatso vs. Jack Donaghy," season 7, episode 6), a number of awkward dancing scenes ("Flu Shot" [season 3, episode 8], "Retreat to Move Forward" [season 3, episode 9], "Black Light Attack!"), or any scene of hearty and unabashed eating. Whether through a throwaway joke or a narrative twist, this active acceptance of her unfeminine body calculatedly pushes against the glamorous ideals of postfeminist womanhood. This resistance has special resonance within the trajectory of Fey's growing popularity and the sexualization of her star text, especially after the 2008 *SNL* Sarah Palin impressions (which occurred during the third season of *30 Rock*), accelerating the contrast of the funny/pretty body.

The episode "Dance Like Nobody's Watching" (season 6, episode 1) is an interesting case in point both for physical comedy and for the outright rejection of the romance narrative, since it *does* include a romance plot. (Lemon has a secret boyfriend.) The latter is decentralized, however, by two factors: first, the big surprise around which the episode is structured is not Lemon's romance but the discovery that she is on the dance team for the Women's National Basketball Association (WNBA). The episode's central comic plot and imagery revolve around Lemon's defiantly self-confident bodily display during some

14.4. Tina Fey in the episode "The Tuxedo Begins," *30 Rock* (2012).

unflattering routines and awkward but enthusiastic dances. Second, the romance is incorporated into the larger narrative not as a "chase" plot (free-agent career woman dating in the city)[51] but as an already established, working relationship that has developed completely outside of the text's diegetic frame; and the fiction never offers up the couple's detailed backstory. This is a rare plot device for central characters in comedy conventions anyway, but considering that Lemon is a version of the "urban single woman" trope (including multiple portrayals of her failed attempts at romance), completely eliminating the romantic comedy narrative from her final romance storyline works, again, as a statement about genre and gender politics. The comic tension is shifted onto the Liz-Jack screwball friendship via the question of how Jack will take this new twist, which is further developed in later episodes.

As all this suggests, the building of comedian comedy and satire on the ruins of postfeminist romance, combined with the shift in Fey's star text, has ramifications for *30 Rock*'s engagement with body politics and feminist concerns. Crucially, the push toward *embodied* (physical, grotesque) satire, located in the female comedian's bodily performance, was nervously received in mainstream feminist media discourses. On the one hand, the exaggerated physical comedy has the tinge of less respectable modes of entertainment, and on the other, it is quite problematic to reconcile with Fey's feminist image as "attractive-yet-smart" (or "smart-yet-attractive") comedian. Thus, both as female-centered quality comedy and as feminist tract, *30 Rock* was embraced ambiguously by its contemporary reviewers.

The other reason for Lemon's and Fey's ambiguous evaluation as feminist "role models" concerns *30 Rock*'s relationship with its own overt portrayal of feminism and postfeminism. That Liz Lemon functions as a parody of an entitled, uninformed feminism rather than, for instance, a reliable mouthpiece of an aspirational feminism (like Poehler's character Leslie Knope on *Parks and Recreation*), is acknowledged in the pilot episode. In a much-quoted tirade, Jack Donaghy recites a summary of Lemon's character: "New York third-wave feminist, college-educated, single and pretending-to-be-happy-about-it, overscheduled, undersexed, you buy any magazine that says 'healthy body image' on the cover, and every two years you take up knitting for . . . a week?" This of course clues the viewer in about the show's parody of *Sex and the City* womanhood and has been discussed by critics and commentators as such.[52] Less frequently noted is the dialogue following this tirade. Upon producer Pete's (Scott Adsit) praise of Donaghy's "dead-on" reading of Lemon, Donaghy, the NBC executive whose job title is Vice President of East Coast Television and Microwave Oven Programming, shares the secret of his skill at profiling: "Years and years of market research," he says. Feminist scholarship's long-standing argument about the postfeminist paradigm, namely that it exists first and foremost through popular media's formulations, is evoked here.[53] Via Donaghy's long-winded job title, and the consistently portrayed connections throughout the series between Liz's confused feminist politics and corporate culture's creation of feminized consumer citizens, the show leaves little doubt that women of Liz's "type," as consumers and target demographic, are calculatedly created by and for the media industries.

However, if the show explicitly states that Liz as a parody of popular feminism is a creation of the media industries, and if it handles the debates around feminism and postfeminism via social satire, then Fey's established *feminist* persona appears in dubious light and its reception renders the series' feminism problematic. Mizejewski's evaluation of *30 Rock*'s gender politics similarly argues that it is hard to treat its intentions as unequivocally feminist, not only due to the dominant sarcastic tone, but also because it takes feminism as (one of) its objects of query. In her assessment, although the series is remarkable in today's television landscape for its unique centralization of feminism and postfeminism as important political issues, it gains its cultural relevance and exceptionality precisely from positioning itself as an outsider, an "observer" of these relations.[54]

As a result, for critics both the author-comedian (Fey) and the fictional character (Lemon) emerge as outsiders, liminal in relation to popular feminism, suggesting that *30 Rock*'s scrutiny of Liz Lemon and feminism is what prevents the series from realizing unambiguously feminist cultural work. Paradoxically, then, the trait that established Fey's popular image as Hollywood's token feminist—namely, the position of outsider-observer and astute satirist of gender relations—seems to work against the "feminist" moniker here. The "social observer" element in Fey's star text had previously foregrounded feminist intervention (calling out sexism and gender discrimination), but in *30 Rock* this scrutiny is partly turned against postmillennial discourses of both feminism and postfeminism. Fey's observational mode of comedy (watching the belly-floppers and writing about them) makes her an unreliable feminist figurehead if the object of scrutiny is the ambiguities of popular feminism projected onto her own comic alter ego. It makes her an "outsider" to feminism, though being the outsider is an ideal location for comedy.

KIMMY SCHMIDT'S "UNBREAKABLE" FEMINISM

In light of *30 Rock*'s ambiguously received cultural work relating to feminist and gender politics, Fey's next project seems to have relieved her critics somewhat in its take on these issues. Cocreated with Robert Carlock, the thirteen-episode first season of the comedy series *Unbreakable Kimmy Schmidt* was originally produced for NBC, which passed the series on to Netflix, reportedly due to the broadcast network's drastic downsizing of its comedy lineup, and to the apparently better fit of the series' tone with the online streaming service's profile.[55] As the first TV program that Fey produced since *30 Rock*, and similarly treated in the mainstream media as an "authorly" text, it is also the first project in a long time in which she does not appear in a central role. So her contribution to the series is a return to her long-established "writerly," or observer, position, without the complications of a centralized and performed alter ego. At the same time, *Kimmy* has been received by critics as a less ambiguously feminist text in its aspirational optimism and focus on a "strong female character," Kimmy Schmidt (Ellie Kemper), a tough-yet-perky survivor

14.5. Nick Kroll in the episode "Kimmy Rides a Bike!," *The Unbreakable Kimmy Schmidt* (2015).

of a misogynistic doomsday cult. This verdict also surfaces through comparisons to *Parks and Recreation*; indeed, Kemper's Kimmy offers herself to be interpreted as a new Leslie Knope, "Except that this is a Leslie Knope who has been to Hell," as one critic puts it.[56]

While debates about the series' politics have shifted onto its problematic treatment of race,[57] its status as "quality" comedy is located not only in its sunny-yet-sarcastic portrayal of post-traumatic stress disorder, but also in its uncompromisingly critical portrayal of white, heterosexual, affluent masculinity.[58] This is evident in whole storylines whose central concern is to unmask the villainy of a white male character in a position of authority. In "Kimmy Goes to School!" (season 1, episode 6), Kimmy keeps trying to cure a grumpy GED prep teacher (Richard Kind) from his presumed disillusionment about education until she realizes that he *wants* his class of underprivileged students to fail for his own selfish purposes. In "Kimmy Rides a Bike!" (season 1, episode 11), her employer, rich and unhappy housewife Jacqueline, gets her to join Spirit Cycle, a SoulCycle-type spinning class led by idolized instructor/lifestyle guru Tristafé (Nick Kroll). Both women use the class as a means to avoid the problems in their lives, which for Kimmy is the ongoing trial of her abductor, the crazy Reverend Richard Wayne Gary Wayne (Jon Hamm), where she is expected to testify. A parodic rendition of the fitness industries' cultivation of self-work and spiritualism, the episode's revelation is that these practices contribute to a denial and glossing over of larger issues—such as women's structural oppression. This is expressed again via the unmasking (here almost literally) and hyperbolic deconstruction of the class instructor as a fraud: Kimmy's energetic intervention and pep talk to class members reveal that Tristafé's real name is Christopher, he holds classes in half darkness to conceal his horrid rashes and zits, and he does not even pedal his bike but sits on it and instead uses it as a toilet behind a screen (hence the abundance of scented candles in the room).

Tristafé's manipulative and parasitic fraudulence, manifested in the physically grotesque comedy, is overtly used as a metaphor for patriarchal control over women's choices in a broader sense. "Why do we keep doing this to ourselves?" Kimmy demands of the women (and sole gay man) of the class, "Replacing one stupid male authority figure with another?" Referring to Jacqueline's controlling and unfaithful husband, she continues: "Is he different than any guy who tells you he'll make you richer or prettier or safer if you just let *him* make all the decisions?" The denouement of the episode also works as a turning point in the serialized narrative: Kimmy realizes that she needs to stand up to the reverend, the ultimate oppressive patriarchal figure overshadowing *her* life (and thus the series).

Examples are numerous in *Kimmy* for the expression of such "inspirational feminist" life lessons dramatized as resistances to white male authority—while *30 Rock* negotiated a compromise with this symbolic figure in the Liz-Jack friendship—thus aligning the series with the recently increased popularity of feminist and antiracist discourses both in the quality television paradigm and more generally in popular media. As feminist activism is once again gaining popular interest, particularly via digital media platforms, "feminism" as contested buzzword has begun circulating in various media sites, with the word's meaning often discussed in relation to the figure of the "feminist" celebrity (Fey's name being reliably prominent in these debates).[59] Further, notions of intersectionality and of feminism's historically problematic relation to race and ethnicity politics are centralized in these discourses: for instance, in debates about "Beyoncé feminism" or in the #SolidarityIsForWhiteWomen hashtag campaign.[60]

These discourses have special resonance in the quality TV environment at a time when representational politics is being evaluated with renewed attention; increasingly, methods of representation shape judgments about quality for high-profile television programming. That is, both media producers and critics grant special attention to the ways in which television texts deal with marginalized social identities (e.g., gender, sexuality, race, age) and political relevance. An appeal to "diversity" once again becomes a basis on which the TV industry conceives its quality products and molds them towards target audiences, best signified in TV producer Shonda Rhimes's career trajectory and her influential production company ShondaLand.[61] Signaling its alignment with these trends, *Kimmy* shows a shift in the trajectory of Fey's celebrity as an author of female-centered quality comedy. The series employs enthusiastic and fight-happy feminist rhetoric to make social observations about patriarchy in the same urban milieu as *30 Rock*, while also frequently narrativizing race and sexuality politics in its plots. Unlike the earlier series, however, it is not concerned with the scrutiny of popular (post)feminism projected onto the female author-comedian's comic persona.

There is an ambiguity at work, then, between the mobilization of feminist rhetoric in Fey's comedy and her self-positioning as a comic performer. Put bluntly, centralizing her own comic body mobilizes a great deal of sarcastic scrutiny of feminism and the feminist/postfeminist female subject, but this becomes muted when she works from a more clearly "observational" position. Further, her celebrity as a female and feminist comedy auteur is now cemented in media discourses and as such is not so deeply entangled in negotiations of her celebrity meaning in the landscape of quality comedy. The changed institutional context (i.e., Netflix's self-branding as catering to female audiences) combined with the changed cultural context (feminism as a hot topic in popular media), allows Fey's comedy to move away from *30 Rock*'s preoccupations with feminism, postfeminism, and the female auteur. Instead, *Kimmy* joins the more directly articulated discourses of (some) recession-era television that center around diversity and feminism, such as *Orange Is the New Black* (Netflix 2013–), *Parks and Recreation*, *Transparent* (Amazon 2014–), and ShondaLand's programming output such as *Scandal* (ABC 2012–) and *How to Get Away with Murder* (ABC 2014–).

CONCLUSION

The novelty of Fey's image as a female comedian was initially a boundary-pushing introduction of the "feminist" persona, mediated through the discursive ambivalence between writer-observer versus

performer-enactor of gender-based comedy. However, the popularization of this figure also demonstrates the limits of its acceptability
in the cultural imagination. My analysis has shown that these limits have to do, as ever, with the connection between femaleness and
bodily performance in comedy: Liz Lemon's increasingly *physical*
parodies of popular feminism and postfeminism became controversial because they worked against popular understandings of feminist
comedy and quality television. Yet the critical and feminist ambivalence about *30 Rock* emerged precisely because of Fey's carefully balanced ambiguity or liminality in both her celebrity and her work as
a writer-performer of comedy—and popular media discourses do not
deal well with ambiguity.

Whether coincidental or not, what's striking in the trajectory
of Fey's star text is the way in which she began to enact physical-
grotesque performances of femininity once she became a household
name as observer/author *and* sexualized feminist icon. In retrospect
this is no surprise, since her comedy has always caricatured political and cultural contradictions, including those of popular feminism and her own image. In Fey's work on *30 Rock*, two seemingly
contradictory practices of women's comedy meet: on the one hand,
self-deprecation and self-scrutiny, which operate to internalize the
"male gaze"; and on the other hand, an observational feminist rhetoric that turns the gaze against the observer. The combination of these
two traditions in Fey's comedy produces a consistently scrutinizing
commentary on popular feminist practices of the early twenty-first
century.

NOTES

1. Virginia Heffernan, "Anchor Woman," *New Yorker*, Mar. 11, 2003, www
.newyorker.com/magazine/2003/11/03/anchor-woman.

2. Fey and Poehler met in the 1990s at Second City, Chicago's renowned comedy theater, where they both studied and performed improvisational comedy. As
a comic double act, they first became popular on *SNL*'s "Weekend Update" as
the show's first (and so far only) all-female news anchor duo (2004–2006). After
this, a number of joint appearances capitalized on their comic chemistry, such as
their pairing in feature films like *Baby Mama* (2008) and *Sisters* (2015) and their
cohosting of the Golden Globe Awards in three consecutive years (2013–2015).
For a representative example of popular media's discussions of their friendship
narrative in terms of female solidarity, cooperation, and appreciation of diverse
comic skills, see Jesse David Fox, "The History of Tina Fey and Amy Poehler's
Best Friendship [Significantly Updated]," *Vulture*, Jan. 8, 2015, www.vulture.com
/2013/01/history-of-tina-and-amys-best-friendship.html.

3. See, for instance, Rebecca Traister, "The Tina Fey Backlash," *Salon*, Apr. 14, 2010, www.salon.com/2010/04/14/tina_fey_backlash/; Maddie Rodriguez, "Three Times Amy Poehler Said 'Yes Please' to Feminism in Her Memoir, and We're On Board, Naturally," *Bustle*, Nov. 6 2014, www.bustle.com/articles/47745-3-times-amy-poehler-said-yes-please-to-feminism-in-her-memoir-and-were-on-board; and Amanda Duberman, "Amy Poehler on Celebrity Feminism Conversation: 'It's an "Attempt to Get Us to Talk Sh*t about Each Other,'" *Huffington Post*, Oct. 28, 2014, www.huffingtonpost.com/2014/10/28/amy-poehler-feminism-celebrity_n_6064350.html.

4. Tina Fey, *Bossypants*, 1st ed. (New York: Little, Brown, 2011).

5. Ibid., 143.

6. The perennially visited question "Can women be funny?" was a hot topic in the latter years of the first decade of the twenty-first century in American media discourses, partly due to the popularization of Fey's and her female *SNL* peers' comedy. See Alessandra Stanley, "Who Says Women Aren't Funny?," *Vanity Fair*, Apr. 2008, 182–251.

7. *Salon* journalist Anna Silman's article about the first official trailer of *Sisters* expresses a similarly contrasting understanding of the two comedians' comic talents, affecting the perception of their feminist credentials. Silman's concern about the film's quality is based on the trailer and on the supposed "swapping" of comic personas (Fey playing an "outrageous" character, Poehler an uptight one) and betrays a discursive conflict between "observational"/writerly and "performed"/physical comedy. After a lament over the loss of feminist authorship in the film's production, she argues: "Fey, the weaker actress of the two, shines best when playing some loose version of herself: Cerebral, discombobulated, acid-tongued. Dating back to her *SNL* days, she has always been at her funniest when she lets her zany intellect shine through, not when she forces herself into dumbed-down slapstick. . . . Conversely, pegging Amy as the buttoned-up straight woman seems a waste of her talents as a virtuoso of voices and gestures and wild characters." Silman, "I'm Worried That Tina Fey and Amy Poehler's 'Sisters' Will Be as Bad as It Looks," *Salon*, July 15, 2015, www.salon.com/2015/07/15/im_worried_that_tina_fey_and_amy_poehlers_sisters_will_be_as_bad_as_it_looks.

8. Linda Mizejewski, *Pretty/Funny: Women Comedians and Body Politics* (Austin: University of Texas Press, 2014), 3, 5.

9. See, for instance, "Top Ten Thinking Man's Sex Symbols," *Daily Beast*, n.d., www.thedailybeast.com/galleries/2008/12/16/top-ten-thinking-man-s-sex-symbols.html.

10. Mizejewski, *Pretty/Funny*, 11.

11. Ibid., 8–9.

12. See more on this in Mizejewski, *Pretty/Funny*, 67–75; Martha Lauzen, "The Funny Business of Being Tina Fey: Constructing a (Feminist) Comedy Icon," *Feminist Media Studies* 14, no. 1 (2014): 106–117, doi:10.1080/14680777.2012.740060; Eleanor Patterson, "Fracturing Tina Fey: A Critical Analysis of Postfeminist Television Comedy Stardom," *Communication Review* 15, no. 3 (July 2012): 232–251, doi:10.1080/10714421.2012.701991.

13. Ibid., 247.

14. Kathleen Rowe (Karlyn), *The Unruly Woman: Gender and the Genres of Laughter* (Austin: University of Texas Press, 1995).

15. Julia Havas, "What's in a Burp? Therapeutic Gross-out Humour in 'Unbreakable Kimmy Schmidt,'" June 30, 2016, *CST Online*, http://cstonline.tv/kimmy-schmidt.

16. In *Bossypants* Fey chalks up her acceptance of the role to public pressure and Lorne Michaels's insistence. And tellingly, this section of the book devotes a few introductory pages to explaining how unskilled and physically unsuitable she was during her tenure at *SNL* to play different characters, even providing photographic evidence from the show to support this statement (197–203). This notion of "accidental performer" further undergirds the writer/performer dualism. The media also lauded the performance by emphasizing the "accidental" aspect of it (i.e., that it was not a calculated choice to showcase her comic impersonation skills).

17. The discursive writer/performer dichotomy is further evident in the fact that while Fey has received a number of awards for acting on the series, she is often keen to point out a supposed contradiction in this: "I wanna thank everyone in the Screen Actors Guild for considering me an actor at all" is the opening remark of her acceptance speech for winning the 2008 SAG Award for Best Actress in a Comedy Series; she continues, "It takes a lot of people to make me look like a good actor." "Tina Fey SAG Awards," *Dailymotion*, Jan. 28, 2008, www.dailymotion.com/video/x46y21_tina-fey-sag-awards_shortfilms.

18. "Tina Fey Monologue—Saturday Night Live," YouTube, Sept. 23, 2013, www.youtube.com/watch?v=AaPZEdVlwZAMizejewski_6434_14_ed2.docx.

19. Michael Z. Newman and Elana Levine, *Legitimating Television: Media Convergence and Cultural Status* (New York: Routledge, 2012).

20. See Jason Mittell, "Narrative Complexity in Contemporary American Television," *Velvet Light Trap* 58, no. 1 (2006): 29–40, doi:10.1353/vlt.2006.0032.

21. It is also worth noting (while not central to my analysis) that *30 Rock* often makes specific thematic references to the writer/performer dichotomy. For instance, a particular storyline utilizes this contrast to build an overarching narrative over several episodes: when comedy writer Lemon is given the opportunity to host her own talk show following the success of a sketch that she wrote, she has a nervous breakdown over the pressure of appearing on TV ("Mamma Mia," "Kidney Now!," "Dealbreakers Talk Show #0001").

22. Diane Negra, "Claiming Feminism: Commentary, Autobiography, and Advice Literature for Women in the Recession," *Journal of Gender Studies* 23, no. 3 (2014): 275–286, doi:10.1080/09589236.2014.913977.

23. Sheryl Sandberg, *Lean In: Women, Work, and the Will to Lead*, 1st ed. (New York: Knopf, 2013); Negra, "Claiming Feminism," 284.

24. Negra, "Claiming Feminism," 282.

25. Fey, *Bossypants*, 172, 194.

26. Ibid., 194.

27. "Abject" or uncomfortable aspects of motherhood are a source of comedy that Fey regularly employs when publicly discussing her own pregnancies and mothering experiences. An extreme example of this is her appearance on Conan O'Brien's talk show in 2011. A few months pregnant, she purported to present a sonogram of the foetus, which turned out to be a disturbing image she described as a "lava monster" (but more reminiscent of an alien parasite straight from *The*

X Files). "Pregnant Tina Fey Gives Sneak Peek of Her Baby, 04/19/11," *TeamCoco,* Apr. 19, 2011, http://teamcoco.com/content/pregnant-tina-fey-gives-sneak-peek -her-baby.

28. See Brett Mills, *The Sitcom* (Edinburgh: Edinburgh University Press, 2009), 134; and Jeremy G. Butler, *Television Style* (New York: Routledge, 2010), 216–218.

29. For the ways in which quality, gender politics, and a relationship to feminism are configured in the MTM production company's 1970s sitcoms, see Jane Feuer, Paul Kerr, and Tise Vahimagi, eds., *MTM: "Quality Television"* (London: BFI, 1984); and Kirsten Marthe Lentz, "Quality versus Relevance: Feminism, Race, and the Politics of the Sign in 1970s Television," *Camera Obscura* (2000) 15(1 43): 45–93, doi:10.1215/02705346-15-1_43–45.

30. See Mizejewski, *Pretty/Funny,* 75–76; Jacques Steinberg, "'30 Rock' Lives, and Tina Fey Laughs," *New York Times,* Sept. 23, 2007, www.nytimes.com/2007 /09/23/arts/television/23stei.html; and Erin Carlson, "*30 Rock* Character Study: Why Tina Fey and Alec Baldwin's Friendship-with-Benefits Worked," *Hollywood Reporter,* Jan. 30, 2013, www.hollywoodreporter.com/news/30-rock-character -study-why-416807.

31. See, for instance, Diane Negra, "'Quality Postfeminism?': Sex and the Single Girl on HBO," *Genders,* no. 39 (2004): n.p., www.genders.org/g39/g39_negra .html; and Jane Arthurs, "*Sex and the City* and Consumer Culture: Remediating Postfeminist Drama," in *Television: The Critical View,* ed. Horace Newcomb, 7th ed. (New York: Oxford University Press, 2007), 315–331.

32. Rowe Karlyn's analysis illuminates the structuring connection between genre traditions and their gendered hierarchies in the history of Hollywood cinema. In the cultural signifying processes of classic genres, female transgressions, and generally centralizations of gender politics, have overwhelmingly been expressed in romantic comedy and melodrama. Kathleen Rowe Karlyn, "Comedy, Melodrama, and Gender: Theorizing the Genres of Laughter," in *Classical Hollywood Comedy,* ed. Kristine Brunovska Karnick and Henry Jenkins (New York: Routledge, 1995), 39–59.

33. For detailed discussions of this tradition, see, for instance, Yvonne Tasker, *Working Girls: Gender and Sexuality in Popular Cinema* (London: Routledge, 1998), 141–144; and Charlotte Brunsdon, *Screen Tastes: Soap Opera to Satellite Dishes* (London: Routledge, 1997), 9–43.

34. See Mittell, "Narrative Complexity"; Butler, *Television Style;* Amanda D. Lotz, *Cable Guys: Television and Masculinities in the Twenty-First Century* (New York: NYU Press, 2014).

35. Mizejewski, *Pretty/Funny,* 26.

36. Molly Marie Griffin, "How Tina Fey Ousted Carrie Bradshaw," *Salon,* May 20, 2010, www.salon.com/2010/05/20/tina_fey_recession_americas_carrie _bradshaw.

37. *Nerdist with Tina Fey,* Youtube, May 15, 2012, www.youtube.com/watch ?v=0qjrmTTPBFI&feature=youtube_gdata_player.

38. Michael McCullers et al., *Baby Mama* "Audio Commentary" (Universal Studios, 2009), DVD.

39. This contrast taps again into the cultural, and equally gendered, hierarchi-

cal dichotomy of the body and mind. As Mizejewski observes, the Judeo-Christian duality of woman as body and man as intellect is the structuring force behind the pretty/funny binary (*Pretty/Funny*, 14–15). For Fey, then, the straddling of the intellectual or brainy kind of comedy with the glamorous celebrity persona becomes especially precarious once the humor turns physical, projected onto her "comic" body.

40. Mizejewski, *Pretty/Funny*, 75.

41. The critique of Lemon was often made through a comparison to Leslie Knope, portrayed by Amy Poehler in *Parks and Recreation*, who was deemed a more "progressive" female figure. This is best expressed in a blog post by Hanna Brooks Olsen, "A Leslie Knope in a World Full of Liz Lemons," *Medium*, Jan. 22, 2015, https://medium.com/@mshannabrooks/a-leslie-knope-in-a-world-full-of-liz -lemons-61726b6c6493#.yf0uhjoa5. Also see Sarah Seltzer, "Knoptimism vs. Liz Lemonism: How 'Parks and Recreation' Took a Different Feminist Route," *Flavorwire*, Feb. 24, 2015, http://flavorwire.com/505916/knoptimism-vs-liz-lem onism-how-parks-and-recreation-took-a-different-feminist-route; Linda Holmes, "The Incredible Shrinking Liz Lemon: From Woman to Little Girl," *NPR*, Feb. 9, 2012, www.npr.org/sections/monkeysee/2012/02/09/146626983/the-incredible -shrinking-liz-lemon-from-woman-to-little-girl; and Sam Adams, "Has Liz Lemon Become 'Dumbass Homer'?," *Slate*, Feb. 10, 2012, www.slate.com/blogs /browbeat/2012/02/10/liz_lemon_and_homer_simpson_is_30_rock_getting _stupider_.html.

42. Traister, "Tina Fey Backlash."

43. Newman and Levine, *Legitimating Television*.

44. Sadie Doyle, "Thirteen Ways of Looking at Liz Lemon," *Tiger Beatdown*, Mar. 24, 2010, http://tigerbeatdown.com/2010/03/24/13-ways-of-looking -at-liz-lemon.

45. Holmes, "Incredible Shrinking Liz"; Adams, "Has Lemon Become 'Dumbass Homer'?"

46. Adams, "Has Lemon Become 'Dumbass Homer'?"

47. Jane Arthurs, "Revolting Women: The Body in Comic Performance," in *Women's Bodies: Discipline and Transgression*, ed. Jane Arthurs and Jean Grimshaw (London: Cassell, 1999), 137–164; Mary Russo, *The Female Grotesque: Risk, Excess, and Modernity* (New York: Routledge, 1995).

48. Arthurs, "Revolting Women," 143.

49. Ibid.

50. "Hey Dummies: An Evening with the *30 Rock* Writers," *The Paley Center for Media*, Feb. 27, 2013, www.paleycenter.org/2013-spring-hey-dummies-an -evening-with-the-30-rock-writers.

51. For serial TV's "chase" narratives and "the comedy of the sexes," see Christine Scodari, "Possession, Attraction, and the Thrill of the Chase: Gendered Myth-making in Film and Television Comedy of the Sexes," *Critical Studies in Mass Communication* 12, no. 1 (1995): 23–39, doi:10.1080/15295039509366917; and Newman and Levine, *Legitimating Television*, 92–97. They argue that the trope of the romantic "chase" for TV comedies (i.e., the narrative tension centralized on the would-be couple's constant fights and forever delayed unity) expresses a masculinized subjectivity. In Newman and Levine's interpretation,

"Television's serialized narratives of sex and romance tend to uphold masculinist conceptions of heterosexual pairings, in that they are often unable—or unwilling—to offer stories of complicated, ongoing, and egalitarian sexual relationships between men and women" (97).

52. See, for instance, Emily Nussbaum, "In Defense of Liz Lemon," *New Yorker*, Feb. 23, 2012, www.newyorker.com/culture/culture-desk/in-defense-of -liz-lemon; Traister, "Tina Fey Backlash"; Carlson, "*30 Rock* Character Study."

53. As a representative example, much feminist analysis has been devoted to mainstream media's frequent assertions in the late 1990s that "feminism is dead," exemplified by the notorious June 28, 1998, *Time* cover. This shows the black-and-white portraits of three prominent women's rights activists (Susan B. Anthony, Betty Friedan, and Gloria Steinem); contrasted with them, at the far right of the cover, is the color image of Calista Flockhart in character as Ally Mc-Beal from the eponymous series (Fox 1997–2002). Under her head shot, the ominous question "Is feminism dead?" is posed in bright red. For the cover's feminist critics, it is precisely the use of a *popular fictional* figure that indicates the extent to which the ideas of postfeminism are inherently media creations, serving the purposes of neoliberal governmentality and consumer culture to argue that feminism is no longer needed (see, e.g., Sarah Projansky, *Watching Rape: Film and Television in Postfeminist Culture* (New York: NYU Press, 2001) 68–70; Kathleen Rowe Karlyn, "Feminism in the Classroom: Teaching Towards the Third Wave," in *Feminism in Popular Culture*, ed. Joanne Hollows and Rachel Moseley (Oxford: Berg, 2006), 57–75; Geraldine Harris, *Beyond Representation: Television Drama and the Politics and Aesthetics of Identity* (Manchester: Manchester University Press, 2011), 34–35; Michele Schreiber, *American Postfeminist Cinema: Women, Romance, and Contemporary Culture* (Edinburgh: Edinburgh University Press, 2014), 3–4.

54. Mizejewski, *Pretty/Funny*, 77.

55. Nellie Andreeva, "Tina Fey and Robert Carlock's *Unbreakable Kimmy Schmidt* Moves from NBC to Netflix with 2-Season Pickup," *Deadline*, Nov. 21, 2014, http://deadline.com/2014/11/unbreakable-kimmy-schmidt-tina-fey-robert -carlock-netflix-2-season-pickup-nbc-1201292254.

56. Emily Nussbaum, "Candy Girl," *New Yorker*, Mar. 30, 2015, www.new yorker.com/magazine/2015/03/30/candy-girl.

57. This criticism initially concerned a production background issue rather than a fictional portrayal: Jane Krakowski plays Kimmy's employer, the Manhattan socialite Jacqueline, who hides her Native American identity then slowly comes to terms with it; the portrayal was deemed offensive because a white actor was cast in the role instead of a Native American. (See Megh Wright, "Tituss Burgess on 'Unbreakable Kimmy Schmidt' Critics: 'If People Aren't Talking about You, You're Not Doing Your Job,'" *Splitsider*, Mar. 13, 2015, http://splitsider .com/2015/03/titus-burgess-on-unbreakable-kimmy-schmidt-critics-if-people -arent-talking-about-you-youre-not-doing-your-job.) A second-season storyline added further fodder to the controversy due to its explicit commentary on the critical backlash: in the episode "Kimmy Goes to a Play!" (season 2, episode 3), Kimmy's roommate, black gay actor Titus (Titus Burgess) claims that he was a Japanese geisha in a past life and puts on a one-man show based on her life. This

includes applying the accoutrements of "traditional" Japanese femininity and performing a reverse version of "blackface," which incites the outrage of online communities for its perceived racism. The narrative stresses that Titus's claim is authentic, underlined by his intense and eventually well-received performance (which, in a departure from the series' overall tone, is not portrayed in a sarcastic or comic mode). Space limits prevent me here from a detailed analysis of these controversies and their repercussions for the series' cultural work. But it is worth noting that these are results of the series' insistence in exploring identity as a malleable cultural construct, always in flux. See also Sonia Saraiya, "Imagine There's No Outrage: 'Unbreakable Kimmy Schmidt' Dreams of a Post-identity Comedy Utopia," *Salon*, Apr. 17, 2016, www.salon.com/2016/04/17/imagine _theres_no_outrage_unbreakable_kimmy_schmidt_dreams_of_a_post_identity _comedy_utopia. This is a position that the producers seem to have extended outside the fiction to the casting process, thus ignoring the political realities of minority actors' on-screen representation.

58. Tyler Coates, "Tina Fey and Race: 'Unbreakable Kimmy Schmidt' Has a Straight, White Male Problem," *Decider*, Mar. 10, 2015, http://decider.com /2015/03/10/tina-fey-race-unbreakable-kimmy-schmidt.

59. On the notion of the feminist celebrity, see Heather Savigny and Helen Warner, eds., *The Politics of Being a Woman: Feminism, Media, and Twenty-First-Century Popular Culture* (New York: Palgrave Macmillan, 2015). Representative of the renewed media fascination with this figure is the self-declared feminist magazine *Bust*'s compilation of twenty-two years of female celebrities' answers to the question, "Are you a feminist?" "'Are You A Feminist?': Celebrities' Answers from BUST Magazine's Twenty-Two-Year Archive May Surprise You," *BUST*, n.d., http://bust.com/are-you-a-feminist-celebrity-answers-from -bust-magazine-s-22-year-archive-may-surprise-you.html. Crucially, *BUST* published this list of quotes as confirmation that in today's media frenzy over the question, their interest is the most authentic since they have been doing it the longest.

60. For Beyoncé's contested "feminism," see Nathalie Weidhase, "'Beyoncé Feminism' and the Contestation of the Black Feminist Body," *Celebrity Studies* 6, no. 1 (2015): 128–131, doi:10.1080/19392397.2015.1005389. For a summary of the "#SolidarityIsForWhiteWomen" campaign, see Mikki Kendall, "#SolidarityIsFor WhiteWomen: Women of Color's Issue with Digital Feminism," *Guardian*, Aug. 14, 2013, www.theguardian.com/commentisfree/2013/aug/14/solidarityisfor whitewomen-hashtag-feminism.

61. See Maureen Ryan, "Why TV Is Finally Embracing the Realities of Race," *Variety*, Feb. 23, 2016, http://variety.com/2016/tv/features/television-race-diver sity-ratings-1201712266; and Wesley Morris and James Poniewozik, "Why 'Diverse TV' Matters: It's Better TV. Discuss," *New York Times*, Feb. 10, 2016, www .nytimes.com/2016/02/14/arts/television/smaller-screens-truer-colors.html.

CHAPTER 15

LENA DUNHAM: CRINGE COMEDY AND BODY POLITICS

MARIA SULIMMA

IN THE 2012 EMMYS OPENING SKIT, host Jimmy Kimmel rushes past female celebrities practicing their acceptance speeches in the women's restroom. Kimmel is crying because of a beauty emergency—his face has swollen up grotesquely after one too many Botox injections. But when a group of women gathers and bursts open the door to a stall, they find not Kimmel but a short-haired, naked white woman with a large tattoo on her arm, sitting cross-legged on the toilet seat and eating a large cake. In response to their mumbled apology, the cheerful woman replies: "That's okay. I don't mind." And in fact, the then twenty-six-year-old Lena Dunham had demonstrated on the television show *Girls* (HBO 2012–2017) that she did not mind appearing nude on-screen. The HBO series had quickly acquired an audience that enjoyed controversies about the show and about Dunham, its high-profile lead actress and showrunner. As former darling of the independent movie scene following the success of *Tiny Furniture* (2010), a film she wrote, directed, and starred in, Dunham's career accelerated with *Girls*, which made her into a mainstream media sensation. By the time *Girls* entered its fifth, penultimate season, Dunham had become a media juggernaut, with an autobiographical essay collection (*Not That Kind of Girl*, 2014), a podcast series (*Women of the Hour*, 2015), a biweekly newsletter, and frequent media appearances.[1]

Investigating Lena Dunham's comedy and star image(s), I follow other contributors to this collection by starting with Kathleen Rowe Karlyn's work on unruly femininity (1995, 2010), as well as with the double bind of "pretty/funny" that Linda Mizejewski claims has historically shaped women's relationship with and spaces within American comedy. As "the unruly woman," Dunham "eats too much and speaks too much,"[2] commanding attention and dominating conversa-

15.1. Nudity and cake: Dunham's appearance during the opening skit of *The 64th Primetime Emmy Awards* (2012).

tions, both when enacting fictional characters and in her celebrity appearances. Also, Dunham's willingness to portray her own nude body on-screen subverts television and cinematic norms about which bodies are deemed "the norm," illustrating the tensions of the "pretty/funny" divide. I begin with Dunham's television authorship and the dense, controversial reception of *Girls*/Dunham by journalism and academia, and then I turn to an exploration of her comedic abilities, arguing that her humor derives from a combination of simultaneous repulsion and relatability to her characters living their lives "one mistake at a time," as *Girls'* first season promotional poster proclaimed. At times, her nonfictional appearances, such as the aforementioned Emmys opening clip, make uncomfortable aspects of her fictional work—her disregard of boundaries, her casualness about exposing her body—more comically accessible. Unlike the other female comedians analyzed in this collection, Dunham is not always perceived as a comedian, since some of her work has more in common with drama than comedy. As suggested by the title of her essay collection, she herself is "not that kind of comedian"—the kind that can be easily categorized, as seen in the prevalent themes and scenarios of her work overall, as well as in the perception of and discourses around her serial star image.

Dunham's self-presentation as a feminist is primarily enacted by the depiction of her body, as well as through female friendship and collaboration, as I argue in the final part of this essay. Dunham's star persona is intricately tied to her self-branding as a representative of urban, millennial "girlhood" and as an increasingly feminist media insider. Such labels are referenced and evoked by her different media texts, but they are also actively employed by her audiences. In this way, her different star personas function as paratextual frames of reception that accompany her films and television shows and manage viewers' expectations towards them. First coined by Gérard Genette in regard to literary texts, the concept of a "paratext" refers to elements such as promotional materials that accompany a text, cue reception, and signal the author's perceived intention.[3] Significantly, Dunham's image(s) is subject to change and evolves with the ongoing criticism that she and the media properties associated with her name receive. In other words, like her serial text *Girls*, Dunham's image progresses in the overlap of media products, reception, and production that scholars of seriality have deemed essential characteristics of contemporary popular culture.[4]

DUNHAM AS TELEVISION AUTEUR

Industry promotion of television series, as well as audiences' readings of those series, frequently centers around the figure of the showrunner as author of the series. The showrunner, previously a relatively invisible figure, holds a loosely defined position in television production as a "hyphenated writer-producer"[5] that has become more prominent with television's increased interest in serial narration and its more complicated materials.[6] While the demographics of U.S. television writers' rooms are notoriously white and male,[7] diversity is even more problematic when it comes to those writers offered as visible personifications of television authorship. In a highly competitive field in which issues of gender, race, ethnicity, and age consistently play out in terms of underrepresentation, few female or nonwhite writers have been showrunners, and even fewer have managed to build up the celebrity status of male showrunners associated with the canon of prestigious television series.[8] Jason Mittell points out that the gendered dimensions of the author function to convey "authority, mastery, and control of fictional universes," qualities that express not only gendered but also racialized perceptions of authorship.[9]

Dunham is unusual as one of the very few highly visible female showrunners able to assume a role of television auteurship. She is also unusual in the number of additional roles she plays in regard

to *Girls'* production. In addition to sharing the showrunner respon-
sibilities with cowriters Jenni Konner and Judd Apatow, she is also
the star of the show, playing an aspiring writer, the protagonist Hannah Horvath. Dunham is, as well, a member of the writers' room, the
director of the majority of episodes, and one of the show's producers. This multiplicity of roles is highly untypical for television's collaborative model of labor division.[10] But the auteur Dunham is also
remarkable for her age. As a New Yorker who was just twenty-five
when she launched *Girls*, Dunham became a figurehead for an urban,
"hipster" lifestyle that is often presented as characteristic of the so-
called millennial generation. The positioning of Dunham as millennial spokesperson and the show as representative of this generation's
lifestyle was anticipated by an ambiguous statement made by protagonist Hannah in the first episode. While feeling high from the actually harmless opium pod tea she drank, Hannah attempts to persuade
her parents to continue to support her financially and argues for the
importance of her writing: "I don't want to freak you out, but I think
that I may be the voice of my generation. Or at least a voice. Of a generation." The sarcasm of this quotation was not always grasped, as
many viewers took this as a genuine claim of Dunham's. Whether or
not the character Hannah or her creator Dunham might be representational of any specific group, the fact that a multitude of viewers—
and particularly critics—are willing to take this quotation at face
value is relevant to how the show's comedy is perceived. The themes
and struggles of twenty-somethings coming-of-age in an urban environment make the show endearing to some and a racist portrayal of
self-centeredness to others.

As such, perhaps it was the show's name—the ominous claim to
represent a universal group of "girls"—that caused many critics to
disparage the lack of racial diversity and the "whitewashing" of New
York.[11] In addition, critics noted that the characters' perceived entitlement and privilege were extended to the actresses who played them—
all daughters of artists and media insiders.[12] Even before the first episode of *Girls* premiered, the show was already the center of much
critical discussion, especially about its representation of race.[13] As
Roxane Gay concludes: "*Girls* is a fine example of someone writing
what she knows and the painful limitations of doing so."[14]

Dunham and her work are firmly positioned not only as part of
the millennial generation but also as part of a generational divide.
This is evident in the series and in Dunham's many self-descriptions

as a "girl," with references to her parents and childhood. It would be easy to read such evocations of childhood as nostalgia for the safety of parental care, generated by anxieties about professional or romantic security. However, I feel it is more helpful to read this representation of girlhood as an intrinsic part of Dunham's star image and her own brand of comedy, opening up tropes of privileged, white girlhood as a source of humor. She presents herself as the weird child grown-up, the awkward teenager and social outcast who asks a lot of her surroundings, and who, while not necessarily having changed after growing up, can at least joke about her past self. In *Tiny Furniture* Aura (Dunham) moves back into her mother's apartment and disrupts the well-attuned living arrangements of her mother and sister (Laurie Simmons and Grace Dunham, respectively), while claiming to others that this is what her family wants and needs. In *Girls* Hannah's parents are frequently shown literally dropping everything they're doing when she calls them during (actual or imagined) emergencies, while she can rarely muster enough attention to listen to what is happening in their lives.

The identification with the younger generation and her label as a "girl" also shape Dunham's interactions with older female stars. Instead of presenting herself as a successor to the female comedians discussed in this book's earlier chapters or to the feminist activists she interviews and discusses on social media, she approaches these women with awe and expresses fan-like worship, again positioning herself as an inexperienced girl with a lot to learn. In her January 2013 acceptance speech at the Golden Globes as Best Actress in Comedy, Dunham described how her fellow nominees inspire her and "have comforted me at the darkest moments of my life. Julia [Louis-Dreyfus], Tina [Fey], Amy [Poehler], and Zooey [Deschanel] have respectively gotten me through middle school, mono, a ruptured eardrum, and the acute food anxiety that populates my entire life." Significantly, Dunham doesn't create the impression that she is a successor to these women. Instead, her gratitude is part of her star image as the anxious, nervous girl whose social awkwardness is a source of her humor. Similarly, in her prominent interviews with Gloria Steinem and Nora Ephron, Dunham presents herself as a younger feminist activist or as a female director asking for advice.[15] Even though the subtitle of her essay collection—*A Young Woman Tells You What She's "Learned"*—seems to aim at keeping others from making the same mistakes, Dunham rarely speaks from an authoritative position.

Consider, too, the crucial difference between the twenty-something Hannah and the thirty-something protagonist of that other female-centered HBO show set in New York, *Sex and the City*'s Carrie Bradshaw (Sarah Jessica Parker).[16] Carrie knows exactly what she is looking for—romance and a pair of Manolo Blahniks—while Hannah is in the midst of figuring things out and "trying to become who I am."[17] Carrie portrays a confident femininity; in voice-overs framing every episode, Carrie explores urban, single womanhood and draws conclusions from her and her friends' experiences. Voice-overs—which signal authority and control of the narrative—are an unknown in the world of *Girls*, in which viewers watch Hannah and her friends performing an unselfconscious girlhood that's open towards experimentation with sexuality, femininity, and relationships as a process of learning by doing.

IS THIS SOMETHING I CAN LAUGH AT?
PUTTING THE CRINGE IN COMEDY

In regard to viewers' relationship to the characters of *Girls*, Betty Kaklamanidou and Margaret Tally argue that "Dunham has deep empathy for her characters, and as a result, we as viewers have empathy for them as well."[18] However, other critics suggest the relationship between the audience and the female characters of this series is more conflicted and entails not only empathy but also disgust and alienation. While ambiguous humor characterizes Dunham's earlier work, *Creative Nonfiction* (2009) and *Tiny Furniture*, in the serial text *Girls* it becomes most distinct. As Todd VanDerWerff comments about his experience of watching: "So maybe that—the often-horrifying lack of emotional distance—is what we talk about when we talk about *Girls*. . . . It moves and wrecks and loves and observes, and it never stops trying to push viewers to a point where the 'comedy' falls out of 'cringe comedy.'"[19] VanDerWerff uses a term from popular journalism, "cringe comedy," to describe comedy that capitalizes on scenes that are humorous but cause viewers to feel uncomfortable. For Gary Susman, *Girls* is a typical example of cringe comedy because of its characters' lack of self-awareness.[20] As interdisciplinary research in humor theory clarifies, it is never entirely clear with whom laughter aligns itself in comedy—that is, if laughter is *with* or *at* the expense of a character or perspective.[21] So in *Girls*, moments in which we are able to relate to characters alternate with moments in which their behavior seems utterly unrelatable and appalling.

A good example of cringe comedy occurs in *Girls'* fourth season, when Hannah works as a substitute teacher at a New York high school and begins an inappropriate friendship with one of her teenage students, Cleo, played by Maude Apatow ("Tad & Loreen & Avi & Shanaz," season 4, episode 8). They decide to get matching tongue piercings, which results in a horrifically gruesome scene almost on par with Hannah rupturing her eardrum with a Q-Tip in the second season. While Cleo proceeds with the piercing, Hannah refuses out of pretend maturity: "Listen, as an older woman and as your friend, a great lesson I can teach you is that it's okay to change your mind." Unsurprisingly but ironically, their friendship is short-lived because of Hannah's overbearing, immature, and needy behavior. When the school principal finds out about Hannah's inappropriate conduct, he asks her to his office to lecture her on the significance of privacy and professionalism. During their conversation, she ignorantly continues to shock her superior with inappropriate confessions, until he wearily reminds her: "You're an adult and I know it sucks, but you just have to start at least trying to keep at least some stuff inside." Hannah remains completely oblivious but nonetheless in a later scene employs his exact phrases to rebuff others.

In her public appearances and interviews, Dunham is likewise known for her lack of boundaries. She dominates conversations and frequently surprises her interview partners by breathlessly delivering unexpected confessions or sarcastic conclusions that function as punch lines. Again, the term "cringe comedy" comes to mind, because both interviewer and audience often respond to her confessions with uncomfortable laughter. This notion of oversharing and overstepping boundaries is central to Dunham's comic persona, exemplified by the opening sketch of the *Saturday Night Live* episode she hosted in March 2014 (season 39, episode 15). While Dunham tries to address the audience and begin the episode, different cast members step up to her to share intimate, personal, and often sexual confessions while ignoring her protests.

Frequently, media texts associated with Dunham's name are also ambiguous in their dealings with sad or serious content, resulting in her work sometimes being categorized as dramedy rather than comedy. This ambiguity is especially pronounced in scenes connected to sexuality and consent. In *Creative Nonfiction*, Ella (Dunham) initiates sex with her classmate Ty (Jeffrey Cristiani) but seems unsure how far to take the encounter. Problematically, Ty tells her: "If you want to have sex, say nothing." During the following sex scene, Ella seems emotionally withdrawn, absently staring at the ceiling and the wall. Afterward, Ty snuggles up to her and suggests a relationship, but the camera shows Ella with her back turned to him, about to cry. In *Girls*, the early sex scenes between Hannah and Adam (Adam Driver), her romantic interest and later boyfriend, include role-playing that entails Hannah's objectification and degradation, which she subjects herself to willingly and out of curiosity. Unlike Ella, Hannah never emotionally retreats or creates the impression of feeling sad or violated during sex scenes, making them more readily available as sources of humor. To her worried friend Marnie (Allison Williams), Hannah jokes about Adam's "abusive rhetoric" as being inspiration for her writing. Hannah seems to explore her sexuality with a childlike curiosity that reinforces her position as a woman not entirely sure of her sexual desires or needs; rather she is a girl still in the midst of figuring things out for herself.

In "I Get Ideas" (season 2, episode 2), after their relationship has ended, Adam enters Hannah's apartment against her will and scares her. Hannah's fear quickly turns to violent anger. She throws Adam out of the apartment in an emotional outburst that is humorous but with serious, alarming undertones. Hannah's screams are childlike— high-pitched and screechy—and her punches carry little weight, illustrating the contrast between Dunham's relative smallness and Driver's large frame towering over her. Despite this, Hannah is able to push him across the kitchen and out the door because Adam is so surprised by the intensity of her anger and aggression. In *Tiny Furniture*, Dunham protagonist Aura similarly explodes into a furious outburst that resembles a childlike temper tantrum, while her mother maintains a poker face and her younger sister struggles visibly to not burst out laughing. These portrayals of exaggerated emotion hover between disturbing and humorous affects.

Such displays of emotion also could be described, in a more problematic way, as hysterical. In the fourth season of *Girls*, when Hannah is a student at the writer's workshop in Iowa ("Female Author," episode 3), she has a confrontation with the class's wunderkind D. August (Ato Essandoh) at a party and calls him out for his male-centric literary canon building. He dismisses her by saying she is "starting to sound a little hysterical here." Aggravated, Hannah snaps back: "Hysteria? Hysteria is how they diagnosed women who they found uppity in the 1800s and had an excuse to remove their ovaries." As the introduction to this anthology points out, the behaviors of the "hysterical" women of comedy would likely in a different time have been framed within the gendered discourse of hysteria, which supposedly accounted for symptoms like nervousness, verbal outbursts, food cravings, and expressions of sexual desire. The concept of "making a spectacle of herself," intrinsic to Kathleen Rowe Karlyn's "unruly woman," demonstrates this relationship; historians have noted the importance of performance in nineteenth-century diagnoses and treatments of hysteria, in which the physician and the patient collaborated in defining and performing the disease.[22]

Although Hannah openly confronts the sexist basis of hysteria in season 4, the behavioral tics of mental illness are seriously explored earlier in the series. As a result of her writer's block and stress in season 2, Hannah develops an obsessive-compulsive disorder and feels compelled to perform gestures, movements, or actions repeatedly while counting them aloud. This is significantly not enacted in a humorous manner, but rather indicates Hannah's worrisome mental state. Hannah's parents persuade her to start seeing a psychiatrist (Bob Balaban), who becomes a recurring character. Her unwillingness to accept her psychiatrist's evaluations and her quickness to criticize and dismiss him as narcissistic provide a source of comedy in ensuing seasons. Importantly, it is not Hannah's OCD that is treated comically but her conversations with others about it. Dunham's representation of mental illness in the show is accompanied by her willingness to talk about her own experiences with therapy in her essay collection or to post photos of her medications on social media.[23] Dunham's matter-of-fact accounts of the challenges of a life with mental illness function to normalize and remove social stigma from this illness. In a television series where we so frequently despise the characters and are appalled by or laugh at their inappropriate behavior, this representation of mental illness makes us empathize and relate to Hannah's struggle.

THIS IS WHAT A FEMINIST LOOKS LIKE: DUNHAM'S FEMINIST STAR PERSONA

In 2012 Lena Dunham expressed her support of Barack Obama by means of a video clip in which, in a serious tone, she instructed younger or inexperienced viewers about their "first time," advising them that it "shouldn't be with just anybody. You wanna do it with a GREAT guy." As the accompanying music becomes upbeat and Dun-

15.2. Jenni Konner, Hillary Clinton, and Lena Dunham in a photo posted on Dunham's social media accounts during Clinton's 2016 presidential campaign.

ham resumes her usual animated style of talking, the punch line becomes obvious: she was not speaking about losing one's virginity but addressing first-time voters. It is easy to see why Dunham as presumed spokesperson for millennials was attractive to Obama's campaigners hoping to target this much-coveted demographic. In the months leading up to the 2016 Iowa caucus, Dunham was again campaigning for a Democratic candidate, and she published an online exclusive interview with Hillary Clinton.

In the interview, Dunham and Clinton are characterized as sister feminists interested in and working towards the same political causes. Overall, the comparison of the Obama clip and the Clinton interview illustrates a shift in Dunham's public image: as Dunham was about to turn thirty, she increasingly sought to expand and enrich her media presence beyond the millennial "girl" persona by means of exploring her feminism, thus countering the trend of female stars who express opinions with a feminist ring but avoid identifying as a feminist.

Dunham's two main strategies of enacting her feminism are the presentation of her body on-screen or in social media and the focus on female friendships or female cooperation on- and off-screen. Significantly, while Dunham claims the label of feminist for herself, *Girls* is not positioned or promoted as explicitly feminist by her, her co-workers, or HBO. Again, the collaborative nature of television would problematize such an equation of the feminist auteur and the feminist text, even though such equations have long been explored and interrogated in television studies and television criticism (as is evident in this collection's chapter on Tina Fey). Further, in the words of Rosalind Gill, "Like the media, gender relations and feminist ideas are themselves changing and in flux."[24] Not only do the texts of contemporary popular culture incorporate multiple, changing understandings of feminism, but frequently feminist elements are positioned within antifeminist and postfeminist dynamics, as Linda Mizejewski has argued about the comedy series *30 Rock*.[25] Dunham and her character Hannah are often conflated, as are Fey and her alter ego, the character Liz Lemon. And like *30 Rock*, *Girls* often struggles with the label of feminist comedy. But the differences between the two series are illuminating. The character Lemon calls herself a feminist, while Hannah seems to sympathize with feminist positions but never refers to herself as such. And in contrast to Fey's real-world reticence about feminist identity, Dunham's avowed feminism has become a significant paratextual frame for the show. My intent here is not to judge the gender politics of *Girls*—which could easily result in what Charlotte Brunsdon has famously referred to as the "Ur-feminist article," an essay primarily concerned with evaluating whether a text, its characters, or themes are able to live up to an author's understanding of feminism.[26] Instead, I am interested in how Dunham's star image of being a feminist is communicated, and how, in turn, it becomes a paratext for the series, her previous work, and her persona as a comedian.

In a productive exploration of *Girls'* humor and feminism, Marcie Bianco finds in it a feminism "that is less aggressive and more reflexive and observational."[27] As examples of the show's feminism, consider, for instance, how in the first season the "girls" support without question the decision of their friend Jessa (Jemima Kirke) to have an abortion; or how in the second season minor character Beedie expresses her frustration at the invisibility of older women in popular culture. However, in *Girls'* third season, during an uncomfortable discussion with Adam about female perception, Hannah's feminist argument is countered by the casual sexism of her friend Shoshanna (Zosia Mamet):

ADAM: I just think that women get stuck in this, like, vortex of guilt and jealousy with each other that keeps them from seeing situations clearly.

HANNAH: "Women get stuck?" Okay, now you sound like one of those guys who thinks a woman should never be president because her menstruation will cloud her judgment.

SHOSHANNA: But they shouldn't, like be president, because it . . . it could . . . their . . . their judgment.

This dialog is characteristic of the way a "feminist-friendly" statement or criticism is often supplemented with vagueness or antifeminist utterances on *Girls*, accounting for the multitude of possible readings of the show. While Hannah does at times adopt a feminist perspective, none of the characters are consistently represented as feminists, and references to feminism are rare.[28] Instead, it is rather the audience that has proven itself willing to read Lena Dunham the television auteur and her brand of feminism into her work, generating lively scholarly conversations and frustrations about *Girls'* lack of diversity, the female characters' lack of empowerment, or their preoccupation with the men in their lives.[29]

The aspect of *Girls* that all feminist readings acclaim is the progressiveness of representing bodies that fall short of television's glamorous ideals, in particular Lena Dunham's own body.[30] Dunham's willingness to portray nudity without glamour has become a hallmark of her performances. While Dunham's characters are often nude in front of their romantic partners, they also undress in front of their friends or family members. Margaret Tally argues that in such scenes "the nudity of a 'regular' female body is not simply to counteract stereotypical images of women in film and television, but as a kind of shorthand way of signifying the emotional intimacy between the girlfriends," thereby complicating the audience's expectation of equating naked female bodies with sexuality or sexualization.[31] However, Dunham's nudity or partial nudity is never portrayed as a source of humor. In a scene from "All Adventurous Women Do" (season 1, episode 3), Hannah and Adam relax in bed postcoitus when he starts making funny sounds and groping her stomach. She stops him, saying, "Maybe I don't want my body to be funny. Has that ever occurred to you?" Alyssa Rosenberg argues that in such sex scenes "it's not [Hannah's] body that's funny, it's [Adam's] pornified fantasies."[32]

Hannah's lack of boundaries in undressing in front of others is amusing, but we laugh not at the way Hannah's body looks, but at things characters say or do in response to or despite of her nudity. In regard to Hannah, it is her behavior, exaggerations, and melodramatic gestures that are the source of humor, not the body that performs them. Of all the show's characters, the most conventionally attractive character, Marnie, is the one with the fewest (partially) nude scenes and some of the most hilariously awkward sex scenes. By contrast, the characters Dunham portrays in *Girls* and her other work are usually the ones with the most (or sole) nude scenes. Her appearance is what many consider "non-normative" for pop-culture texts because her body type is slightly heavier than that of the average Hollywood female star, but on the other hand far more typical of American female bodies. Describing her own body, Dunham says:

> On good days I am sturdy bordering on slim and on less good days I am chubby. On all days I have a high waist, a wide ass and fairly long legs. I feel lucky to have thin wrists and ankles, and less lucky to have three rolls of flesh on my stomach that don't budge even in the face of extreme measures.[33]

Echoing a frequent response to this aspect of Dunham's work, Michelle Dean remarks that "by consistently putting that 'imperfection' in front of us, [the show] is demanding that we interrogate our devotion to our beauty standards."[34] It is highly significant that Dean places the word "imperfection" in quotation marks, because it is the lack of diverse and average-looking bodies on screen that situates Dunham in the space of the "non-normative." We can applaud Dunham for the representation of her non-thin body, while understanding that many other bodies still need to be represented, and not as sources of shame or humor, in film and television. The non-normative appearance of Dunham's characters further stems from cinematic and televisual standards of heavy makeup, special lighting, or editing to make already conventionally attractive bodies look even more flawless. Critic Emily Nussbaum points out that Dunham

> lets herself look like hell. Dunham films herself nude, with her skin breaking out, her belly in folds, chin doubled, or flat on her back with her feet in a gynecologist's stirrups. These scenes shouldn't shock,

but they do, if only because in a culture soaked in Photoshop and Botox, few powerful women open themselves up so aggressively to the judgment of voyeurs.[35]

Whenever she's praised in this manner for her nudity on-screen, Dunham herself has frequently responded that this is not something she finds extraordinary or something that she is uncomfortable with, continuing to normalize such representation. In an interview on the *Ellen* show in 2014, she explained: "And so I feel like I'm always getting all these props for being brave, and I'm like I didn't do anything brave, I feel totally cool about being naked."

Dunham's nudity on *Girls* and in her other work still remains controversial, with a disturbing amount of sexism, body shaming, and misogyny being expressed in social media. Radio host Howard Stern famously likened the experience of seeing this "little fat girl" naked to rape, a comment he would later apologize for.[36] Dunham has vigorously responded to this line of criticism; she opens an episode of her podcast series on "The Body" by reading horrific online comments about her body, and she makes the sexism of anonymous online degradation a theme in her work.[37] During the Television Critics Association press tour in 2014, a journalist caused a controversy when he asked Dunham about the "purpose" of her character's nudity on the

15.3. "Let's talk about you being naked on television": Lena Dunham as a guest on *The Ellen Show* (2014).

15.4. Dunham's appearance in the February 2014 issue of *Vogue* caused a controversy.

show.[38] The journalist's question seemed to echo online discussions about whether Dunham is attractive enough to appear nude on television, a (sexist) question that generated especially heated debate after the second-season episode "One Man's Trash" (episode 5). This episode focused exclusively on Hannah's sexual encounter with the attractive doctor Joshua (Patrick Wilson). Several viewers found it highly unlikely that a woman who looks like Hannah could be sexually attractive to a conventionally good-looking and professionally successful character like Joshua,[39] ignoring the long tradition of male comedians being romantically paired off with more attractive actresses. While this controversy was heating up, Dunham appeared on the cover of *Vogue*, and the self-identified feminist online magazine *Jezebel* offered a high sum of money for unedited pictures from her shoot. The website was heavily criticized for this policing of Dunham's body, which its editor claimed was not done to question the uncharacteristically glamorous portrayal of Dunham but to draw attention to problematic beauty norms. Previously, *Jezebel* had reported on Dunham starting to work out with a celebrity fitness trainer and expressed worry that in trying to reshape her body, Dunham might succumb to mainstream beauty images after all.[40] So despite the feminist embrace of Dunham's body politics, this incident suggests the policing not just of Dunham's body but of her feminism as well, similar to feminist criticism of Tina Fey described in chapter 14 in this collection. Curiously, this type of critique entails a rhetoric of "exposing the truth" and reads like investigative journalism, asking if the celebrity and her media texts are behaving consistently enough to allow her to call herself a feminist.

Finally, central to Dunham's star image as a feminist is the theme of female friendship as a focal point in her work, as well as in her public celebration of the friends and women who inspire her.[41] Dunham shares pictures of these women and their work on her social media and includes them in her films and series. Her longtime friend Jemima Kirke stars in *Girls* and *Tiny Furniture*. Another friend, political strategist Audrey Gelman, stars in *Creative Nonfiction* and in *Delusional Downtown Divas* (2009); Dunham explored the origins of their friendship in her essay collection *Not That Kind of Girl*, where we learn that Gelman's mother was Dunham's therapist. The relationship that has gotten most media attention, however, is Dunham's friendship with celebrity singer Taylor Swift, with Dunham appearing in Swift's music video "Bad Blood" and joining her onstage during concerts.[42]

In the podcast series *Women of the Hour*, which Dunham hosted and produced in cooperation with the website *BuzzFeed* in 2015, female collaborations and friendships figure prominently. The podcast episodes have titles such as "Friendship," "The Body," "Love & Sex," "Work," or "The Big Picture" that correlate with the structure of Dunham's autobiographical essay collection. Instead of rehashing her essays, Dunham focuses less on her childhood and college time and more on her current life and the beginning of her career. As such, the podcasts illustrate her attempt to shift her image from "girlhood" towards a mature enactment of professional, feminist womanhood. A few months prior to the podcasts, Dunham and her co-showrunner Jenni Konner launched a free e-mail subscription newsletter, "Lenny," which promises its subscribers an "email newsletter where there's no

15.5. The friends reconcile in an impromptu performance of their drunken dance routine in the episode "Beach House," *Girls* (2014).

such thing as too much information." The biweekly newsletter publishes articles and interviews on "Feminism, style, health, politics, friendship, and everything else," written by Dunham, Konner, and a large group of guest contributors, among them political activists and industry insiders. Following up on their joint foundation of a production company to specifically target gender in film and television and support women in the industry, the newsletter highlights Konner and Dunham's productive partnership and friendship, exemplifying Dunham's celebration of female collaboration.[43]

Dunham's films and series are distinctive in exploring not just supportive female friendships but also rivalry, jealousy, annoyance, and miscommunication among female friends. In *Creative Nonfiction* Ella is hurt to find her friend and confidante Carly (Slaine Jenkins) in bed with her crush, and in *Tiny Furniture* Aura seems overwhelmed by the neediness and envious personality of her friend Charlotte (Jemima Kirke). While the friendships in *Sex and the City* were depicted as a stable, unchanging background to the women's quest for love, in *Girls* romantic relationships typically take a narrative backseat to the friendships that increasingly fracture during the course of the show. While each episode of *SATC* included at least one scene of all four protagonists getting together for a dinner at a restaurant, a *Girls* season typically includes only one or two scenes that feature all four main characters together. The episode "Beach House" (season 3, episode 7) stands out from the rest of the series in this regard. Marnie invites the other three women to spend a weekend outside the city to reconnect and "you know, prove to everyone via Instagram that we can still have fun as a group." The night ends in a drunken confrontation in which the female characters scream out their dislike of and frustration with each other. The next morning the embarrassed women run into each other in the kitchen and silently work together to clean up. Their awkward silence continues as they sit waiting at the bus stop, but soon they begin to perform the gestures of a dance choreography they learned the night before. The scene indicates that—despite all their frustration and miscommunication—it is in small moments of shared activities and experiences rather than grand declarations on Instagram that their friendship can be expressed. Tally refers to this as "realistic portraits of friendships between twenty-something women that inevitably have conflicts" and argues that in this regard "*Girls* can be understood as trying to portray something that has not been previously depicted in mainstream or cable television."[44] I agree with Tally that such portrayals of the highs and lows of female friendship are few in our contemporary televisual (and cinematic) media landscape. Further, the portrayal of friendship in *Girls* is also paratextually accompanied by Dunham's public friendships and collaborations. As such, a media text like *Girls* is crucially shaped by its creator's star image. When watching the women in the show mistreat their friends or grow apart from them, viewers can easily evoke paratextual discourses as counterexamples that extend the theme of friendship from the fictional to the realm of the nonfictional by means of Dunham's feminist persona.

CONCLUSION

The title of Dunham's essay collection, *Not That Kind of Girl*, not only raises the question of what "kind of girl" Dunham might be but also winks at a cliché about how "good" girls are supposed to behave. Dunham writes female characters who behave badly—they talk too much, share too much intimate information, or are too self-involved—and Dunham's star persona shares most of these traits as well. Audiences respond to such transgressions with a mixture of disgust, empathy, or laughter, thus making ambiguity a hallmark of Dunham's comedy. The most significant transgression, however, is

Dunham's nudity, which challenges the disturbingly narrow body image allowed by mainstream culture; her comedy never makes the "non-normative" body a target but rather challenges the norms by means of the other characters' and audiences' responses to it. Lena Dunham is also notable for the multitude of roles she fills in the creation of the media texts associated with her name. The ways she is perceived and performs her public persona(s)—as television auteur; comedian; spokesperson for millennials; representative of white, privileged girlhood; and professional, feminist media entrepreneur—form a significant paratextual frame for her comedy. As such, my chapter has illustrated the productivity of considering how practices of reception and production overlap to create Dunham's celebrity status, a star text that draws from as well as informs her television show and films.

While Dunham would not position herself as a successor to the female comedians covered in this anthology, her work draws from their unruly histories of performances that disrupt social scenarios and norms of gender, beauty, and sexuality. In an anthology that aims to correct cultural amnesia about this history, the final example of Dunham—the only millennial-generation comedian included in this book—points towards an interesting future for women's comedy. Currently, she shares her celebrity as feminist comedian with performers such as Amy Schumer, Samantha Bee, Amy Poehler, and Tig Notaro; with writers such as Jill Soloway; and with her age peers, *Broad City* (Comedy Central 2014–) creators Ilana Glazer and Abbi Jacobson. These women illustrate how the comedian willing to position herself as a feminist is a multitasker, a "Jackie-of-all-trades," who expands her media presence (and feminism) into a variety of media platforms and embraces controversy yet admits her own privilege and limited possibility to speak for others, making her own reception a source of her comedy. These women continue to target sexist social and media norms regarding age or non-normative beauty, and their success points towards an exciting time for hysterically funny feminist comedy.

NOTES

1. Dunham gained her first experiences with short experimental YouTube videos, web series (*Tight Shots, Delusional Downtown Divas*), and her feature-length film *Creative Nonfiction*.

2. Kathleen Rowe (Karlyn), *The Unruly Woman: Gender and Genres of Laughter* (Austin: University of Texas Press, 1995), 37; and Rowe Karlyn, *Unruly*

Girls, Unrepentant Mothers: Redefining Feminism on Screen (Austin: University of Texas Press, 2010).

3. Gérard Genette, *Paratexts: Thresholds of Interpretation*, trans. Jane E. Lewin (Cambridge: Cambridge University Press, 1997). Expanding upon Genette, Jonathan Gray explored how paratexts—promotional posters, DVD extras, opening credits, trailers, etc.—manage media consumption and embed films, TV shows, or video games with meanings and value. See Jonathan Gray, *Show Sold Separately: Promos, Spoilers, and Other Media Paratexts* (New York: NYU Press, 2010).

4. See contributions to Frank Kelleter, ed., *Populäre Serialität: Narration—Evolution—Distinktion: Zum seriellen Erzählen seit dem 19. Jahrhundert* (Bielefeld, Germany: Transcript, 2012).

5. Michael Z. Newman and Elana Levine, *Legitimating Television: Media Convergence and Cultural Studies* (New York: Routledge, 2011), 49.

6. Jason Mittell, *Complex TV: The Poetics of Contemporary Television Storytelling* (New York: NYU Press, 2015), 88–90; and Newman and Levine, *Legitimating Television*, 40–41.

7. In their staffing brief of 2015, the Writers Guild of America West documents the underrepresentation of female writers at two to one (29 percent) and writers of color at three to one (13.7 percent) for the 2013–2014 season; both statistics signal a slight decline from previously higher numbers. Darnell Hunt, "Writers Guild of America/WGAW 2015 TV Staffing Brief." WGAW.org, Aug. 20, 2015, www.wga.org/. . ./who_we. . ./tvstaffingbrief2015.pdf.

8. Among popular and visible showrunners are Shonda Rhimes, Tina Fey (see chapter 14), and Mindy Kaling. Showrunners like Julie Plec, Amy Sherman Palladino, Jenji Kohan, Michelle King, and Liz Meriwether have managed to maintain a public profile due to the dedicated fan followings of their shows. Whereas women like Carol Mendelsohn, Pam Veasey, and Ann Donahue (*CSI* franchise); Jam Nash (*Rizzoli & Isles*); Michelle Ashford (*Masters of Sex*); and Kerry Ewin (*Bates Motel*), just to name a few, are relatively absent from popular discussions of televisual authorship and showrunner-ship.

9. Mittell, *Complex TV*, 103–104.

10. As of this writing the show has entered its sixth and final season. Surveying the first four seasons, I find that Dunham had directed a third of all episodes, had single writing credits for ten of forty-two episodes, and is the first woman to have won a Directors Guild of America award for comedy. The only other current media persona of similar influence on a series is Louis C.K., who also writes, directs, stars in, and edits the majority of episodes of *Louie*.

11. Rebecca Carroll, "White Girls, Big City: What HBO's New Show Misses," *Daily Beast*, Apr. 20, 2012, www.thedailybeast.com/articles/2012/04/20/white-girls-big-city what-hbo-s-new-show-misses.html.

12. Dunham's mother is the successful photographer and artist Laurie Simmons (and her father the less-well-known painter Carroll Dunham), Zosia Mamet is the daughter of playwright David Mamet, Allison Williams is the daughter of former *NBC Nightly News* anchor Brian Williams, and Jemima Kirke is the daughter of drummer Simon Kirke of the band Bad Company. One of Dunham's early works explicitly comments on entitlement and nepotism: the web series *De-*

lusional Downtown Divas follows a group of three women who are attempting to "make it" in the New York art world. The short, episodic installments follow the characters as they encounter a successful artist in each episode and attempt to develop strategies to finally achieve the fame they feel they are entitled to.

13. See Anna Holmes, "White *Girls*," *New Yorker*, Apr. 23, 2012, www.new yorker.com/culture/culture-desk/white-girls; Kendra James, "Dear Lena Dunham: I Exist," *Racialicious*, Apr. 19, 2012, www.racialicious.com/2012/04/19 /dear-lena-dunham-i-exist; Jenna Wortham, "Where (My) Girls At?," *The Hairpin*, Apr. 16, 2012, http://thehairpin.com/2012/04/where-my-girls-at.

14. Roxane Gay, *Bad Feminist: Essays* (New York: Harper Perennial, 2014), 56. Overall, academic analysis of this "virtual industry of *Girls* criticism" (Kaklamanidou and Tally 1) is underway; both Nikita Hamilton and Faye Woods productively weed a path through the controversial discourse of TV criticism and feuilleton, while Boké Saisi targets social media discussions. Nikita T. Hamilton, "So They Say You Have a Race Problem? You're in Your Twenties, You Have Way More Problems Than That," in *HBO's Girls: Questions of Gender, Politics, and Millennial Angst*, ed. Betty Kaklamanidou and Margaret Tally (Newcastle upon Tyne: Cambridge Scholars Publishing, 2014), 43–58. Also see Faye Woods, "Girls Talk: Authorship and Authenticity in the Reception of Lena Dunham's *Girls*," *Critical Studies in Television* 10, no. 2 (2015): 37–54; Boké Saisi, "(Just White) Girls? Underrepresentation and Active Audiences in HBO's *Girls*," in Kaklamanidou and Tally, *HBO's Girls*, 59–72.

15. Lena Dunham, "Seeing Nora Everywhere," *New Yorker*, June 28, 2012; Lena Dunham, "Lena Dunham Interviews Gloria Steinem," *Harper's BAZAAR*, Jan. 2015.

16. The sheer number of articles published that discuss *Girls* as either an update to, new version of, or an inferior copy of *Sex and the City* is overwhelming. The show actively encouraged such comparisons as promotional opportunities, for instance, by having *Girls'* character Shoshanna elaborate on her *Sex and the City* fandom.

17. Marcie Bianco, "Hannah's Self-Writing: Satirical Aesthetics, Unfashionable Ethics, and a Poetics of Cruel Optimism," in Kaklamanidou and Tally, *HBO's Girls*, 76.

18. Kaklamanidou and Tally, introduction to *HBO's Girls*, 5.

19. Todd VanDerWerff, "What We Talk about When We Talk about Girls," *TV Club*, Mar. 14, 2013, www.avclub.com/article/what-we-talk-about-when-we-talk -about-igirlsi93685.

20. Gary Susman, "Discomfort Zone: Ten Great Cringe Comedies," *Time*, May 12, 2013, http://entertainment.time.com/2013/05/13/discomfort-zone-10 -great cringecomedies/slide/intro/print.

21. See Brett Mills, "Studying Comedy," in *The Television Genre Book*, ed. Toby Miller et al. (London: BFI, 2011), 62.

22. Georges Didi-Huberman, *Invention of Hysteria: Charcot and the Photographic Iconography of the Salpêtrière*, trans. Alisa Hartz (Cambridge, MA: MIT Press, 2003); see also Christina Wald, *Hysteria, Trauma, and Melancholia: Performative Maladies in Contemporary Anglophone Drama* (New York: Palgrave Macmillan, 2007).

23. Lena Dunham, *Not That Kind of Girl: A Young Woman Tells You What She's "Learned"* (New York: Random House, 2014).

24. Rosalind Gill, *Gender and the Media* (Cambridge, UK: Polity Press, 2007), 3.

25. Linda Mizejewski, *Pretty/Funny: Women Comedians and Body Politics* (Austin: University of Texas Press, 2014), 27–28.

26. Charlotte Brunsdon, "The Feminist in the Kitchen: Martha, Martha, and Nigella" in *Feminism in Popular Culture*, ed. Joanne Hollows and Rachel Moseley (New York: Berg, 2006), 44.

27. Bianco, "Hannah's Self-Writing," 74–75.

28. This is aside from a caricature of a feminist: in the submerged story-within-a-story, the play that Ella is writing and discussing with her friends in *Creative Nonfiction*, the central character, "the girl," is on the run, picked up and aided in her escape by a "radical feminist" who provides her with long, baggy clothing and instructs her to avoid patriarchal institutions like the police.

29. See Lauren J. DeCarvalho, "Hannah and Her Entitled Sisters: (Post)Feminism, (Post)Recession, and *Girls*," *Feminist Media Studies* 13, no. 2 (2013): 367–370; Serena Daalmans, "'I'm Busy Trying to Become Who I Am': Self-Entitlement and the City in HBO's *Girls*," *Feminist Media Studies* 13, no. 2 (2013): 359–362; Katherine Bell, "Obvie, We're the Ladies! Postfeminism, Privilege, and HBO's Newest Girls," *Feminist Media Studies* 13, no. 2 (2013): 363–366.

30. See Soraya Roberts, "Naked if I Want To: Lena Dunham's Body Politic," *Salon*, Feb. 10, 2013, www.salon.com/2013/02/09/naked_if_i_want_to_lena_dunhams_body_politic; Michelle Dean, "'Girls' Whiplash Report: Why, Despite Everything, Lena Dunham's Nudity Is Radical," *Flavorwire*, Jan. 10, 2014, http://flavorwire.com/432925/girls-whiplash-report why-despite-everything-lena - dunhams-nudity-is -radical.

31. Margaret Tally, "Post-Modernity, Emerging Adulthood, and the Exploration of Female Friendships on *Girls*," in Kaklamanidou and Tally, *HBO's Girls*, 31; See also Stefania Marghitu and Conrad Ng, "Body Talk: Reconsidering The Post-feminist Discourse and Critical Reception of Lena Dunham's *Girls*," *Gender Forum*, no. 45 (2013): n.p., www.genderforum.org/issues/special-issue-early-career -researchers-i/body-talk   reconsidering-the-post-feminist-discourse-and-critical -reception-of-lena-dunhams-girls.

32. Alyssa Rosenberg, "Lena Dunham's Looks, the Misogyny of the 'Girls' Backlash, and Staying in Your Assigned Story," *Thinkprogress*, May 29, 2012, http://thinkprogress.org/alyssa/2012/05/29/491372/lena-dunham-girls.

33. Sheila Heti et al., *Women in Clothes* (New York: Blue Rider Press, 2014), 88.

34. Dean, "'Girls' Whiplash."

35. Emily Nussbaum, "It's Different for 'Girls,'" *New Yorker*, Mar. 25, 2012, http://nymag.com/arts/tv/features/girls-lena-dunham-2012-4.

36. Joyce Chen, "Howard Stern Calls Lena Dunham 'Little Fat Girl,' Likens Girls Sex Scenes to 'Rape,'" *US Weekly*, Jan. 12, 2013, www.usmagazine.com /celebrity-news/news/howard-stern-calls-lena-dunham-little-fat-girl-likens-girls -sex-scenes-to-rape-2013121.

37. In one of her early YouTube clips (*The Fountain*), Dunham bathes and

brushes her teeth in a campus water fountain while wearing a bikini. The non-fiction clip was included in *Tiny Furniture*, where Aura shows it to her estranged childhood friend Charlotte as an example of her film work. Charlotte seems more fascinated with the hateful comments viewers of the clip have left, all of which target Aura's body. A similar scenario occurs in *Girls'* fourth season ("She Said OK," episode 3), in which aspiring singer Marnie shows her horrifically bad You-Tube music video to her girlfriends Shoshanna and Hannah. Shoshanna begins to read the comments targeting and objectifying Marnie's body.

38. Tim Molloy, "Judd Apatow and Lena Dunham Get Mad at Me for Asking Why She's Naked So Much on 'Girls'," *The Wrap*, Jan. 9, 2014, www.thewrap.com /judd-apatow-lena-dunham-get-mad-asking-shes-naked-much-girls.

39. See David Haglund and Daniel Engber, "Guys on Girls, Season 2: Was That the Worst Episode of *Girls* Ever?," *Slate*, Feb. 10, 2013, www.slate.com /articles/arts/tv_club/features/2013/girls_season_2/week_5/girls_o_hbo_one _man_s_trash_episode_5_of_season_2_ viewed_by_guys.html; Peter Martin, "The *Girls* Recap for Men: Self-Indulgent Dreaming," *Esquire*, Feb. 10, 2013, www.esquire.com/blogs/culture/girls-season-2-episode-5-recap.

40. Jessica Coen, "We're Offering $10,000 for Unretouched Images of Lena Dunham in Vogue," *Jezebel*, Jan. 16, 2014, http://jezebel.com/were-offering-10 -000-for-unretouched-images-of-lena-d-1502000514; Kelsey Wallace, "Why Jeze-bel Was Wrong to Put a Bounty on Lena Dunham's Photos," *Bitchmedia*, Jan. 20, 2014, https://bitchmedia.org/post/why-jezebel-was-wrong-to put-a-bounty-on -those-lena-dunham-photos; Tracie Egan Morrissey, "Tracy Anderson Is Not Allowed to Transform Lena Dunham's Body . . . Yet," *Jezebel*, Sept. 12, 2013, http://jezebel.com/tracy-anderson-is-not-allowed-to-transform-lena-dunham -1300322086.

41. In a piece for *Glamour* magazine published in February 2015, Dunham lists the ten women who "changed her life": among these are poet and activist Audre Lorde, Shonda Rhimes, Facebook COO Sheryl Sandberg, and transgender activist CeCe McDonald, but she also lists women who are both her friends and conspir-ators, such as Jenni Konner, writer Ashley C. Ford, or the aforementioned Audrey Gelman. "Lena Dunham Opens Up: The Ten Women Who Changed Her Life," *Glamour*, Feb. 17, 2015, www.glamour.com/entertainment/2015/02/lena-dunham -talks-inspiring-women shonda-rhimes-jenni-konner-and-others.

42. During Swift's music video and concert performances, again, Dunham physically stands out from the slim, high-heeled models, musicians, and actresses who also appear as part of Swift's clique or "squad" of friends.

43. Ramin Setoodeh, "How Lena Dunham Is Launching an Empire for Co-medic Women," *Variety*, Apr. 21, 2015, http://variety.com/2015/tv/news/lena -dunham-girls-hbo-production company-girls-a- casual-romance-1201476138.

44. Tally, "Post-Modernity, Emerging Adulthood," 39.

Adams, Sam. "Has Liz Lemon Become 'Dumbass Homer'?" *Slate*, Feb. 10, 2012. www.slate.com/blogs/browbeat/2012/02/10/liz_lemon_and_homer_simpson _is_30_rock_getting_stupider_.html.

Allen, Robert C. *Horrible Prettiness: Burlesque and American Culture*. Chapel Hill: University of North Carolina Press, 1991.

Altman, Rick. *Film Genre*. London: BFI, 1999.

Anderson, Benedict. *Imagined Communities: Reflections on the Origin and Spread of Nationalism*. Rev. ed. London: Verso, 2006.

Anderson, Mark Lynn. "Reading Mabel Normand's Library." *Film History* 18, no. 2 (2006): 209–221.

Anderson, Sam. "Irony Maiden: How Sarah Silverman Is Raping American Comedy." *Slate*, Nov. 10, 2005. www.slate.com/articles/arts/culturebox/2005/11 /irony_maiden.html.

———. "Silent Comediennes and 'The Tragedy of Being Funny.'" In *Researching Women in Silent Cinema: New Findings and Perspectives*, edited by Monica Dall'Asta, Victoria Duckett, and Lucia Tralli, 231–245. Bologna: Dipartimento delle Arti—DAR, Alma Mater Studiorum Università di Bologna, 2013. http:// amsacta.unibo.it/3811.

Andreeva, Nellie. "NBC Eyes 10/90 Order for Roseanne Barr Comedy Co-Written by Linda Wallem." *Deadline Hollywood*, June 28, 2013. www.deadline.com /2013/06/roseanne-barr-comedy-series-order-near-nbc-linda-wallem.

———. "Tina Fey and Robert Carlock's 'Unbreakable Kimmy Schmidt' Moves from NBC to Netflix with 2-Season Pickup." *Deadline*, Nov. 21, 2014. http:// deadline.com/2014/11/unbreakable-kimmy-schmidt-tina-fey-robert-carlock -netflix 2-season-pickup-nbc-1201292254.

Ang, Ien. "Melodramatic Identifications: Television Fiction and Women's Fantasy." In *Television and Women's Culture: The Politics of the Popular*, edited by Mary Ellen Brown, 75–88. London: Sage, 1990.

Anker, Elisabeth R. *Orgies of Feeling: Melodrama and the Politics of Freedom*. Durham, NC: Duke University Press, 2014.

"'Are You A Feminist?': Celebrities' Answers from *BUST* Magazine's Twenty-Two-Year Archive May Surprise You." *BUST*, n.d. http://bust.com/feminism/14540 -are-you-a-feminist-celebrity-answers-from-bust magazine-s-22-year-archive -may-surprise-you.html.

Arnold, Roseanne. *Roseanne: My Lives*. London: Century, 1994.

Arthurs, Jane. "Revolting Women: The Body in Comic Performance." In *Women's Bodies: Discipline and Transgression*, edited by Jane Arthurs and Jean Grimshaw, 137–164. London: Cassell, 1999.

———. "*Sex and the City* and Consumer Culture: Remediating Postfeminist Drama." In *Television: The Critical View*, edited by Horace Newcomb, 7th ed., 315–331. New York: Oxford University Press, 2007.

Bacalzo, Dan. "The One That She Wants: Margaret Cho, Mediatization, and Autobiographical Performance." In *Embodying Asian American Sexualities*, edited by Gina Masequesmay and Sean Metzger, 43–50. Lanham, MD: Lexington Books, 2009.

Bakhtin, Mikhail. *Rabelais and His World* (1965). Translated by Hélène Iswolsky. Bloomington: Indiana University Press, 1984.

Banks, Miranda J. "I Love Lucy: The Writer-Producer." In *How to Watch Television*, edited by Ethan Thompson and Jason Mittell, 244–252. New York: NYU Press, 2013.

Banner, Lois. *American Beauty*. Chicago: University of Chicago Press, 1984.

Barnes, Brooks. "Easy, Breezy, Trending: Ellen DeGeneres, TV and Twitter Hit, Ready to Host Oscars." *New York Times*, Jan. 17, 2014. www.nytimes.com /2014/01/19/arts/television/ellen-degeneres-tv-and-twitter-hit-ready-to-host -oscars.html?_r=1.

Barr, Roseanne. *Roseanne: My Life as a Woman*. New York: Harper and Row, 1989.

———. *Roseannearchy: Dispatches from the Nut Farm*. New York: Gallery Books, 2011.

Barreca, Regina, ed. *Last Laughs: Perspectives on Women and Comedy*. New York: Gordon and Breach, 1988.

———, ed. *New Perspectives on Women and Comedy*. New York: Gordon and Breach, 1992.

———. *They Used to Call Me Snow White . . . But I Drifted: Women's Strategic Use of Humor*. New York: Viking, 1991.

Bartlett, Randolph. "Would You Have Ever Suspected It? *Photoplay* 14, no. 3 (Aug. 1918): 43–44.

"Beauty into Buffoon." *Life*, Feb. 1952, 93–97.

"Behind the Laughter of Jackie 'Moms' Mabley." *Ebony*, Aug. 1962, 89–91.

Bell, Elizabeth. "Somatexts at the Disney Shop: Constructing the Pentimentos of Women's Animated Bodies." In *From Mouse to Mermaid: The Politics of Film, Gender, and Culture*, edited by Elizabeth Bell, Lynda Haas, and Laura Sells, 107–124. Bloomington: Indiana University Press, 1995.

Bell, Katherine. "Obvie, We're the Ladies! Postfeminism, Privilege, and HBO's Newest Girls." *Feminist Media Studies* 13, no. 2 (2013): 363–366.

Berg, A. Scott. *Goldwyn: A Biography*. New York: Ballantine Books, 1989.

Bergson, Henri. *Laughter: An Essay on the Meaning of the Comic*. Translated by Cloudesley Brereton and Fred Rothwell. Boston: IndyPublish, 2008; and Rockville, MD: Arc Manor, 2008.

Berlant, Lauren Gail. *Cruel Optimism*. Durham, NC: Duke University Press, 2011.

———, and Michael Warner. "Sex in Public." *Critical Inquiry* 24, no. 2 (1998): 547–566.

Bianco, Marcie. "Hannah's Self-Writing: Satirical Aesthetics, Unfashionable Ethics, and a Poetics of Cruel Optimism." In Kaklamanidou and Tally, *HBO's Girls: Questions of Gender, Politics, and Millennial Angst*, 73–90.

Birmingham, Frederic. "A Carol Is a Song Is a Burnett." *Saturday Evening Post*, Sept. 1976, 54+.

Bogle, Donald. *Toms, Coons, Mulattoes, Mammies, and Bucks: An Interpretative History of Blacks in American Films.* 1st. ed. New York: Viking Press, 1973; 3rd ed. London: Continuum International, 1996.

Brady, Kathleen. *Lucille: The Life of Lucille Ball.* New York: Billboard Books, 2001.

Breuer, Josef, and Sigmund Freud. *Studies on Hysteria* (1895). Translated and edited by James Strachey. New York: Basic Books, 1957.

Brevard, Lisa Pertillar. *Whoopi Goldberg on Stage and Screen.* Jefferson, NC: Mc-Farland, 2013.

Brewster, Eugene V. "The Coming Screen Year." *Motion Picture Classic,* Oct. 1925, 27.

Brodkey, Harold. "Why Is This Woman Funny?" *Esquire,* June 1972, 122+.

Brooks, Peter. *The Melodramatic Imagination: Balzac, Henry James, Melodrama, and the Mode of Excess.* New Haven, CT: Yale University Press, 1976.

Brooks Olsen, Hanna. "A Leslie Knope in a World Full of Liz Lemons." *Medium,* Jan. 22, 2015. https://medium.com/@mshannabrooks/a-leslie-knope-in-a-world -full-of-liz-lemons-61726b6c6493#.yf0uhjoa5.

Brown, Mary Ellen. *Soap Opera and Women's Talk: The Pleasure of Resistance.* Thousand Oaks, CA: Sage, 1994.

Brunsdon, Charlotte. "The Feminist in the Kitchen: Martha, Martha, and Nigella." In *Feminism in Popular Culture,* edited by Joanne Hollows and Rachel Moseley, 41–56. New York: Berg, 2006.

———. *Screen Tastes: Soap Opera to Satellite Dishes.* London: Routledge, 1997.

Burnett, Carol. *Carrie and Me: A Mother-Daughter Love Story.* New York: Simon and Schuster, 2011.

———. *One More Time: A Memoir.* New York: Random House, 1986. Reprinted by Random House Trade Paperbacks, 2003.

———. *This Time Together: Laughter and Reflection.* New York: Three Rivers, 2010.

Butler, Jeremy G. *Television Style.* New York: Routledge, 2010.

Butler, Judith. *Precarious Life: The Powers of Mourning and Violence.* London: Verso, 2004.

Camp, David. "Why Late Night Comedy Is Better Than Ever." *Vanity Fair,* Oct. 2015.

"Carol Burnett: The Fresh Air Interview." *Fresh Air.* NPR, Nov. 15, 2013.

"Carol Burnett: The Kennedy Center Mark Twain Prize." PBS, Nov. 24, 2013.

Carroll, Jeffrey. "Margaret Cho, Jake Shimabukuro, and Rhetorics in a Minor Key." In *Representations: Doing Asian American Rhetoric,* edited by Luming Mao and Morris Young, 266–278. Logan: Utah State University Press, 2008.

Carroll, Rebecca. "White Girls, Big City: What HBO's New Show Misses." *Daily Beast,* Apr. 20, 2012. www.thedailybeast.com/articles/2012/04/20/white-girls -big-city what-hbo-s-new-show-misses.html.

Castells, Manuel. *Communication Power.* Oxford: Oxford University Press, 2009.

Castelluccio, Frank, and Alvin Walker. *The Other Side of Ethel Mertz: The Life Story of Vivian Vance.* Manchester, CT: Knowledge, Ideas & Trends, 1998.

Chen, Joyce. "Howard Stern Calls Lena Dunham 'Little Fat Girl,' Likens *Girls* Sex Scenes to 'Rape.'" *US Weekly,* Jan. 12, 2013. www.usmagazine.com

/celebrity-news/news/howard-stern-calls-lena-dunham-little-fat-girl-likens
-girls-sex-scenes-to-rape-2013121.

Cho, Margaret. "Aroma Smells Like Bigotry." *Margaret Cho: Blog*, Mar. 25, 2013. http://margaretcho.com/2013/03/25/aroma-smells-like-bigotry.

———. *Assassin*. Directed by Kerry Asmussen. Cho Taussig Productions, 2005. Video.

———. *Beautiful*. Directed by Lorene Machado. Clownery Productions, 2009. Video.

———. *Drunk with Power*. San Francisco: Uproar, 1996. Audio recording.

———. *I Have Chosen to Stay and Fight*. New York: Penguin, 2005.

———. *I'm the One That I Want*. New York: Ballantine Books, 2001.

———. "Introduction: The Kindness of Gay Men." In *Out on the Edge: America's Rebel Comics*, edited by Mike Player, 1–2. New York: Alyson Books, 2008.

———. "Margaret Cho: Bio." http://margaretcho.com/bio. Accessed June 12, 2014.

———. "Margaret Cho Talks about Her Pride in Being Called a 'Queer Icon,' in Light of Michelle Shocked's Anti-gay Rant." *xoJane*, Mar. 21, 2013. www .xojane.com/issues/margaret-cho-talks-about-her-pride-in-being-called a-queer -icon-in-light-of-michelle-shockeds-anti-gay-rant.

———. *Notorious C.H.O.* Directed by Lorene Machado. Wellspring Media, 2002. Video.

———. *Revolution*. Directed by Lorene Machado. Wellspring Media, 2004. Video.

Cixous, Helene. "The Laugh of the Medusa." Translated by Keith Cohen and Paula Cohen. *Signs* 1, no. 4 (Summer 1976): 875–893.

———, and Catherine Clément. *The Newly Born Woman (La Jeune Née)* (1975). Translated by Betsy Wing. Minneapolis: University of Minnesota Press, 1986.

Clark, Danae. "Commodity Lesbianism." In *The Lesbian and Gay Studies Reader*, edited by Henry Abelove, Michèle Aina Barale, and David M. Halperin, 186–201. New York: Routledge, 1993.

Coates, Tyler. "Tina Fey and Race: 'Unbreakable Kimmy Schmidt' Has a Straight, White Male Problem." *Decider*, Mar. 10, 2015. http://decider.com/2015/03/10/ tina-fey-race unbreakable-kimmy-schmidt.

Coen, Jessica. "We're Offering $10,000 for Unretouched Images of Lena Dunham in Vogue." *Jezebel*, Jan. 16, 2014. http://jezebel.com/were-offering-10–000-for -unretouched-images-of-lena-d-1502000514.

Collins, Patricia Hill. *Black Feminist Thought: Knowledge, Consciousness, and the Politics of Empowerment*. New York: Routledge, 2000.

Crenshaw, Kimberle. "Intersectionality: The Double Bind of Race and Gender." *Perspectives* magazine, 2004, 2.

Curry, Ramona. "Mae West and Film Censorship." In Karnick and Jenkins, *Classical Hollywood Comedy*, 211–237.

———. *Too Much of a Good Thing: Mae West as Cultural Icon*. Minneapolis: University of Minnesota Press, 1996.

Daalmans, Serena. "'I'm Busy Trying to Become Who I Am': Self-Entitlement and the City in HBO's *Girls*." *Feminist Media Studies* 13, no. 2 (2013): 359–362.

Dale, Joshua Paul, Joyce Goggin, Julia Leyda, Anthony P. McIntyre, and Diane

Negra. "The Aesthetics and Affects of Cuteness." In *The Aesthetics and Affects of Cuteness*, edited by Joshua Paul Dale et al., 1–34. New York: Routledge, 2017.

Dean, Michelle. "'Girls' Whiplash Report: Why, Despite Everything, Lena Dunham's Nudity Is Radical." *Flavorwire*, Jan. 10, 2014. http://flavorwire .com/432925/girls-whiplash-report why-despite-everything-lena- dunhams -nudity-is-radical.

DeCarvalho, Lauren J. "Hannah and Her Entitled Sisters: (Post)Feminism, (Post) Recession, and *Girls*." *Feminist Media Studies* 13, no. 2 (2013): 367–370.

Deleuze, Gilles, and Félix Guattari. *Kafka: Toward a Minor Literature.* Minneapolis: University of Minnesota Press, 1986.

Denny, Margaret. "How Fay Tincher Regards Her Profession." *Motion Picture Magazine*, Aug. 1916, 77–80.

Deuze, Mark. *Media Work.* Malden, MA: Polity Press, 2007.

Devereux, Cecily. "Hysteria, Feminism, and Gender Revisited: The Case of the Second Wave." *English Studies in Canada* 40, no. 1 (2014): 19–45.

Dickinson, Peter, et al., eds. *Women and Comedy.* Lanham, MD: Fairleigh Dickinson University Press, 2013.

Didi-Huberman, Georges. *Invention of Hysteria: Charcot and the Photographic Iconography of the Salpêtrière.* Translated by Alisa Hartz. Cambridge, MA: MIT Press, 2003.

Dolan, Jill. "'Finding Our Feet in the Shoes of (One An) Other': Multiple Character Solo Performers and Utopian Performatives." *Modern Drama* 45, no. 4 (Winter 2002): 495–518.

Doty, Alexander. "The Cabinet of Lucy Ricardo: Lucille Ball's Star Image." *Cinema Journal* 29 (1990): 3–22.

Doyle, Billy H. *The Ultimate Directory of the Silent Screen Performers: A Necrology of Births and Deaths and Essays on Fifty Lost Players.* Metuchen, NJ: Scarecrow Press, 1995.

Doyle, Sadie. "Thirteen Ways of Looking at Liz Lemon." *Tiger Beatdown*, Mar. 24, 2010. http://tigerbeatdown.com/2010/03/24/13-ways-of-looking-at-liz-lemon.

Duberman, Amanda. "Amy Poehler on Celebrity Feminism Conversation: It's an 'Attempt to Get Us to Talk Sh*t about Each Other.'" *Huffington Post*, Oct. 28, 2014. www.huffingtonpost.com/2014/10/28/amy-poehler-feminismcelebrity_n _6064350.html.

Duggan, Lisa. *The Twilight of Equality? Neoliberalism, Cultural Politics, and the Attack on Democracy.* New York: Beacon Press, 2003.

Dunham, Lena. "Lena Dunham Interviews Gloria Steinem." *Harper's BAZAAR*, Jan. 2015. www.harpersbazaar.com/culture/features/a12838/lena-dunham-glo ria-steinem interview-1215.

———. "Lena Dunham Opens Up: The Ten Women Who Changed Her Life." *Glamour*, Feb. 17, 2015. www.glamour.com/entertainment/2015/02/lena-dun ham-talks-inspiring-women shonda-rhimes-jenni-konner-and-others.

———. *Not That Kind of Girl: A Young Woman Tells You What She's "Learned."* New York: Random House, 2014.

———. "Seeing Nora Everywhere." *New Yorker*, June 28, 2012. www.newyorker .com/culture/culture-desk/seeing-nora-everywhere.

Duralde, Alonso. "Thoroughly Modern Lily." *Advocate*, Mar. 15, 2005, 56–59.

Dworkin, Susan. "Carol Burnett: Getting On with It." *Ms.* 12, no. 3 (Sept. 1983): 43+.

Dyer, Richard. *Heavenly Bodies: Film Stars and Society*. 2nd ed. London: Routledge, 2004.

———. *Stars*. London: BFI, 1998.

———. *White*. London: Routledge, 1997.

Ehrbar, Ned. "Stop Asking Tina Fey If Women Are Funny." *Metro*, Mar. 2, 2016.

Engstrom, Erika. "'Knope We Can!': Primetime Feminist Strategies in NBC's *Parks and Recreation*." *Media Report to Women* 41, no. 4 (Fall 2013): 6–21.

Ephron, Nora. "Carol Burnett, Cockeyed Optimist." *Good Housekeeping*, Oct. 1968, 68+.

Esther, John. "The Incredible Never-Shrinking Lily Tomlin." *Lesbian News* 28, no. 12 (July 2003): 26–27.

Ewen, Stuart. *Captains of Consciousness: Advertising and the Social Roots of the Consumer Culture*. New York: McGraw Hill, 1976.

Fairclough, Kirsty. "Nothing Less Than Perfect: Female Celebrity, Ageing, and Hyper-scrutiny in the Gossip Industry." *Celebrity Studies* 3, no. 1 (2012): 90–103.

Fallon, Kevin. "Sarah and Susan Silverman: Comedian and Rabbi Are Perfect Sisters." *Daily Beast*, Mar. 31, 2014. www.thedailybeast.com/articles/2014/03/31/sarah-and-susan-silverman-comedian-and-rabbi-are-perfect-sisters.html.

"Fay Tincher—An Ingenuish Vampire." *Theatre Magazine*, June 1919.

Feuer, Jane, Paul Kerr, and Tise Vahimagi, eds. *MTM: "Quality Television."* London: BFI, 1984.

Fey, Tina. *Bossypants*. 1st ed. New York: Little, Brown, 2011.

Finney, Gail, ed. *Look Who's Laughing: Gender and Comedy*. New York: Gordon and Breach, 1994.

Fox, Jesse David. "The History of Tina Fey and Amy Poehler's Best Friendship [Significantly Updated]." *Vulture*, Jan. 8, 2015. www.vulture.com/2013/01/history-of-tina-and-amys-best-friendship.html.

Freed, Rosanne. "The Gripes of Wrath: Roseanne's Bitter Comedy of Class." *Television Quarterly* 30, no. 2 (Fall 1999): 90–99.

Freedman, Jonathan. "Transformations of a Jewish Princess: Salomé and the Remaking of the Jewish Female Body from Sarah Bernhardt to Betty Boop." *Philological Quarterly* 92, no. 1 (Winter 2013): 89–114.

Freud, Sigmund. *Jokes and Their Relation to the Unconscious* (1905). Translated by James Strachey. New York: Norton, 1963.

———. "The Uncanny." In *The Collected Papers of Sigmund Freud*. 10 vols. Edited by Philip Rieff, translated by Alix Strachey, 10:19–60. New York: Collier, 1963.

Fussell, Betty Harper. *Mabel: The Life of Mabel Normand*. New York: Limelight Editions, 1992.

Gassaway, Gordon. "Where Are the Funny Girls?" *Picture-Play* magazine 18, no. 4 (June 1923): 4–44, 86.

Gay, Roxane. *Bad Feminist: Essays*. New York: Harper Perennial, 2014.

Genette, Gérard. *Paratexts: Thresholds of Interpretation*. Translated by Jane E. Lewin. Cambridge, UK: Cambridge University Press, 1997.

Genz, Stephanie. "Under the Knife: Feminism and Cosmetic Surgery in Contemporary Culture." In *Women on Screen: Feminism and Femininity in Visual Culture*, edited by Melanie Waters, 123–135. Basingstoke, UK: Palgrave Macmillan, 2011.

Gilbert, Joanne R. *Performing Marginality: Humor, Gender, and Cultural Critique*. Detroit: Wayne State University Press, 2004.

Gill, Rosalind. *Gender and the Media*. Cambridge, UK: Polity Press, 2007.

———, and Christina Scharff. Introduction to *New Femininities: Postfeminism, Neoliberalism, and Subjectivity*, edited by Rosalind Gill and Christina Scharff, 1–17. London: Palgrave Macmillan, 2011.

Gilman, Sander, ed. "The Image of the Hysteric." In *Hysteria Beyond Freud*, 345–452. Berkeley: University of California Press, 1993.

Gilson, Erinn. *The Ethics of Vulnerability: A Feminist Analysis of Social Life and Practice*. New York: Routledge, 2014.

———. "Vulnerability, Ignorance, and Oppression." *Hypatia* 26, no. 2 (2011): 308–332.

Gledhill, Christine. "The Melodramatic Field: An Investigation." In *Home Is Where the Heart Is: Studies in Melodrama and the Woman's Film*, edited by Christine Gledhill, 5–39. London: British Film Institute, 1987.

———. "Rethinking Genre." In *Reinventing Film Studies*, eds. Linda Williams and Christine Gledhill, 221–243. London: Edward Arnold, 2000.

Glenn, Susan. *Female Spectacle: The Theatrical Roots of Modern Feminism*. Cambridge, MA: Harvard University Press, 2000.

Goldberg, Whoopi. *Book*. New York: R Weisbach Books, 1997.

———, dir. *Moms Mabley: I Got Somethin' to Tell You*. Whoop/One Ho Productions, 2013. Film.

Gray, Frances. *Women and Laughter*. Charlottesville: University of Virginia Press, 1994.

Gray, Jonathan. *Show Sold Separately: Promos, Spoilers, and Other Media Paratexts*. New York: NYU Press, 2010.

Griffin, Molly Marie. "How Tina Fey Ousted Carrie Bradshaw." *Salon*, May 20, 2010. www.salon.com/2010/05/20/tina_fey_recession_americas_carrie_bradshaw.

Griffith, Linda A. "The Comments and Criticisms of a Free-Lance, Re-enter Miss Normand." *Film Fun* 349 (May 1918): 11.

Grimm, David. *Citizen Canine: Our Evolving Relationship with Cats and Dogs*. New York: Public Affairs, 2014.

Gross, Terry. "Sarah Silverman: Turning Ignorance into Comedy." *Fresh Air*. NPR, July 15, 2011.

Grossman, Andrew. "Fay Tincher." *Senses of Cinema* 23 (Dec. 2002). www.sensesofcinema.com/contents/02/23/symposium3.html.

Grossman, Barbara. *Funny Woman: The Life and Times of Fanny Brice*. Bloomington: Indiana University Press, 1991.

Haggins, Bambi. *Laughing Mad: The Black Comic Persona in Post-Soul America*. New Brunswick, NJ: Rutgers University Press, 2007.

Haglund, David, and Daniel Engber. "Guys on Girls, Season 2: Was That the Worst Episode of *Girls* Ever?" *Slate*, Feb. 10, 2013. www.slate.com/articles/arts/tv_club/features/2013/girls_season_2/week_5/girls_o_hbo_one_man_s_trash_episode_5_of_season_2_viewed_by_guys.html.

Haiken, Elizabeth. "The Making of the Modern Face: Cosmetic Surgery." *Social Research* 67, no. 1 (Spring 2000): 81–97.

Halberstam, Judith. *Female Masculinity*. Durham, NC: Duke University Press, 1998.

Hamilton, Marybeth. *"When I'm Bad, I'm Better": Mae West, Sex, and American Entertainment*. Berkeley: University of California Press, 1997.

Hamilton, Nikita T. "So They Say You Have a Race Problem? You're in Your Twenties, You Have Way More Problems Than That." In Kaklamanidou and Tally, *HBO's Girls: Questions of Gender, Politics, and Millennial Angst*, 43–58.

Hansen, Miriam. "Adventures of Goldilocks: Spectatorship, Consumerism, and Public Life." *Camera Obscura* 8, no. 1 (1990): 50–72.

Haraway, Donna Jeanne. *When Species Meet*. Minneapolis: University of Minnesota Press, 2008.

Harris, Daniel. *Cute, Quaint, Hungry, and Romantic: The Aesthetics of Consumerism*. New York: Basic Books, 2000.

Harris, Geraldine. *Beyond Representation: Television Drama and the Politics and Aesthetics of Identity*. Manchester, UK: Manchester University Press, 2011.

Harrison, Louis Reeves. "The Love Pirate, A Two-Reel Reliance Presenting Woman's Character from a Utilitarian Standpoint." *Moving Picture World*, Feb. 13, 1915, n.p.

Harvie, Ian. "Funny Boi." In *Out on the Edge: America's Rebel Comics*, edited by Mike Player. New York: Alyson Books, 2008.

Havas, Julia. "What's in a Burp? Therapeutic Gross-out Humour in *Unbreakable Kimmy Schmidt*." *CST Online*, June 30, 2016. http://cstonline.tv/kimmy-schmidt.

Havemann, Ernest. "Only Girl Who Acts with Her Back and Front, Too: Carol Burnett." *Life*, Feb. 22, 1963, 85+.

Heap, Chad. *Slumming: Sexual and Racial Encounters in American Nightlife, 1885–1940*. Chicago: University of Chicago Press, 2010.

Heffernan, Virginia. "Anchor Woman." *New Yorker*, Mar. 11, 2003. www.newyorker.com/magazine/2003/11/03/anchor-woman.

Heti, Sheila, Heidi Julavits, Leanne Shapton, and 639 Others. *Women in Clothes*. New York: Blue Rider Press, 2014.

"Hey Dummies: An Evening with the *30 Rock* Writers." *The Paley Center for Media*, Feb. 27, 2013. www.paleycenter.org/2013-spring-hey-dummies-an-evening-with-the-30-rock writers.

Higashi, Sumiko. "The New Woman and Consumer Culture." In *The Silent Cinema Reader*, edited by Lee Grieveson and Peter Kramer, 305–317. London: Routledge, 2004.

Hitchens, Christopher. "Why Women Aren't Funny." *Vanity Fair*. Jan. 2007.

Hogan, Kate. "Creating the Lesbian Mammy: Boys on the Side and the Politics of AIDS." *Women's Studies Quarterly* 30 (Spring/Summer 2002): 88–102.

Hollinger, Karen. *In the Company of Women: Contemporary Female Friendship Films*. Minneapolis: University of Minnesota Press, 1998.

Holmes, Anna. "White 'Girls'." *New Yorker*, Apr. 23, 2012. www.newyorker.com/culture/culture-desk/white-girls.

Holmes, Linda. "The Incredible Shrinking Liz Lemon: From Woman to Little Girl."

NPR, Feb. 9, 2012. www.npr.org/sections/monkeysee/2012/02/09/146626983 /the-incredible-shrinking-liz-lemon-from-woman-to-little-girl.

Holmlund, Chris. *Impossible Bodies: Femininity and Masculinity at the Movies.* London: Routledge, 2002.

Hone, Liana S. E., William Hurwitz, and Debra Lieberman. "Sex Differences in Preferences for Humor." *Evolutionary Psychology,* Feb. 10, 2015.

hooks, bell. *Black Looks.* Boston: South End Press, 1992.

Hopper, De Wolf. *Reminiscences of De Wolf Hopper: Once a Clown, Always a Clown.* Boston: Little Brown, 1927.

Horowitz, Susan. *Queens of Comedy: Lucille Ball, Phyllis Diller, Carol Burnett, Joan Rivers, and the New Generation of Funny Women.* London: Routledge, 1997.

Horst, Carole. "Organically Grown Woes." *Variety,* Oct. 22, 2013, 47–48.

Hosey, Sara. "Canaries and Coalmines: Toxic Discourse in *The Incredible Shrinking Woman* and *Safe.*" *Feminist Formations* 23, no. 2 (Summer 2011): 77–97.

Hughes, Langston. "When the Negro Was in Vogue." In *The Collected Works of Langston Hughes,* vol. 13. Edited by Joseph McLaren. Columbia: University of Missouri Press, 2002.

Hunt, Darnell. "Writers Guild of America/WGAW 2015 TV Staffing Brief." WGAW.org, Aug. 20, 2015. www.wga.org/.../who_we.../tvstaffingbrief2015.pdf.

Hurston, Zora Neale. "The Characteristics of Negro Expression" (1934). In *"Sweat,"* edited by Cheryl A. Wall, 55–72. New Brunswick, NJ: Rutgers University Press, 1997.

Hutcheon, Linda. *The Politics of Postmodernism.* 2nd ed. New York: Routledge, 1989.

Illouz, Eva. *Why Love Hurts: A Sociological Explanation.* Cambridge, UK: Polity, 2012.

"Immortalizing Andy." *Picture-Play* magazine 12, no. 6 (Aug. 1925): 99.

"The Independent Woman." *United States of Television: America in Primetime.* BBC 2013, season 1, episode 3.

Jacobs, Lea. *The Decline of Sentiment: American Film in the 1920s.* Berkeley: University of California Press, 2008.

James, Kendra. "Dear Lena Dunham: I Exist." *Racialicious,* Apr. 19, 2012. www .racialicious.com/2012/04/19/dear-lena-dunham-i-exist.

Jenkins, Henry. *What Made Pistachio Nuts? Early Sound Comedy and the Vaudeville Aesthetic.* New York: Columbia University Press, 1992.

Johnson, Julian. "Close-Ups." *Photoplay* 8, no. 5 (Oct. 1915): 105.

———. "The Shadow Stage." *Photoplay* 9, no. 4 (Mar. 1916): 110.

———. "The Shadow Stage." *Photoplay* 10, no. 4 (Sept. 1916): 122.

Kaklamanidou, Betty, and Margaret Tally. Introduction to *HBO's Girls: Questions of Gender, Politics, and Millennial Angst.* Edited by Betty Kaklamanidou and Margaret Tally, 1–9. Newcastle upon Tyne: Cambridge Scholars, 2014.

Kanfer, Stefan. *Ball of Fire: The Tumultuous Life and Comic Art of Lucille Ball.* New York: Knopf, 2003.

Karlyn, Kathleen Rowe. "Feminism in the Classroom: Teaching Towards the Third Wave." In *Feminism in Popular Culture,* edited by Joanne Hollows and Rachel Moseley, 57–75. Oxford: Berg, 2006.

———. "Roseanne: Unruly Woman as Domestic Goddess." In *Critiquing the Sit-*

com: A Reader, edited by Joanne Morreale, 251–261. Syracuse, NY: Syracuse University Press, 2003.

———. *Unruly Girls, Unrepentant Mothers: Redefining Feminism on Screen.* Austin: University of Texas Press, 2010.

Karnick, Kristine Brunovska, and Henry Jenkins, eds. *Classical Hollywood Comedy.* New York: Routledge, 1995.

Katkov, Norman. *The Fabulous Fanny: The Story of Fanny Brice.* New York: Knopf, 1953.

Katz, Lee Michael. "Funny Girl." *Washingtonian*, June 11, 2010. www.washing tonian.com/articles/people/funny-girl.

Kelleter, Frank, ed. *Populäre Serialität: Narration—Evolution—Distinktion: Zum seriellen Erzählen seit dem 19. Jahrhundert.* Bielefeld, Germany: Transcript, 2012.

Kellner, Douglas. "Cultural Studies, Multiculturalism, and Media Culture." In *Gender, Race, and Class in Media: A Critical Reader*, edited by Gail Dines and Jean M. Humez, 7–18. Thousand Oaks, CA: Sage, 2011.

Kelly, Lisa W. "For Us, By Us? Gender, Privilege, and Race in HBO's *Girls*." *CST Online*, 2013. http://cstonline.tv/for-us-by-us-gender-privilege-race.

Khazan, Olga. "Plight of the Funny Female." *Atlantic*, Nov. 19, 2015.

Kibler, M. Alison. *Rank Ladies: Gender and Cultural Hierarchy in American Vaudeville.* Chapel Hill: University of North Carolina Press, 1999.

King, Rob. *The Fun Factory: The Keystone Film Factory and the Emergence of Mass Culture.* Berkeley: University of California Press, 2009.

Kissling, Elizabeth Arveda. "On the Rag on Screen: Menarche in Film and Television." *Sex Roles* 46, nos. 1/2 (Jan. 2002): 5–12.

Kline, Wendy. *Building a Better Race: Gender, Sexuality, and Eugenics from the Turn of the Century to the Baby Boom.* Berkeley: University of California Press, 2005.

Koestler, Arthur. *The Act of Creation.* New York: Macmillan, 1964.

Kohen, Yael. *We Killed: The Rise of Women in American Comedy.* New York: Sarah Crichton Books, 2012.

Kramer, Gary M., ed., *Independent Queer Cinema: Reviews and Interviews.* New York: Harrington Park Press, 2006.

Krefting, Rebecca. *All Joking Aside: American Humor and Its Discontents.* Baltimore: Johns Hopkins University Press, 2014.

Lahr, John. "Dealing with Roseanne." *New Yorker*, July 17, 1995, 42–61.

Lahue, Kalton C., and Samuel Gill. "Fay Tincher." In *Clown Princes and Court Jesters.* London: Thomas Yoseloff, 1970.

Landay, Lori. *I Love Lucy.* Detroit: Wayne State University Press, 2010.

———. "*I Love Lucy*, Television, and Gender in Postwar Domestic Ideology." In *The Sitcom Reader: America Viewed and Skewed*, edited by Mary M. Dalton and Laura R. Linder, 87–97. Albany: SUNY Press, 2005.

———. *Madcaps, Screwballs, and Con Women: The Female Trickster in American Culture.* Philadelphia: University of Pennsylvania Press, 1998.

Langer, John. "Television's 'Personality System.'" *Media, Culture & Society* 4 (1981): 351–365.

Latham, Angela J. *Posing a Threat: Flappers, Chorus Girls, and Other Brazen Per-

formers of the American 1920s. Hanover, NH: University Press of New England, 2000.

Lauzen, Martha. "The Funny Business of Being Tina Fey: Constructing a (Feminist) Comedy Icon." *Feminist Media Studies* 14, no. 1 (2014): 106–117. doi: 10.1080/14680777.2012.740060.

Lavin, Suzanne. *Women and Comedy in Solo Performance.* New York: Routledge, 2004.

Lavitt, Pamela Brown. "First of the Red Hot Mamas: 'Coon Shouting' and the Jewish Ziegfeld Girl." *American Jewish History* 87, no. 4 (Dec. 1999): 253–290.

Lee, Janet. "Subversive Sitcoms: *Roseanne* as Inspiration for Feminist Resistance." In *Gender, Race, and Class in Media: A Text-Reader,* edited by Gail Dines and Jean M. Humez, 469–475. London: Sage, 1995.

Lee, Judith Yaross. *Twain's Brand: Humor in Contemporary American Culture.* Jackson: University Press of Mississippi, 2012.

Leitch, Will. "Animal Magnetism." *NYMag.com,* Apr. 11, 2010. http://nymag.com/arts/books/features/65351.

Lentz, Kirsten Marthe. "Quality versus Relevance: Feminism, Race, and the Politics of the Sign in 1970s Television." *Camera Obscura* (2000) 15 (1 43): 45–93. doi:10.1215/02705346-15-1.

Lewis, Paul. "Beyond Empathy: Sarah Silverman and the Limits of Comedy." *Tikkun* 22, no. 5 (2007): 88–89.

Lieber, Leslie. "Lucy's Ready-Made Faces." *L.A. Times This Week Magazine,* May 1954.

"Lily . . . Ernestine . . . Tess . . . Lupe . . . Edith Ann . . ." *Time,* March 28, 1977, 68.

Little, Judy. *Comedy and the Woman Writer: Woolf, Spark, and Feminism.* Lincoln: University of Nebraska Press, 1983.

Lloyd, John. "Let Fay Try It!" *Photoplay* 10, no. 1 (June 1916): 53–56.

Loos, Anita. *Cast of Thousands.* New York: Grosset and Dunlap, 1977.

Lott, Eric. *Love and Theft: Blackface Minstrelsy and the American Working Class.* New York: Oxford University Press, 1993.

Lotz, Amanda D. *Cable Guys: Television and Masculinities in the Twenty-First Century.* New York: NYU Press, 2014.

Louvish, Simon. *Mae West: It Ain't No Sin.* New York: St. Martin's Griffin, 2007.

Lovece, Frank. "Sarah Silverman Gives Voice to Disney Girl in 'Wreck-It Ralph.'" *Newsday,* Oct. 24, 2012. www.newsday.com/entertainment/movies/sarah-silverman-gives-voice-to-disney-girl-in-wreck-it-ralph-1.4145392.

Lowe, Lisa. *Immigrant Acts: On Asian American Cultural Politics.* Durham, NC: Duke University Press, 1996.

Lusk, Norbert. "The Girl on the Cover: Mabel Normand Discloses a New Plan for Making Magnates Laugh." *Picture-Play,* Feb. 1918.

Macdonald, Myra. *Representing Women: Myths of Femininity in the Popular Media.* London: Edward Arnold, 1995.

Mack, Grace Lee. "The Girl Who Put Stripes in Comedy." *Photoplay* 15, no. 6 (June 1919): 37.

Mahar, Karen Ward. *Women Filmmakers in Early Hollywood.* Baltimore: Johns Hopkins University Press, 2006.

Marantz, Andrew. "Ready for Prime Time: After Twenty-Five Years as a Road Comic, Leslie Jones Becomes a Star." *New Yorker*, Jan. 4, 2016.

Marc, David. "Carol Burnett: The Last of the Big-Time Comedy-Variety Stars." *Quarterly Review of Film and Video* 14, nos. 1–2 (1992): 149–156.

"Margaret Cho, Jeffrey Ross, Richard Lewis and Kamail Nanjiani." *The Green Room with Paul Provenza*, season 2, episode 5, Aug. 11, 2011. www.youtube .com/watch?v=bmr1khDeah4.

Marghitu, Stefania, and Conrad Ng. "Body Talk: Reconsidering the Post-feminist Discourse and Critical Reception of Lena Dunham's *Girls*." *Gender Forum*, no. 45 (2013): n.p. www.genderforum.org/issues/special-issue-early-career-re searchers-i/body-talk reconsidering-the-post-feminist-discourse-and-critical -reception-of-lena-dunhams-girls.

Marshall, Garry, with Lori Marshall. *Wake Me When It's Funny: How to Break into Show Business and Stay*. New York: HarperCollins, 1997.

Marshall, P. David. "The Promotion and Presentation of the Self: Celebrity as Marker of Presentational Media." *Celebrity Studies* 1, no. 1 (2010): 35–48.

———. "Seriality and Persona." *M/C Journal* [online] 17, no. 3 (June 11, 2014): n.p. http://journal.media-culture.org.au/index.php/mcjournal/article/viewArticle /802.

Martin, Emily. *Flexible Bodies: Tracking Immunity in American Culture—From the Days of Polio to the Age of AIDS*. Boston: Beacon Press, 1994.

Martin, Pete. "Backstage with Carol Burnett." *Saturday Evening Post* 235, no. 10 (Mar. 10, 1962).

Martin, Peter. "The *Girls* Recap for Men: Self-Indulgent Dreaming." *Esquire*, Feb. 10, 2013. www.esquire.com/blogs/culture/girls-season-2-episode-5-recap.

Martinez, Ernesto Javier. *On Making Sense: Queer Race Narratives of Intelligibility*. Stanford, CA: Stanford University Press, 2012.

Mask, Mia. *Divas on Screen: Black Women in American Film*. Urbana: University of Illinois Press, 2009.

Massa, Steve. "Some Job: The Film Career of Fay Tincher." In *Lame Brains and Lunatics*, 147–173. Albany, GA: Bear Manor Media, 2013.

Mast, Gerald. *The Comic Mind: Comedy and the Movies*. Indianapolis, IN: Bobbs-Merrill, 1973.

McCullers, Michael, et al. *Baby Mama* "Audio Commentary." Universal Studios, 2009. DVD.

McElravy, Robert C. Review of *A Perfect 36. Moving Picture World*, Dec. 28, 1918.

McGovern, James. "The American Woman's Pre–World War I Freedom in Manners and Morals." *Journal of American History* 55, no. 2 (Sept. 1968): 315–333.

McIntyre, Anthony P. "Isn't She Adorkable! Cuteness as Political Neutralization in the Star-Text of Zooey Deschanel." *Television and New Media* 16, no. 5 (2015): 422–438.

———. "*Ted, Wilfred*, and the Guys: Twenty-First-Century Masculinities, Raunch Culture, and the Affective Ambivalences of Cuteness." In *The Aesthetics and Affects of Cuteness*, ed. Joshua Paul Dale et al., 274–294. New York: Routledge, 2017.

McRobbie, Angela. "Post-Feminism and Popular Culture." *Feminist Media Studies* 4, no. 3 (2004): 255–264.

Mellencamp, Patricia. "Situation Comedy, Feminism, and Freud: Discourses of

Gracie and Lucy." In *Star Texts: Image and Performance in Film and Television*, edited by Jeremy G. Butler. Detroit: Wayne State University Press, 1991. Originally published in *Studies in Entertainment: Critical Approaches to Mass Culture*, edited by Tania Modleski, 80–95. Bloomington: Indiana University Press, 1986.

Merish, Lori. "Cuteness and Commodity Aesthetics: Tom Thumb and Shirley Temple." In *Freakery: Cultural Spectacles of the Extraordinary Body*, edited by Rosemarie Garland-Thomson, 185–203. New York: New York University Press, 1996.

Meryman, Richard. "Carol Burnett's Own Story." *McCalls* 105 (1978): 126+.

Meyer, Michaela. "'Maybe I Could Play a Hooker in Something!': Asian American Identity, Gender, and Comedy in the Rhetoric of Margaret Cho." In *Representations: Doing Asian American Rhetoric*, edited by LuMing Mao and Morris Young, 279–292. Logan: Utah State University Press, 2008.

Micale, Mark S. "Hysteria and its Historiography." *History of Science* 27, no. 4 (1989): 319–351.

Mills, Brett. *The Sitcom*. Edinburgh: Edinburgh University Press, 2009.

———. "Studying Comedy." In *The Television Genre Book*, edited by Toby Miller et al., 61–62. London: British Film Institute, 2011.

Mittell, Jason. *Complex TV: The Poetics of Contemporary Television Storytelling*. New York: NYU Press, 2015.

———. "Narrative Complexity in Contemporary American Television." *Velvet Light Trap* 58, no. 1 (2006), 29–40. doi:10.1353/vlt.2006.0032.

Mizejewski, Linda. "Feminism, Postfeminism, Liz Lemonism: Comedy and Gender Politics on *30 Rock*." *Genders* 55 (Spring 2012). www.genders.org/g55/g55_mizejewski.html.

———. *Pretty/Funny: Women Comedians and Body Politics*. Austin: University of Texas Press, 2014.

———. "Queen Latifah, Unruly Women, and the Bodies of Romantic Comedy." *Genders* 46 (2007). www.genders.org/g46/g46_mizejewski.html.

———. *Ziegfeld Girl: Image and Icon in Culture and Cinema*. Durham, NC: Duke University Press, 1999.

Mock, Roberta. *Jewish Women on Stage, Film, and Television*. Basingstoke, UK: Palgrave Macmillan, 2007.

———. "Stand-up Comedy and the Legacy of the Mature Vagina." *Women and Performance: A Journal of Feminist Theory* 22, no. 1 (2012), 9–28.

Molloy, Tim. "Judd Apatow and Lena Dunham Get Mad at Me for Asking Why She's Naked So Much on 'Girls.'" *The Wrap*, Jan. 9, 2014. www.thewrap.com/judd-apatow-lena-dunham-get-mad-asking-shes-naked-much-girls.

Moore, Barbara, Marvin R. Bensman, and Jim van Dyke. *Prime-Time Television: A Concise History*. Westport, CT: Praeger, 2006.

Moore, Candace. "Resisting, Reiterating, and Dancing Through: The Swinging Closet Doors of Ellen DeGeneres' Televised Personalities." In *Televising Queer Women: A Reader*, edited by Rebecca Beirne, 17–32. New York: Palgrave Macmillan, 2008.

Morreale, Joanne. "Television in the 1990s and Beyond." In *Critiquing the Sitcom: A Reader*, edited by Joanne Morreale, 247–250. New York: Syracuse University Press, 2003.

Morrison, Toni. *The Bluest Eye*. New York: Pocket Books, 1972.

Morrissey, Tracie Egan. "Tracy Anderson Is Not Allowed to Transform Lena Dunham's Body . . . Yet." *Jezebel*, Sept. 12, 2013. http://jezebel.com/tracy-anderson-is-not-allowed-to-transform-lena-dunham-1300322086.

Negra, Diane. "Claiming Feminism: Commentary, Autobiography, and Advice Literature for Women in the Recession." *Journal of Gender Studies* 23, no. 3 (2014): 275–286. doi:10.1080/09589236.2014.913977.

———. "'Quality Postfeminism?': Sex and the Single Girl on HBO." *Genders*, no. 39 (2004): n.p. www.genders.org/g39/g39_negra.html.

———. *What a Girl Wants? Fantasizing the Reclamation of Self in Postfeminism*. London: Routledge, 2009.

———, and Su Holmes. "Going Cheap? Female Celebrity in the Reality, Tabloid and Scandal Genres." *Genders* 48 (2008): n.p. www.genders.org/g48/g48_negraholmes.html.

Nelson, Patricia. "Character Crossings: Sexuality and Intersectional Comedy in Lily Tomlin's Early Variety Specials." Paper delivered at the SCMS annual conference, Seattle, Mar. 2014.

Nesteroff, Kliph. "Moms Mabley—Agitation in Moderation." *WEMU's Beware of the Blog*, Aug. 26, 2007. http://blog.wfmu.org/freeform/2007/08/moms-mabley---a.html.

Newman, Michel Z., and Elana Levine. *Legitimating Television: Media Convergence and Cultural Studies*. New York: Routledge, 2011.

Ngai, Sianne. *Our Aesthetic Categories: Zany, Cute, Interesting*. Cambridge, MA: Harvard University Press, 2012.

Notkin, Melanie. "Study Uncovers 23 Million Generous Women Society Overlooks." *Psychology Today*, Dec. 1, 2012. www.psychologytoday.com/blog/savvy-auntie/201212/study-uncovers-23-million-generous-women-society-overlooks.

Nussbaum, Emily. "Candy Girl." *New Yorker*, Mar. 30, 2015. www.newyorker.com/magazine/2015/03/30/candy-girl.

———. "In Defense of Liz Lemon." *New Yorker*, Feb. 23, 2012. www.newyorker.com/culture/culture-desk/in-defense-of-liz-lemon.

———. "It's Different for 'Girls.'" *New Yorker*, Mar. 25, 2012. http://nymag.com/arts/tv/features/girls-lena-dunham-2012-4.

Oppenheimer, Jess, with Gregg Oppenheimer. *Laughs, Luck, and Lucy: How I Came to Create the Most Popular Sitcom of All Time*. Syracuse: Syracuse University Press, 1996.

Orgeron, Marsha. "Making *It* in Hollywood: Clara Bow, Fandom, and Consumer Culture." *Cinema Journal* 42, no. 4 (Summer 2003): 76–97.

Oursler, Fulton. "Give Mabel Normand a Chance!" *Movie Weekly*, Feb. 2, 1924.

Page, Alison. "'This Baby Sloth Will Inspire You to Keep Going': Capital, Labor, and the Affective Power of Cute Animal Videos." In *The Aesthetics and Affects of Cuteness*, edited by Joshua Paul Dale et al., 75–94. New York: Routledge, 2017.

Palmer, Gareth. "'The New You': Class and Transformation in Lifestyle Television." In *Understanding Reality Television*, edited by Su Holmes and Deborah Jermyn, 173–190. London: Routledge, 2004.

Patterson, Eleanor. "Fracturing Tina Fey: A Critical Analysis of Postfeminist Television Comedy Stardom." *Communication Review* 15, no. 3 (July 2012): 232–251. doi:10.1080/10714421.2012.701991.

Patterson, James T. *Brown v. Board of Education: A Civil Rights Milestone and Its Troubled Legacy.* New York: Oxford University Press, 2001.

Paul, William. *Laughing Screaming: Modern Hollywood Horror and Comedy.* New York: Columbia University Press, 1994.

Pearson, Roberta. "Anatomising Gilbert Grisson: The Structure and Function of the Televisual Character." In *Reading CSI: Crime TV under the Microscope,* edited by Michael Allen, 39–56. London: I.B. Tauris, 2007.

Peiss, Kathy. *Cheap Amusements: Working Women in Turn-of-the-Century New York.* Philadelphia: Temple University Press, 1986.

Pellegrini, Ann. "Women on Top, Boys on the Side, but Some of Us Are Brave: Blackness, Lesbianism, and the Visible." *College Literature* 24, no. 1 (1997): 83–97.

Plotz, David. "Domestic Goddess Dethroned: How Roseanne Lost It." *Slate,* May 18, 1997. www.slate.com/articles/news_and_politics/assessment/1997/05/domestic_goddess_dethroned.html.

Prieto, Jenaro. *The Partner.* Trans. Blanca de Roig and Guy Dowler. London: Thornton Butterworth, 1931.

Projansky, Sarah. *Watching Rape: Film and Television in Postfeminist Culture.* New York: NYU Press, 2001.

Rabinovitz, Lauren. *For the Love of Pleasure: Women, Movies, and Culture in Turn-of-the-Century Chicago.* New Brunswick, NJ: Rutgers University Press, 1998.

Reed, Jennifer. "Lily: Sold Out! The Queer Feminism of Lily Tomlin." *Genders* 49 (2009). www.genders.org/g49/g49_reed.html.

———. "Lily Tomlin's *Appearing Nitely*: Performing Difference before Difference Was Cool." *Journal of Popular Culture* 37, no. 3 (2004): 436–449.

———. *The Queer Cultural Work of Lily Tomlin and Jane Wagner.* New York: Palgrave Macmillan, 2013.

Roberts, Chadwick. "Lily 'White': Commodity Racism and the Construction of Female Domesticity in *The Incredible Shrinking Woman*." *Journal of Popular Culture* 43, no. 4 (2010): 801–819.

Roberts, Martin. "The Fashion Police: Governing the Self in *What Not to Wear*." In *Interrogating Postfeminism: Gender and the Politics of Popular Culture,* edited by Yvonne Tasker and Diane Negra, 227–248. Durham, NC: Duke University Press, 2007.

Roberts, Soraya. "Naked if I Want To: Lena Dunham's Body Politic." *Salon,* Feb. 10, 2013. www.salon.com/2013/02/09/naked_if_i_want_to_lena_dunhams_body_politic.

Robertson, Pamela. *Guilty Pleasures: Feminist Camp from Mae West to Madonna.* Durham, NC: Duke University Press, 1996.

———. "Mae West's Maids: Race, 'Authenticity,' and the Discourse of Camp." In *Camp: Queer Aesthetics and the Performing Subject, A Reader,* ed. Fabio Cleto. Ann Arbor: University of Michigan Press, 1999.

Rodriguez, Maddie. "Three Times Amy Poehler Said 'Yes Please' to Feminism

in Her Memoir, and We're on Board, Naturally." *Bustle*, Nov. 6, 2014. www
.bustle.com/articles/47745-3-times-amy-poehler-said-yes-please-to-feminism
in-her-memoir-and-were-on-board.

Romero, Ramon. "The Town of Forgotten Faces." *New Movie* magazine, Aug. 1932, 39.

Rosenberg, Alyssa. "Lena Dunham's Looks, the Misogyny of the 'Girls' Backlash, and Staying in Your Assigned Story." *Thinkprogress*, May 29, 2012. http://thinkprogress.org/alyssa/2012/05/29/491372/lena-dunham-girls.

Rosenblatt, Yaakov. "An Open Letter to Sarah Silverman." *Jewish Press*, Oct. 11, 2012. www.jewishpress.com/indepth/opinions/dear-sarah-silverman/2012/10/11.

Rousseau, G. S. "'A Strange Pathology': Hysteria in the Early Modern World, 1500–1800." *Hysteria beyond Freud*. Edited by Sander L. Gilman et al., 91–221. Berkeley: University of California Press, 1993.

Rowe (Karlyn), Kathleen. "Comedy, Melodrama, and Gender: Theorizing the Genres of Laughter." In Karnick and Jenkins, *Classical Hollywood Comedy*, 39–59.

———. *The Unruly Woman: Gender and the Genres of Laughter.* Austin: University of Texas Press, 1995.

Rudnick, Paul. "Fun with Nuns." *New Yorker*, July 20, 2009. www.newyorker.com/magazine/2009/07/20/fun-with-nuns.

Russo, Mary. *The Female Grotesque: Risk, Excess, and Modernity.* New York: Routledge, 1995.

Ryan, Maureen. "Why TV Is Finally Embracing the Realities of Race." *Variety*, Feb. 23, 2016. http://variety.com/2016/tv/features/television-race-diversity-ratings-1201712266.

Saisi, Boké. "(Just White) Girls? Underrepresentation and Active Audiences in HBO's *Girls*." In Kaklamanidou and Tally, *HBO's Girls: Questions of Gender, Politics, and Millennial Angst*, 59–72.

Sandberg, Sheryl. *Lean In: Women, Work, and the Will to Lead.* 1st ed. New York: Knopf, 2013.

Saraiya, Sonia. "Imagine There's No Outrage: 'Unbreakable Kimmy Schmidt' Dreams of a Post-Identity Comedy Utopia." *Salon*, Apr. 17, 2016. www.salon.com/2016/04/17/imagine_theres_no_outrage_unbreakable_kimmy_schmidt_dreams_of_a_post_identity_comedy_utopia.

Savigny, Heather, and Helen Warner, eds. *The Politics of Being a Woman: Feminism, Media, and Twenty-First-Century Popular Culture.* New York: Palgrave Macmillan, 2015.

Schatz, Thomas. "Desilu, I Love Lucy, and the Rise of Network TV." In *Making Television: Authorship and the Production Process*, edited by Robert J. Thompson and Gary Burns, 117–136. New York: Praeger, 1990.

Schreiber, Michele. *American Postfeminist Cinema: Women, Romance, and Contemporary Culture.* Edinburgh: Edinburgh University Press, 2014.

Scodari, Christine. "Possession, Attraction, and the Thrill of the Chase: Gendered Myth-making in Film and Television Comedy of the Sexes." *Critical Studies in Mass Communication* 12, no. 1 (1995): 23–39. doi:10.1080/15295039509366917.

Sedgwick, Eve Kosofsky. *Tendencies.* Durham, NC: Duke University Press, 1993.

Seidman, Robert. "Syndicated TV Ratings Top 25: Charlie Sheen's 'Two and a

Half Men' Still a Beast in Syndication." *TV by the Numbers*, Feb. 15, 2011. tvbythenumbers.zap2it.com.

Seidman, Steve. *Comedian Comedy: A Tradition in Hollywood Film*. Ann Arbor: University of Michigan Research Press, 1981.

Seldes, Gilbert. *The Movies Come from America*. New York: Charles Scribner's Sons, 1937.

Seltzer, Sarah. "Knoptimism vs. Liz Lemonism: How 'Parks and Recreation' Took a Different Feminist Route." *Flavorwire*, Feb. 24, 2015. http://flavorwire.com/505916/knoptimism-vs-liz-lemonism-how-parks-and-recreation-took-a-different-feminist-route.

Sennett, Mack. *King of Comedy*. As told to Cameron Shipp. San Francisco: Mercury House, 1954.

Senzani, Alessandra. "Class and Gender as a Laughing Matter? The Case of *Roseanne*." *Humor* 23, no. 2 (2010): 229–253.

Setoodeh, Ramin. "How Lena Dunham Is Launching an Empire for Comedic Women." *Variety*, Apr. 21, 2015. http://variety.com/2015/tv/news/lena-dunham-girls-hbo-production company-girls-a- casual-romance-1201476138.

Sherman, William Thomas. "Mabel Normand: An Introductory Biography." www.mn-hp.com/mn.html.

———. *Mabel Normand: A Source Book to Her Life and Films*, 2015. https://archive.org/details/MabelNormandASourceBookToHerLifeAndFilms.

Shores, Robert J. "The History of Don Quixote." *Motion Picture Magazine* 11, no. 1 (Feb. 1916): 34–46.

Shulman, Randy. "Interview with Lily Tomlin." *MetroWeekly*, Apr. 26, 2006.

Showalter, Elaine. *The Female Malady: Women, Madness, and English Culture 1830–1980*. New York: Pantheon, 1985.

———. "Hysteria, Feminism, and Gender." In *Hysteria beyond Freud*, edited by Sander L. Gilman et al., 286–344. Berkeley: University of California Press, 1993.

Silman, Anna. "I'm Worried That Tina Fey and Amy Poehler's 'Sisters' Will Be as Bad as It Looks." *Salon*, July 15, 2015. www.salon.com/2015/07/15/im_worried_that_tina_fey_and_amy_poehlers_sisterswill_be_as_bad_as_it_looks.

Silverman, Sarah. *The Bedwetter: Stories of Courage, Redemption, and Pee*. New York: Harper, 2010.

Simon, John. "Affectionately Yours." *New Yorker*, Nov. 11, 2002, 106–107.

Skeggs, Beverley. *Class, Self, Culture*. London: Routledge, 2004.

Slide, Anthony. *The Encyclopedia of Vaudeville*. Westport, CT: Greenwood Press, 1994.

Smith, Bob. "Lily Tomlin's Take on Customer Service." *Management Review*, July 1994, 17–20.

Smith-Rosenberg, Carroll. *Disorderly Conduct: Visions of Gender in Victorian America*. New York: Oxford University Press, 1986.

Snead, James. *White Screens, Black Images: Hollywood from the Dark Side*. New York: Routledge, 1994.

Sochen, June, ed. *Women's Comic Visions*. Detroit: Wayne State University Press, 1991.

Sorensen, Jeff. *Lily Tomlin: Woman of a Thousand Faces*. New York: St Martin's, 1989.

Spangler, Lynn C. *Television Women from Lucy to Friends: Fifty Years of Sitcoms and Feminism.* Westport, CT: Praeger, 2003.

Spelman, Elizabeth. "Anger and Insubordination." In *Women, Knowledge, and Reality: Explorations in Feminist Philosophy,* edited by Ann Garry and Marilyn Pearsall, 263–274. Boston: Unwin Hyman, 1989.

Springer, Kimberly. "Divas, Evil Black Bitches, and Bitter Black Women: African American Women in Postfeminist and Post-Civil-Rights Popular Culture." In *Interrogating Postfeminism: Gender and the Politics of Popular Culture,* edited by Yvonne Tasker and Diane Negra, 249–276. Durham, NC: Duke University Press, 2007.

Standing, Guy. *The Precariat: A New Dangerous Class.* London: Bloomsbury Academic Press, 2011.

Stanley, Alessandra. "Who Says Women Aren't Funny?" *Vanity Fair,* Apr. 2008, 182–251.

Steele, Claude M. *Whistling Vivaldi and Other Clues to How Stereotypes Affect Us.* New York: Norton, 2010.

Stransky, Tanner. "20 Years Ago This Week . . . Roseanne Marries Tom Arnold." *Entertainment Weekly,* Jan. 29, 2010, 8.

Sturtevant, Victoria. "Getting Hysterical: *Thelma & Louise* and Laughter." *Thelma & Louise Live! The Cultural Aftermath of an American Film,* edited by Bernie Cook, 43–64. Austin: University of Texas Press, 2007.

———. *A Great Big Girl Like Me: The Films of Marie Dressler.* Urbana: University of Illinois Press, 2009.

Sutherland, Sidney. "Madcap Mabel Normand, Part Three." *Liberty* magazine, Sept. 20, 1930, 44+.

———. "Madcap Mabel Normand, Part Four." *Liberty* magazine, Sept. 27, 1930.

Susman, Gary. "Discomfort Zone: Ten Great Cringe Comedies." *Time,* May 12, 2013. http://entertainment.time.com/2013/05/13/discomfort-zone-10-great cringecomedies/slide/intro/print.

Tally, Margaret. "Post-Modernity, Emerging Adulthood, and the Exploration of Female Friendships on *Girls.*" In Kaklamanidou and Tally, *HBO's Girls: Questions of Gender, Politics, and Millennial Angst,* 28–42.

Taraborrelli, J. Randy. *Laughing Till It Hurts: The Complete Life and Career of Carol Burnett.* New York: William Morrow, 1988.

Tasca, Cecilia, et al. "Women and Hysteria in the History of Mental Health." *Clinical Practice and Epidemiology in Mental Health* 8, (2012): 110–119. www.ncbi.nlm.nih.gov/pmc/articles/PMC3480686.

Tasker, Yvonne. *Working Girls: Gender and Sexuality in Popular Cinema.* London: Routledge, 1998.

———, and Diane Negra. *Interrogating Postfeminism: Gender and the Politics of Popular Culture.* Durham, NC: Duke University Press, 2007.

Teachout, Terry. "Saturday Night Strive." *Commentary* 36, no. 1 (July 2013): 70–73.

Tillman, Aaron. "'Through the Rube Goldberg Crazy Straw': Ethnic Mobility and Narcissistic Fantasy in *Sarah Silverman: Jesus Is Magic.*" *Studies in American Humor* 3, no. 20 (2009): 58–84.

"Top Ten Thinking Man's Sex Symbols." *Daily Beast,* n.d. www.thedailybeast.com/galleries/2008/12/16/top-ten-thinking-man-s-sex symbols.html.

Turner, Victor. *The Ritual Process: Structure and Anti-Structure*. Ithaca, NY: Cornell University Press, 1969.

Tyler, Imogen. "'Chav Mum Chav Scum': Class Disgust in Contemporary Britain." *Feminist Media Studies* 8, no. 1 (2008): 17–34.

"Uncle Bin's Gift." *Motion Picture News* 28 (Sept. 8, 1923): 1245.

VanDerWerff, Todd. "What We Talk about When We Talk about Girls." *TV Club*, Mar. 14, 2013. www.avclub.com/article/what-we-talk-about-when-we-talk-about-igirlsi93685.

Wade, Peter. "The Girl on the Cover." *Motion Picture Magazine*, Apr. 1917, 167.

Wagner, Kristen Anderson. "'Have Women a Sense of Humor?': Comedy and Femininity in Early Twentieth-Century Film." *Velvet Light Trap* 68 (Fall 2011): 35.

Wald, Christina. *Hysteria, Trauma, and Melancholia: Performative Maladies in Contemporary Anglophone Drama*. New York: Palgrave Macmillan, 2007.

Walker, Alice. *The Same River Twice: Honoring the Difficult*. New York: Scribner's, 1996.

Walker, Brent E. *Mack Sennett's Fun Factory*. Jefferson, NC: McFarland, 2013.

Walker, Nancy A. "Toward Solidarity: Women's Humor and Group Identity." In *Women's Comic Visions*, edited by June Sochen. Detroit: Wayne State University Press, 1991.

———. *A Very Serious Thing: Women's Humor and American Culture*. Minneapolis: University of Minnesota Press, 1988.

———, and Zita Dresner, eds. Introduction to *Redressing the Balance: American Women's Literary Humor from Colonial Times to the 1980s*. Jackson: University Press of Mississippi, 1988.

Wallace, Kelsey. "Why Jezebel Was Wrong to Put a Bounty on Lena Dunham's Photos." *Bitchmedia*, Jan. 20, 2014. https://bitchmedia.org/post/why-jezebel-was-wrong-to put-a-bounty-on-those-lena-dunham-photos.

Wallace-Sanders, Kimberly. *Mammy: A Century of Race, Gender, and Southern Memory*. Ann Arbor: University of Michigan Press, 2008.

Wanzo, Rebecca. "Beyond a 'Just' Syntax: Black Actresses, Hollywood, and Complex Personhood." *Women and Performance* 16, no. 1 (2006): 135–152.

Waters, Harry F. "A Comedy Comeback." *Newsweek*, June 18, 1990, 64.

Watkins, Mel. *On the Real Side: Laughing, Lying, and Signifying—The Underground Tradition of African American Humor That Transformed American Culture, from Slavery to Richard Pryor*. New York: Simon and Schuster, 1994.

Weber, Brenda. "Imperialist Projections: Manners, Makeovers, and Models of Nationality." In *Women on Screen: Feminism and Femininity in Visual Culture*, edited by Melanie Waters, 136–152. Basingstoke, UK: Palgrave Macmillan, 2011.

Weidhase, Nathalie. "'Beyoncé Feminism' and the Contestation of the Black Feminist Body." *Celebrity Studies* 6, no. 1 (2015): 128–131. doi:10.1080/19392397.2015.1005389.

Weinman, Jaime J. "Fast-forward to the Reruns." *Maclean's*, July 29, 2013, 1.

West, Mae. *The Constant Sinner*. London: Virago Press, 1995.

———. *Goodness Had Nothing to Do with It*. Englewood Cliffs, NJ: Prentice-Hall, 1969.

———. *Three Plays by Mae West: Sex, The Drag, The Pleasure Man*. Edited by Lillian Schlissel. New York: Routledge, 1997.

Wexman, Virginia Wright. "Kinesics and Film Acting: Humphrey Bogart in *The Maltese Falcon* and *The Big Sleep*." *Journal of Popular Film and Television* 7, no. 1 (1978): 42–55.

Williams, Elsie A. *The Humor of Jackie "Moms" Mabley: An African American Comedy Tradition*. New York: Garland, 1995.

Williams, Linda. "Melodrama Revised." In *Refiguring American Film Genres: Theory and History*, edited by Nick Browne, 42–88. Berkeley: University of California Press, 1998.

———. *Playing the Race Card: Melodramas of Black and White from Uncle Tom's Cabin to O. J. Simpson*. Princeton, NJ: Princeton University Press, 2001.

Wilson, Margaret Gibbons. *The American Woman in Transition: The Urban Influence, 1870–1920*. Westport, CT: Greenwood Press, 1979.

Wittkower, Dylan E. "On the Origins of the Cute as a Dominant Aesthetic." In *Putting Knowledge to Work and Letting Information Play*, edited by Timothy W. Luke and Jeremy Hunsinger, 212–229. Blacksburg, VA: Center for Digital Discourse and Culture, 2009.

Woo, Michelle. "Twenty Years Later Margaret Cho Looks Back on *All-American Girl*." *KoreAm Journal*, Sept. 15, 2014. http://iamkoream.com/20-years-later-margaret-cho-looks-back-on-all-american-girl.

Woods, Faye. "Girls Talk: Authorship and Authenticity in the Reception of Lena Dunham's *Girls*." *Critical Studies in Television* 10, no. 2 (2015): 37–54.

Wortham, Jenna. "Where (My) Girls At?" *The Hairpin*, Apr. 16, 2012. http://thehairpin.com/2012/04/where-my-girls-at.

Wright, Megh. "Tituss Burgess on 'Unbreakable Kimmy Schmidt' Critics: 'If People Aren't Talking about You, You're Not Doing Your Job.'" *Splitsider*, Mar. 13, 2015. http://splitsider.com/2015/03/titus-burgess-on-unbreakable-kimmy-schmidt-critics-if people-arent-talking-about-you-youre-not-doing-your-job.

Yano, Christine. *Pink Globalization: Hello Kitty's Trek across the Pacific*. Durham, NC: Duke University Press, 2013.

Zeidman, Bennie Lubinbille. "The Unexploited Series That Exploited Itself." *Photoplayers Weekly* 2, no. 7 (Apr. 23, 1915): 7–8.

Zwagerman, Sean. "A Cautionary Tale: Ann Coulter and the Failure of Humor." In Dickinson et al., *Women and Comedy*, 171–183.

BAMBI HAGGINS is an associate professor of film and media studies at the University of California, Irvine. Her research engages issues of gender, race, and sexuality in American film and television. Her book *Laughing Mad: The Black Comic Persona in Post-Soul America* (2007) won the Katherine Singer Kovacs Book Award from the Society for Cinema and Media Studies. Professor Haggins's recent film credits include writing for Showtime's *Why We Laugh: Funny Women* (2013) and working as a historical consultant and on-screen talent for HBO's *Whoopi Goldberg Presents Moms Mabley* (2013). Her current project examines comedy and blackness in the age of Obama.

KRISTEN HATCH is associate professor in the Department of Film and Media Studies and in the visual studies program at the University of California, Irvine. She is the author of *Shirley Temple and the Performance of Girlhood* (2015), as well as contributing numerous essays to book collections and journals.

JULIA HAVAS earned her PhD in the School of Arts, Media and American Studies at the University of East Anglia. Her research investigates the ways in which feminism is represented in contemporary American "quality" television. A specific concern of her work is the relationship between television aesthetics and gender politics—how popular cultural debates around issues of feminism and postfeminism become interconnected with discourses about quality television.

KATHLEEN ROWE KARLYN is an emerita professor of English at the University of Oregon. She is the author of *The Unruly Woman: Gender and the Genres of Laughter* (1995) and *Unruly Girls, Unrepentant Mothers: Redefining Feminism on Screen* (2011), as well as contributing many articles in scholarly journals and anthologies.

KRISTINE BRUNOVSKA KARNICK is associate professor of communication studies at Indiana University–Purdue University Indianapolis. She has written widely on film and television history, silent era comedy, and gender and film comedy. She is the coeditor of *Classical Hollywood Comedy* (1995).

REBECCA KREFTING is an associate professor of American studies at Skidmore College. She is the author of *All Joking Aside: American Humor and Its Discontents* (2014). Her work has been published in journals such as *Studies in American Humor* and *Comedy Studies* and in edited collections, including *The Laughing Stalk: Live Comedy and Its Audiences* (2012), *Transgressive Humor of American Women Writers* (2017), and *Taking a Stand: American Stand-up Comedians as Public Intellectuals* (forthcoming). Her current research investigates the impact of social media platforms and emergent technologies on the comedy industry.

LORI LANDAY is professor of cultural studies at Berklee College of Music and an interdisciplinary scholar and new media artist exploring the making of visual meaning in twentieth- and twenty-first-century culture. She is the author of *I Love Lucy* (2010) and *Madcaps, Screwballs, and Con Women: The Female Trickster in American Culture* (1998), as well as articles on television culture, digital narrative, silent film, LEGO transmedia, and other topics. Her creative work includes animation, machinima, and interactive virtual art. Her current project considers animation, presence, and the "virtual kino-eye," extending inquiry from her NEH Enduring Questions Grant for "What Is Being?" (2010–2012).

JOSELYN K. LEIMBACH is a lecturer with the Institute for Women's Studies at the University of Georgia. She received her PhD in gender studies from Indiana University. Her work explores queer performances at the intersections of gender, sexuality, and race in popular culture. She focuses on depictions of explicitly lesbian identities, same-gender sexual and romantic desire between women, and characterizations that disrupt singular definitions of womanhood. Her publications include "Strengthening as They Undermine: Rachel Maddow and Suze Orman's Homonormative Lesbian Identities" in *In the Limelight and under the Microscope* (2011).

SUZANNE LEONARD is associate professor of English at Simmons College and co-coordinator of the college's interdisciplinary minor in cinema and media studies. She is the author of *Fatal Attraction* (2009) and co-editor of *Fifty Hollywood Directors* (2015). Her monograph, *Wife, Inc.: The Business of Marriage in Twenty-First-Century American Culture*, is forthcoming from New York University Press.

ANTHONY P. MCINTYRE is an associate lecturer in film studies at University College Dublin. He is a coeditor of *The Aesthetics and Affects of Cuteness* (2016), and his work has appeared in numerous scholarly edited collections as well as the journal *Television and New Media*. He is currently finishing a monograph, *Millennial Tensions: Generational Affect and Contemporary Screen Cultures*.

LINDA MIZEJEWSKI is professor of women's, gender, and sexuality studies at the Ohio State University. She is the author of *Divine Decadence: Fascism, Female Spectacle, and the Makings of Sally Bowles* (1992); *Ziegfeld Girl: Image and Icon in Culture and Cinema* (1999); *Hardboiled and High Heeled: The Woman Detective in Popular Culture* (2004); *It Happened One Night* (2010); and, most recently, *Pretty Funny: Woman Comedians and Body Politics* (2014).

JOANNA E. RAPF is an emerita professor of English and film and media studies from the University of Oklahoma. She is coeditor of Blackwell's *A Companion to Film Comedy* (2013) and (focusing on comedy) has published on Buster Keaton, Marie Dressler, Harry Langdon, Jimmy Durante, Jerry Lewis, and Woody Allen.

VICTORIA STURTEVANT is associate professor of film and media studies and associate dean of the College of Arts and Sciences at the University of Oklahoma. Her first book, *A Great Big Girl Like Me: The Films of Marie Dressler*, was published in 2009. As *Hysterical!* goes to press, she is happily immersed in writing her next manuscript, a study of representations of pregnancy in American film and television comedy.

MARIA SULIMMA is a PhD candidate and faculty member of the Department of Culture at the John F. Kennedy Institute for North American Studies (Free University Berlin). She has written a book on media representations of female politicians (*Die anderen Ministerpräsidenten*, 2014) and has published articles on digital seriality and gaming communities, crossmedia franchises, and gender and race in political television shows. In her dissertation project, Maria is examining the production of gender in and around contemporary U.S. cable television series as a serial phenomenon invested in specific discourses of authorship and criticism, as well as in social networks.

KRISTEN ANDERSON WAGNER received her PhD in critical studies from the University of Southern California's School of Cinematic Arts. She is the author of *Comic Venus: Women and Comedy in American Silent Film* (2017). She has also published essays in *Not So Silent: Women in Cinema Before Sound* (2010), Blackwell's *A Companion to Film Comedy* (2013), and the *Velvet Light Trap*, and she co-edited the spring 2017 special issue of *Feminist Media Histories* on gender and comedy.

REBECCA WANZO is associate professor of women, gender, and sexuality studies at Washington University in St. Louis. She is the author of *The Suffering Will Not Be Televised: African American Women and Sentimental Political Storytelling* (2009). Her research interests include African American studies, feminist theory, feminist media studies, and graphic storytelling. Her essays have appeared in various edited collections and journals including *Journal of Popular Culture*, *Women and Performance*, *differences: A Journal of Feminist Cultural Studies*, and *Camera Obscura*.

BRENDA R. WEBER is professor and chair of the Department of Gender Studies at Indiana University. Her books include *Makeover TV: Selfhood, Citizenship, and Celebrity* (2009); *Women and Literary Celebrity in the Nineteenth Century: The Transatlantic Construction of Fame and Gender* (2012); and *Reality Gendervision: Sexuality and Gender on Transatlantic Reality Television* (2014).

ROSIE WHITE is senior lecturer at Northumbria University, Newcastle (UK). She has published in journals such as *Feminist Media Studies* and *Women: A Cultural Review*, and in edited collections such as *Twenty-First Century Feminism: Forming and Performing Femininity* (2015) and *Ageing, Popular Culture, and Contemporary Feminism: Harleys and Hormones* (2014). Her first monograph was *Violent Femmes: Women as Spies in Popular Culture* (2007), and she is completing a book for I. B. Tauris on *Television Comedy and Femininity: Queering Gender*.

Page numbers followed by f indicate figures.